Class Model Notation — Advanced

Ternary Association:

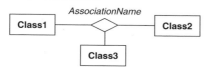

Visibility:

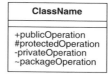

ClassName
+publicOperation
#protectedOperation
-privateOperation
~packageOperation

Abstract and Concrete Class:

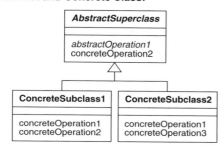

Aggregation:

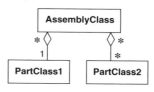

Multiple Inheritance, Disjoint:

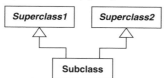

Composition:

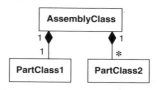

Constraint on Objects:

Class
attrib1
attrib2

$\{ \text{attrib1} \geq 0 \}$

Multiple Inheritance, Overlapping:

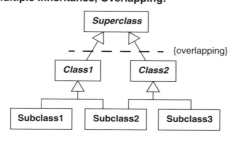

Constraint on Links:

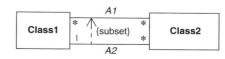

Derived Class:

/ ClassName

Derived Association:

Derived Attribute:

Class
/ attribute

Object-Oriented Modeling and Design with UML™

Second Edition

What Others Have Said About Object-Oriented Modeling and Design with UML, Second Edition

"The first edition of *Object-Oriented Modeling and Design* by James Rumbaugh, Michael Blaha, and their colleagues is already a classic. It has influenced me more than any other book on modeling. I have successfully applied their ideas in large university project courses for over ten years now, and I am glad to see an updated version of this landmark book. It is bound to shape the thinking habits of another generation of software designers and modelers."

— *Bernd Bruegge, Technical University Munich*

"Blaha & Rumbaugh have done it again. They've updated their classic book for our current times, showing again that by their simple and straightforward explanations, their precise insights, and their key examples and exercises, that the adoption of object-oriented methodology need not be difficult. A must to have, read, and study by any practitioner."

— *Michael J. Chonoles*

"Our Master and Doctoral programs in information systems are adopting the *Object-Oriented Modeling and Design with UML* (OOMD) methodology. The book, written by two of the leading experts in the field, covers all aspects of OOMD with deep insight, many fine points, and up to date examples. It offers great value to our programs."

— *Peter H. Chang, Lawrence Technological University*

"If you are looking for a book that introduces UML, has a simple and useful object-oriented analysis and design process, and also includes details about important object-oriented concepts, then I strongly recommend that you study this excellent text."

— *Mikael Berndtsson, University of Skövde*

Object-Oriented Modeling and Design with UML™

Second Edition

Michael Blaha
Modelsoft Consulting Corporation

James Rumbaugh
IBM

Upper Saddle River, New Jersey 07458

Library of Congress Cataloging-in-Publication Data

Blaha, Michael.
   Object-oriented modeling and desgin with UML /
   Michael Blaha, James Rumbaugh.
     p. cm.
   Rev. ed of Object-oriented modeling and design /
   James Rumbaugh. 1991.
   Includes bibliographical references and index.
   ISBN 0-13-015920-4
   1. Object-oriented methods (Computer science) 2. UML (Computer science)
   I. Rumbaugh, James. II. Rumbaugh James. Object-oriented modeling and design.
   III. Title.
QA76.9.O35B562005
005.1'17--dc22

2004057348

Vice President and Editorial Director, ECS: *Marcia Horton*
Publisher: *Alan Apt*
Associate Editor: *Toni Holm*
Vice President and Director of Production and Manufacturing, ESM: *David W. Riccardi*
Executive Managing Editor: *Vince O'Brien*
Managing Editor: *Camille Trentacoste*
Production Editor: *Irwin Zucker*
Manufacturing Manager: *Trudy Pisciotti*
Manufacturing Buyer: *Lisa McDowell*
Director of Creative Services: *Paul Belfanti*
Art Director: *Heather Scott*
Cover Design: *Marjory Dressler*
Executive Marketing Manager: *Pamela Hersperger*
Marketing Assistant: *Barrie Reinhold*

© 2005, 1991 by Pearson Education, Inc.
Pearson Prentice Hall
Pearson Education, Inc.
Upper Saddle River, New Jersey 07458

Printed in the United States of America

10 9 8 7 6 5 4 3 2 1

ISBN 0-13-015920-4

Pearson Education Ltd., *London*
Pearson Education Australia Pty. Ltd., *Sydney*
Pearson Education Singapore Pte. Ltd.
Pearson Education North Asia Ltd. *Hong Kong*
Pearson Education Canada Inc., *Toronto*
Pearson Educación de Mexico, S.A. de C.V.
Pearson Education—Japan, Inc., *Tokyo*
Pearson Education—Malaysia Pte. Ltd.
Pearson Education Inc., *Upper Saddle River, New Jersey*

Contents

Preface

Welcome to the second edition of *Object-Oriented Modeling and Design*. Much has changed since we finished the first book (1991). Back then object-oriented (OO) technology was considered new. Despite the excitement and enthusiasm, there was concern whether OO was really practical or just a passing fad. Consider all that has changed:

- **OO languages**. C++ is now established and Java has also become popular. The dominant programming languages are now OO.

- **OO databases**. Somewhat surprisingly, OO databases have faded, but relational databases are now including some OO features.

- **OO modeling**. The Unified Modeling Language (UML) standard from the Object Management Group has consolidated the multiple competing notations.

- **OO methodology**. Development methodologies now routinely incorporate OO ideas and concepts.

OO technology has truly become part of the computing mainstream. OO technology is no longer the exception; rather it is the usual practice.

What You Will Find

This book presents an object-oriented approach to software development based on modeling objects from the real world and then using the model to build a language-independent design organized around those objects. Object-oriented modeling and design promote better understanding of requirements, cleaner designs, and more maintainable systems. We describe a set of object-oriented concepts and a language-independent graphical notation that can be used to analyze problem requirements, design a solution to the problem, and then implement the solution in a programming language or database. Our approach allows the same concepts and notation to be used throughout the entire software development process. The software developer does not need to translate into a new notation at each development stage.

We show how to use object-oriented concepts throughout the entire software life cycle, from analysis through design to implementation. The book is not primarily about object-oriented languages or coding. Instead we stress that coding is the last stage in a process of development that includes stating a problem, understanding its requirements, planning a solution, and implementing a program in a particular language. A good design technique defers implementation details until later stages of design to preserve flexibility. Mistakes in the front of the development process have a large impact on the ultimate product and on the time needed to finish. We describe the implementation of object-oriented designs in object-oriented languages and relational databases.

The book emphasizes that object-oriented technology is more than just a way of programming. Most importantly, it is a way of thinking abstractly about a problem using real-world concepts, rather than computer concepts. We have found this to be a difficult transition for some people. Books that emphasize object-oriented programming often fail to help the programmer learn to think abstractly. We have found that a graphical notation helps the software developer visualize a problem without prematurely resorting to implementation.

We show that object-oriented technology provides a practical, productive way to develop software for most applications, regardless of the final implementation language. We take an informal approach in this book; there are no proofs or formal definitions with Greek letters. We attempt to foster a pragmatic approach to problem solving by drawing upon the intuitive sense that object-oriented technology captures and by providing a notation and methodology for using it systematically on real problems. We provide tips and examples of good and bad design to help the software developer avoid common pitfalls.

Who Should Read This Book?

This book is intended for both software professionals and students. The reader will learn how to apply object-oriented concepts to all stages of the software development life cycle. We do not assume any prior knowledge of object-oriented concepts. We do assume that the reader is familiar with basic computing concepts, but an extensive formal background is not required. Even existing object-oriented programmers will benefit from learning how to design programs systematically; they may be surprised to discover that certain common object-oriented coding practices violate principles of good design.

The database designer will find much of interest here. Although object-oriented programming languages have received the most attention, object-oriented design of databases is also compelling and immediately practical. We include an entire chapter describing how to implement an object-oriented model using relational databases.

This book can be used as a textbook for a graduate or advanced undergraduate course on software engineering or object-oriented technology. It can be used as a supplementary text for courses on databases or programming languages. Prerequisites include exposure to modern programming languages and a knowledge of basic computer science terms and concepts, such as syntax, semantics, recursion, set, procedure, graph, and state; a detailed formal background is not required.

Our emphasis differs from that of some in the object-oriented programming community but is in accord with the information modeling and design methodology communities. We emphasize object-oriented constructs as models of real things, rather than as techniques for programming. We elevate interobject relationships to the same semantic level as classes, rather than hiding them as pointers inside objects. We place somewhat less emphasis on inheritance and methods. We downplay fine details of inheritance mechanisms. We come down strongly in favor of typing, classes, modeling, and advance planning. We also show how to apply object-oriented concepts to state machines.

The book contains four parts. Part 1 presents object-oriented concepts in a high-level, language-independent manner. These concepts are fundamental to the rest of the book, although advanced material can be skipped initially. The UML notation is introduced in Part 1 and used throughout the book. Part 2 describes a step-by-step object-oriented methodology of software development from problem statement through analysis, system design, and class design. All but the final stages of the methodology are language independent. Part 3 describes the implementation of object-oriented designs in object-oriented languages and relational databases. It describes the considerations applicable to different environments, although it is not intended to replace books on object-oriented programming. Part 4 describes software engineering practices needed for successful object-oriented development.

The authors have used object-oriented analysis, design, programming, and database modeling for many years now on a variety of applications. We are enthusiastic about the object-oriented approach and have found it appropriate to almost any kind of application. We have found that the use of object-oriented concepts, together with a graphical notation and a development methodology, can greatly increase the quality, flexibility, and understandability of software. We hope that this book can help get that message across.

The book has a rich variety of exercises that cover a range of application domains and implementation targets. We suggest that you try working some of them as you go along. Ultimately, OO technology is not learned by reading about it, but by trying to practice it. Answers to selected exercises are included at the back of the book.

Comparison With Other Books

There are many books on the market that cover object-oriented technology. This book differs from most in that it teaches how to think about object-oriented modeling, rather than just presenting the mechanics of a programming language or modeling notation.

Many of the available object-oriented books are about programming issues, often from the point of view of a single language. Some of these books do discuss design issues, but they are still mainly about programming. Few books focus on object-oriented analysis or design. We show that object-oriented concepts can and should be applied throughout the entire software life cycle.

In addition there are a number of books that present the concepts of the UML. This book is different than most in that it not only explains the concepts, but it also explains their fundamental purpose and shows how to use them to build software. We do not explain every concept and nuance, but we do strive to explain the core of UML—enough to help you learn how to use the UML to build better software.

Changes From the First Edition

It has been fourteen years since we completed the first edition of this book. In the meantime there have been many advances in technology, leading to many changes in this second edition.

- **Notation**. We have replaced the OMT notation with the UML notation, specifically UML 2.0. The UML is now the dominant and standard language for OO modeling.

- **Process**. The second edition adds more content to the software development process. We now distinguish between domain analysis and application analysis. We have added implementation modeling. By intent, we have kept the process simple and lightweight so that it is approachable to students. This book's process is a subset of heavyweight processes, such as IBM Rational's RUP.

- **The three models**. We have carried forward the first edition's focus on "the three models" because we believe such an emphasis is helpful for teaching and learning OO modeling. However, we dropped the functional model, because it was not as useful as we had expected. In its place, we added the interaction model to incorporate use cases and sequence diagrams and to give a more holistic understanding of behavior among several objects.

- **Software engineering**. Part 4 covers several important software engineering topics: iterative development, management of models, and treatment of legacy systems.

- **Programming languages**. Programming languages have changed dramatically over the past decade and a half. Smalltalk has faded, while C and Fortran have diminished in importance. C++ and Java are now the dominant OO programming languages, and we have focused on them accordingly.

- **Databases**. OO models provide a sound basis not only for programming code, but also for relational databases. This book has an entire chapter that shows how to build efficient, correct, and extensible databases from UML models.

- **Case studies**. When the first edition was published, we felt a need to justify OO technology, so we included several case studies. Today, many case studies are available in the literature, so we have eliminated them from this book.

In this second edition, we have attempted to carry forward the first edition's style, emphasis on practical ideas, many examples, and many exercises.

Web Site

We are posting materials relevant to this book at www.modelsoftcorp.com.

Acknowledgements

Over the years we have worked with a number of people who have taught us about their business, given us the opportunity to try our ideas, and helped us learn in the process. We would like to thank these many individuals, starting with our former management at the General Electric R&D Center and continuing to our recent business friends and clients.

Although only two of us have written this second edition, the first edition had three additional authors—Bill Premerlani, Fred Eddy, and Bill Lorensen. We thank them for their past contribution on which this second edition builds. We also thank them for their support and encouragement in our writing of this second edition.

Chris Kelsey had an important role in the second edition that deserves special mention. She is the primary author of Chapter 18 on OO programming languages and also was an active reviewer.

We are grateful to our other reviewers (Mikael Berndtsson, Peter Chang, Bill Premerlani, and John Putnam) for taking the time to read our manuscript and provide thoughtful criticism.

Finally we wish to thank our families and colleagues for being patient with our many distractions and diversions during the writing of this book.

Michael Blaha
Chesterfield, Missouri
blaha@computer.org

James Rumbaugh
Cupertino, California

1

Introduction

Object-oriented modeling and design is a way of thinking about problems using models organized around real-world concepts. The fundamental construct is the object, which combines both data structure and behavior. Object-oriented models are useful for understanding problems, communicating with application experts, modeling enterprises, preparing documentation, and designing programs and databases. This book presents an object-oriented notation and process that extends from analysis through design to implementation. The same notation applies at all stages of the process as development proceeds.

1.1 What Is Object-Orientation?

Superficially the term *object-oriented (OO)* means that we organize software as a collection of discrete objects that incorporate both data structure and behavior. This contrasts with previous programming approaches in which data structure and behavior are only loosely connected. There is some dispute about exactly what characteristics are required by an OO approach, but they generally include four aspects: identity, classification, inheritance, and polymorphism.

Identity means that data is quantized into discrete, distinguishable entities called *objects*. The *first paragraph in this chapter*, *my workstation*, and the *white queen in a chess game* are examples of objects. Figure 1.1 shows some additional objects. Objects can be concrete, such as a *file* in a file system, or conceptual, such as a *scheduling policy* in a multiprocessing operating system. Each object has its own inherent identity. In other words, two objects are distinct even if all their attribute values (such as name and size) are identical.

In the real world an object simply exists, but within a programming language each object has a unique handle by which it can be referenced. Languages implement the handle in various ways, such as an address, array index, or artificial number. Such object references are uniform and independent of the contents of the objects, permitting mixed collections of objects to be created, such as a file system directory that contains both files and subdirectories.

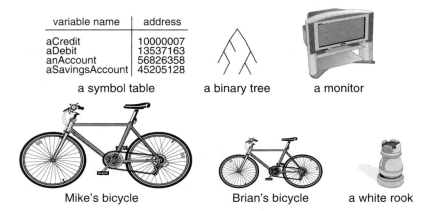

Figure 1.1 Objects. Objects lie at the heart of object-oriented technology.

Classification means that objects with the same data structure (*attributes*) and behavior (*operations*) are grouped into a class. *Paragraph*, *Monitor*, and *ChessPiece* are examples of classes. A *class* is an abstraction that describes properties important to an application and ignores the rest. Any choice of classes is arbitrary and depends on the application.

Each class describes a possibly infinite set of individual objects. Each object is said to be an *instance* of its class. An object has its own value for each attribute but shares the attribute names and operations with other instances of the class. Figure 1.2 shows two classes and some of their respective instances. An object contains an implicit reference to its own class; it "knows what kind of thing it is."

Inheritance is the sharing of attributes and operations (*features*) among classes based on a hierarchical relationship. A *superclass* has general information that *subclasses* refine and elaborate. Each subclass incorporates, or inherits, all the features of its superclass and adds its own unique features. Subclasses need not repeat the features of the superclass. For example, *ScrollingWindow* and *FixedWindow* are subclasses of *Window*. Both subclasses inherit the features of *Window,* such as a visible region on the screen. *ScrollingWindow* adds a scroll bar and an offset. The ability to factor out common features of several classes into a superclass can greatly reduce repetition within designs and programs and is one of the main advantages of OO technology.

Polymorphism means that the same operation may behave differently for different classes. The *move* operation, for example, behaves differently for a pawn than for the queen in a chess game. An *operation* is a procedure or transformation that an object performs or is subject to. *RightJustify*, *display*, and *move* are examples of operations. An implementation of an operation by a specific class is called a *method*. Because an OO operator is polymorphic, it may have more than one method implementing it, each for a different class of object.

In the real world, an operation is simply an abstraction of analogous behavior across different kinds of objects. Each object "knows how" to perform its own operations. In an OO programming language, however, the language automatically selects the correct method to

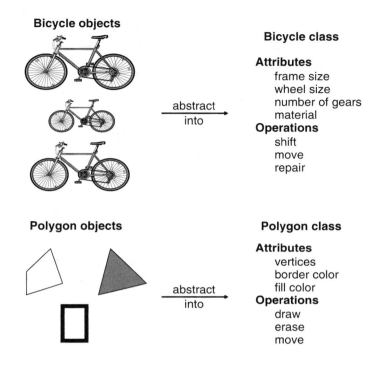

Figure 1.2 Objects and classes. Each class describes a possibly infinite set of individual objects.

implement an operation based on the name of the operation and the class of the object being operated on. The user of an operation need not be aware of how many methods exist to implement a given polymorphic operation. Developers can add new classes without changing existing code, as long as they provide methods for each applicable operation.

1.2 What Is OO Development?

This book is about OO development as a way of thinking about software based on abstractions that exist in the real world as well as in the program. In this context *development* refers to the software life cycle: analysis, design, and implementation. The essence of OO development is the identification and organization of application concepts, rather than their final representation in a programming language. Brooks observes that the hard part of software development is the manipulation of its *essence,* owing to the inherent complexity of the problem, rather than the *accidents* of its mapping into a particular language [Brooks-95].

This book does not explicitly address integration, maintenance, and enhancement, but a clean design in a precise notation facilitates the entire software life cycle. The OO concepts and notation used to express a design also provide useful documentation.

1.2.1 *Modeling Concepts, Not Implementation*

In the past, much of the OO community focused on programming languages, with the literature emphasizing implementation rather than analysis and design. OO programming languages were first useful in alleviating the inflexibility of traditional programming languages. In a sense, however, this emphasis was a step backward for software engineering—it focuses excessively on implementation mechanisms, rather than the underlying thought process that they support.

The real payoff comes from addressing front-end conceptual issues, rather than back-end implementation details. Design flaws that surface during implementation are more costly to fix than those that are found earlier. A premature focus on implementation restricts design choices and often leads to an inferior product. An OO development approach encourages software developers to work and think in terms of the application throughout the software life cycle. It is only when the inherent concepts of the application are identified, organized, and understood that the details of data structures and functions can be addressed effectively.

OO development is a conceptual process independent of a programming language until the final stages. OO development is fundamentally a way of thinking and not a programming technique. Its greatest benefits come from helping specifiers, developers, and customers express abstract concepts clearly and communicate them to each other. It can serve as a medium for specification, analysis, documentation, and interfacing, as well as for programming.

1.2.2 *OO Methodology*

We present a process for OO development and a graphical notation for representing OO concepts. The process consists of building a model of an application and then adding details to it during design. The same seamless notation is used from analysis to design to implementation, so that information added in one stage of development need not be lost or translated for the next stage.The methodology has the following stages.

- **System conception**. Software development begins with business analysts or users conceiving an application and formulating tentative requirements.

- **Analysis**. The analyst scrutinizes and rigorously restates the requirements from system conception by constructing models. The analyst must work with the requestor to understand the problem, because problem statements are rarely complete or correct. The analysis model is a concise, precise abstraction of *what* the desired system must do, not *how* it will be done. The analysis model should not contain implementation decisions. For example, a *Window* class in a workstation windowing system would be described in terms of its visible attributes and operations.

    The analysis model has two parts: the ***domain model***, a description of the real-world objects reflected within the system; and the ***application model***, a description of the parts of the application system itself that are visible to the user. For example, domain objects for a stockbroker application might include stock, bond, trade, and commission. Application objects might control the execution of trades and present the results. Application experts who are not programmers can understand and criticize a good model.

■ **System design**. The development team devise a high-level strategy—the *system architecture*—for solving the application problem. They also establish policies that will serve as a default for the subsequent, more detailed portions of design. The system designer must decide what performance characteristics to optimize, choose a strategy of attacking the problem, and make tentative resource allocations. For example, the system designer might decide that changes to the workstation screen must be fast and smooth, even when windows are moved or erased, and choose an appropriate communications protocol and memory buffering strategy.

■ **Class design**. The class designer adds details to the analysis model in accordance with the system design strategy. The class designer elaborates both domain and application objects using the same OO concepts and notation, although they exist on different conceptual planes. The focus of class design is the data structures and algorithms needed to implement each class. For example, the class designer now determines data structures and algorithms for each of the operations of the *Window* class.

■ **Implementation**. Implementers translate the classes and relationships developed during class design into a particular programming language, database, or hardware. Programming should be straightforward, because all of the hard decisions should have already been made. During implementation, it is important to follow good software engineering practice so that traceability to the design is apparent and so that the system remains flexible and extensible. For example, implementers would code the *Window* class in a programming language, using calls to the underlying graphics system on the workstation.

OO concepts apply throughout the system development life cycle, from analysis through design to implementation. You can carry the same classes from stage to stage without a change of notation, although they gain additional details in the later stages. The analysis and implementation models of *Window* are both correct, but they serve different purposes and represent a different level of abstraction. The same OO concepts of identity, classification, polymorphism, and inheritance apply throughout development.

Note that we are not suggesting a waterfall development process—first capturing requirements, then analyzing, then designing, and finally implementing. For any particular part of a system, developers must perform each stage in order, but they need not develop each part of the system in tandem. We advocate an iterative process—developing part of the system through several stages and then adding capability.

Some classes are not part of analysis but are introduced during design or implementation. For example, data structures such as *trees, hash tables,* and *linked lists* are rarely present in the real world and are not visible to users. Designers introduce them to support particular algorithms. Such data structure objects exist within a computer and are not directly observable.

We do not consider testing as a distinct step. Testing is important, but it must be part of an overall philosophy of quality control that occurs throughout the life cycle. Developers must check analysis models against reality. They must verify design models against various kinds of errors, in addition to testing implementations for correctness. Confining quality control to a separate step is more expensive and less effective.

1.2.3 Three Models

We use three kinds of models to describe a system from different viewpoints: the class model for the objects in the system and their relationships; the state model for the life history of objects; and the interaction model for the interactions among objects. Each model applies during all stages of development and acquires detail as development progresses. A complete description of a system requires models from all three viewpoints.

The *class model* describes the static structure of the objects in a system and their relationships. The class model defines the context for software development—the universe of discourse. The class model contains class diagrams. A *class diagram* is a graph whose nodes are classes and whose arcs are relationships among classes.

The *state model* describes the aspects of an object that change over time. The state model specifies and implements control with state diagrams. A *state diagram* is a graph whose nodes are states and whose arcs are transitions between states caused by events.

The *interaction model* describes how the objects in a system cooperate to achieve broader results. The interaction model starts with use cases that are then elaborated with sequence and activity diagrams. A *use case* focuses on the functionality of a system—that is, what a system does for users. A *sequence diagram* shows the objects that interact and the time sequence of their interactions. An *activity diagram* elaborates important processing steps.

The three models are separate parts of the description of a complete system but are cross-linked. The class model is most fundamental, because it is necessary to describe *what* is changing or transforming before describing *when* or *how* it changes.

1.3 OO Themes

Several themes pervade OO technology. Although these themes are not unique to OO systems, they are particularly well supported.

1.3.1 Abstraction

Abstraction lets you focus on essential aspects of an application while ignoring details. This means focusing on what an object is and does, before deciding how to implement it. Use of abstraction preserves the freedom to make decisions as long as possible by avoiding premature commitments to details. Most modern languages provide data abstraction, but inheritance and polymorphism add power. The ability to abstract is probably the most important skill required for OO development.

1.3.2 Encapsulation

Encapsulation (also *information hiding*) separates the external aspects of an object, that are accessible to other objects, from the internal implementation details, that are hidden from other objects. Encapsulation prevents portions of a program from becoming so interdependent that a small change has massive ripple effects. You can change an object's implementation without affecting the applications that use it. You may want to change the implementation of an object to improve performance, fix a bug, consolidate code, or support porting. Encapsulation is not unique to OO languages, but the ability to combine data structure and behavior in a single entity makes encapsulation cleaner and more powerful than in prior languages, such as Fortran, Cobol, and C.

1.3.3 Combining Data and Behavior

The caller of an operation need not consider how many implementations exist. Operator polymorphism shifts the burden of deciding what implementation to use from the calling code to the class hierarchy. For example, non-OO code to display the contents of a window must distinguish the type of each figure, such as polygon, circle, or text, and call the appropriate procedure to display it. An OO program would simply invoke the *draw* operation on each figure; each object implicitly decides which procedure to use, based on its class. Maintenance is easier, because the calling code need not be modified when a new class is added. In an OO system, the data structure hierarchy matches the operation inheritance hierarchy (Figure 1.3).

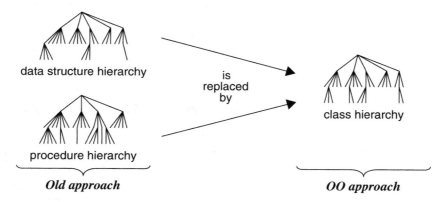

Figure 1.3 OO vs. prior approach. An OO approach has one unified
hierarchy for both data and behavior.

1.3.4 Sharing

OO techniques promote sharing at different levels. Inheritance of both data structure and behavior lets subclasses share common code. This sharing via inheritance is one of the main advantages of OO languages. More important than the savings in code is the conceptual clarity from recognizing that different operations are all really the same thing. This reduces the number of distinct cases that you must understand and analyze.

   OO development not only lets you share information within an application, but also offers the prospect of reusing designs and code on future projects. OO development provides the tools, such as abstraction, encapsulation, and inheritance, to build libraries of reusable components. Unfortunately, reuse has been overemphasized as a justification for OO technology. Reuse does not just happen; developers must plan by thinking beyond the immediate application and investing extra effort in a more general design.

1.3.5 Emphasis on the Essence of an Object

OO technology stresses what an object *is,* rather than how it is *used.* The uses of an object depend on the details of the application and often change during development. As requirements evolve, the features supplied by an object are much more stable than the ways it is used, hence software systems built on object structure are more stable in the long run. OO development places a greater emphasis on data structure and a lesser emphasis on procedure structure than functional-decomposition methodologies. In this respect, OO development is similar to information modeling techniques used in database design, although OO development adds the concept of class-dependent behavior.

1.3.6 Synergy

Identity, classification, polymorphism, and inheritance characterize OO languages. Each of these concepts can be used in isolation, but together they complement each other synergistically. The benefits of an OO approach are greater than they might seem at first. The emphasis on the essential properties of an object forces the developer to think more carefully and deeply about what an object is and does. The resulting system tends to be cleaner, more general, and more robust than it would be if the emphasis were only on the use of data and operations.

1.4 Evidence for Usefulness of OO Development

Our work on OO development began with internal applications at the General Electric Research and Development Center. We used OO techniques for developing compilers, graphics, user interfaces, databases, an OO language, CAD systems, simulations, metamodels, control systems, and other applications. We used OO models to document programs that are ill-structured and difficult to understand. Our implementation targets ranged from OO languages to non-OO languages to databases. We successfully taught this approach to others and used it to communicate with application experts.

Since the mid 1990s we have expanded our practice of OO technology beyond General Electric to companies throughout the world. When we wrote the first edition of this book, object orientation and OO modeling were relatively new approaches without much large-scale experience. OO technology can no longer be considered a fad or a speculative approach. It is now part of the computer science and software engineering mainstream.

The annual OOPSLA (Object-Oriented Programming Systems, Languages, and Applications), ECOOP (European Conference on Object-Oriented Programming), and TOOLS (Technology of Object-Oriented Languages and Systems) conferences are important forums for disseminating new OO ideas and application results. The conference proceedings describe many applications that have benefited from an OO approach. Articles on OO systems have also appeared in major publications, such as *IEEE Computer* and *Communications of the ACM.*

1.5 OO Modeling History

Our work at GE R&D led to the development of the Object Modeling Technique (OMT), which the previous edition of this book introduced in 1991. OMT was a success, but so were several other approaches. The popularity of OO modeling led to a new problem—a plethora of alternative notations. The notations expressed similar ideas but had different symbols, confusing developers and making communication difficult.

As a result, the software community began to focus on consolidating the various notations. In 1994 Jim Rumbaugh joined Rational (now part of IBM) and began working with Grady Booch on unifying the OMT and Booch notations. In 1995, Ivar Jacobson also joined Rational and added Objectory to the unification work.

In 1996 the Object Management Group (OMG) issued a request for proposals for a standard OO modeling notation. Several companies responded, and eventually the competing proposals were coalesced into a final proposal. Rational led the final proposal team, with Booch, Rumbaugh, and Jacobson deeply involved. The OMG unanimously accepted the resulting Unified Modeling Language (UML) as a standard in November 1997. The participating companies transferred UML rights to the OMG, which owns the trademark and specification for UML and controls its future development.

The UML was highly successful and replaced the other notations in most publications. Most of the authors of other methods adopted UML notation, willingly or because of market pressure. The UML has ended the OO notation wars and is now clearly *the* accepted OO notation. We have used UML in this book because it is now the standard notation.

In 2001 OMG members started work on a revision to add features missing from the initial specification and to fix problems that were discovered by experience with UML 1. This book is based on the UML 2.0 revision approved in 2004. For access to the official specification documents, see the OMG Web site at www.omg.org.

1.6 Organization of This Book

The remainder of this book is organized into four parts: modeling concepts, analysis/design, implementation, and software engineering. Appendices provide a glossary of terms and answer some of the exercises. The inside covers summarize the notation used in the book.

Part 1 explains OO concepts and presents a graphical notation for expressing them. Chapter 2 introduces modeling and three kinds of models—class, state, and interaction. Chapters 3 and 4 describe the class model, which deals with the structural "data" aspects of a system—these chapters are the heart of Part 1, and mastery of the class model is essential for successful OO development. Chapters 5 and 6 present the state model, which concerns the control aspects of a system. Chapters 7 and 8 describe the interaction model, which captures the interactions among different objects in a system. Chapter 9 summarizes the three models and how they relate to each other. The concepts dealt with in Part 1 permeate the software development cycle, applying equally to analysis, design, and implementation. The entire book uses the notation described in Part 1.

Part 2 shows how to prepare an OO model and use it to analyze and design a system. Chapter 10 summarizes the process, and then Chapter 11 discusses system conception, the invention of an application. Chapters 12 and 13 discuss analysis, the process of describing and understanding the application. Analysis begins with a problem statement from the customer. The analyst incorporates customer information and application knowledge to construct domain and application models. Chapter 14 addresses system design, which is primarily a task of partitioning a system into subsystems and making high-level policy decisions. Chapter 15 presents class design, the augmentation of the analysis model with design decisions. These decisions include the specification of algorithms, assigning functionality to objects, and optimization. Chapter 16 summarizes the process.

Part 3 addresses implementation, with Chapter 17 discussing issues apart from the target language. Chapters 18 and 19 address C++, Java, and databases. Chapter 20 presents guidelines for enhancing readability, reusability, and maintainability using good OO programming style.

Part 4 focuses on software engineering. Although Part 2 presents the stages in a linear order, as a book must, we do not believe that development should proceed in a waterfall fashion. Chapter 21 describes iterative development, in which the process stages are repeated multiple times to build the complete system. Chapter 22 provides advice for managing models. It is easiest to understand and to apply OO development on a new system, but most projects do not have the luxury of working on a clean slate. Chapter 23 describes issues involved in working with existing systems.

Most chapters contain exercises. Selected answers are included in the back of the book. We suggest that you try to work the exercises as you read this book, even if you are not a student. The exercises bring out many subtle points. They provide practice with OO technology and serve as a stepping stone to applications.

abstraction	encapsulation	object-oriented (OO)
analysis	identity	polymorphism
class design	implementation	state model
class model	inheritance	system design
classification	interaction model	

Figure 1.4 Key concepts for Chapter 1

Bibliographic Notes

[Taylor-98] provides a well-written overview of OO technology. [Meyer-97] is also an informative source, even though it is primarily an OO language book. [Love-93] presents examples of industrial projects that have used OO technology.

The purpose of this book is to teach OO concepts and thinking, not serve as a UML reference manual (see [Rumbaugh-05] for that). A textbook should emphasize important concepts, not fine details. We therefore present the most useful aspects of the UML, but we do not try to describe everything. You will learn faster by focusing on core concepts.

We have made a similar condensation of the development process. The process we describe is simple and aimed at small and medium projects. It contains highlights of the Unified Process (see [Jacobson-99]).

The UML contains the concept of a *classifier*, a more general form of a class that abstracts various kinds of modeling entities. For most purposes, there is little difference between a class and a classifier. In this book, we use the word *class* in preference to *classifier*, because modelers will work mostly with classes.

References

[Brooks-95] Frederick P. Brooks, Jr. *The Mythical Man-Month, Anniversary Edition*. Boston: Addison-Wesley, 1995.

[Jacobson-99] Ivar Jacobson, Grady Booch, James Rumbaugh. *The Unified Software Development Process*. Boston: Addison-Wesley, 1999.

[Love-93] Tom Love. *Object Lessons: Lessons Learned in Object-Oriented Development Practices*. New York: SIGS Books, 1993.

[Meyer-97] Bertrand Meyer. *Object-Oriented Software Construction, Second Edition*. Hertfordshire, England: Prentice Hall International, 1997.

[Rumbaugh-05] James Rumbaugh, Ivar Jacobson, Grady Booch. *The Unified Modeling Language Reference Manual, Second Edition*. Boston: Addison-Wesley, 2005.

[Taylor-98] David A. Taylor. *Object Technology: A Manager's Guide, Second Edition*. Boston: Addison-Wesley, 1998.

Exercises

The number in parentheses next to each exercise indicates the difficulty, from 1 (easy) to 10 (very difficult).

1.1   (3) What major problems have you encountered during past software projects? Estimate what percentage of your time you spend on analysis, design, coding, and testing/debugging/fixing. How do you go about estimating how much effort a project will require?

1.2   (3) Recall a past system that you created. Briefly describe it. What obstacles did you encounter in the design? What software engineering methodology, if any, did you use? What were your reasons for choosing or not choosing a methodology? Are you satisfied with the system as it exists? How difficult is it to add new features to the system? Is it maintainable?

1.3   (3) Describe a recent large software system that was behind schedule, over budget, or failed to perform as expected. What factors were blamed? How could the failure have been avoided?

1.4   (3) From a user's point of view, criticize a hardware or software system that has a flaw that especially annoys you. For example, some cars require the bumper to be removed to replace a tail light. Describe the system, the flaw, how it was overlooked, and how it could have been avoided with a bit more thought during design.

1.5   (5) All objects have identity and are distinguishable. However, for large collections of objects, it may not be a trivial matter to devise a scheme to distinguish them. Furthermore, a scheme may depend on the purpose of the distinction. For each of the following collections of objects, describe how they could be distinguished.
a. All persons in the world for the purpose of sending mail
b. All persons in the world for the purpose of criminal investigations
c. All customers with safe deposit boxes in a given bank
d. All telephones in the world for making telephone calls
e. All customers of a telephone company for billing purposes
f. All electronic mail addresses throughout the world
g. All employees of a company to restrict access for security reasons

1.6   (4) Prepare a list of classes that you would expect each of the following systems to handle.
a. A program for laying out a newspaper
b. A program to compute and store bowling scores
c. A telephone voice mail system with delivery options, message forwarding, and group lists
d. A controller for a video cassette recorder
e. A catalog store order entry system

1.7   (6) Classes and operations are listed below. For each class, select the operations that make sense for objects in that class. You may place an operation in multiple classes. Discuss the behavior of each operation.
Classes:
variable-length array — ordered collection of objects, indexed by an integer, whose size can vary at run time
symbol table — a table that maps text keywords into descriptors
set — unordered collection of objects with no duplicates
Operations:
append — add an object to the end of a collection
copy — make a copy of a collection
count — return the number of elements in a collection
delete — remove an element from a collection
index — retrieve an object from a collection at a given position
intersect — determine the common elements of two collections
insert — place an object into a collection at a given position
update — add an element to a collection, writing over whatever is already there

1.8   (4) Discuss what the classes in each of the following lists have in common. You may add more classes to each list.
a. scanning electron microscope, eyeglasses, telescope, bomb sight, binoculars
b. pipe, check valve, faucet, filter, pressure gauge
c. bicycle, sailboat, car, truck, airplane, glider, motorcycle, horse
d. nail, screw, bolt, rivet
e. tent, cave, shed, garage, barn, house, skyscraper

Part 1

Modeling Concepts

Part 1 describes the concepts and notations involved in object-oriented modeling. The concepts and notation apply to analysis, design, and implementation.

Chapter 2 discusses modeling in general and then introduces the three kinds of object-oriented models—class, state, and interaction.

Chapter 3 presents the class model which describes the static structure of a system. The class model provides the context for the other two kinds of models. Chapter 4 covers advanced class modeling concepts that you can skip upon a first reading of the book.

Chapter 5 explains the state model which describes the aspects of a system that change over time as well as control behavior. Chapter 6 covers advanced state modeling concepts that you can also skip upon a first reading.

Chapter 7 presents the interaction model and completes the treatment of the three models. The interaction model describes how objects collaborate to achieve overall results. Chapter 8 is an advanced chapter on interaction modeling that you can skip upon an initial reading.

Chapter 9 briefly summarizes the three kinds of models and how they relate to each other.

After reading Part 1, you will understand object-oriented concepts and the UML notation for expressing them. You will be ready to apply the concepts to software development in subsequent parts of the book.

2

Modeling as a Design Technique

A *model* is an abstraction of something for the purpose of understanding it before building it. Because a model omits nonessential details, it is easier to manipulate than the original entity. Abstraction is a fundamental human capability that permits us to deal with complexity. Engineers, artists, and craftsmen have built models for thousands of years to try out designs before executing them. Development of hardware and software systems is no exception. To build complex systems, the developer must abstract different views of the system, build models using precise notations, verify that the models satisfy the requirements of the system, and gradually add detail to transform the models into an implementation.

2.1 Modeling

Designers build many kinds of models for various purposes before constructing things. Examples include architectural models to show customers, airplane scale models for wind-tunnel tests, pencil sketches for composition of oil paintings, blueprints of machine parts, storyboards of advertisements, and outlines of books. Models serve several purposes.

■ **Testing a physical entity before building it**. The medieval masons did not know modern physics, but they built scale models of the Gothic cathedrals to test the forces on the structure. Engineers test scale models of airplanes, cars, and boats in wind tunnels and water tanks to improve their dynamics. Recent advances in computation permit the simulation of many physical structures without the need to build physical models. Not only is simulation cheaper, but it provides information that is too fleeting or inaccessible to be measured from a physical model. Both physical models and computer models are usually cheaper than building a complete system and enable early correction of flaws.

■ **Communication with customers**. Architects and product designers build models to show their customers. Mock-ups are demonstration products that imitate some or all of the external behavior of a system.

- **Visualization**. Storyboards of movies, television shows, and advertisements let writers see how their ideas flow. They can modify awkward transitions, dangling ends, and unnecessary segments before detailed writing begins. Artists' sketches let them block out their ideas and make changes before committing them to oil or stone.

- **Reduction of complexity**. Perhaps the main reason for modeling, which incorporates all the previous reasons, is to deal with systems that are too complex to understand directly. The human mind can cope with only a limited amount of information at one time. Models reduce complexity by separating out a small number of important things to deal with at a time.

2.2 Abstraction

Abstraction is the selective examination of certain aspects of a problem. The goal of abstraction is to isolate those aspects that are important for some purpose and suppress those aspects that are unimportant. Abstraction must always be for some purpose, because the purpose determines what is, and is not, important. Many different abstractions of the same thing are possible, depending on the purpose for which they are made.

All abstractions are incomplete and inaccurate. Reality is a seamless web. Anything we say about it, any description of it, is an abridgement. All human words and language are abstractions—incomplete descriptions of the real world. This does not destroy their usefulness. The purpose of an abstraction is to limit the universe so we can understand. In building models, therefore, you must not search for absolute truth but for adequacy for some purpose. There is no single "correct" model of a situation, only adequate and inadequate ones.

A good model captures the crucial aspects of a problem and omits the others. Most computer languages, for example, are poor vehicles for modeling algorithms because they force the specification of implementation details that are irrelevant to the algorithm. A model that contains extraneous detail unnecessarily limits your choice of design decisions and diverts attention from the real issues.

2.3 The Three Models

We find it useful to model a system from three related but different viewpoints, each capturing important aspects of the system, but all required for a complete description. The *class model* represents the static, structural, "data" aspects of a system. The *state model* represents the temporal, behavioral, "control" aspects of a system. The *interaction model* represents the collaboration of individual objects, the "interaction" aspects of a system. A typical software procedure incorporates all three aspects: It uses data structures (class model), it sequences operations in time (state model), and it passes data and control among objects (interaction model). Each model contains references to entities in other models. For example, the class model attaches operations to classes, while the state and interaction models elaborate the operations.

The three kinds of models separate a system into distinct views. The different models are not completely independent—a system is more than a collection of independent parts—but each model can be examined and understood by itself to a large extent. The different models have limited and explicit interconnections. Of course, it is always possible to create bad designs in which the three models are so intertwined that they cannot be separated, but a good design isolates the different aspects of a system and limits the coupling between them.

Each of the three models evolves during development. First analysts construct a model of the application without regard for eventual implementation. Then designers add solution constructs to the model. Implementers code both application and solution constructs. The word *model* has two dimensions—a view of a system (class model, state model, or interaction model) and a stage of development (analysis, design, or implementation). The meaning is generally clear from context.

2.3.1   Class Model

The *class model* describes the structure of objects in a system—their identity, their relationships to other objects, their attributes, and their operations. The class model provides context for the state and interaction models. Changes and interactions are meaningless unless there is something to be changed or with which to interact. Objects are the units into which we divide the world, the molecules of our models.

Our goal in constructing a class model is to capture those concepts from the real world that are important to an application. In modeling an engineering problem, the class model should contain terms familiar to engineers; in modeling a business problem, terms from the business; in modeling a user interface, terms from the application. An analysis model should not contain computer constructs unless the application being modeled is inherently a computer problem, such as a compiler or an operating system. The design model describes how to solve a problem and may contain computer constructs.

Class diagrams express the class model. Generalization lets classes share structure and behavior, and associations relate the classes. Classes define the attribute values carried by each object and the operations that each object performs or undergoes.

2.3.2   State Model

The *state model* describes those aspects of objects concerned with time and the sequencing of operations—events that mark changes, states that define the context for events, and the organization of events and states. The state model captures *control*, the aspect of a system that describes the sequences of operations that occur, without regard for what the operations do, what they operate on, or how they are implemented.

State diagrams express the state model. Each state diagram shows the state and event sequences permitted in a system for one class of objects. State diagrams refer to the other models. Actions and events in a state diagram become operations on objects in the class model. References between state diagrams become interactions in the interaction model.

2.3.3 Interaction Model

The *interaction model* describes interactions between objects—how individual objects collaborate to achieve the behavior of the system as a whole. The state and interaction models describe different aspects of behavior, and you need both to describe behavior fully.

Use cases, sequence diagrams, and activity diagrams document the interaction model. Use cases document major themes for interaction between the system and outside actors. Sequence diagrams show the objects that interact and the time sequence of their interactions. Activity diagrams show the flow of control among the processing steps of a computation.

2.3.4 Relationship Among the Models

Each model describes one aspect of the system but contains references to the other models. The class model describes data structure on which the state and interaction models operate. The operations in the class model correspond to events and actions. The state model describes the control structure of objects. It shows decisions that depend on object values and causes actions that change object values and state. The interaction model focuses on the exchanges between objects and provides a holistic overview of the operation of a system.

There are occasional ambiguities about which model should contain a piece of information. This is natural, because any abstraction is only a rough cut at reality; something will inevitably straddle the boundaries. Some properties of a system may be poorly represented by the models. This is also normal, because no abstraction is perfect; the goal is to simplify the system description without loading down the model with so many constructs that it becomes a burden and not a help. For those things that the model does not adequately capture, natural language or application-specific notation is still perfectly acceptable.

2.4 Chapter Summary

Models are abstractions built to understand a problem before implementing a solution. All abstractions are subsets of reality selected for a particular purpose.

We recommend three kinds of models. The class model describes the static structure of a system in terms of classes and relationships. The state model describes the control structure of a system in terms of events and states. The interaction model describes how individual objects collaborate to achieve the behavior of the system as a whole. Different problems place different emphasis on the three kinds of models.

abstraction	modeling
class model	relationship among models
interaction model	state model

Figure 2.1 Key concepts for Chapter 2

Bibliographic Notes

The first edition of this book also had three models (object, dynamic, and functional), but they were organized differently than those in this second edition.

The object model in the first edition is the same as the class model presented here. We have changed the name to *class model* to stress that the modeling entities are descriptors (classes and relationships) rather than instances (objects and links). Our presentation of the class model in this book also includes constraint modeling, which was missing from the first edition.

Similarly, the dynamic model in the first edition is the same as the state model in this book. We changed the name to *state model* to avoid confusion with other representations of dynamic behavior. The UML contains multiple kinds of models with various degrees of overlap—we cover the most important ones in this book.

We have dropped the functional model from the second edition. Certainly, the eventual software has functionality, but we seldom capture it with data flow diagrams as was shown in the first edition. We included data flow diagrams in the first edition for continuity with the structured analysis / structured design approach of the past. The functional model was not as useful as we envisioned, so we have now dropped it.

In its place, the second edition adds the interaction model. State diagrams do express dynamic behavior fully, but often in an inscrutable manner. Each state diagram focuses on a single class. When many classes have a significant state diagram, it can be difficult to understand an entire system. The interaction model focuses on collaboration and helps a software developer obtain a more comprehensive understanding than with state diagrams alone.

Exercises

2.1   (1) Some characteristics of an automotive tire are its size, material, internal construction (bias ply, steel belted, for example), tread design, cost, expected life, and weight. Which factors are important in deciding whether or not to buy a tire for your car? Which ones might be relevant to someone simulating the performance of a computerized anti-skid system for cars? Which ones are important to someone constructing a swing for a child?

2.2   (2) Suppose your bathroom sink is clogged and you have decided to try to unclog it by pushing a wire into the drain. You have several types of wire available around the house, some insulated and some not. Which of the following wire characteristics would you need to consider in selecting a wire for the job? Explain your answers.
   a. Immunity to electrical noise
   b. Color of the insulation
   c. Resistance of the insulation to salt water
   d. Resistance of the insulation to fire
   e. Cost
   f. Stiffness
   g. Ease of stripping the insulation

    h. Weight
    i. Availability
    j. Strength
    k. Resistance to high temperatures
    l. Resistance to stretching

2.3   (3) Wire is used in the following applications. For each application, prepare a list of wire characteristics that are relevant and explain why each is important for the application.
    a. Selecting wire for a transatlantic cable
    b. Choosing wire that you will use to create colorful artwork
    c. Designing the electrical system for an airplane
    d. Hanging a bird feeder from a tree
    e. Designing a piano
    f. Designing the filament for a light bulb

2.4   (3) If you were designing a protocol for transferring computer files from one computer to another over telephone lines, which of the following details would you select as relevant? Explain how they are relevant.
    a. Electrical noise on the communication lines
    b. The speed at which serial data is transmitted
    c. Availability of a database
    d. Availability of a good full-screen editor
    e. Buffering and flow control, such as an XON/XOFF protocol to regulate an incoming stream of data
    f. Number of tracks and sectors on a disk drive
    g. Character interpretation, such as special handling of control characters
    h. File organization, linear stream of bytes versus record-oriented, for example
    i. Math co-processor

2.5   (2) There are several models used in the analysis and design of electrical motors. An electrical model involves voltages, currents, electromagnetic fields, inductance, and resistance. A mechanical model considers stiffness, density, motion, forces, and torques. A thermal model handles heat dissipation and heat transfer. A fluid model describes the flow of cooling air. Which model(s) can answer the following questions? Discuss your conclusions.
    a. How much power is required to run a motor? How much of it is wasted as heat?
    b. How much does a motor weigh?
    c. How hot does a motor get?
    d. How much vibration does a motor create?
    e. How long will it take for the bearings of a motor to wear out?

2.6   (3) Decide which model(s) (class, state, interaction) are relevant for the following aspects of a computer chess player. A video display will show the board and pieces. A cursor controlled by a mouse will indicate human moves. Of course, in some cases, more than one model may apply. Explain your answers.
    a. User interface that displays computer moves and accepts human moves
    b. Representation of a configuration of pieces on the board
    c. Consideration of a sequence of possible legal moves
    d. Validation of a move requested by the human player

3

Class Modeling

A class model captures the static structure of a system by characterizing the objects in the system, the relationships between the objects, and the attributes and operations for each class of objects. The class model is the most important of the three models. We emphasize building a system around objects rather than around functionality, because an object-oriented system more closely corresponds to the real world and is consequently more resilient with respect to change. Class models provide an intuitive graphic representation of a system and are valuable for communicating with customers.

Chapter 3 discusses basic class modeling concepts that will be used throughout the book. We define each concept, present the corresponding UML notation, and provide examples. Some important concepts that we consider are object, class, link, association, generalization, and inheritance. You should master the material in this chapter before proceeding in the book.

3.1 Object and Class Concepts

3.1.1 Objects

The purpose of class modeling is to describe objects. For example, *Joe Smith*, *Simplex company*, *process number 7648*, and *the top window* are objects.

An *object* is a concept, abstraction, or thing with identity that has meaning for an application. Objects often appear as proper nouns or specific references in problem descriptions and discussions with users. Some objects have real-world counterparts (Albert Einstein and the General Electric company), while others are conceptual entities (simulation run 1234 and the formula for solving a quadratic equation). Still others (binary tree 634 and the array bound to variable *a*) are introduced for implementation reasons and have no correspondence to physical reality. The choice of objects depends on judgment and the nature of a problem; there can be many correct representations.

All objects have identity and are distinguishable. Two apples with the same color, shape, and texture are still individual apples; a person can eat one and then eat the other. Similarly, identical twins are two distinct persons, even though they may look the same. The term *identity* means that objects are distinguished by their inherent existence and not by descriptive properties that they may have.

3.1.2 Classes

An object is an *instance*—or occurrence—of a class. A *class* describes a group of objects with the same properties (attributes), behavior (operations), kinds of relationships, and semantics. *Person*, *company*, *process*, and *window* are all classes. Each person has name and birthdate and may work at a job. Each process has an owner, priority, and list of required resources. Classes often appear as common nouns and noun phrases in problem descriptions and discussions with users.

Objects in a class have the same attributes and forms of behavior. Most objects derive their individuality from differences in their attribute values and specific relationships to other objects. However, objects with identical attribute values and relationships are possible. The choice of classes depends on the nature and scope of an application and is a matter of judgment.

The objects in a class share a common semantic purpose, above and beyond the requirement of common attributes and behavior. For example, a barn and a horse may both have a cost and an age. If barn and horse were regarded as purely financial assets, they could belong to the same class. If the developer took into consideration that a person paints a barn and feeds a horse, they would be modeled as distinct classes. The interpretation of semantics depends on the purpose of each application and is a matter of judgment.

Each object "knows" its class. Most OO programming languages can determine an object's class at run time. An object's class is an implicit property of the object.

If objects are the focus of modeling, why bother with classes? The notion of abstraction is at the heart of the matter. By grouping objects into classes, we abstract a problem. Abstraction gives modeling its power and ability to generalize from a few specific cases to a host of similar cases. Common definitions (such as class name and attribute names) are stored once per class rather than once per instance. You can write operations once for each class, so that all the objects in the class benefit from code reuse. For example, all ellipses share the same procedures to draw them, compute their areas, and test for intersection with a line; polygons would have a separate set of procedures. Even special cases, such as circles and squares, can use the general procedures, though more efficient procedures are possible.

3.1.3 Class Diagrams

We began this chapter by discussing some basic modeling concepts, specifically *object* and *class*. We have described these concepts with examples and prose. This approach is vague and insufficient for dealing with the complexity of applications. We need a means for expressing models that is coherent, precise, and easy to formulate. There are two kinds of models of structure—class diagrams and object diagrams.

Class diagrams provide a graphic notation for modeling classes and their relationships, thereby describing possible objects. Class diagrams are useful both for abstract modeling and for designing actual programs. They are concise, easy to understand, and work well in practice. We will use class diagrams throughout this book to represent the structure of applications.

We will also occasionally use object diagrams. An *object diagram* shows individual objects and their relationships. Object diagrams are helpful for documenting test cases and discussing examples. A class diagram corresponds to an infinite set of object diagrams.

Figure 3.1 shows a class (left) and instances (right) described by it. Objects *JoeSmith*, *MarySharp*, and an anonymous person are instances of class *Person*. The UML symbol for an object is a box with an object name followed by a colon and the class name. The object name and class name are both underlined. Our convention is to list the object name and class name in boldface.

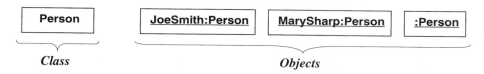

Class   *Objects*

Figure 3.1 A class and objects. Objects and classes are the focus of class modeling.

The UML symbol for a class also is a box. Our convention is to list the class name in boldface, center the name in the box, and capitalize the first letter. We use singular nouns for the names of classes.

Note how we run together multiword names, such as *JoeSmith*, separating the words with intervening capital letters. This is the convention we use for referring to objects, classes, and other constructs. Alternative conventions would be to use intervening spaces (Joe Smith) or underscores (Joe_Smith). The mixed capitalization convention is popular in the OO literature but is not a UML requirement.

3.1.4 Values and Attributes

A *value* is a piece of data. You can find values by examining problem documentation for examples. An *attribute* is a named property of a class that describes a value held by each object of the class. You can find attributes by looking for adjectives or by abstracting typical values. The following analogy holds: Object is to class as value is to attribute. Structural constructs—that is, classes and relationships (to be explained)—dominate class models. Attributes are of lesser importance and serve to elaborate classes and relationships.

Name, *birthdate*, and *weight* are attributes of *Person* objects. *Color*, *modelYear*, and *weight* are attributes of *Car* objects. Each attribute has a value for each object. For example, attribute *birthdate* has value "21 October 1983" for object *JoeSmith*. Paraphrasing, Joe Smith was born on 21 October 1983. Different objects may have the same or different values for a given attribute. Each attribute name is unique within a class (as opposed to being unique across all classes). Thus class *Person* and class *Car* may each have an attribute called *weight*.

Do not confuse values with objects. An attribute should describe values, not objects. Unlike objects, values lack identity. For example, all occurrences of the integer "17" are indistinguishable, as are all occurrences of the string "Canada." The country Canada is an object, whose *name* attribute has the value "Canada" (the string).

Figure 3.2 shows modeling notation. Class *Person* has attributes *name* and *birthdate*. *Name* is a string and *birthdate* is a date. One object in class *Person* has the value "Joe Smith" for name and the value "21 October 1983" for birthdate. Another object has the value "Mary Sharp" for name and the value "16 March 1950" for birthdate.

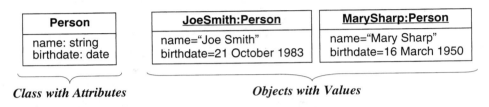

Figure 3.2 Attributes and values. Attributes elaborate classes.

The UML notation lists attributes in the second compartment of the class box. Optional details, such as type and default value, may follow each attribute. A colon precedes the type. An equal sign precedes the default value. Our convention is to show the attribute name in regular face, left align the name in the box, and use a lowercase letter for the first letter.

You may also include attribute values in the second compartment of object boxes. The notation is to list each attribute name followed by an equal sign and the value. We also left align attribute values and use regular type face.

Some implementation media require that an object have a unique identifier. These identifiers are implicit in a class model—you need not and should not list them explicitly. Figure 3.3 emphasizes the point. Most OO languages automatically generate identifiers with which to reference objects. You can also readily define them for databases. Identifiers are a computer artifact and have no intrinsic meaning.

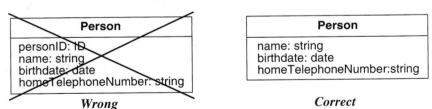

Figure 3.3 Object identifiers. Do not list object identifiers; they are implicit in models.

Do not confuse internal identifiers with real-world attributes. Internal identifiers are purely an implementation convenience and have no application meaning. In contrast, tax payer number, license plate number, and telephone number are not internal identifiers because they have meaning in the real world. Rather they are legitimate attributes.

3.1.5 Operations and Methods

An **operation** is a function or procedure that may be applied to or by objects in a class. *Hire, fire,* and *payDividend* are operations on class *Company. Open, close, hide,* and *redisplay* are operations on class *Window.* All objects in a class share the same operations.

Each operation has a target object as an implicit argument. The behavior of the operation depends on the class of its target. An object "knows" its class, and hence the right implementation of the operation.

The same operation may apply to many different classes. Such an operation is **polymorphic;** that is, the same operation takes on different forms in different classes. A **method** is the implementation of an operation for a class. For example, the class *File* may have an operation *print.* You could implement different methods to print ASCII files, print binary files, and print digitized picture files. All these methods logically perform the same task—printing a file; thus you may refer to them by the generic operation *print.* However, a different piece of code may implement each method.

An operation may have arguments in addition to its target object. Such arguments may be placeholders for values, or for other objects. The choice of a method depends entirely on the class of the target object and not on any object arguments that an operation may have. (A few OO languages, notably CLOS, permit the choice of method to depend on any number of arguments, but such generality leads to considerable semantic complexity, which we shall not explore.)

When an operation has methods on several classes, it is important that the methods all have the same **signature**—the number and types of arguments and the type of result value. For example, *print* should not have *fileName* as an argument for one method and *filePointer* for another. The behavior of all methods for an operation should have a consistent intent. It is best to avoid using the same name for two operations that are semantically different, even if they apply to distinct sets of classes. For example, it would be unwise to use the name *invert* to describe both a matrix inversion and turning a geometric figure upside-down. In a large project, some form of name scoping may be necessary to accommodate accidental name clashes, but it is best to avoid any possibility of confusion.

In Figure 3.4, the class *Person* has attributes *name* and *birthdate* and operations *changeJob* and *changeAddress. Name, birthdate, changeJob,* and *changeAddress* are features of *Person.* **Feature** is a generic word for either an attribute or operation. Similarly, *File* has a *print* operation. *GeometricObject* has *move, select,* and *rotate* operations. *Move* has argument *delta,* which is a *Vector; select* has one argument *p,* which is of type *Point* and returns a *Boolean;* and *rotate* has argument *angle,* which is an input of type float with a default value of 0.0.

The UML notation is to list operations in the third compartment of the class box. Our convention is to list the operation name in regular face, left align the name in the box, and use a lowercase letter for the first letter. Optional details, such as an argument list and result type, may follow each operation name. Parentheses enclose an argument list; commas separate the arguments. A colon precedes the result type. An empty argument list in parentheses shows explicitly that there are no arguments; otherwise you cannot draw conclusions. We do not list operations for objects, because they do not vary among objects of the same class.

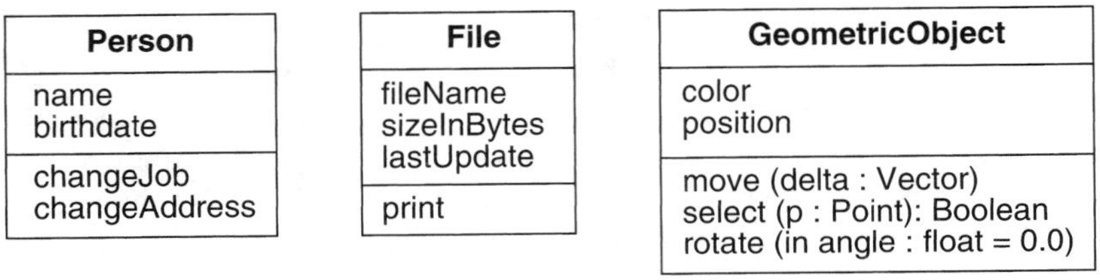

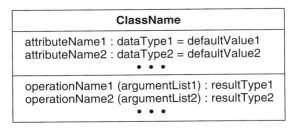

Figure 3.4 Operations. An operation is a function or procedure that may
be applied to or by objects in a class.

3.1.6 Summary of Notation for Classes

Figure 3.5 summarizes the notation for classes. A box represents a class and may have as
many as three compartments. The compartments contain, from top to bottom: class name,
list of attributes, and list of operations. Optional details such as type and default value may
follow each attribute name. Optional details such as argument list and result type may follow
each operation name.

ClassName
attributeName1 : dataType1 = defaultValue1 attributeName2 : dataType2 = defaultValue2 • • •
operationName1 (argumentList1) : resultType1 operationName2 (argumentList2) : resultType2 • • •

Figure 3.5 Summary of modeling notation for classes. A box represents
a class and may have as many as three compartments.

Figure 3.6 shows that each argument may have a direction, name, type, and default value. The *direction* indicates whether an argument is an input (*in*), output (*out*), or an input
argument that can be modified (*inout*). A colon precedes the type. An equal sign precedes the
default value. The default value is used if no argument is supplied for the argument.

direction argumentName : type = defaultValue

Figure 3.6 Notation for an argument of an operation. The direction, type,
and default value are optional. Direction may be *in*, *out*, or *inout*.

The attribute and operation compartments of class boxes are optional, and you may or
may not show them. A missing attribute compartment means that attributes are unspecified.
Similarly, a missing operation compartment means that operations are unspecified. In contrast,
an empty compartment means that attributes (operations) are specified and that there are none.

3.2 Link and Association Concepts

Links and associations are the means for establishing relationships among objects and classes.

3.2.1 Links and Associations

A *link* is a physical or conceptual connection among objects. For example, Joe Smith *Works-For* Simplex company. Most links relate two objects, but some links relate three or more objects. This chapter discusses only binary associations; Chapter 4 discusses n-ary associations. Mathematically, we define a link as a tuple—that is, a list of objects. A link is an instance of an association.

An *association* is a description of a group of links with common structure and common semantics. For example, a person *WorksFor* a company. The links of an association connect objects from the same classes. An association describes a set of potential links in the same way that a class describes a set of potential objects. Links and associations often appear as verbs in problem statements.

Figure 3.7 is an excerpt of a model for a financial application. Stock brokerage firms need to perform tasks such as recording ownership of various stocks, tracking dividends, alerting customers to changes in the market, and computing margin requirements. The top portion of the figure shows a class diagram and the bottom shows an object diagram.

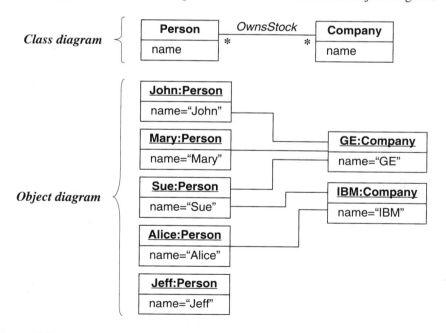

Figure 3.7 Many-to-many association. An association describes a set of potential links in the same way that a class describes a set of potential objects.

In the class diagram, a person may own stock in zero or more companies; a company may have multiple persons owning its stock. The object diagram shows some examples. John, Mary, and Sue own stock in the GE company. Sue and Alice own stock in the IBM company. Jeff does not own stock in any company and thus has no link. The asterisk is a multiplicity symbol. Multiplicity specifies the number of instances of one class that may relate to a single instance of another class and is discussed in the next section.

The UML notation for a link is a line between objects; a line may consist of several line segments. If the link has a name, it is underlined. For example, John owns stock in the GE company. An association connects related classes and is also denoted by a line (with possibly multiple line segments). For example, persons own stock in companies. Our convention is to show link and association names in italics and to confine line segments to a rectilinear grid. It is good to arrange the classes in an association to read from left-to-right, if possible.

The association name is optional, if the model is unambiguous. Ambiguity arises when a model has multiple associations among the same classes (*person works for company* and *person owns stock in company*). When there are multiple associations, you must use association names or association end names (Section 3.2.3) to resolve the ambiguity.

Associations are inherently bidirectional. The name of a binary association usually reads in a particular direction, but the binary association can be traversed in either direction. For example, *WorksFor* connects a person to a company. The inverse of *WorksFor* could be called *Employs,* and it connects a company to a person. In reality, both directions of traversal are equally meaningful and refer to the same underlying association; it is only the names that establish a direction.

Developers often implement associations in programming languages as references from one object to another. A *reference* is an attribute in one object that refers to another object. For example, a data structure for *Person* might contain an attribute *employer* that refers to a *Company* object, and a *Company* object might contain an attribute *employees* that refers to a set of *Person* objects. Implementing associations as references is perfectly acceptable, but you should not model associations this way.

A link is a relationship among objects. Modeling a link as a reference disguises the fact that the link is not part of either object by itself, but depends on both of them together. A company is not part of a person, and a person is not part of a company. Furthermore, using a pair of matched references, such as the reference from *Person* to *Company* and the reference from *Company* to a set of *Persons,* hides the fact that the forward and inverse references depend on each other. Therefore, you should model all connections among classes as associations, even in designs for programs.

The OO literature emphasizes encapsulation, that implementation details should be kept private to a class, and we certainly agree with this. Associations are important, precisely because they break encapsulation. Associations cannot be private to a class, because they transcend classes. Failure to treat associations on an equal footing with classes can lead to programs containing hidden assumptions and dependencies. Such programs are difficult to extend and the classes are difficult to reuse.

Although modeling treats associations as bidirectional, you do not have to implement them in both directions. You can readily implement associations as references if they are only traversed in a single direction. Chapter 17 discusses some trade-offs to consider when implementing associations.

3.2.2 *Multiplicity*

Multiplicity specifies the number of instances of one class that may relate to a single instance of an associated class. Multiplicity constrains the number of related objects. The literature often describes multiplicity as being "one" or "many," but more generally it is a (possibly infinite) subset of the nonnegative integers. UML diagrams explicitly list multiplicity at the ends of association lines. The UML specifies multiplicity with an interval, such as "1" (exactly one), "1..*" (one or more), or "3..5" (three to five, inclusive). The special symbol "*" is a shorthand notation that denotes "many" (zero or more).

Figure 3.7 illustrates many-to-many multiplicity. A person may own stock in many companies. A company may have multiple persons holding its stock. In this particular case, John and Mary own stock in the GE company; Alice owns stock in the IBM company; Sue owns stock in both companies; Jeff does not own any stock. GE stock is owned by three persons; IBM stock is owned by two persons.

Figure 3.8 shows a one-to-one association and some corresponding links. Each country has one capital city. A capital city administers one country. (In fact, some countries, such as The Netherlands and Switzerland, have more than one capital city for different purposes. If this fact were important, the model could be modified by changing the multiplicity or by providing a separate association for each kind of capital city.)

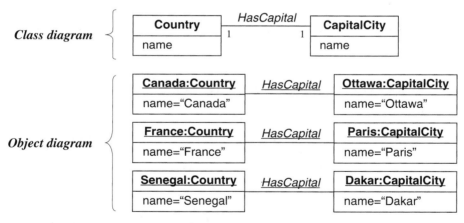

Figure 3.8 One-to-one association. Multiplicity specifies the number of instances of one class that may relate to a single instance of an associated class.

Figure 3.9 illustrates zero-or-one multiplicity. A workstation may have one of its windows designated as the console to receive general error messages. It is possible, however, that no console window exists. (The word "console" on the diagram is an association end name, discussed in Section 3.2.3.)

Figure 3.9 Zero-or-one multiplicity. It may be optional whether an object
is involved in an association.

Do not confuse "multiplicity" with "cardinality." Multiplicity is a *constraint* on the size
of a collection; cardinality is the *count* of elements that are actually in a collection. Therefore, multiplicity is a constraint on the cardinality.

A multiplicity of "many" specifies that an object may be associated with multiple objects. However, for each association there is at most one link between a given pair of objects
(except for bags and sequences, see Section 3.2.5). As Figure 3.10 and Figure 3.11 show, if
you want two links between the same objects, you must have two associations.

Figure 3.10 Association vs. link. A pair of objects can be instantiated at
most once per association (except for bags and sequences).

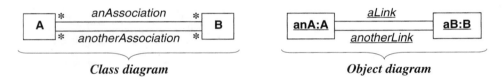

Figure 3.11 Association vs. link. You can use multiple associations to
model multiple links between the same objects.

Multiplicity depends on assumptions and how you define the boundaries of a problem.
Vague requirements often make multiplicity uncertain. Do not worry excessively about multiplicity early in software development. First determine classes and associations, then decide
on multiplicity. If you omit multiplicity notation from a diagram, multiplicity is considered
to be unspecified.

Multiplicity often exposes hidden assumptions built into a model. For example, is the
WorksFor association between *Person* and *Company* one-to-many or many-to-many? It depends on the context. A tax collection application would permit a person to work for multiple
companies. On the other hand, the member records for an auto workers' union may consider
second jobs irrelevant. Class diagrams help to elicit these hidden assumptions, making them
visible and subject to scrutiny.

The most important multiplicity distinction is between "one" and "many." Underesti-
mating multiplicity can restrict the flexibility of an application. For example, many programs

cannot accommodate persons with multiple phone numbers. On the other hand, overestimating multiplicity imposes overhead and requires the application to supply additional information to distinguish among the members of a "many" set. In a true hierarchical organization, for example, it is better to represent "boss" with a multiplicity of "zero or one," rather than allow for nonexistent matrix management.

3.2.3 Association End Names

Our discussion of multiplicity implicitly referred to the ends of associations. For example, a one-to-many association has two ends—an end with a multiplicity of "one" and an end with a multiplicity of "many." The notion of an **association end** is an important concept in the UML. You can not only assign a multiplicity to an association end, but you can give it a name as well. (Chapter 4 discusses additional properties of association ends.)

Association end names often appear as nouns in problem descriptions. As Figure 3.12 shows, a name appears next to the association end. In the figure *Person* and *Company* participate in association *WorksFor*. A person is an *employee* with respect to a company; a company is an *employer* with respect to a person. Use of association end names is optional, but it is often easier and less confusing to assign association end names instead of, or in addition to, association names.

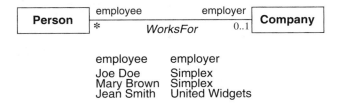

Figure 3.12 Association end names. Each end of an association can have a name.

Association end names are especially convenient for traversing associations, because you can treat each one as a pseudo attribute. Each end of a binary association refers to an object or set of objects associated with a source object. From the point of view of the source object, traversal of the association is an operation that yields related objects. Association end names provide a means of traversing an association, without explicitly mentioning the association. Section 3.5 talks further about traversing class models.

Association end names are necessary for associations between two objects of the same class. For example, in Figure 3.13 *container* and *contents* distinguish the two usages of *Directory* in the self-association. A directory may contain many lesser directories and may optionally be contained itself. Association end names can also distinguish multiple associations between the same pair of classes. In Figure 3.13 each directory has exactly one user who is an owner and many users who are authorized to use the directory. When there is only a single association between a pair of distinct classes, the names of the classes often suffice, and you may omit association end names.

Figure 3.13 Association end names. Association end names are necessary for associations between two objects of the same class. They can also distinguish multiple associations between a pair of classes.

Association end names let you unify multiple references to the same class. When constructing class diagrams you should properly use association end names and not introduce a separate class for each reference, as Figure 3.14 shows. In the wrong model, two instances represent a person with a child, one for the child and one for the parent. In the correct model, one person instance participates in two or more links, twice as a parent and zero or more times as a child. (In the correct model, we must show a child as having an optional parent, so that the recursion eventually terminates.)

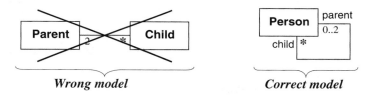

Figure 3.14 Association end names. Use association end names to model multiple references to the same class.

Because association end names distinguish objects, all names on the far end of associations attached to a class must be unique. Although the name appears next to the destination object on an association, it is really a pseudo attribute of the source class and must be unique within it. For the same reason, no association end name should be the same as an attribute name of the source class.

3.2.4 Ordering

Often the objects on a "many" association end have no explicit order, and you can regard them as a set. Sometimes, however, the objects have an explicit order. For example, Figure 3.15 shows a workstation screen containing a number of overlapping windows. Each window on a screen occurs at most once. The windows have an explicit order, so only the topmost window is visible at any point on the screen. The ordering is an inherent part of the association. You can indicate an ordered set of objects by writing "{ordered}" next to the appropriate association end.

Figure 3.15 Ordering the objects for an association end. Ordering sometimes occurs for "many" multiplicity.

3.2.5 Bags and Sequences

Ordinarily a binary association has at most one link for a pair of objects. However, you can permit multiple links for a pair of objects by annotating an association end with *{bag}* or *{sequence}*. A **bag** is a collection of elements with duplicates allowed. A **sequence** is an ordered collection of elements with duplicates allowed. In Figure 3.16 an itinerary is a sequence of airports and the same airport can be visited more than once. Like the *{ordered}* indication, *{bag}* and *{sequence}* are permitted only for binary associations.

Figure 3.16 An example of a sequence. An itinerary may visit multiple airports, so you should use *{sequence}* and not *{ordered}*.

UML1 did not permit multiple links for a pair of objects. Some modelers misunderstood this restriction with ordered association ends and constructed incorrect models, assuming that there could be multiple links. With UML2 the modeler's intent is now clear. If you specify *{bag}* or *{sequence}*, then there can be multiple links for a pair of objects. If you omit these annotations, then the association has at most one link for a pair of objects.

Note that the *{ordered}* and the *{sequence}* annotations are the same, except that the first disallows duplicates and the other allows them. A sequence association is an ordered bag, while an ordered association is an ordered set.

3.2.6 Association Classes

Just as you can describe the objects of a class with attributes, so too you can describe the links of an association with attributes. The UML represents such information with an association class. An **association class** is an association that is also a class. Like the links of an association, the instances of an association class derive identity from instances of the constituent classes. Like a class, an association class can have attributes and operations and participate in associations. You can find association classes by looking for adverbs in a problem statement or by abstracting known values.

In Figure 3.17, *accessPermission* is an attribute of *AccessibleBy*. The sample data at the bottom of the figure shows the value for each link. The UML notation for an association class is a box (a class box) attached to the association by a dashed line.

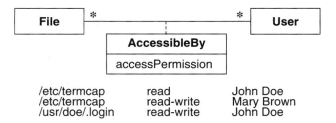

Figure 3.17 An association class. The links of an association can have attributes.

Many-to-many associations provide a compelling rationale for association classes. Attributes for such associations unmistakably belong to the link and cannot be ascribed to either object. In Figure 3.17, *accessPermission* is a joint property of *File* and *User* and cannot be attached to either *File* or *User* alone without losing information.

Figure 3.18 presents attributes for two one-to-many associations. Each person working for a company receives a salary and has a job title. The boss evaluates the performance of each worker. Attributes may also occur for one-to-one associations.

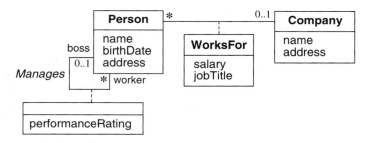

Figure 3.18 Association classes. Attributes may also occur for one-to-many
and one-to-one associations.

Figure 3.19 shows how it is possible to fold attributes for one-to-one and one-to-many associations into the class opposite a "one" end. This is not possible for many-to-many associations. As a rule, you should not fold such attributes into a class because the multiplicity of the association might change. Either form in Figure 3.19 can express a one-to-many association. However, only the association class form remains correct if the multiplicity of *WorksFor* is changed to many-to-many.

Figure 3.20 shows an association class participating in an association. Users may be authorized on many workstations. Each authorization carries a priority and access privileges. A user has a home directory for each authorized workstation, but several workstations and users can share the same home directory. Association classes are an important aspect of class modeling because they let you specify identity and navigation paths precisely.

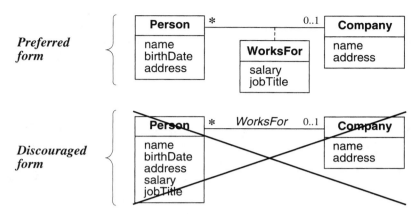

Figure 3.19 Proper use of association classes. Do not fold attributes of an association into a class.

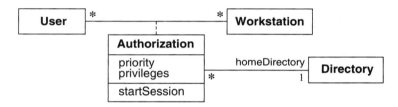

Figure 3.20 An association class participating in an association. Association classes let you specify identity and navigation paths precisely.

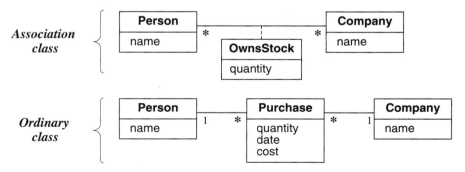

Figure 3.21 Association class vs. ordinary class. An association class is much different than an ordinary class.

Do not confuse an association class with an association that has been promoted to a class. Figure 3.21 highlights the difference. The association class has only one occurrence for each pairing of *Person* and *Company*. In contrast there can be any number of occurrences of a *Purchase* for each *Person* and *Company*. Each purchase is distinct and has its own quantity, date, and cost.

3.2.7 Qualified Associations

A **qualified association** is an association in which an attribute called the **qualifier** disambiguates the objects for a "many" association end. It is possible to define qualifiers for one-to-many and many-to-many associations. A qualifier selects among the target objects, reducing the effective multiplicity, from "many" to "one." Qualified associations with a target multiplicity of "one" or "zero-or-one" specify a precise path for finding the target object from the source object.

Figure 3.22 illustrates the most common use of a qualifier— for associations with one-to-many multiplicity. A bank services multiple accounts. An account belongs to a single bank. Within the context of a bank, the account number specifies a unique account. *Bank* and *Account* are classes and *accountNumber* is the qualifier. Qualification reduces the effective multiplicity of this association from one-to-many to one-to-one.

Qualified   *Not qualified*

Figure 3.22 Qualified association. Qualification increases the precision of a model.

Both models are acceptable, but the qualified model adds information. The qualified model adds a multiplicity constraint, that the combination of a bank and an account number yields at most one account. The qualified model conveys the significance of account number in traversing the model, as methods will reflect. You first find the bank and then specify the account number to find the account.

The notation for a qualifier is a small box on the end of the association line near the source class. The qualifier box may grow out of any side (top, bottom, left, right) of the source class. The source class plus the qualifier yields the target class. In Figure 3.22 *Bank* + *accountNumber* yields an *Account*, therefore *accountNumber* is listed in a box contiguous to *Bank*.

Figure 3.23 provides another example of qualification. A stock exchange lists many companies. However, a stock exchange lists only one company with a given ticker symbol. A company may be listed on many stock exchanges, possibly under different symbols. (We are presuming this is true. If every stock had a single ticker symbol that was invariant across exchanges, we would make *tickerSymbol* an attribute of *Company*.)

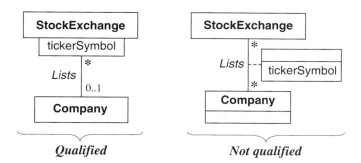

Figure 3.23 Qualified association. Qualification also facilitates traversal of class models.

3.3 Generalization and Inheritance

3.3.1 Definition

Generalization is the relationship between a class (the *superclass*) and one or more variations of the class (the *subclasses*). Generalization organizes classes by their similarities and differences, structuring the description of objects. The superclass holds common attributes, operations, and associations; the subclasses add specific attributes, operations, and associations. Each subclass is said to *inherit* the features of its superclass. Generalization is sometimes called the "is-a" relationship, because each instance of a subclass is an instance of the superclass as well.

Simple generalization organizes classes into a hierarchy; each subclass has a single immediate superclass. (Chapter 4 discusses a more complex form of generalization in which a subclass may have multiple immediate superclasses.) There can be multiple levels of generalizations.

Figure 3.24 shows several examples of generalization for equipment. Each piece of equipment is a pump, heat exchanger, or tank. There are several kinds of pumps: centrifugal, diaphragm, and plunger. There are several kinds of tanks: spherical, pressurized, and floating roof. The fact that the tank generalization symbol is drawn below the pump generalization symbol is not significant. Several objects are displayed at the bottom of the figure. Each object inherits features from one class at each level of the generalization. Thus *P101* embodies the features of equipment, pump, and diaphragm pump. *E302* has the properties of equipment and heat exchanger.

A large hollow arrowhead denotes generalization. The arrowhead points to the superclass. You may directly connect the superclass to each subclass, but we normally prefer to group subclasses as a tree. For convenience, you can rotate the triangle and place it on any side, but if possible you should draw the superclass on top and the subclasses on the bottom. The curly braces denote a UML comment, indicating that there are additional subclasses that the diagram does not show.

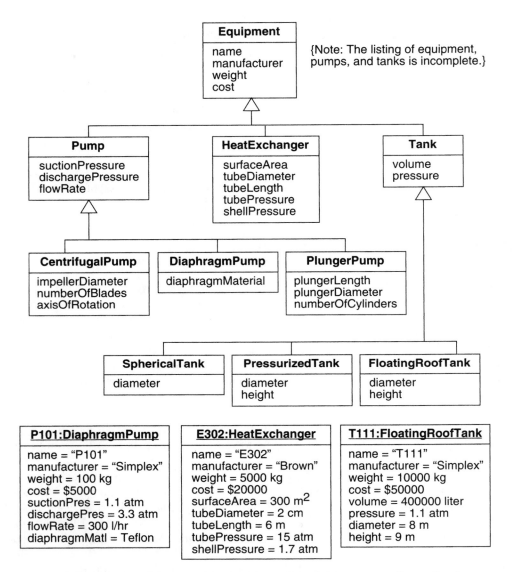

Figure 3.24 A multilevel inheritance hierarchy with instances. Generalization organizes classes by their similarities and differences, structuring the description of objects.

Generalization is transitive across an arbitrary number of levels. The terms *ancestor* and *descendant* refer to generalization of classes across multiple levels. An instance of a subclass is simultaneously an instance of all its ancestor classes. An instance includes a value for every attribute of every ancestor class. An instance can invoke any operation on any ancestor class. Each subclass not only inherits all the features of its ancestors but adds its own specific features as well. For example, *Pump* adds attributes *suctionPressure*, *dischargePressure*, and *flowRate*, which other kinds of equipment do not share.

Figure 3.25 shows classes of geometric figures. This example has more of a programming flavor and emphasizes inheritance of operations. *Move*, *select*, *rotate*, and *display* are operations that all subclasses inherit. *Scale* applies to one-dimensional and two-dimensional figures. *Fill* applies only to two-dimensional figures.

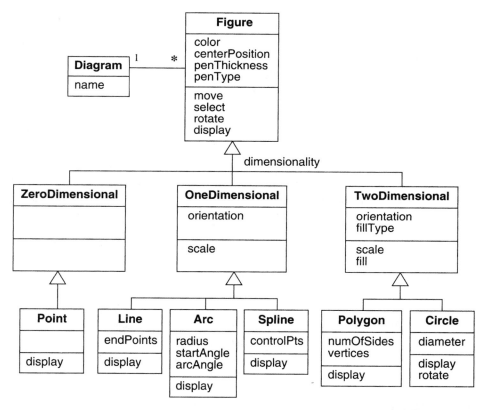

Figure 3.25 Inheritance for graphic figures. Each subclass inherits the attributes, operations, and associations of its superclasses.

The word written next to the generalization line in the diagram—*dimensionality*—is a generalization set name. A **generalization set name** is an enumerated attribute that indicates which aspect of an object is being abstracted by a particular generalization. You should generalize only one aspect at a time. For example, the means of propulsion (wind, fuel, animal, gravity) and the operating environment (land, air, water, outer space) are two aspects for class *Vehicle*. Generalization set values are inherently in one-to-one correspondence with the subclasses of a generalization. The generalization set name is optional.

Do not nest subclasses too deeply. Deeply nested subclasses can be difficult to under-stand, much like deeply nested blocks of code in a procedural language. Often, with some careful thought and a little restructuring, you can reduce the depth of an overextended inher-itance hierarchy. In practice, whether or not a subclass is "too deeply nested" depends upon judgment and the particular details of a problem. The following guidelines may help: An in-heritance hierarchy that is two or three levels deep is certainly acceptable; ten levels deep is probably excessive; five or six levels may or may not be proper.

3.3.2 Use of Generalization

Generalization has three purposes, one of which is support for polymorphism. You can call an operation at the superclass level, and the OO language compiler automatically resolves the call to the method that matches the calling object's class. Polymorphism increases the flexibility of software—you add a new subclass and automatically inherit superclass behav-ior. Furthermore, the new subclass does not disrupt existing code. Contrast the OO situation with procedural code, where addition of a new type can cause a ripple of changes.

The second purpose of generalization is to structure the description of objects. When you use generalization, you are making a conceptual statement—you are forming a taxono-my and organizing objects on the basis of their similarities and differences. This is much more profound than modeling each class individually and in isolation from other classes.

The third purpose is to enable reuse of code—you can inherit code within your applica-tion as well as from past work (such as a class library). Reuse is more productive than re-peatedly writing code from scratch. Generalization also lets you adjust the code, where necessary, to get the precise desired behavior. Reuse is an important motivator for inherit-ance, but the benefits are often oversold as Chapter 14 explains.

The terms generalization, specialization, and inheritance all refer to aspects of the same idea. *Generalization* and *specialization* concern a relationship among classes and take oppo-site perspectives, viewed from the superclass or from the subclasses. The word *generaliza-tion* derives from the fact that the superclass generalizes the subclasses. *Specialization* refers to the fact that the subclasses refine or specialize the superclass. *Inheritance* is the mecha-nism for sharing attributes, operations, and associations via the generalization/specialization relationship. In practice, there is little danger of confusion between the terms.

3.3.3 Overriding Features

A subclass may **override** a superclass feature by defining a feature with the same name. The overriding feature (the subclass feature) refines and replaces the overridden feature (the su-perclass feature). There are several reasons why you may wish to override a feature: to spec-ify behavior that depends on the subclass, to tighten the specification of a feature, or to improve performance. For example, in Figure 3.25, each leaf subclass must implement *dis-play*, even though *Figure* defines it. Class *Circle* improves performance by overriding oper-ation *rotate* to be a null operation.

You may override methods and default values of attributes. You should never override the *signature*, or form, of a feature. An override should preserve attribute type, number and type of arguments to an operation, and operation return type. Tightening the type of an attribute or operation argument to be a subclass of the original type is a form of restriction and must be done with care. It is common to boost performance by overriding a general method with a special method that takes advantage of specific information but does not alter the operation semantics (such as *Circle.rotate* in Figure 3.25).

You should never override a feature so that it is inconsistent with the original inherited feature. A subclass *is* a special case of its superclass and should be compatible with it in every respect. A common, but unfortunate, practice in OO programming is to "borrow" a class that is similar to a desired class and then modify it by changing and ignoring some of its features, even though the new class is not really a special case of the original class. This practice can lead to conceptual confusion and hidden assumptions built into programs.

3.4   A Sample Class Model

Figure 3.26 shows a class model of a workstation window management system. This model is greatly simplified—a real model would require a number of pages—but it illustrates many class modeling constructs and shows how they fit together.

Class *Window* defines common parameters of all kinds of windows, including a rectangular boundary defined by the attributes *x1, y1, x2, y2*, and operations to display and undisplay a window and to raise it to the top (foreground) or lower it to the bottom (background) of the entire set of windows.

A canvas is a region for drawing graphics. It inherits the window boundary from *Window* and adds the dimensions of the underlying canvas region defined by attributes *cx1, cy1, cx2, cy2*. A canvas contains a set of elements, shown by the association to class *Shape*. All shapes have color and line width. Shapes can be lines, ellipses, or polygons, each with their own parameters. A polygon consists of a list of vertices. Ellipses and polygons are both closed shapes, which have a fill color and a fill pattern. Lines are one dimensional and cannot be filled. Canvas windows have operations to add and delete elements.

TextWindow is a kind of a *ScrollingWindow,* which has a two-dimensional scrolling offset within its window, as specified by *xOffset* and *yOffset,* as well as an operation *scroll* to change the scroll value. A text window contains a string and has operations to insert and delete characters. *ScrollingCanvas* is a special kind of canvas that supports scrolling; it is both a *Canvas* and a *ScrollingWindow.* This is an example of *multiple inheritance,* to be explained in Chapter 4.

A *Panel* contains a set of *PanelItem* objects, each identified by a unique *itemName* within a given panel, as shown by the qualified association. Each panel item belongs to a single panel. A panel item is a predefined icon with which a user can interact on the screen. Panel items come in three kinds: buttons, choice items, and text items. A button has a string that appears on the screen; a button can be pushed by the user and has an attribute *depressed*. A choice item allows the user to select one of a set of predefined choices, each of which is a *ChoiceEntry* containing a string to be displayed and a value to be returned if the entry is selected. There are two associations between *ChoiceItem* and *ChoiceEntry*; a one-to-many as-

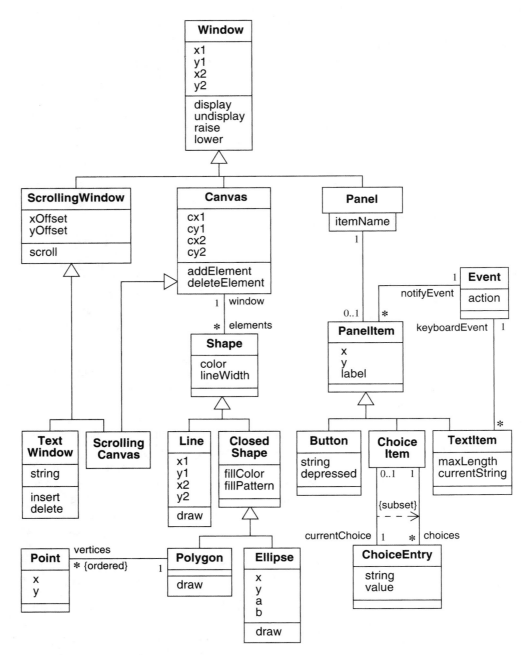

Figure 3.26 Class model of a windowing system

sociation defines the set of allowable choices, while a one-to-one association identifies the current choice. The current choice must be one of the allowable choices, so one association is a subset of the other as shown by the arrow between them labeled "{subset}." This is an example of a constraint, to be explained in Chapter 4.

When a panel item is selected by the user, it generates an *Event,* which is a signal that something has happened together with an action to be performed. All kinds of panel items have *notifyEvent* associations. Each panel item has a single event, but one event can be shared among many panel items. Text items have a second kind of event, which is generated when a keyboard character is typed while the text item is selected. The association with end name *keyboardEvent* shows these events. Text items also inherit the *notifyEvent* from super-class *PanelItem;* the *notifyEvent* is generated when the entire text item is selected with a mouse.

There are many deficiencies in this model. For example, perhaps we should define a type *Rectangle*, which can then be used for the window and canvas boundaries, rather than having two similar sets of four position attributes. Maybe a line should be a special case of a polyline (a connected series of line segments), in which case both *Polyline* and *Polygon* could be sub-classes of a new superclass that defines a list of points. Many attributes, operations, and classes are missing from a description of a realistic windowing system. Certainly the windows have associations among themselves, such as overlapping one another. Nevertheless, this simple model gives a flavor of the use of class modeling. We can criticize its details because it says something precise. It would serve as the basis for a fuller model.

3.5 Navigation of Class Models

So far we have shown how class models can express the structure of an application. Now we show how they can also express the behavior of navigating among classes. Navigation is important because it lets you exercise a model and uncover hidden flaws and omissions so that you can repair them. You can perform navigation manually (an informal technique) or write navigation expressions (as we will explain).

Consider the simple model for credit card accounts in Figure 3.27. An institution may issue many credit card accounts, each identified by an account number. Each account has a maximum credit limit, a current balance, and a mailing address. The account serves one or more customers who reside at the mailing address. The institution periodically issues a statement for each account. The statement lists a payment due date, finance charge, and minimum payment. The statement itemizes various transactions that have occurred throughout the billing interval: cash advances, interest charges, purchases, fees, and adjustments to the account. The name of the merchant is printed for each purchase.

We can pose a variety of questions against the model.

- What transactions occurred for a credit card account within a time interval?

- What volume of transactions were handled by an institution in the last year?

- What customers patronized a merchant in the last year by any kind of credit card?

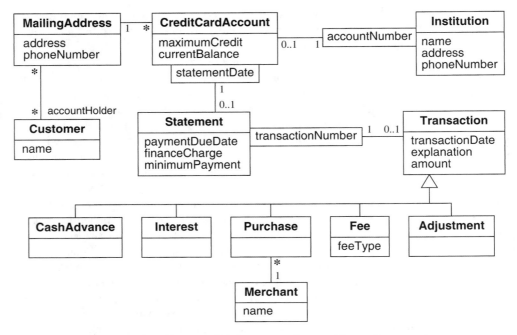

Figure 3.27 Class model for managing credit card accounts

■ How many credit card accounts does a customer currently have?

■ What is the total maximum credit for a customer, for all accounts?

The UML incorporates a language that can express these kinds of questions—the **Object Constraint Language (OCL)** [Warmer-99]. The next two sections discuss the OCL, and Section 3.5.3 then expresses the credit card questions using the OCL. By no means do we cover the complete OCL; we just cover the portions relevant to traversing class models.

3.5.1 OCL Constructs for Traversing Class Models

The OCL can traverse the constructs in class models.

■ **Attributes**. You can traverse from an object to an attribute value. The syntax is the source object, followed by a dot, and then the attribute name. For example, the expression *aCreditCardAccount.maximumCredit* takes a *CreditCardAccount* object and finds the value of *maximumCredit*. (We use the convention of preceding a class name by "a" to refer to an object.) Similarly, you can access an attribute for each object in a collection, returning a collection of attribute values. In addition, you can find an attribute value for a link, or a collection of attribute values for a collection of links.

■ **Operations**. You can also invoke an operation for an object or a collection of objects. The syntax is the source object or object collection, followed by a dot, and then the operation. An operation must be followed by parentheses, even if it has no arguments, to avoid confusion with attributes. You may invoke operations from your class model or predefined operations that are built into the OCL.

The OCL has special operations that operate on entire collections (as opposed to operating on each object in a collection). For example, you can count the objects in a collection or sum a collection of numeric values. The syntax for a collection operation is the source object collection, followed by "->", and then the operation.

- **Simple associations**. A third use of the *dot* notation is to traverse an association to a target end. The target end may be indicated by an association end name or, where there is no ambiguity, a class name. In the example, *aCustomer.MailingAddress* yields a set of addresses for a customer (the target end has "many" multiplicity). In contrast, *aCredit-CardAccount.MailingAddress* yields a single address (the target end has multiplicity of one).

- **Qualified associations**. A qualifier lets you make a more precise traversal. The expression *aCreditCardAccount.Statement[30 November 1999]* finds the statement for a credit card account with the statement date of 30 November 1999. The syntax is to enclose the qualifier value in brackets. Alternatively, you can ignore the qualifier and traverse a qualified association as if it were a simple association. Thus the expression *aCredit-CardAccount.Statement* finds the multiple statements for a credit card account. (The multiplicity is "many" when the qualifier is not used.)

- **Association classes**. Given a link of an association class, you can find the constituent objects. Alternatively, given a constituent object, you can find the multiple links of an association class.

- **Generalizations**. Traversal of a generalization hierarchy is implicit for the OCL notation.

- **Filters**. There is often a need to filter the objects in a set. The OCL has several kinds of filters, the most common of which is the *select* operation. The *select* operation applies a predicate to each element in a collection and returns the elements that satisfy the predicate. For example, *aStatement.Transaction->select(amount>$100)* finds the transactions for a statement in excess of $100.

3.5.2 Building OCL Expressions

The real power of the OCL comes from combining primitive constructs into expressions. For example, an OCL expression could chain together several association traversals. There could be several qualifiers, filters, and operators as well.

With the OCL, a traversal from an object through a single association yields a singleton or a set (or a bag if the association has the annotation *{bag}* or *{sequence}*). In general, a traversal through multiple associations can yield a bag (depending on the multiplicities), so you must be careful with OCL expressions. A set is a collection of elements without duplicates. A bag is a collection of elements with duplicates allowed.

The example in Figure 3.28 illustrates how an OCL expression can yield a bag. A company might want to send a single mailing to each stockholder address. Starting with the GE company, we traverse the *OwnsStock* association and get a set of three persons. Starting with

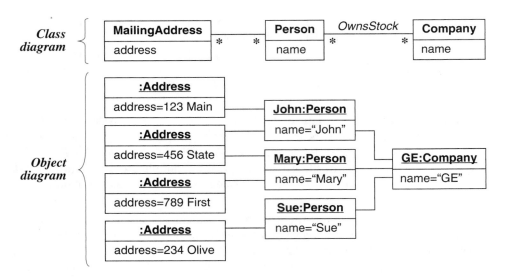

Figure 3.28 A sample model and examples. Traversal of multiple associations can yield a bag.

these three persons and traversing to mailing address, we get a bag obtaining the address *456 State* twice.

[Warmer-99] does not mention null values, since they only discuss the specification of constraints for a correctly implemented system. (***Null*** is a special value denoting that an attribute value is unknown or not applicable.) Handling of exceptions and run-time errors is also outside the scope of their book.

In contrast, the purpose in this chapter is not to specify constraints, but rather to discuss navigation of class models. Nulls do not arise for properly phrased and valid constraints. But they certainly do arise with model navigation. For example, a person may lack a mailing address. We extend the meaning of OCL expressions to accommodate nulls—a traversal may yield a null value, and an OCL expression evaluates to null if the source object is null.

3.5.3 Examples of OCL Expressions

We can use the OCL to answer the credit card questions.

■ What transactions occurred for a credit card account within a time interval?

```
aCreditCardAccount.Statement.Transaction->
select(aStartDate <= transactionDate and
transactionDate <= anEndDate)
```

The expression traverses from a *CreditCardAccount* object to *Statement* and then to *Transaction*, resulting in a set of transactions. (Traversal of the two associations results in a set, rather than a bag, because both associations are one-to-many.) Then we use the OCL *select* operator (a collection operator) to find the transactions within the time interval bounded by *aStartDate* and *anEndDate*.

■ What volume of transactions were handled by an institution in the last year?

```
anInstitution.CreditCardAccount.Statement.Transaction->
select(aStartDate <= transactionDate and
transactionDate <= anEndDate).amount->sum()
```

The expression traverses from an *Institution* object to *CreditCardAccount*, then to *Statement*, and then to *Transaction*. (Traversal results in a set, rather than a bag, because all three associations are one-to-many.) The OCL *select* operator finds the transactions within the time interval bounded by *aStartDate* and *anEndDate*. (We choose to make the time interval more general than *last year*.) Then we find the amount for each transaction and compute the total with the OCL *sum* operator (a collection operator).

■ What customers patronized a merchant in the last year by any kind of credit card?

```
aMerchant.Purchase->
select(aStartDate <= transactionDate and
transactionDate <= anEndDate).Statement.
CreditCardAccount.MailingAddress.Customer->asSet()
```

The expression traverses from a *Merchant* object to *Purchase*. The OCL *select* operator finds the transactions within the time interval bounded by *aStartDate* and *anEndDate*. (Traversal across a generalization, from *Purchase* to *Transaction*, is implicit in the OCL.) For these transactions, we then traverse to *Statement*, then to *CreditCardAccount*, then to *MailingAddress*, and finally to *Customer*. The association from *MailingAddress* to *Customer* is many-to-many, so traversal to *Customer* yields a bag. The OCL *asSet* operator converts a bag of customers to a set of customers, resulting in our answer.

■ How many credit card accounts does a customer currently have?

```
aCustomer.MailingAddress.CreditCardAccount->size()
```

Given a *Customer* object, we find a set of *MailingAddress* objects. Then, given the set of *MailingAddress* objects, we find a set of *CreditCardAccount* objects. (This traversal yields a set, and not a bag, because each *CreditCardAccount* pertains to a single *MailingAddress*.) For the set of *CreditCardAccount* objects we apply the OCL *size* operator, which returns the cardinality of the set.

■ What is the total maximum credit for a customer, for all accounts?

```
aCustomer.MailingAddress.CreditCardAccount.
maximumCredit->sum()
```

The expression traverses from a *Customer* object to *MailingAddress*, and then to *CreditCardAccount*, yielding a set of *CreditCardAccount* objects. For each *CreditCardAccount*, we find the value of *maximumCredit* and compute the total with the OCL *sum* operator.

Note that these kinds of questions exercise a model and uncover hidden flaws and omissions that can then be repaired. For example, the query on the number of credit card accounts suggests that we may need to differentiate past accounts from current accounts.

Keep in mind that the OCL was originally intended as a constraint language (see Chapter 4). However, as we explain here, the OCL is also useful for navigating models.

3.6 Practical Tips

We have gleaned the following tips for constructing class models from our application work. Many of these tips have been mentioned throughout the chapter.

- **Scope**. Don't begin class modeling by merely jotting down classes, associations, and inheritance. First, you must understand the problem to be solved. The content of a model is driven by relevance to the solution. You must exercise judgment in deciding which objects to show and which objects to ignore. A model represents only the relevant aspects of a problem. (Section 3.1.1)

- **Simplicity**. Strive to keep your models simple. A simple model is easier to understand and takes less development effort. Try to use a minimal number of classes that are clearly defined and not redundant. Be suspicious of classes that are difficult to define. You may need to reconsider such classes and restructure the model.

- **Diagram layout**. Draw your diagrams in a manner that elicits symmetry. Often there is a superstructure to a problem that lies outside the notation. Try to position important classes so that they are visually prominent on a diagram. Try to avoid crossing lines.

- **Names**. Carefully choose names. Names are important and carry powerful connotations. Names should be descriptive, crisp, and unambiguous. Do not bias names toward one aspect of an object. Choosing good names is one of the most difficult aspects of modeling. You should use singular nouns for the names of classes.

- **References**. Do not bury object references inside objects as attributes. Instead, model these as associations. This is clearer and captures the true intent rather than an implementation approach. (Section 3.2.1)

- **Multiplicity**. Challenge association ends with a multiplicity of one. Often the object on either end is optional and zero-or-one multiplicity may be more appropriate. Other times "many" multiplicity is needed. (Section 3.2.2)

- **Association end names**. Be alert for multiple uses of the same class. Use association end names to unify references to the same class. (Section 3.2.3)

- **Bags and sequences**. An ordinary binary association has at most one link for a pair of objects. However, you can permit multiple links for a pair of objects by annotating an association end with *{bag}* or *{sequence}*. (Section 3.2.5)

- **Attributes of associations**. During analysis, do not collapse attributes of associations into one of the related classes. You should directly describe the objects and links in your models. During design and implementation, you can always combine information for more efficient execution. (Section 3.2.6)

- **Qualified associations**. Challenge association ends with a multiplicity of "many." A qualifier can often improve the precision of an association and highlight important navigation paths. (Section 3.2.7)

- **Generalization levels**. Try to avoid deeply nested generalizations. (Section 3.3.1)

- **Overriding features**. You may override methods and default values of attributes. However, you should never override a feature so that it is inconsistent with the signature or semantics of the original inherited feature. (Section 3.3.3)

- **Reviews**. Try to get others to review your models. Expect that your models will require revision. Class models require revision to clarify names, improve abstraction, repair errors, add information, and more accurately capture structural constraints. Nearly all of our models have required several revisions.

- **Documentation**. Always document your models. The diagram specifies the structure of a model but cannot describe the rationale. The written explanation guides the reader and explains subtle reasons for why the model was constructed a particular way.

3.7 Chapter Summary

Class models describe the static data structure of objects and their relationships to one another. The content of a model is a matter of judgment and is driven by the needs of an application. An object is a concept, abstraction, or thing with identity that has meaning for an application. A class describes a group of objects with the same attributes, behavior, kinds of relationships, and semantics. An attribute is a named property of a class that describes a value held by each object of the class. An operation is a function or procedure that may be applied to or by objects in a class.

A link is a physical or conceptual connection among objects and is an instance of an association. An association is a description of a group of links with common structure and semantics. An association describes a set of potential links in the same way that a class describes a set of potential objects. An association is a logical construct, of which a reference is an implementation alternative. There are other ways of implementing associations besides using references.

You can refer to an end of an association and give it a name and multiplicity. Multiplicity specifies the number of instances of one class that may relate to a single instance of an associated class. An association class is an association that is also a class; an association class may have attributes, operations, and participate in associations. A qualified association is an association in which the objects in a "many" association end are partially or fully disambiguated by an attribute called the qualifier. The qualifier selects among the target objects, reducing the effective multiplicity, often from "many" to "one." Names are often qualifiers.

Generalization is the relationship between a class (the superclass) and one or more variations of the class (the subclasses). Generalization organizes classes by their similarities and differences, structuring the description of objects. A subclass inherits the attributes, operations, and associations of its superclasses. Through inheritance, a subclass can reuse superclass properties or override them; a subclass can add new properties.

Generalization is an important construct for both conceptual modeling and implementation. During conceptual modeling, generalization lets the developer organize classes on the basis of similarities and differences. During implementation, inheritance facilitates polymorphism and code reuse. Inheritance may occur across an arbitrary number of levels, where each level represents one aspect of an object. An object accumulates attributes, operations, and associations from each level of a generalization hierarchy.

Class models are useful for more than just data structure. In particular, navigation of class models lets you express certain behavior. Furthermore, navigation exercises a class model and uncovers hidden flaws and omissions, which you can then repair. The UML incorporates a language that can be used for navigation, the Object Constraint Language (OCL).

The various class modeling constructs work together to describe a complex system precisely, as shown by our example of a model for a windowing system. Once a model is available, even a simplified one, you can compare it against the requirements of an application, criticize it, and improve it.

ancestor	default value	link	polymorphism
association	descendant	method	qualified association
association class	direction	multiplicity	qualifier
association end	feature	navigation	sequence
attribute	generalization	object	signature
bag	generalization set name	object diagram	specialization
class	identity	operation	subclass
class diagram	inheritance	ordering	superclass
class model	instance	override	value

Figure 3.29 Key concepts for Chapter 3

Bibliographic Notes

The class modeling approach described in this book builds on the OMT notation originally proposed in [Loomis-87], which has now been superseded by the UML [Booch-99] [Rumbaugh-05] [UML]. The UML *class model* corresponds to the *OMT notation* discussed in [Loomis-87]. [Blaha-98] also covers the UML class modeling notation with an emphasis on the constructs that are relevant to database applications.

The class modeling notation is one of a score of approaches descended from the seminal entity-relationship (ER) model of [Chen-76]. All the descendants attempt to improve on the ER approach. Enhancements to the ER model have been pursued for several reasons. The ER technique has been successful for database modeling and as a result, there has been great demand for additional power. Also, ER modeling addresses only database design and not programming. There are too many extensions to ER for us to discuss them here.

A noteworthy aspect of the OMT notation and its successor UML is the emphasis on associations. As with inheritance, associations are important for conceptual modeling and implementation. [Rumbaugh-87] is the original source of the association ideas. The use of the term *relation* in [Rumbaugh-87] is synonymous with our use of *association* in this book.

In the data modeling notations, such as ER and IDEF1X, a binary association has at most one link for a pair of objects. UML1 follows the data modeling convention and also restricts a binary association to at most one link for a pair of objects. Note that UML2 has an exception to this behavior. In UML2 a binary association with the annotation *{bag}* or *{sequence}* can have multiple links for a pair of objects.

[Khoshafian-86] defines the concept of object identity and its importance to programming languages and database systems.

[Warmer-99] is the reference for the Object Constraint Language (OCL) that is part of the UML. We use the OCL in this chapter for navigating class models.

[Rayside-00] compares OO concepts with philosophy. He emphasizes the importance of crisp names and clear thinking.

[Chonoles-03], [Fowler-00], and [Larman-02] are additional books that you can read to help you learn about the UML. We thank Michael Chonoles for the example (Figure 3.10, Figure 3.11) clarifying that each association has at most one link between a given pair of objects (other than bags and sequences).

References

[Blaha-98] Michael Blaha and William Premerlani. *Object-Oriented Modeling and Design for Database Applications*. Upper Saddle River, NJ: Prentice Hall, 1998.

[Booch-99] Grady Booch, James Rumbaugh, and Ivar Jacobson. *The Unified Modeling Language User Guide*. Boston: Addison-Wesley, 1999.

[Chen-76] P.P.S. Chen. The Entity-Relationship model—toward a unified view of data. *ACM Transactions on Database Systems 1*, 1 (March 1976), 9–36.

[Chonoles-03] Michael Jesse Chonoles and James A. Schardt. *UML2 for Dummies*. New York: Wiley, 2003.

[Fowler-00] Martin Fowler. *UML Distilled, Second Edition*. Boston: Addison-Wesley, 2000.

[Khoshafian-86] S.N. Khoshafian and G.P. Copeland. Object identity. *OOPLSA '86 as ACM SIGPLAN 21*, 11 (November 1986), 406–416.

[Larman-02] Craig Larman. *Applying UML and Patterns: An Introduction to Object-Oriented Analysis and Design and the Unified Process*. Upper Saddle River, NJ: Prentice Hall, 2002.

[Loomis-87] Mary E.S. Loomis, Ashwin V. Shah, and James E. Rumbaugh. An object modeling technique for conceptual design. *European Conference on Object-Oriented Programming*, Paris, France, June 15–17, 1987, published as *Lecture Notes in Computer Science, 276,* Springer-Verlag, 192–202.

[Rayside-00] Derek Rayside and Gerard Campbell. An Aristotelian understanding of object-oriented programming. *OOPLSA '00 as ACM SIGPLAN 35*, 10 (October 2000), 337–353.

[Rumbaugh-87] James E. Rumbaugh. Relations as semantic constructs in an object-oriented language. *OOPSLA '87 as ACM SIGPLAN 22*, 12 (December1987), 466–481.

[Rumbaugh-05] James Rumbaugh, Ivar Jacobson, Grady Booch. *The Unified Modeling Language Reference Manual, Second Edition*. Boston: Addison-Wesley, 2005.

[UML] www.uml.org

[Warmer-99] Jos Warmer and Anneke Kleppe. *The Object Constraint Language*. Boston: Addison-Wesley, 1999.

Exercises

3.1   (3) Prepare a class diagram from the object diagram in Figure E3.1.

Spain:Country	*Borders*	**France:Country**	*Borders*	**Belgium:Country**
name="Spain"		name="France"		name="Belgium"

Figure E3.1 Object diagram for a portion of Europe

3.2   (5) Prepare a class diagram from the object diagram in Figure E3.2. Explain your multiplicity decisions. Each point has an x coordinate and a y coordinate. What is the smallest number of points required to construct a polygon? Does it make a difference whether or not a point may be shared between polygons? Your answer should address the fact that points are ordered.

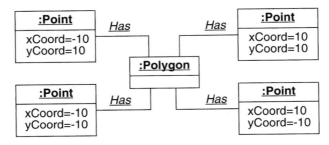

Figure E3.2   Object diagram for a polygon that happens to be a square

3.3   (5) Using your class diagram for Exercise 3.2, prepare an object diagram for two triangles with a common side under the following conditions.
        a. A point belongs to exactly one polygon.
        b. A point belongs to one or more polygons.

3.4   (5) Prepare a class diagram from the object diagram in Figure E3.3. How does your diagram express the fact that points are ordered? Assume that a point belongs to at most one polygon.

3.5   (2) Prepare a written description for the class diagrams from Exercise 3.2 and Exercise 3.4.

3.6   (6) Prepare a class diagram from the object diagram in Figure E3.4.

3.7   (5) Prepare a class diagram from the object diagram in Figure E3.5. This particular document has 4 pages. The first page has a red point and a yellow square displayed on it. The second page contains a line and an ellipse. An arc, a circle, and a rectangle appear on the last two pages. In preparing your diagram, use one or more generalizations.

3.8   (4) Figure E3.6 is a partially completed class diagram of an air transportation system. Multiplicity has been omitted. Add multiplicity to the diagram. Demonstrate how multiplicity decisions depend on your perception of the world.

3.9   (3) Add association names to the unlabeled associations in Figure E3.6.

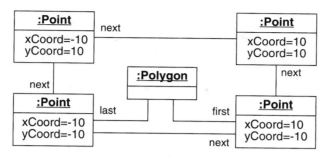

Figure E3.3 Object diagram for a polygon that happens to be a square

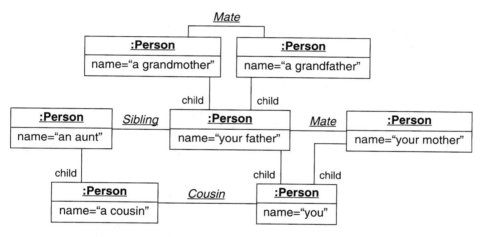

Figure E3.4 Object diagram for part of your family tree

3.10 (3) Add association end names to Figure E3.6. Add only meaningful names that are different from the class names. You should add at least six association end names to the diagram.

3.11 (2) Add the following operations to the class diagram in Figure E3.6: heat, hire, fire, refuel, reserve, clean, de-ice, take off, land, repair, cancel, delay. It is permissible to add an operation to more than one class.

3.12 (6) Prepare an object diagram for an imaginary round trip you took last weekend to London. Include at least one instance of each class. Fortunately, direct flights on a hypersonic plane were available. A friend went with you but decided to stay a while and is still there. Captain Johnson was your pilot on both flights. You had a different seat each way, but you noticed it was on the same plane because of a distinctive dent in the tail section. Students should indicate unknown values with a "?".

3.13 Prepare a class diagram for each group of classes. Add at least 10 relationships (associations and generalizations) to each diagram. Use association names and association end names where

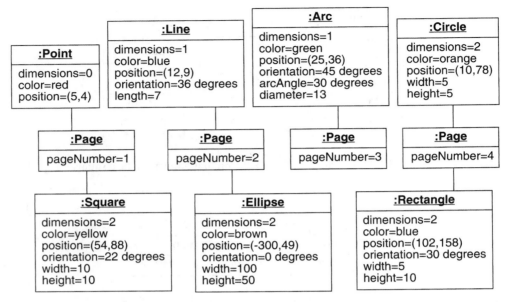

Figure E3.5 Object diagram for a geometrical document

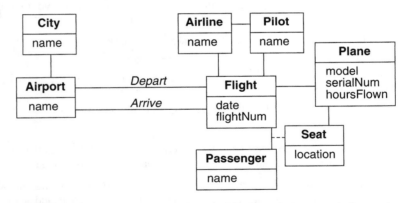

Figure E3.6 Partially completed class model of an air transportation system

needed. Also use qualified associations and show multiplicity. You do not need to show attributes or operations. As you prepare the diagrams, you may add classes. Be sure to explain
your diagrams.

a. (6) school, playground, principal, school board, classroom, book, student, teacher, cafeteria,
   restroom, computer, desk, chair, ruler, door, swing
b. (4) automobile, engine, wheel, brake, brake light, door, battery, muffler, tail pipe
c. (4) castle, moat, drawbridge, tower, ghost, stairs, dungeon, floor, corridor, room, window,
   stone, lord, lady, cook

d. (8) expression, constant, variable, function, argument list, relational operator, term, factor, arithmetic operator, statement, computer program

e. (6) file system, file, ASCII file, binary file, directory file, disc, drive, track, sector

f. (4) gas furnace, blower, blower motor, room thermostat, furnace thermostat, humidifier, humidity sensor, gas control, blower control, hot air vent

g. (7) chess piece, rank, file, square, board, move, tree of moves

h. (4) sink, freezer, refrigerator, table, light, switch, window, smoke alarm, burglar alarm, cabinet, bread, cheese, ice, door, kitchen

3.14 (4) Add at least 10 attributes and at least 5 methods to each of the class diagrams you prepared in the previous exercise.

3.15 (6) Figure E3.7 is a portion of a class diagram for a computer program for playing several types of card games. Deck, hand, discard pile, and draw pile are collections of cards. The initial size of a hand depends on the type of game. Each card has a suit and rank. Add the following operations to the diagram: *display*, *shuffle*, *deal*, *initialize*, *sort*, *topOfPile*, *bottomOfPile*, *insert*, *draw*, and *discard*. Some operations may appear in more than one class. For each class in which an operation appears, describe the arguments to the operation and what the operation should do to an instance of that class.

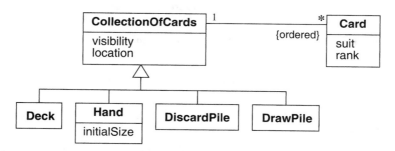

Figure E3.7 Portion of a class diagram for a card-playing system

3.16 (5) Figure E3.8 is a portion of a class diagram for a computer system for laying out a newspaper. The system handles newspaper pages which may contain, among other things, columns of text. The user may edit the width and length of a column of text, move it around on a page, or move it from one page to another. As shown, a column is displayed on exactly one page.

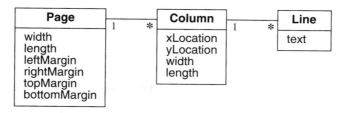

Figure E3.8 Portion of a class diagram for a newspaper publishing system

Modify the class diagram so that portions of the same column may appear on more than one page. If the user edits the text on one page, the changes should appear automatically on other pages. You should change *x* location and *y* location into attributes of an association.

3.17 (6) Figure E3.9 is a class diagram that might be used in developing a system to simplify the scheduling and scoring of judged athletic competitions such as gymnastics, diving, and figure skating. There are multiple events and competitors. Each competitor may enter several events and each event has many competitors.

Each event has several judges who subjectively rate the performance of competitors in that event. A judge rates every competitor for an event. In some cases, a judge may score more than one event.

Trials are the focus of the competition. Each trial is an attempt by one competitor to perform his or her best in one event. A trial is scored by the panel of judges for that event and a net score determined. Add multiplicity to the diagram.

Figure E3.9 Portion of a class diagram for an athletic-event scoring system

3.18 (3) Add the following attributes to Figure E3.9: address, age, date, difficulty factor, score, and name. In some cases, you may wish to use the same attribute in more than one class.

3.19 (3) Add an association to Figure E3.9 to make it possible to determine a competitor's intended events before trials are held.

3.20 (6) Prepare a class model to describe undirected graphs. An undirected graph consists of a set of vertices and a set of edges. Edges connect pairs of vertices. Your model should capture only the structure of graphs (i.e., connectivity) and need not be concerned with layout such as location of vertices or lengths of edges. Figure E3.10 shows a typical undirected graph.

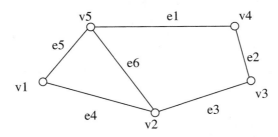

Figure E3.10 Sample undirected graph

3.21 (4) Prepare an object diagram for Figure E3.10. [Instructor's note: You may want to give the students our answer to Exercise 3.20.]

3.22   (5) Extend the class diagram you prepared in Exercise 3.20 with layout details, including loca-
        tions of vertices and thickness and color of edges. Also add names of vertices and edges. [In-
        structor's note: You may want to give the students our answer to Exercise 3.20.]

3.23   (7) Prepare a class model to describe directed graphs. A directed graph is similar to an undirect-
        ed graph, except the edges are oriented. Figure E3.11 shows a typical directed graph.

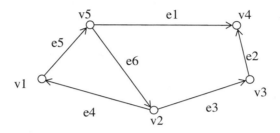

Figure E3.11 Sample directed graph

3.24   (4) Prepare an object diagram for Figure E3.11. [Instructor's note: You may want to give the
        students our answer to Exercise 3.23.]

3.25   (7) Several classes shown in Figure E3.12 have attributes that are really references to other
        classes and could be replaced with associations. A person may have up to three companies as
        employers. Each person has an ID. A car is assigned an ID. Cars may be owned by persons,
        companies, or banks. Owner ID refers to the ID of the person, company, or bank who owns the
        car. A car loan may be involved in the purchase of a car.
            Burying object references as references is the incorrect way to construct a model. Prepare a
        class diagram without IDs and using association and generalization. Try to assign multiplicities.
        You may need to add one or more classes of your own.

Person	Car	CarLoan	Company	Bank
name birthdate employer1ID employer2ID employer3ID personID address	ownerID vehicleID ownerType model year	vehicleID customerType customerID accountNumber bankID interestRate currentBalance	name companyID	name bankID

Figure E3.12 Classes with some attributes that are references.

3.26   (4) A problem arises when several independent systems need to identify the same object. For
        example, the department of motor vehicles, an insurance company, a bank, and the police may
        wish to identify a given motor vehicle. Discuss the relative merits of using the following iden-
        tification methods:
        a. Identify by its owner
        b. Identify by attributes such as manufacturer, model, and year

c. Use the vehicle identification number (VIN) assigned to the car by its manufacturer

d. Use IDs generated internally by each interested agency

3.27 (7) Prepare a class model that might be used to troubleshoot a 4-cycle lawn mower engine. Use three separate diagrams for the model, with one diagram for each of the following paragraphs.

Power is developed in such an engine by the combustion of a mixture of air and gasoline against a piston. The piston is attached to a crankshaft via a connecting rod, and it moves up and down inside a cylinder as the shaft rotates. As the piston moves down, an intake valve opens, allowing the piston to draw a mixture of fuel and air into the cylinder. At the bottom of the stroke, the intake valve closes. The piston compresses and heats the mixture as it moves upward. Rings in grooves around the piston rub against the cylinder wall, providing a seal necessary for compression and spreading lubricating oil. At the top of the stroke, an electrical spark from a spark plug detonates the mixture. The expanding gases develop power during the downward stroke. At the bottom, an exhaust valve is opened. On the next upward stroke, the exhaust gases are driven out.

Fuel is mixed with air in a carburetor. Dust and dirt in the air, which could cause excessive mechanical wear, are removed by an air filter. The optimum ratio of fuel to air is set by adjusting a tapered mixture screw. A throttle plate controls the amount of mixture pulled into the cylinder. The throttle plate, in turn, is controlled through springs by the operator throttle control and a governor, a mechanical device which stabilizes the engine speed under varying mechanical loads. Intake and exhaust valves are normally held closed by springs and are opened at the right time by a cam shaft, which is gear driven by the crankshaft.

The electrical energy for the spark is provided and timed by a magnet, coil, condenser, and a normally closed switch called the points. The coil has a low-voltage primary circuit connected to the points and a high-voltage secondary connected to the spark plug. The magnet is mounted on a flywheel and as it rotates past the coil, it induces a current in the shorted primary circuit. The points are driven open at the right instant by a cam on the crankshaft. With the aid of the condenser, they interrupt the current in the primary circuit, inducing a high-voltage pulse in the secondary.

3.28 (6) Prepare a class diagram for the dining philosopher problem. There are 5 philosophers and 5 forks around a circular table. Each philosopher has access to 2 forks, one on either side. Each fork is shared by 2 philosophers. Each fork may be either on the table or in use by one philosopher. A philosopher must have 2 forks to eat.

3.29 (7) The tower of Hanoi is a problem frequently used to teach recursive programming techniques. The goal is to move a stack of disks from one of three long pegs to another, using the third peg for maneuvering. Each disk is a different size. Disks may be moved from the top of a stack on a peg to the top of the stack on any other peg, one at a time, provided a disk is never placed on another disk that is smaller than itself. The details of the algorithm for listing the series of required moves depend on the structure of the class diagram used. Prepare class diagrams for each of the following descriptions. Show classes and associations. Do not show attributes or operations:

a. A tower consists of 3 pegs. Each peg has several disks on it, in a certain order.

b. A tower consists of 3 pegs. Disks on the pegs are organized into subsets called stacks. A stack is an ordered set of disks. Every disk is in exactly one stack. A peg may have several stacks on it, in order.

c. A tower consists of 3 pegs. Disks on the pegs are organized into subsets called stacks, as in (b), with several stacks on a peg. However, the structure of a stack is recursive. A stack consists of one disk (the disk that is physically on the bottom of the stack) and zero or one stack, depending on the height of the stack.

    d. Similar to (c), except only one stack is associated with a peg. Other stacks on the peg are associated in a linked list.

3.30 (8) The recursive algorithm for producing the series of moves described in the previous exercise focuses on a stack of disks. To move a stack of height N, where $N > 1$, first move the stack of height $N - 1$ to the free peg using a recursive call. Then move the bottom disk to the desired peg. Finally, move the stack on the free peg to the desired peg. The recursion terminates, because moving a stack of height 1 is trivial. Which one of the several class diagrams that you prepared in the previous exercise is best suited for this algorithm? Discuss why. Also, add attributes and operations to the diagram. What are the arguments for each operation? Describe what each operation is supposed to do to each class for which it is defined.

3.31 (6) Consider Figure E3.6. Write an OCL expression to compute the set of names of airlines that a person flew in a given year. Assume you have a function *getYear(date)* that extracts the year given a date. (Instructor's note: You should give the students our answer to Exercise 3.10 as the basis for this exercise.)

3.32 (6) Consider Figure E3.6. Write an OCL expression to find the nonstop flights from *aCity1* to *aCity2*. (Instructor's note: You should give the students our answer to Exercise 3.10 as the basis for this exercise.)

3.33 (6) Consider Figure E3.9. Write an OCL expression to find the total score a competitor received from a judge. (Instructor's note: You should give the students our answer to Exercise 3.18 as the basis for this exercise.)

3.34 (6) Compare the class models in Figure E3.13. The left model represents *Subscription* as an association class; the right model treats *Subscription* as an ordinary class.

    A person may have multiple magazine subscriptions. A magazine has multiple subscribers. For each subscription, it is important to track the date and amount of each payment as well as the current expiration date.

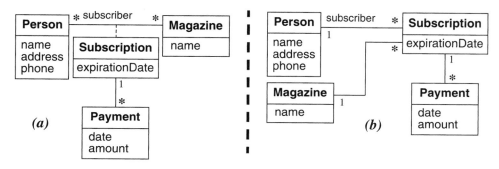

Figure E3.13 Class diagram for magazine subscriptions

4

Advanced Class Modeling

Chapter 4 continues our discussion of class modeling concepts with a treatment of advanced topics. This chapter provides subtleties for improved modeling that you can skip upon a first reading of this book.

4.1 Advanced Object and Class Concepts

4.1.1 Enumerations

A data type is a description of values. Data types include numbers, strings, and enumerations. An **enumeration** is a data type that has a finite set of values. For example, the attribute *accessPermission* in Figure 3.17 is an enumeration with possible values that include *read* and *read-write*. Figure 3.25 also has some enumerations that Figure 4.1 illustrates. *Figure.penType* is an enumeration that includes *solid*, *dashed*, and *dotted*. *TwoDimensional.fillType* is an enumeration that includes *solid*, *grey*, *none*, *horizontal lines*, and *vertical lines*.

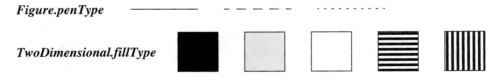

Figure 4.1 Examples of enumerations. Enumerations often occur and are important to users. Implementations must enforce the finite set of values.

When constructing a model, you should carefully note enumerations, because they often occur and are important to users. Enumerations are also significant for an implementation;

you may display the possible values with a pick list and you must restrict data to the legitimate values.

Do not use a generalization to capture the values of an enumerated attribute. An enumeration is merely a list of values; generalization is a means for structuring the description of objects. You should introduce generalization only when at least one subclass has significant attributes, operations, or associations that do not apply to the superclass. As Figure 4.2 shows, you should not introduce a generalization for *Card*, because most games do not differentiate the behavior of spades, clubs, hearts, and diamonds.

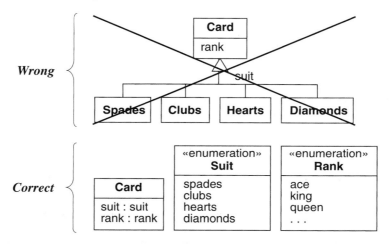

Figure 4.2   Modeling enumerations. Do not use a generalization to capture the values of an enumerated attribute.

In the UML an enumeration is a data type. You can declare an enumeration by listing the keyword *enumeration* in guillemets («») above the enumeration name in the top section of a box. The second section lists the enumeration values.

4.1.2 Multiplicity

Multiplicity is a constraint on the cardinality of a set. Chapter 3 explained multiplicity for associations. Multiplicity also applies to attributes.

It is often helpful to specify multiplicity for an attribute, especially for database applications. ***Multiplicity for an attribute*** specifies the number of possible values for each instantiation of an attribute. The most common specifications are a mandatory single value [1], an optional single value [0..1], and many [*]. Multiplicity specifies whether an attribute is mandatory or optional (in database terminology whether an attribute can be null). Multiplicity also indicates if an attribute is single valued or can be a collection. If not specified, an attribute is assumed to be a mandatory single value ([1]). In Figure 4.3 a person has one name, one or more addresses, zero or more phone numbers, and one birthdate.

Person
name : string [1] address : string [1..*] phoneNumber : string [*] birthDate : date [1]

Figure 4.3 Multiplicity for attributes. You can specify whether an attribute
is single or multivalued, mandatory or optional.

4.1.3 Scope

Chapter 3 presented features for individual objects. This is the default usage, but there can
also be features for an entire class. The *scope* indicates if a feature applies to an object or a
class. An underline distinguishes features with class scope (static) from those with object
scope. Our convention is to list attributes and operations with class scope at the top of the
attribute and operation boxes, respectively.

It is acceptable to use an attribute with class scope to hold the ***extent*** of a class (the set
of objects for a class)—this is common with OO databases. Otherwise, you should avoid attributes with class scope because they can lead to an inferior model. It is better to model
groups explicitly and assign attributes to them. For example, the upper model in Figure 4.4
shows a simple model of phone mail. Each message has an owner mailbox, date recorded,
time recorded, priority, message contents, and a flag indicating if it has been received. A message may have a mailbox as the source or it may be from an external call. Each mailbox has
a phone number, password, and recorded greeting. For the *PhoneMessage* class we can store
the maximum duration for a message and the maximum days a message will be retained. For
the *PhoneMailbox* class we can store the maximum number of messages that can be stored.

The upper model is inferior, however, because the maximum duration, maximum days
retained, and maximum message count have a single value for the entire phone mail system.
In the lower model these limits can vary for different kinds of users, yielding a more flexible
and extensible phone mail system.

In contrast to attributes, it is acceptable to define operations of class scope. The most
common use of class-scoped operations is to create new instances of a class. Sometimes it is
convenient to define class-scoped operations to provide summary data. You should be careful
with the use of class-scoped operations for distributed applications.

4.1.4 Visibility

Visibility refers to the ability of a method to reference a feature from another class and has
the possible values of *public*, *protected*, *private*, and *package*. The precise meaning depends
on the programming language. (See Chapter 18 for details.) Any method can freely access
public features. Only methods of the containing class and its descendants via inheritance can
access ***protected*** features. (Protected features also have package accessibility in Java.) Only
methods of the containing class can access ***private*** features. Methods of classes defined in
the same package as the target class can access ***package*** features.

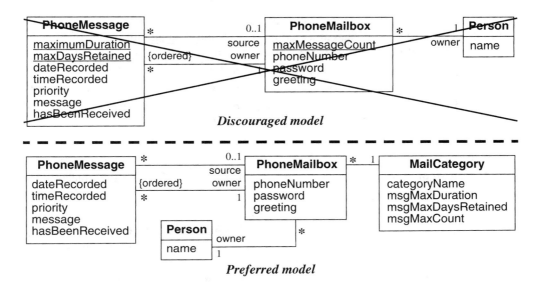

Figure 4.4 Attribute scope. Instead of assigning attributes to classes, model groups explicitly.

The UML denotes visibility with a prefix. The character "+" precedes public features. The character "#" precedes protected features. The character "-" precedes private features. And the character "~" precedes package features. The lack of a prefix reveals no information about visibility.

There are several issues to consider when choosing visibility.

- **Comprehension**. You must understand all public features to understand the capabilities of a class. In contrast, you can ignore private, protected, and package features—they are merely an implementation convenience.

- **Extensibility**. Many classes can depend on public methods, so it can be highly disruptive to change their signature (number of arguments, types of arguments, type of return value). Since fewer classes depend on private, protected, and package methods, there is more latitude to change them.

- **Context**. Private, protected, and package methods may rely on preconditions or state information created by other methods in the class. Applied out of context, a private method may calculate incorrect results or cause the object to fail.

4.2 Association Ends

As the name implies, an ***association end*** is an end of an association. A binary association has two ends, a ternary association (Section 4.3) has three ends, and so forth. Chapter 3 discussed the following properties.

- **Association end name**. An association end may have a name. The names disambiguate multiple references to a class and facilitate navigation. Meaningful names often arise, and it is useful to place the names within the proper context.
- **Multiplicity**. You can specify multiplicity for each association end. The most common multiplicities are "1" (exactly one), "0..1" (at most one), and "*" ("many"—zero or more).
- **Ordering**. The objects for a "many" association end are usually just a set. However, sometimes the objects have an explicit order.
- **Bags and sequences**. The objects for a "many" association end can also be a bag or sequence.
- **Qualification**. One or more qualifier attributes can disambiguate the objects for a "many" association end.

Association ends have some additional properties.

- **Aggregation**. The association end may be an aggregate or constituent part (Section 4.4). Only a binary association can be an aggregation; one association end must be an aggregate and the other must be a constituent.
- **Changeability**. This property specifies the update status of an association end. The possibilities are *changeable* (can be updated) and *readonly* (can only be initialized).
- **Navigability**. Conceptually, an association may be traversed in either direction. However, an implementation may support only one direction. The UML shows navigability with an arrowhead on the association end attached to the target class. Arrowheads may be attached to zero, one, or both ends of an association.
- **Visibility**. Similar to attributes and operations (Section 4.1.4), association ends may be *public*, *protected*, *private*, or *package*.

4.3 N-ary Associations

Chapter 3 presented binary associations (associations between two classes). However, you may occasionally encounter ***n-ary associations*** (associations among three or more classes.) You should try to avoid n-ary associations—most of them can be decomposed into binary associations, with possible qualifiers and attributes. Figure 4.5 shows an association that at first glance might seem to be an n-ary but can readily be restated as binary associations.

A nonatomic n-ary association—a person makes the purchase of stock in a company...

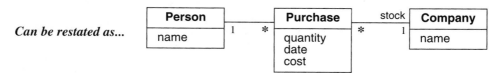

Figure 4.5 Restating an n-ary association. You can decompose most
n-ary associations into binary associations.

Figure 4.6 shows a genuine n-ary (ternary) association: Programmers use computer languages on projects. This n-ary association is an atomic unit and cannot be subdivided into binary associations without losing information. A programmer may know a language and work on a project, but might not use the language on the project. The UML symbol for n-ary associations is a diamond with lines connecting to related classes. If the association has a name, it is written in italics next to the diamond.

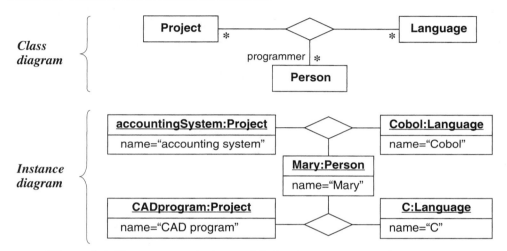

Figure 4.6 Ternary association and links. An n-ary association can have association end names, just like a binary association.

As Figure 4.6 illustrates, an n-ary association can have a name for each end just like a binary association. End names are necessary if a class participates in an n-ary association more than once. You cannot traverse n-ary associations from one end to another as with binary associations, so end names do not represent pseudo attributes of the participating classes. The OCL [Warmer-99] does not define notation for traversing n-ary associations.

Figure 4.7 shows another ternary association: A professor teaches a listed course during a semester. The resulting delivered course has a room number and any number of textbooks.

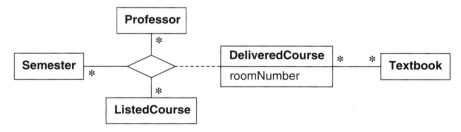

Figure 4.7 Another ternary association. N-ary associations are full-fledged associations and can have association classes.

The typical programming language cannot express n-ary associations. Thus if you are programming, you will need to promote n-ary associations to classes as Figure 4.8 does for *DeliveredClass*. Be aware that you change the meaning of a model, when you promote an n-ary association to a class. An n-ary association enforces that there is at most one link for each combination—for each combination of *Professor*, *Semester*, and *ListedCourse* in Figure 4.7 there is one *DeliveredCourse*. In contrast a promoted class permits any number of links—for each combination of *Professor*, *Semester*, and *ListedCourse* in Figure 4.8 there can be many *DeliveredCourses*. If you were implementing Figure 4.8, special application code would have to enforce the uniqueness of *Professor* + *Semester* + *ListedCourse*.

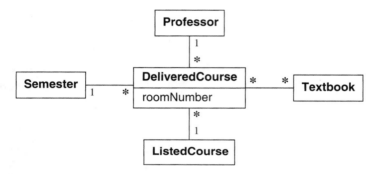

Figure 4.8 Promoting an n-ary association. Programming languages cannot express n-ary associations, so you must promote them to classes.

4.4 Aggregation

Aggregation is a strong form of association in which an aggregate object is *made of* constituent parts. Constituents are *part of* the aggregate. The aggregate is semantically an extended object that is treated as a unit in many operations, although physically it is made of several lesser objects.

We define an aggregation as relating an assembly class to *one* constituent part class. An assembly with many kinds of constituent parts corresponds to many aggregations. For example, a *LawnMower* consists of a *Blade*, an *Engine*, many *Wheels*, and a *Deck*. *LawnMower* is the assembly and the other parts are constituents. *LawnMower* to *Blade* is one aggregation, *LawnMower* to *Engine* is another aggregation, and so on. We define each individual pairing as an aggregation so that we can specify the multiplicity of each constituent part within the assembly. This definition emphasizes that aggregation is a special form of binary association.

The most significant property of aggregation is ***transitivity***—that is, if *A* is part of *B* and *B* is part of *C*, then *A* is part of *C*. Aggregation is also ***antisymmetric***—that is, if *A* is part of *B*, then *B* is not part of *A*. Many aggregate operations imply transitive closure[*] and operate on both direct and indirect parts.

4.4.1 Aggregation Versus Association

Aggregation is a special form of association, not an independent concept. Aggregation adds semantic connotations. If two objects are tightly bound by a part-whole relationship, it is an aggregation. If the two objects are usually considered as independent, even though they may often be linked, it is an association. Some tests include:

- Would you use the phrase *part of*?
- Do some operations on the whole automatically apply to its parts?
- Do some attribute values propagate from the whole to all or some parts?
- Is there an intrinsic asymmetry to the association, where one class is subordinate to the other?

Aggregations include bill-of-materials, part explosions, and expansions of an object into constituent parts. Aggregation is drawn like association, except a small diamond indicates the assembly end. In Figure 4.9 a lawn mower consists of one blade, one engine, many wheels, and one deck. The manufacturing process is flexible and largely combines standard parts, so blades, engines, wheels, and decks pertain to multiple lawn mower designs.

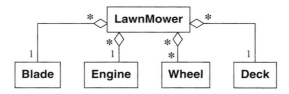

Figure 4.9   Aggregation. Aggregation is a kind of association in
which an aggregate object is made of constituent parts.

The decision to use aggregation is a matter of judgment and can be arbitrary. Often it is not obvious if an association should be modeled as an aggregation. To a large extent this kind of uncertainty is typical of modeling; modeling requires seasoned judgment and there are few hard and fast rules. Our experience has been that if you exercise careful judgment and are consistent, the imprecise distinction between aggregation and ordinary association does not cause problems in practice.

4.4.2 Aggregation Versus Composition

The UML has two forms of part-whole relationships: a general form called *aggregation* and a more restrictive form called *composition*.

---

* Transitive closure is a term from graph theory. If E denotes an edge and N denotes a node and S is the set of all pairs of nodes connected by an edge, then S^+ (the transitive closure of S) is the set of all pairs of nodes directly or indirectly connected by a sequence of edges. Thus S^+ includes all nodes that are directly connected, nodes connected by two edges, nodes connected by three edges, and so forth.

Composition is a form of aggregation with two additional constraints. A constituent part can belong to at most one assembly. Furthermore, once a constituent part has been assigned an assembly, it has a coincident lifetime with the assembly. Thus composition implies ownership of the parts by the whole. This can be convenient for programming: Deletion of an assembly object triggers deletion of all constituent objects via composition. The notation for composition is a small *solid* diamond next to the assembly class (vs. a small *hollow* diamond for the general form of aggregation).

In Figure 4.10 a company consists of divisions, which in turn consist of departments; a company is indirectly a composition of departments. A company is not a composition of its employees, since company and person are independent objects of equal stature.

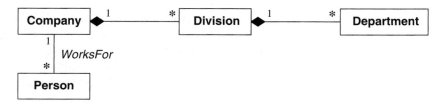

Figure 4.10 Composition. With composition a constituent part belongs to at
most one assembly and has a coincident lifetime with the assembly.

4.4.3 *Propagation of Operations*

Propagation (also called **triggering**) is the automatic application of an operation to a network of objects when the operation is applied to some starting object [Rumbaugh-88].[†] For example, moving an aggregate moves its parts; the move operation propagates to the parts. Propagation of operations to parts is often a good indicator of aggregation.

Figure 4.11 shows an example of propagation. A person owns multiple documents. Each document consists of paragraphs that, in turn, consist of characters. The copy operation propagates from documents to paragraphs to characters. Copying a paragraph copies all the characters in it. The operation does not propagate in the reverse direction; a paragraph can be copied without copying the whole document. Similarly, copying a document copies the owner link but does not spawn a copy of the person who is owner.

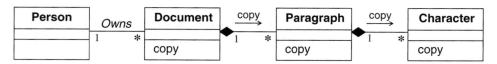

Figure 4.11 Propagation. You can propagate operations across aggregations
and compositions.

---

† The term *association* as used in this book is synonymous with the term *relation* used in [Rumbaugh-88].

Most other approaches present an all-or-nothing option: copy an entire network with deep copy, or copy the starting object and none of the related objects with shallow copy. The concept of propagation of operations provides a concise and powerful way for specifying a continuum of behavior. You can think of an operation as starting at some initial object and flowing from object to object through links according to propagation rules. Propagation is possible for other operations including save/restore, destroy, print, lock, and display.

You can indicate propagation on class models with a small arrow indicating the direction and operation name next to the affected association. The notation binds propagation behavior to an association (or aggregation), direction, and operation. Note that this notation is not part of the UML and is a special notation.

4.5 Abstract Classes

An **abstract class** is a class that has no direct instances but whose descendant classes have direct instances. A **concrete class** is a class that is instantiable; that is, it can have direct instances. A concrete class may have abstract subclasses (but they, in turn, must have concrete descendants). Only concrete classes may be leaf classes in an inheritance tree.

All the occupations shown in Figure 4.12 are concrete classes. *Butcher, Baker,* and *CandlestickMaker* are concrete classes because they have direct instances. *Worker* also is a concrete class because some occupations may not be specified.

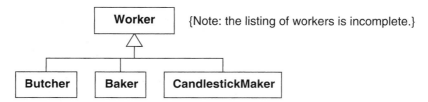

Figure 4.12 Concrete classes. A concrete class is instantiable; that is, it
can have direct instances.

Class *Employee* in Figure 4.13 is an example of an abstract class. All employees must be either full-time or part-time. *FullTimeEmployee* and *PartTimeEmployee* are concrete classes because they can be directly instantiated. In the UML notation an abstract class name is listed in an italic font. Or you may place the keyword *{abstract}* below or after the name.

You can use abstract classes to define methods that can be inherited by subclasses. Alternatively, an abstract class can define the signature for an operation without supplying a corresponding method. We call this an **abstract operation**. (Recall that an operation specifies the form of a function or procedure; a method is the actual implementation.) An abstract operation defines the signature of an operation for which each concrete subclass must provide its own implementation. A concrete class may not contain abstract operations, because objects of the concrete class would have undefined operations.

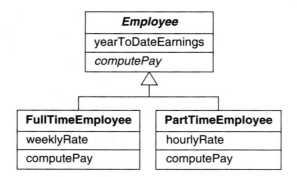

Figure 4.13 Abstract class and abstract operation. An abstract class is
a class that has no direct instances

Figure 4.13 shows an abstract operation. An abstract operation is designated by italics or the keyword *{abstract}*. *ComputePay* is an abstract operation of class *Employee*; its signature but not its implementation is defined. Each subclass must supply a method for this operation.

Note that the abstract nature of a class is always provisional, depending on the point of view. You can always refine a concrete class into subclasses, making it abstract. Conversely, an abstract class may become concrete in an application in which the difference among its subclasses is unimportant.

As a matter of style, it is a good idea to avoid concrete superclasses. Then, abstract and concrete classes are readily apparent at a glance; all superclasses are abstract and all leaf subclasses are concrete. Furthermore, you will avoid awkward situations where a concrete superclass must both specify the signature of an operation for descendant classes and also provide an implementation for its concrete instances. You can always eliminate concrete superclasses by introducing an *Other* subclass, as Figure 4.14 shows.

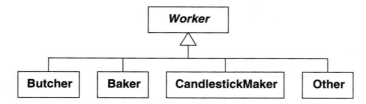

Figure 4.14 Avoiding concrete superclasses. You can always eliminate
concrete superclasses by introducing an *Other* subclass.

4.6 Multiple Inheritance

Multiple inheritance permits a class to have more than one superclass and to inherit features from all parents. Then you can mix information from two or more sources. This is a more complicated form of generalization than single inheritance, which restricts the class hierarchy to a tree. The advantage of multiple inheritance is greater power in specifying classes and an increased opportunity for reuse. The disadvantage is a loss of conceptual and implementation simplicity.

The term *multiple inheritance* is used somewhat imprecisely to mean either the conceptual relationship between classes or the language mechanism that implements that relationship. Whenever possible, we try to distinguish between *generalization* (the conceptual relationship) and *inheritance* (the language mechanism), but the term "multiple inheritance" is more widely used than the term "multiple generalization."

4.6.1 Kinds of Multiple Inheritance

The most common form of multiple inheritance is from sets of disjoint classes. Each subclass inherits from one class in each set. In Figure 4.15 *FullTimeIndividualContributor* is both *FullTimeEmployee* and *IndividualContributor* and combines their features. *FullTimeEmployee* and *PartTimeEmployee* are disjoint; each employee must belong to exactly one of these. Similarly, *Manager* and *IndividualContributor* are also disjoint and each employee must be one or the other. The model does not show it, but we could define three additional combinations: *FullTimeManager*, *PartTimeIndividualContributor*, and *PartTimeManager*. The appropriate combinations depend on the needs of an application.

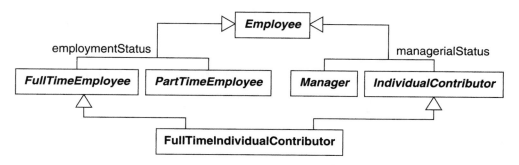

Figure 4.15 Multiple inheritance from disjoint classes. This is the most common form of multiple inheritance.

Each generalization should cover a single aspect. You should use multiple generalizations if a class can be refined on several distinct and independent aspects. In Figure 4.15, class *Employee* independently specializes on employment status and managerial status. Consequently the model has two separate generalization sets.

A subclass inherits a feature from the same ancestor class found along more than one path only once; it is the same feature. For example, in Figure 4.15 *FullTimeIndividualContributor* inherits *Employee* features along two paths, via *employmentStatus* and *managerialStatus*. However, each *FullTimeIndividualContributor* has only a single copy of *Employee* features.

Conflicts among parallel definitions create ambiguities that implementations must resolve. In practice, you should avoid such conflicts in models or explicitly resolve them, even if a particular language provides a priority rule for resolving conflicts. For example, suppose that *FullTimeEmployee* and *IndividualContributor* both have an attribute called *name*. *FullTimeEmployee.name* could refer to the person's full name while *IndividualContributor.name* might refer to the person's title. In principle, there is no obvious way to resolve such clashes. The best solution is to try to avoid them by restating the attributes as *FullTimeEmployee.personName* and *IndividualContributor.title*.

Multiple inheritance can also occur with overlapping classes. In Figure 4.16, *AmphibiousVehicle* is both *LandVehicle* and *WaterVehicle*. *LandVehicle* and *WaterVehicle* overlap, because some vehicles travel on both land and water. The UML uses a constraint (see Section 4.9) to indicate an overlapping generalization set; the notation is a dotted line cutting across the affected generalizations with keywords in braces. In this example, *overlapping* means that an individual vehicle may belong to more than one of the subclasses. *Incomplete* means that all possible subclasses of vehicle have not been explicitly named.

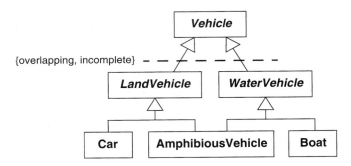

Figure 4.16 Multiple inheritance from overlapping classes. This form of multiple inheritance occurs less often than with disjoint classes.

4.6.2 *Multiple Classification*

An instance of a class is inherently an instance of all ancestors of the class. For example, an instructor could be both faculty and student. But what about a Harvard Professor taking classes at MIT? There is no class to describe the combination (it would be artificial to make one). This is an example of multiple classification, in which one instance happens to participate in two overlapping classes.

The UML permits multiple classification, but most OO languages handle it poorly. As Figure 4.17 shows, the best approach using conventional languages is to treat *Person* as an object composed of multiple *UniversityMember* objects. This workaround replaces inheritance with delegation (discussed in the next section). This is not totally satisfactory, because there is a loss of identity between the separate roles, but the alternatives involve radical changes in many programming languages [McAllester-86].

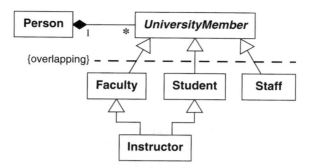

Figure 4.17 Workaround for multiple classification. OO languages do not handle this well, so you must use a workaround.

4.6.3 Workarounds

Dealing with lack of multiple inheritance is really an implementation issue, but early restructuring of a model is often the easiest way to work around its absence. We list some restructuring techniques below. Two of the approaches make use of **delegation**, which is an implementation mechanism by which an object forwards an operation to another object for execution. See Chapter 15 for a further discussion of delegation.

- **Delegation using composition of parts**. You can recast a superclass with multiple independent generalizations as a composition in which each constituent part replaces a generalization. This approach is similar to that for multiple classification in the previous section. This approach replaces a single object having a unique ID by a group of related objects that compose an extended object. Inheritance of operations across the composition is not automatic. The composite must catch operations and delegate them to the appropriate part.

    For example, in Figure 4.18 *EmployeeEmployment* becomes a superclass of *FullTimeEmployee* and *PartTimeEmployee*. *EmployeeManagement* becomes a superclass of *Manager* and *IndividualContributor*. Then you can model *Employee* as a composition of *EmployeeEmployment* and *EmployeeManagement*. An operation sent to an *Employee* object would have to be redirected to the *EmployeeEmployment* or *EmployeeManagement* part by the *Employee* class.

    In this approach, you need not create the various combinations (such as *FullTimeIndividualContributor*) as explicit classes. All combinations of subclasses from the different generalizations are possible.

- **Inherit the most important class and delegate the rest**. Figure 4.19 preserves identity and inheritance across the most important generalization. You degrade the remaining generalizations to composition and delegate their operations as in the previous alternative.

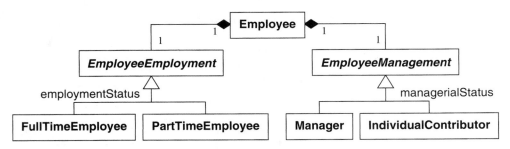

Figure 4.18 Workaround for multiple inheritance—delegation

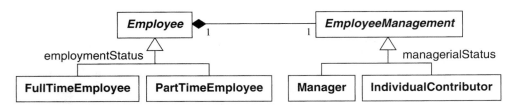

Figure 4.19 Workaround for multiple inheritance—inheritance and delegation

■ **Nested generalization.** Factor on one generalization first, then the other. This approach multiplies out all possible combinations. For example, in Figure 4.20 under *FullTime-Employee* and *PartTimeEmployee*, add two subclasses for managers and individual contributors. This preserves inheritance but duplicates declarations and code and violates the spirit of OO programming.

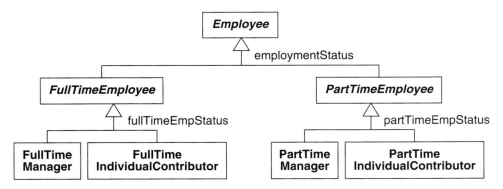

Figure 4.20 Workaround for multiple inheritance—nested generalization

Any of these workarounds can be made to work, but they all compromise logical structure and maintainability. There are several issues to consider when selecting the best workaround.

- **Superclasses of equal importance**. If a subclass has several superclasses, all of equal importance, it may be best to use delegation (Figure 4.18) and preserve symmetry in the model.

- **Dominant superclass**. If one superclass clearly dominates and the others are less important, preserve inheritance through this path (Figure 4.19 or Figure 4.20).

- **Few subclasses**. If the number of combinations is small, consider nested generalization (Figure 4.20). If the number of combinations is large, avoid it.

- **Sequencing generalization sets**. If you use nested generalization (Figure 4.20), factor on the most important criterion first, the next most important second, and so forth.

- **Large quantities of code**. Try to avoid nested generalization (Figure 4.20) if you must duplicate large quantities of code.

- **Identity**. Consider the importance of maintaining strict identity. Only nested generalization (Figure 4.20) preserves this.

4.7 Metadata

Metadata is data that describes other data. For example, a class definition is metadata. Models are inherently metadata, since they describe the things being modeled (rather than *being* the things). Many real-world applications have metadata, such as parts catalogs, blueprints, and dictionaries. Computer-language implementations also use metadata heavily.

Figure 4.21 shows an example of metadata and data. A car model has a model name, year, base price, and a manufacturer. Some examples of car models are a 1969 Ford Mustang and a 1975 Volkswagen Rabbit. A physical car has a serial number, color, options, and an owner. As an example of physical cars, John Doe may own a blue Ford with serial number *1FABP* and a red Volkswagen with serial number *7E81F*. A car model describes many physical cars and holds common data. A car model is metadata relative to a physical car, which is data.

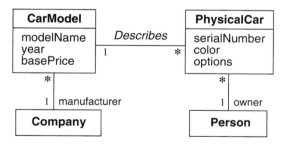

Figure 4.21 Example of metadata. Metadata often arises in applications.

You can also consider classes as objects, but classes are meta-objects and not real-world objects. Class descriptor objects have features, and they in turn have their own classes, which are called *metaclasses*. Treating everything as an object provides a more uniform implementation and greater functionality for solving complex problems. Languages vary in their accessibility for metadata. Some languages, like Lisp and Smalltalk, let metadata be inspected and altered by programs at run time. In contrast, languages like C++ and Java deal with metadata at compile time but do not make the metadata explicitly available at run time.

4.8 Reification

Reification is the promotion of something that is not an object into an object. Reification is a helpful technique for meta applications because it lets you shift the level of abstraction. On occasion it is useful to promote attributes, methods, constraints, and control information into objects so you can describe and manipulate them as data.

As an example of reification, consider a database manager. A developer could write code for each application so that it can read and write from files. Instead, for many applications, it is a better idea to reify the notion of data services and use a database manager. A database manager has abstract functionality that provides a general-purpose solution to accessing data reliably and quickly for multiple users.

For another example, consider state-transition diagrams (see the next two chapters). You can use a state-transition diagram to specify control and then implement it by writing the corresponding code. Alternatively, you can prepare a metamodel and store a state-transition model as data. A general-purpose interpreter reads the contents of the metamodel and executes the intent.

Figure 4.22 promotes the *substanceName* attribute to a class to capture the many-to-many relationship between *Substance* and *SubstanceName*. A chemical substance may have multiple aliases. For example, propylene may be referred to as *propylene* and C_3H_6. Also, an alias may pertain to multiple chemical substances. Various mixtures of ethylene glycol and automotive additives may have the alias of *antifreeze*.

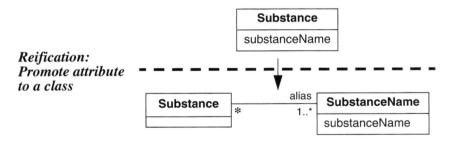

Figure 4.22 Reification. Reification is the promotion of something that is not an object into an object and can be helpful for meta applications.

4.9 Constraints

A *constraint* is a boolean condition involving model elements, such as objects, classes, attributes, links, associations, and generalization sets. A constraint restricts the values that elements can assume. You can express constraints with natural language or a formal language such as the Object Constraint Language (OCL) [Warmer-99].

4.9.1 Constraints on Objects

Figure 4.23 shows several examples of constraints. No employee's salary can exceed the salary of the employee's boss (a constraint between two things at the same time). No window can have an aspect ratio (length/width) of less than 0.8 or greater than 1.5 (a constraint between attributes of a single object). The priority of a job may not increase (constraint on the same object over time). You may place simple constraints in class models.

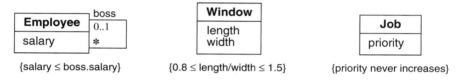

Figure 4.23 Constraints on objects. The structure of a model expresses many constraints, but sometimes it is helpful to add explicit constraints.

4.9.2 Constraints on Generalization Sets

Class models capture many constraints through their very structure. For example, the semantics of generalization imply certain structural constraints. With single inheritance the subclasses are mutually exclusive. Furthermore, each instance of an abstract superclass corresponds to exactly one subclass instance. Each instance of a concrete superclass corresponds to at most one subclass instance.

Figure 4.16 and Figure 4.17 use a constraint to help express multiple inheritance. The UML defines the following keywords for generalization sets.

- **Disjoint**. The subclasses are mutually exclusive. Each object belongs to exactly one of the subclasses.

- **Overlapping**. The subclasses can share some objects. An object may belong to more than one subclass.

- **Complete**. The generalization lists all the possible subclasses.

- **Incomplete**. The generalization may be missing some subclasses.

4.9.3 Constraints on Links

Multiplicity is a constraint on the cardinality of a set. Multiplicity for an association restricts the number of objects related to a given object. Multiplicity for an attribute specifies the number of values that are possible for each instantiation of an attribute.

Qualification also constrains an association. A qualifier attribute does not merely describe the links of an association but is also significant in resolving the "many" objects at an association end.

An association class implies a constraint. An association class is a class in every right; for example, it can have attributes and operations, participate in associations, and participate in generalizations. But an association class has a constraint that an ordinary class does not; it derives identity from instances of the related classes.

An ordinary association presumes no particular order on the objects of a "many" end. The constraint *{ordered}* indicates that the elements of a "many" association end have an explicit order that must be preserved.

Figure 4.24 shows an explicit constraint that is not part of the model's structure. The chair of a committee must be a member of the committee; the *ChairOf* association is a subset of the *MemberOf* association.

Figure 4.24 Subset constraint between associations.

4.9.4 Use of Constraints

We favor expressing constraints in a declarative manner. Declaration lets you express a constraint's intent, without supposing an implementation. Typically, you will need to convert constraints to procedural form before you can implement them in a programming language, but this conversion is usually straightforward.

Constraints provide one criterion for measuring the quality of a class model; a "good" class model captures many constraints through its structure. It often requires several iterations to get the structure of a model right from the perspective of constraints. Also, in practice, you cannot enforce every constraint with a model's structure, but you should try to enforce the important ones.

The UML has two alternative notations for constraints. You can either delimit a constraint with braces or place it in a "dog-eared" comment box (Figure 4.26). Either way, you should try to position constraints near the affected elements. You can use dashed lines to connect constrained elements. A dashed arrow can connect a constrained element to the element on which it depends.

4.10 Derived Data

A ***derived element*** is a function of one or more elements, which in turn may be derived. A derived element is redundant, because the other elements completely determine it. Ultimately, the derivation tree terminates with base elements. Classes, associations, and attributes may be derived. The notation for a derived element is a slash in front of the element name. You should also show the constraint that determines the derivation.

Figure 4.25 shows a derived attribute. Age can be derived from birthdate and the current date.

Figure 4.25 Derived attribute. A derived attribute is a function of one or more elements.

In Figure 4.26, a machine consists of several assemblies that in turn consist of parts. An assembly has a geometrical offset with respect to machine coordinates; each part has an offset with respect to assembly coordinates. We can define a coordinate system for each part that is derived from machine coordinates, assembly offset, and part offset. This coordinate system can be represented as a derived class called *Offset* related to each part by a derived association called *NetOffset*.

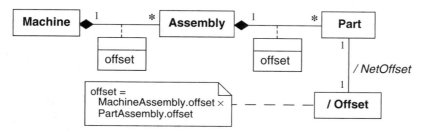

Figure 4.26 Derived object and association. Derived data can complicate implementation, so only use derived data where it truly is compelling.

It is useful to distinguish operations with side effects from those that merely compute a functional value without modifying any objects. The latter kind of operation is called a ***query***. You can regard queries with no arguments except the target object as derived attributes. For example, you can compute the width of a box from the positions of its sides. In many cases, an object has a set of attributes with interrelated values, of which only a fixed number of values can be chosen independently. A class model should generally distinguish independent *base attributes* from dependent *derived attributes*. The choice of base attributes is arbitrary but should be made to avoid overspecifying the state of the object.

Some developers tend to include many derived elements. Generally, this is not helpful and clutters a model. You should only include derived elements when they are important application concepts or substantially ease implementation. It can be quite difficult to keep derived elements consistent with the base data, so only use derived elements for implementation where they are clearly compelling.

4.11 Packages

You can fit a class model on a single page for many small and medium-sized problems. However, it is often difficult to grasp the entirety of a large model. We recommend that you partition large models so that people can understand them.

A **package** is a group of elements (classes, associations, generalizations, and lesser packages) with a common theme. A package partitions a model, making it easier to understand and manage. Large applications may require several tiers of packages. Packages form a tree with increasing abstraction toward the root, which is the application, the top-level package. As Figure 4.27 shows, the notation for a package is a box with a tab. The purpose of the tab is to suggest the enclosed contents, like a tabbed folder.

Figure 4.27 Notation for a package. Packages let you organize large
models so that persons can more readily understand them.

There are various themes for forming packages: dominant classes, dominant relationships, major aspects of functionality, and symmetry. For example, many business systems have a *Customer* package or a *Part* package; *Customer* and *Part* are dominant classes that are important to the business of a corporation and appear in many applications. In an engineering application we used a dominant relationship, a large generalization for many kinds of equipment, to divide a class model into packages. Equipment was the focus of the model, and the attributes and relationships varied greatly across types of equipment. You could divide the class model of a compiler into packages for lexical analysis, parsing, semantic analysis, code generation, and optimization. Once some packages have been established, symmetry may suggest additional packages.

We can offer the following tips for devising packages.

- **Carefully delineate each package's scope.** The precise boundaries of a package are a matter of judgment. Like other aspects of modeling, defining the scope of a package requires planning and organization. Make sure that class and association names are unique within each package, and use consistent names across packages as much as possible.

- **Define each class in a single package.** The defining package should show the class name, attributes, and operations. Other packages that refer to a class can use a class icon, a box that contains only the class name. This convention makes it easier to read class models, because a class is prominent in its defining package. Readers are not distracted by definitions that may be inconsistent or misled by forgetting a prior class definition. This convention also makes it easier to develop packages concurrently.

- **Make packages cohesive.** Associations and generalizations should normally appear in a single package, but classes can appear in multiple packages, helping to bind them. Try to limit appearances of classes in multiple packages. Typically no more than 20–30% of classes should appear in multiple packages.

4.12 Practical Tips

Here are tips for constructing class models in addition to those from Chapter 3.

- **Enumerations.** When constructing a model, you should declare enumerations and their values, because they often occur and are important to users. Do not create unnecessary generalizations for attributes that are enumerations. Only specialize a class when the subclasses have distinct attributes, operations, or associations. (Section 4.1.1)

- **Class-scoped (static) attributes.** It is acceptable to use an attribute with class scope to hold the extent of a class. Otherwise, you should avoid attributes with class scope because they can lead to an inferior model. You can improve a model by explicitly modeling groups and assigning attributes to them. (Section 4.1.3)

- **N-ary associations.** Try to avoid n-ary associations. Most n-ary associations can be decomposed into binary associations. (Section 4.3)

- **Concrete superclasses.** As a matter of style, it is best to avoid concrete superclasses. Then, abstract and concrete classes are readily apparent at a glance—all superclasses are abstract and all leaf subclasses are concrete. You can always eliminate concrete superclasses by introducing an *Other* subclass. (Section 4.5)

- **Multiple inheritance.** Limit your use of multiple inheritance to that which is essential for a model. (Section 4.6)

- **Constraints.** You may be able to restructure a class model to improve clarity and capture additional constraints. (Section 4.9)

- **Derived elements.** You should always indicate when an element is derived. Use derived elements sparingly. (Section 4.10)

- **Large models.** Use packages to organize large models so that the reader can understand portions of the model at a time, rather than having to deal with the whole model at once. (Section 4.11)

- **Defining classes.** Define each class in a single package and show its features there. Other packages that refer to the class should use a class icon, a box that contains only the class name. This convention makes it easier to read class models and facilitates concurrent development. (Section 4.11)

4.13 Chapter Summary

This chapter covers several diverse topics that explain subtleties of class modeling. You will not need these concepts for simple models, but they can be important for complex applications. Remember, application needs should drive the content of any model. Only use the advanced concepts in this chapter if they truly add to your application, either by improving clarity, tightening structural constraints, or permitting expression of a difficult concept.

A data type is a description of values; you must assign every attribute a data type before a model can be implemented. Enumerations are a special data type that constrains the permissible values; enumerated values are often prominent in user interfaces.

Multiplicity is a constraint on the cardinality of a set. It applies to attributes as well as associations. Multiplicity for an association restricts the number of objects related to a given object. Multiplicity for an attribute specifies the number of values that are possible for each attribute instantiation.

You should try to avoid n-ary associations—you can decompose most of them into binary associations. Only use n-ary associations that are atomic and cannot be decomposed. Be aware that most programming languages will force you to promote n-ary associations to classes.

Aggregation is a strong form of association in which an aggregate object is made of constituent parts. Aggregation has the properties of transitivity and antisymmetry that differentiate it from association. Operations on an aggregate often propagate to the constituent parts.

Composition is a form of aggregation with two additional constraints. A constituent part can belong to at most one assembly. Furthermore, once a constituent part has been assigned an assembly, it has a coincident lifetime with the assembly. Composition implies ownership of a part by an assembly.

An abstract class has no direct instances. A concrete class may have direct instances. Abstract classes can define methods in one place for use by several subclasses. You can also use abstract classes to define the signature of an operation, leaving the implementation to each subclass.

Multiple inheritance permits a subclass to inherit features from more than one superclass. Each generalization should discriminate a single aspect You should arrange subclasses into more than one generalization if their superclass specializes on more than one aspect. A subclass may combine classes from different generalizations, or it may combine classes from an overlapping generalization, but it may not combine classes from the same disjoint generalization.

Metadata is data that describes other data. Classes are metadata, since they describe objects. Metadata is a useful concept for two reasons: It occurs in the real world and it is a powerful tool for implementing complex systems. Metadata can be confusing to model, because it blurs the distinction between descriptor and referent. Reification, the promotion of something that is not an object into an object, can be a helpful technique for meta applications.

Explicit constraints on classes, associations, and attributes can increase the precision of a model. Generalization and multiplicity are examples of constraints built into the fabric of class modeling. Derived elements may appear in a model but do not add fundamental information.

A package is a group of classes, associations, generalizations, and lesser packages with a common theme. A package partitions a large model, making it easier to understand and manage.

abstract class	concrete class	generalization	package
abstract operation	constraint	metadata	propagation
aggregation	delegation	multiple inheritance	reification
association end	derived element	multiplicity (of an attribute)	scope
composition	enumeration	n-ary association	visibility

Figure 4.28 Key concepts for Chapter 4

Bibliographic Notes

[Rumbaugh-05] explains many subtleties of the UML, some of which we cover in this chapter. [Warmer-99] is the authoritative reference for the Object Constraint Language (OCL).

The previous edition of this book used candidate keys to specify multiplicity for n-ary associations. In this context, a candidate key is a minimal set of association ends that uniquely identifies a link. This edition omits discussion of candidate keys because they are seldom needed for programming. Also, the notion of a *scope* subsumes the terms *class attribute* and *class operation* in the previous edition.

References

[McAllester-86] David McAllester, Ramin Zabih. Boolean classes. *OOPSLA'87* as *SIGPLAN 22*, 12 (December 1987), 417–424.

[Rumbaugh-88] James E. Rumbaugh. Controlling propagation of operations using attributes on relations. *OOPSLA'88* as *ACM SIGPLAN 23*, 11 (November 1988), 285–296.

[Rumbaugh-05] James Rumbaugh, Ivar Jacobson, Grady Booch. *The Unified Modeling Language Reference Manual, Second Edition*. Boston: Addison-Wesley, 2005.

[Warmer-99] Jos Warmer and Anneke Kleppe. *The Object Constraint Language*. Boston: Addison-Wesley, 1999.

Exercises

4.1 (3) The class diagram in Figure E4.1 is a partial representation of the structure of an automobile. Improve it by changing some of the associations to aggregations.

4.2 (4) Figure E4.2 is a partially completed class diagram for an interactive diagram editor. A sheet is a collection of lines and boxes. A line is a series of line segments that connect two boxes. Each line segment is specified by two points. A point may be shared by a vertical and a horizontal line segment in the same line. A selection is a collection of lines and boxes that have been high-

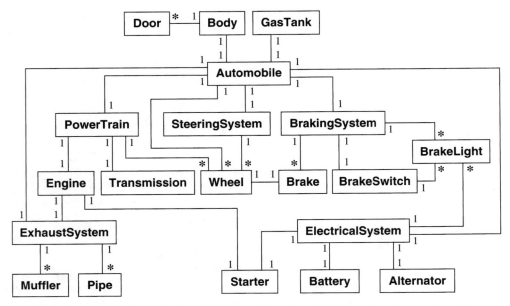

Figure E4.1   Portion of a class diagram of the assembly hierarchy of an automobile

lighted in anticipation of an editing operation. A buffer is a collection of lines and boxes that have been cut or copied from the sheet.

As it stands, the diagram does not express the constraint that a line or a box belongs to exactly one buffer or one selection or one sheet. Revise the class diagram and use generalization to express the constraint by creating a superclass for the classes *Buffer*, *Selection*, and *Sheet*. Discuss the merits of the revision.

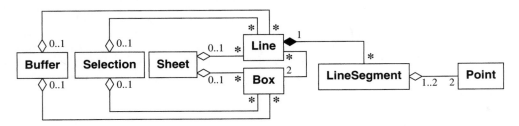

Figure E4.2   Portion of a class diagram for a simple diagram editor

4.3   (3) Categorize the following relationships into generalization, aggregation, or association. Beware, there may be n-ary associations in the list, so do not assume every relationship involving three or more classes is a generalization. Explain your answers.

a. A country has a capital city.

b. A dining philosopher uses a fork.

c. A file is an ordinary file or a directory file.

     d. Files contain records.

     e. A polygon is composed of an ordered set of points.

     f. A drawing object is text, a geometrical object, or a group.

     g. A person uses a computer language on a project.

     h. Modems and keyboards are input/output devices.

     i. Classes may have several attributes.

     j. A person plays for a team in a certain year.

     k. A route connects two cities.

     l. A student takes a course from a professor.

4.4 (7) Prepare a class diagram for a graphical document editor that supports grouping. Assume that a document consists of several sheets. Each sheet contains drawing objects, including text, geometrical objects, and groups. A group is simply a set of drawing objects, possibly including other groups. A group must contain at least two drawing objects. A drawing object can be a direct member of at most one group. Geometrical objects include circles, ellipses, rectangles, lines, and squares.

4.5 (7) The following is a partial taxonomy of rotating electrical machines. Electrical machines may be categorized for analysis purposes into alternating current (ac) or direct current (dc). Some machines run on ac, some on dc, and some will run on either. A few examples of electrical machines include large synchronous motors, small induction motors, universal motors, and permanent magnet motors. Most motors found in the home are usually induction or universal.

An ac machine may be synchronous or induction. Universal motors are typically used where high speed is needed, such as in blenders or vacuum cleaners. They will run on either ac or dc. Permanent-magnet motors are frequently used in toys and will work only on dc.

Prepare a class diagram showing how the categories and the machines just described relate to one another. Use multiple inheritance where it is appropriate to do so.

4.6 (7) Revise the class diagram that you prepared for the previous exercise to eliminate use of multiple inheritance.

4.7 (8) Prepare a metamodel that supports only the following UML concepts: class, attribute, association, association end, multiplicity, class name, and attribute name. Use only these constructs to build your metamodel.

4.8 (8) Prepare an object diagram of the metamodel you prepared in the previous diagram. Treat the metamodel as a class diagram that can be represented by instances of the classes of the metamodel.

4.9 (5) Use generalization to revise your answer from Exercise 4.7 so that an attribute belongs to either a class or an association, but not both at the same time.

4.10 (7) Figure E4.3 is a portion of a metamodel that describes generalization. A generalization is associated with several generalization roles, which are the roles that classes play in generalizations. Role type is either subclass or superclass. Does this model support multiple inheritance? Explain your answer.

4.11 (8) Describe how to find which class is the superclass of a generalization using the metamodel in Figure E4.3. Revise the metamodel to simplify the query. Describe how to determine the superclass of a generalization using your revised metamodel. Make sure that your revised metamodel supports multiple inheritance. Write OCL queries for Figure E4.3 and your model to find a superclass, given a generalization.

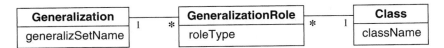

Figure E4.3   Metamodel of generalization

4.12   (7) How well does the metamodel in Figure E4.3 enforce the constraint that every generalization has exactly one superclass? Revise it to improve the enforcement of the constraint.

4.13   (7) Figure E4.3 is a metamodel that describes class models such as in Figure E4.4. Prepare an object diagram using the classes from the metamodel to describe the model in Figure E4.4.

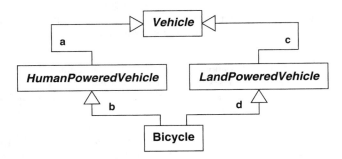

Figure E4.4   Class diagram with multiple inheritance

4.14   (6) Prepare a portion of a class diagram for a library book checkout system that shows the late charges for an overdue book as a derived attribute.

4.15   (10) Prepare a metamodel of Backus-Naur (BNF) representations of computer languages. A compiler-compiler (such as the UNIX program YACC) could use the model. The compiler-compiler accepts these representations in graphical form as input and produces a compiler for the represented language.

   Figure E4.5 shows an example of a Backus-Naur form that the compiler-compiler will accept. Rectangles denote nonterminals, and circles or rectangles with rounded corners denote terminals. Single characters are in circles, and sequences of several characters are in rounded rectangles. Arrows indicate the direction of flow through the diagram. Where several directed paths diverge, it is permissible to take any one of them. The name of the nonterminal being described appears at the beginning of its representation.

4.16   (7) Prepare a simple class model, sufficient for representing recipes. Use the recipe in Figure E4.6 as a basis. This exercise is an example of reification. In one sense the tasks of a recipe could be operations; in another sense they could be data in a class model.

4.17   (9) Extend your class model of recipes to handle alternate ingredients. For example, some lasagna recipes allow cottage cheese to be substituted for ricotta cheese.

4.18   (8) The North American Securities Administrators Association (NASAA, www.nasaa.org) seeks to protect investors and educate them about trading in securities. NASAA recommends

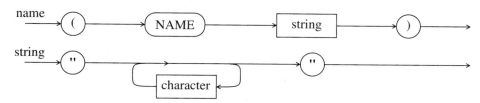

Figure E4.5 Portion of a BNF diagram

Lasagna

2.5 tbsp. salad oil for browning
1 cup minced onion
1 clove garlic
1 lb. ground beef
2 tsp. salt
3.5 cups whole tomatoes (large can)

1 tsp. oregano
.5 box lasagna noodles
1 lb. ricotta cheese
1 cup grated mozzarella cheese
.5 cup parmesan cheese
2 cans tomato paste

Cook onion, clove garlic, ground beef, 1 tsp. salt in salad oil until meat is browned. Add tomatoes, tomato paste, 1 tsp salt, oregano, and simmer, covered, 1 hour until thick. Cook noodles 15 minutes in water until tender. Drain and blanch. Butter 12×8 inch pan and place in layers of noodles, sauce, mozzarella, ricotta cheese, and parmesan. Bake at 350 degrees for 45 to 60 minutes.

Figure E4.6 A simple recipe

that investors take notes when talking to a broker using the form in Figure E4.7. (Use multiple forms when the broker makes multiple recommendations in a call.) Suppose that it is desirable to automate this form with software. Prepare a class model for the form.

4.19 (9) Prepare a model for words in a dictionary. Include the following: alternative spellings, antonyms, dictionary, grammar type (noun, verb, adjective, adverb), historical derivation, hyphenation, meanings, miscellaneous comments, prioritization by frequency of use, pronunciation, and synonyms.

Some sample definitions are as follows (from *Webster's New World Dictionary*):

■ **been** (bin; *also, chiefly Brit.*, bēn &, *esp. if unstressed*, ben), pp. of **be**.

■ **kum·quat** (kum′kwot), *n.* [< Chin. *chin-chü*, golden orange], 1. a small, orange-colored, oval fruit, with a sour pulp and a sweet rind, used in preserves, 2. the tree that it grows on. Also sp. **cumquat**.

■ **lac·y** (lās′i), *adj.* [-IER, -IEST], 1. of lace. 2. like lace; having a delicate open pattern. — **lac′i·ly**, *adv.* —**lac′i·ness**, *n.*

■ **Span·ish** (span′ish), *adj.* of Spain, its people, their language, etc. *n.* 1. the Romance language of Spain and Spanish America. 2. the Spanish people.

Figure E4.8 shows a partial answer to the problem showing classes and relationships. Add attributes and ordering to the associations where appropriate.

The *RelatedWord, Synonym,* and *Antonym* associations are not quite right and have a problem. Comment on them.

Date _____ Time _____

☐ Call made ☐ Call received ☐ Meeting   Location _____

Name of Broker _____ Phone _____

Broker's Firm _____ Phone _____

Broker's CRD No. _____   ☐ Obtained CRD Report

Investment Recommendation

I asked to receive written information about the investment before making a decision.

☐ Buy ☐ Sell

☐ Yes ☐ No

Name of Security _____

I will get:

_____

☐ a prospectus

_____

☐ an offering memorandum

Reasons for recommendation _____

☐ most recent Annual Report

_____

☐ most recent quarterly or interim reports

_____

☐ research reports

_____

☐ other information

How does this meet my investment objectives? _____

Proposed Trade

_____

Number of shares/units _____

_____

Price per share $ _____

_____

Total cost $ _____

_____

commission _____

What are the risks? _____

My instructions

_____

☐ Do nothing ☐ Buy ☐ Sell

_____

Number   Price

_____

$ _____

Notes _____

_____

_____

Notes made by: _____

Figure E4.7 NASAA form for broker calls

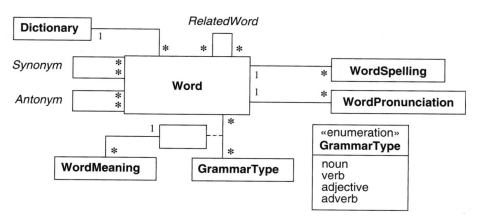

Figure E4.8 Partial model for words in a dictionary

5

State Modeling

You can best understand a system by first examining its static structure—that is, the structure of its objects and their relationships to each other at a single moment in time (the class model). Then you should examine changes to the objects and their relationships over time (the state model). The state model describes the sequences of operations that occur in response to external stimuli, as opposed to what the operations do, what they operate on, or how they are implemented.

The state model consists of multiple state diagrams, one for each class with temporal behavior that is important to an application. The state diagram is a standard computer science concept (a graphical representation of finite state machines) that relates events and states. Events represent external stimuli and states represent values of objects. You should master the material in this chapter before proceeding in the book.

5.1 Events

An *event* is an occurrence at a point in time, such as *user depresses left button* or *flight 123 departs from Chicago*. Events often correspond to verbs in the past tense (*power turned on, alarm set*) or to the onset of some condition (*paper tray becomes empty, temperature becomes lower than freezing*). By definition, an event happens instantaneously with regard to the time scale of an application. Of course, nothing is really instantaneous; an event is simply an occurrence that an application considers atomic and fleeting. The time at which an event occurs is an implicit attribute of the event. Temporal phenomena that occur over an interval of time are properly modeled with a state.

One event may logically precede or follow another, or the two events may be unrelated. Flight 123 must depart Chicago before it can arrive in San Francisco; the two events are causally related. Flight 123 may depart before or after flight 456 departs Rome; the two events are causally unrelated. Two events that are causally unrelated are said to be *concurrent;* they have no effect on each other. If the communications delay between two locations exceeds the difference in event times, then the events must be concurrent because they cannot influence each other. Even if the physical locations of two events are not distant, we consider the events concurrent if they do not affect each other. In modeling a system we do not try to establish an ordering between concurrent events because they can occur in any order.

Events include error conditions as well as normal occurrences. For example, *motor jammed, transaction aborted,* and *timeout* are typical error events. There is nothing different about an error event; only our interpretation makes it an "error."

The term *event* is often used ambiguously. Sometimes it refers to an instance, at other times to a class. In practice, this ambiguity is usually not a problem and the precise meaning is apparent from the context. If necessary, you can say *event occurrence* or *event type* to be precise.

There are several kinds of events. The most common are the signal event, the change event, and the time event.

5.1.1 Signal Event

A *signal* is an explicit one-way transmission of information from one object to another. It is different from a subroutine call that returns a value. An object sending a signal to another object may expect a reply, but the reply is a separate signal under the control of the second object, which may or may not choose to send it.

A *signal event* is the event of sending or receiving a signal. Usually we are more concerned about the receipt of a signal, because it causes effects in the receiving object. Note the difference between *signal* and *signal event*—a signal is a message between objects while a signal event is an occurrence in time.

Every signal transmission is a unique occurrence, but we group them into *signal classes* and give each signal class a name to indicate common structure and behavior. For example, *UA flight 123 departs from Chicago on January 10, 1991* is an instance of signal class *Flight-Departure*. Some signals are simple occurrences, but most signal classes have attributes indicating the values they convey. For example, as Figure 5.1 shows, *FlightDeparture* has attributes *airline, flightNumber, city,* and *date*. The UML notation is the keyword *signal* in guillemets («») above the signal class name in the top section of a box. The second section lists the signal attributes.

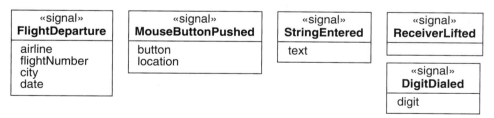

Figure 5.1 Signal classes and attributes. A signal is an explicit one-way transmission of information from one object to another.

5.1.2 Change Event

A *change event* is an event that is caused by the satisfaction of a boolean expression. The intent of a change event is that the expression is continually tested—whenever the expression changes from false to true, the event happens. Of course, an implementation would not *continuously* check a change event, but it must check often enough so that it seems continuous from an application perspective.

The UML notation for a change event is the keyword *when* followed by a parenthesized boolean expression. Figure 5.2 shows several examples of change events.

```
■ when (room temperature < heating set point)
■ when (room temperature > cooling set point)
■ when (battery power < lower limit)
■ when (tire pressure < minimum pressure)
```

Figure 5.2 Change events. A change event is an event that is caused by the satisfaction of a boolean expression.

5.1.3 Time Event

A *time event* is an event caused by the occurrence of an absolute time or the elapse of a time interval. As Figure 5.3 shows, the UML notation for an absolute time is the keyword *when* followed by a parenthesized expression involving time. The notation for a time interval is the keyword *after* followed by a parenthesized expression that evaluates to a time duration.

```
■ when (date = January 1, 2000)
■ after (10 seconds)
```

Figure 5.3 Time events. A time event is an event caused by the occurrence of an absolute time or the elapse of a time interval.

5.2 States

A *state* is an abstraction of the values and links of an object. Sets of values and links are grouped together into a state according to the gross behavior of objects. For example, the state of a bank is either solvent or insolvent, depending on whether its assets exceed its liabilities. States often correspond to verbs with a suffix of "ing" (*Waiting*, *Dialing*) or the duration of some condition (*Powered*, *BelowFreezing*).

Figure 5.4 shows the UML notation for a state—a rounded box containing an optional state name. Our convention is to list the state name in boldface, center the name near the top of the box, and capitalize the first letter.

Figure 5.4   States. A state is an abstraction of the values and links of an object.

In defining states, we ignore attributes that do not affect the behavior of the object, and lump together in a single state all combinations of values and links with the same response to events. Of course, every attribute has some effect on behavior or it would be meaningless, but often some attributes do not affect the sequence of control and you can regard them as simple parameter values within a state. Recall that the purpose of modeling is to focus on qualities that are relevant to the solution of an application problem and abstract away those that are irrelevant. The three UML models (class, state, and interaction) present different views of a system for which the particular choice of attributes and values are not equally important. For example, except for leading 0s and 1s, the exact digits dialed do not affect the control of the phone line, so we can summarize them all with state *Dialing* and track the phone number as a parameter. Sometimes, all possible values of an attribute are important, but usually only when the number of possible values is small.

The objects in a class have a finite number of possible states—one or possibly some larger number. Each object can only be in one state at a time. Objects may parade through one or more states during their lifetime. At a given moment of time, the various objects for a class can exist in a multitude of states.

A state specifies the response of an object to input events. All events are ignored in a state, except those for which behavior is explicitly prescribed. The response may include the invocation of behavior or a change of state. For example, if a digit is dialed in state *Dial tone,* the phone line drops the dial tone and enters state *Dialing*; if the receiver is replaced in state *Dial tone*, the phone line goes dead and enters state *Idle*.

There is a certain symmetry between events and states as Figure 5.5 illustrates. Events represent points in time; states represent intervals of time. A state corresponds to the interval between two events received by an object. For example, after the receiver is lifted and before the first digit is dialed, the phone line is in state *Dial tone*. The state of an object depends on past events, which in most cases are eventually hidden by subsequent events. For example, events that happened before the phone is hung up do not affect future behavior; the *Idle* state "forgets" events received prior to the receipt of the *hang up* signal.

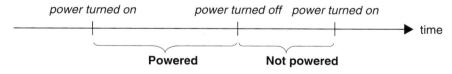

Figure 5.5   Event vs. state. Events represent points in time; states represent intervals of time.

Both events and states depend on the level of abstraction. For example, a travel agent planning an itinerary would treat each segment of a journey as a single event; a flight status board in an airport would distinguish departures and arrivals; an air traffic control system would break each flight into many geographical legs.

You can characterize a state in various ways, as Figure 5.6 shows for the state *Alarm ringing* on a watch. The state has a suggestive name and a natural-language description of its purpose. The event sequence that leads to the state consists of setting the alarm, doing anything that doesn't clear the alarm, and then having the target time occur. A declarative condition for the state is given in terms of parameters, such as *current* and *target time*; the alarm stops ringing after 20 seconds. Finally, a stimulus-response table shows the effect of events *current time* and *button pushed*, including the response that occurs and the next state. The different descriptions of a state may overlap.

State: *AlarmRinging*

Description: alarm on watch is ringing to indicate target time

Event sequence that produces the state:

    setAlarm (*targetTime*)

    any sequence not including *clearAlarm*

    when (*currentTime* = *targetTime*)

Condition that characterizes the state:

    alarm = on, alarm set to *targetTime*, *targetTime* ≤ *currentTime* ≤ *targetTime* + 20 seconds, and no button has been pushed since *targetTime*

Events accepted in the state:

event	response	next state
when (*currentTime* = *targetTime* + 20)	*resetAlarm*	*normal*
buttonPushed (any button)	*resetAlarm*	*normal*

Figure 5.6 Various characterizations of a state. A state specifies the response of an object to input events.

Can links have state? In as much as they can be considered objects, links can have state. As a practical matter, it is generally sufficient to associate state only with objects.

5.3 Transitions and Conditions

A *transition* is an instantaneous change from one state to another. For example, when a called phone is answered, the phone line transitions from the *Ringing* state to the *Connected* state. The transition is said to *fire* upon the change from the source state to the target state. The origin and target of a transition usually are different states, but may be the same. A transition fires when its event occurs (unless an optional guard condition causes the event to be ignored). The choice of next state depends on both the original state and the event received.

An event may cause multiple objects to transition; from a conceptual point of view such transitions occur concurrently.

A **guard condition** is a boolean expression that must be true in order for a transition to occur. For example, a traffic light at an intersection may change only if a road has cars waiting. A guarded transition fires when its event occurs, but only if the guard condition is true. For example, "when you go out in the morning (event), if the temperature is below freezing (condition), then put on your gloves (next state)." A guard condition is checked only once, at the time the event occurs, and the transition fires if the condition is true. If the condition becomes true later, the transition does not then fire. Note that a guard condition is different from a change event—a guard condition is checked only once while a change event is, in effect, checked continuously.

Figure 5.7 shows guarded transitions for traffic lights at an intersection. One pair of electric eyes checks the north-south left turn lanes; another pair checks the east-west turn lanes. If no car is in the north-south and/or east-west turn lanes, then the traffic light control logic is smart enough to skip the left turn portion of the cycle.

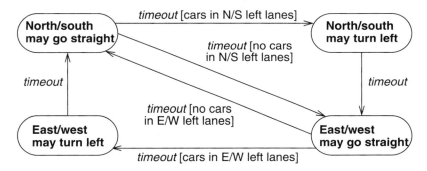

Figure 5.7 Guarded transitions. A transition is an instantaneous change from one state to another. A guard condition is a boolean expression that must be true in order for a transition to occur.

The UML notation for a transition is a line from the origin state to the target state. An arrowhead points to the target state. The line may consist of several line segments. An event may label the transition and be followed by an optional guard condition in square brackets. By convention, we usually confine line segments to a rectilinear grid. We italicize the event name and show the condition in normal font.

5.4 State Diagrams

A **state diagram** is a graph whose nodes are states and whose directed arcs are transitions between states. A state diagram specifies the state sequences caused by event sequences. State names must be unique within the scope of a state diagram. All objects in a class execute the state diagram for that class, which models their common behavior. You can implement state diagrams by direct interpretation or by converting the semantics into equivalent programming code.

The *state model* consists of multiple state diagrams, one state diagram for each class with important temporal behavior. The state diagrams must match on their interfaces—events and guard conditions. The individual state diagrams interact by passing events and through the side effects of guard conditions. Some events and guard conditions appear in a single state diagram; others appear in multiple state diagrams for the purpose of coordination. This chapter covers only individual state diagrams; Chapter 6 discusses state models of interacting diagrams.

A class with more than one state has important temporal behavior. Similarly, a class is temporally important if it has a single state with multiple responses to events. You can represent state diagrams with a single state in a simple nongraphical form—a stimulus–response table listing events and guard conditions and the ensuing behavior.

5.4.1 Sample State Diagram

Figure 5.8 shows a state diagram for a telephone line. The diagram concerns a phone line and not the caller nor callee. The diagram contains sequences associated with normal calls as well as some abnormal sequences, such as timing out while dialing or getting busy lines. The UML notation for a state diagram is a rectangle with its name in a small pentagonal tag in the upper left corner. The constituent states and transitions lie within the rectangle.

At the start of a call, the telephone line is idle. When the phone is removed from the hook, it emits a dial tone and can accept the dialing of digits. Upon entry of a valid number, the phone system tries to connect the call and route it to the proper destination. The connection can fail if the number or trunk are busy. If the connection is successful, the called phone begins ringing. If the called party answers the phone, a conversation can occur. When the called party hangs up, the phone disconnects and reverts to idle when put on hook again.

Note that the receipt of the signal *onHook* causes a transition from any state to *Idle* (the bundle of transitions leading to *Idle*). Chapter 6 will show a more general notation that represents events applicable to groups of states with a single transition.

States do not totally define all values of an object. For example, state *Dialing* includes all sequences of incomplete phone numbers. It is not necessary to distinguish between different numbers as separate states, since they all have the same behavior, but the actual number dialed must of course be saved as an attribute.

If more than one transition leaves a state, then the first event to occur causes the corresponding transition to fire. If an event occurs and no transition matches it, then the event is ignored. If more than one transition matches an event, only one transition will fire, but the choice is nondeterministic.

5.4.2 One-shot State Diagrams

State diagrams can represent continuous loops or one-shot life cycles. The diagram for the phone line is a continuous loop. In describing ordinary usage of the phone, we do not know or care how the loop is started. (If we were describing installation of new lines, the initial state would be important.)

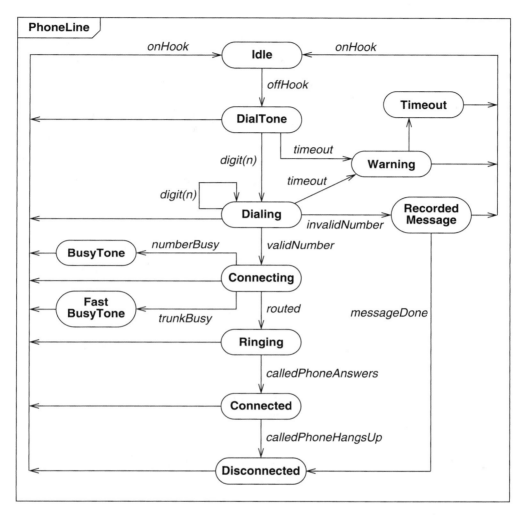

Figure 5.8 State diagram for a telephone line. A state diagram specifies
the state sequences caused by event sequences.

One-shot state diagrams represent objects with finite lives and have initial and final
states. The initial state is entered on creation of an object; entry of the final state implies destruction of the object. Figure 5.9 shows a simplified life cycle of a chess game with a default
initial state (solid circle) and a default final state (bull's eye).

As an alternate notation, you can indicate initial and final states via entry and exit points.
In Figure 5.10 the *start* entry point leads to white's first turn, and the chess game eventually
ends with one of three possible outcomes. Entry points (hollow circles) and exit points (circles enclosing an "x") appear on the state diagram's perimeter and may be named.

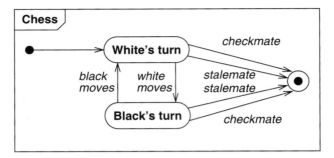

Figure 5.9 State diagram for chess game. One-shot diagrams represent objects with finite lives.

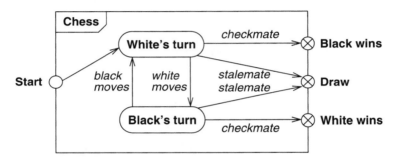

Figure 5.10 State diagram for chess game. You can also show one-shot diagrams by using entry and exit points.

5.4.3 Summary of Basic State Diagram Notation

Figure 5.11 summarizes the basic UML syntax for state diagrams.

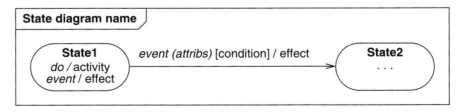

Figure 5.11 Summary of basic notation for state diagrams.

■ **State**. Drawn as a rounded box containing an optional name. A special notation is available for initial states (a solid circle) and final states (a bull's-eye or encircled "x").

■   **Transition**. Drawn as a line from the origin state to the target state. An arrowhead points to the target state. The line may consist of several line segments.

■   **Event**. A signal event is shown as a label on a transition and may be followed by parenthesized attributes. A change event is shown with the keyword *when* followed by a parenthesized boolean expression. A time event is shown with the keyword *when* followed by a parenthesized expression involving time or the keyword *after* followed by a parenthesized expression that evaluates to a time duration.

■   **State diagram**. Enclosed in a rectangular frame with the diagram name in a small pentagonal tag in the upper left corner.

■   **Guard condition**. Optionally listed in square brackets after an event.

■   **Effects** (to be explained in next section). Can be attached to a transition or state and are listed after a slash ("/"). Multiple effects are separated with a comma and are performed concurrently. (You can create intervening states if you want multiple effects to be performed in sequence.)

We also recommend some style conventions. We list the state name in boldface with the first letter capitalized. We italicize event names with the initial letter in lower case. Guard conditions and effects are in normal font and also have the initial letter in lower case. We try to confine transition line segments to a rectilinear grid.

5.5   State Diagram Behavior

State diagrams would be of little use if they just described events. A full description of an object must specify what the object does in response to events.

5.5.1 *Activity Effects*

An *effect* is a reference to a behavior that is executed in response to an event. An ***activity*** is the actual behavior that can be invoked by any number of effects. For example, *disconnect-PhoneLine* might be an activity that is executed in response to an *onHook* event for Figure 5.8. An activity may be performed upon a transition, upon the entry to or exit from a state, or upon some other event within a state.

Activities can also represent internal control operations, such as setting attributes or generating other events. Such activities have no real-world counterparts but instead are mechanisms for structuring control within an implementation. For example, a program might increment an internal counter every time a particular event occurs.

The notation for an activity is a slash ("/") and the name (or description) of the activity, following the event that causes it. The keyword *do* is reserved for indicating an ongoing activity (to be explained) and may not be used as an event name. Figure 5.12 shows the state diagram for a pop-up menu on a workstation. When the right button is depressed, the menu is displayed; when the right button is released, the menu is erased. While the menu is visible, the highlighted menu item is updated whenever the cursor moves.

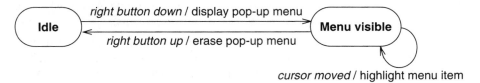

Figure 5.12 Activities for pop-up menu. An activity is behavior that can be executed in response to an event.

5.5.2 Do-Activities

A **do-activity** is an activity that continues for an extended time. By definition, a do-activity can only occur within a state and cannot be attached to a transition. For example, the warning light may flash during the *Paper jam* state for a copy machine (Figure 5.13). Do-activities include continuous operations, such as displaying a picture on a television screen, as well as sequential operations that terminate by themselves after an interval of time, such as closing a valve.

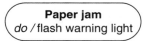

Figure 5.13 Do-activity for a copy machine. A do-activity is an activity that continues for an extended time.

The notation "*do /*" denotes a do-activity that may be performed for all or part of the duration that an object is in a state. A do-activity may be interrupted by an event that is received during its execution; such an event may or may not cause a transition out of the state containing the do-activity. For example, a robot moving a part may encounter resistance, causing it to cease moving.

5.5.3 Entry and Exit Activities

As an alternative to showing activities on transitions, you can bind activities to entry or to exit from a state. There is no difference in expressive power between the two notations, but frequently all transitions into a state perform the same activity, in which case it is more concise to attach the activity to the state.

For example, Figure 5.14 shows the control of a garage door opener. The user generates *depress* events with a pushbutton to open and close the door. Each event reverses the direction of the door, but for safety the door must open fully before it can be closed. The control generates *motor up* and *motor down* activities for the motor. The motor generates *door open* and *door closed* events when the motion has been completed. Both transitions entering state *Opening* cause the door to open.

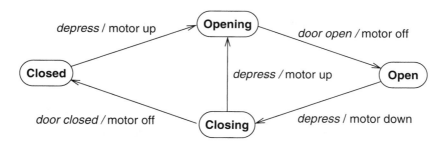

Figure 5.14 Activities on transitions. An activity may be bound to an
event that causes a transition.

Figure 5.15 shows the same model using activities on entry to states. An entry activity
is shown inside the state box following the keyword *entry* and a "/" character. Whenever the
state is entered, by any incoming transition, the entry activity is performed. An entry activity
is equivalent to attaching the activity to every incoming transition. If an incoming transition
already has an activity, its activity is performed first.

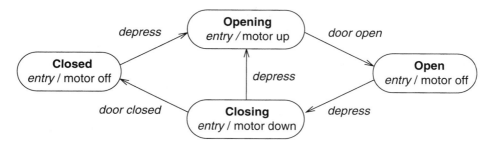

Figure 5.15 Activities on entry to states. An activity may also be bound
to an event that occurs within a state.

Exit activities are less common than entry activities, but they are occasionally useful. An
exit activity is shown inside the state box following the keyword *exit* and a "/" character.
Whenever the state is exited, by any outgoing transition, the exit activity is performed first.

If a state has multiple activities, they are performed in the following order: activities on
the incoming transition, entry activities, do-activities, exit activities, activities on the outgoing transition. Events that cause transitions out of the state can interrupt do-activities. If a do-
activity is interrupted, the exit activity is still performed.

In general, any event can occur within a state and cause an activity to be performed. *Entry* and *exit* are only two examples of events that can occur. As Figure 5.16 shows, there is a
difference between an event within a state and a self-transition; only the self-transition causes the entry and exit activities to be executed.

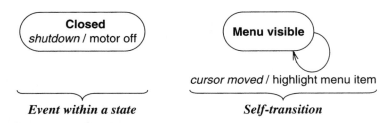

Figure 5.16 **Event within a state vs. self-transition**. A self-transition causes entry
and exit activities to be executed. An event within a state does not.

5.5.4 Completion Transition

Often the sole purpose of a state is to perform a sequential activity. When the activity is completed, a transition to another state fires. An arrow without an event name indicates an automatic transition that fires when the activity associated with the source state is completed. Such unlabeled transitions are called **completion transitions** because they are triggered by the completion of activity in the source state.

A guard condition is tested only once, when the event occurs. If a state has one or more completion transitions, but none of the guard conditions are satisfied, then the state remains active and may become "stuck"—the completion event does not occur a second time, therefore no completion transition will fire later to change the state. If a state has completion transitions leaving it, normally the guard conditions should cover every possible outcome. You can use the special condition *else* to apply if all the other conditions are false. Do not use a guard condition on a completion transition to model waiting for a change of value. Instead model the waiting as a change event.

5.5.5 Sending Signals

An object can perform the activity of sending a signal to another object. A system of objects interacts by exchanging signals.

The activity "send *target.S(attributes)*" sends signal *S* with the given attributes to the target object or objects. For example, the phone line sends a *connect(phone number)* signal to the switcher when a complete phone number has been dialed. A signal can be directed at a set of objects or a single object. If the target is a set of objects, each of them receives a separate copy of the signal concurrently, and each of them independently processes the signal and determines whether to fire a transition. If the signal is always directed to the same object, the diagram can omit the target (but it must be supplied eventually in an implementation, of course).

If an object can receive signals from more than one object, the order in which concurrent signals are received may affect the final state; this is called a **race condition**. For example, in Figure 5.15 the door may or may not remain open if the button is pressed at about the time the door becomes fully open. A race condition is not necessarily a design error, but concurrent systems frequently contain unwanted race conditions that must be avoided by careful design. A requirement of two signals being received simultaneously is never a meaningful condition in the real world, as slight variations in transmission speed are inherent in any distributed system.

5.5.6 Sample State Diagram with Activities

Figure 5.17 adds activities to the state diagram from Figure 5.8.

5.6 Practical Tips

The precise content of all models depends on application needs. The chapter has already mentioned the following practical tips, and we summarize them here for your convenience.

- ■ **Abstracting values into states**. Consider only *relevant* attributes when defining a state. State diagrams need not use all attributes shown in a class model. (Section 5.2)

- ■ **Parameters**. Parameterize events for incidental data that do not affect the flow of control. (Section 5.2)

- ■ **Granularity of events and states**. Consider application needs when deciding on the granularity of events and states. (Section 5.2)

- ■ **When to use state diagrams**. Construct state diagrams only for classes with meaningful temporal behavior. A class has important temporal behavior if it responds differently to various events or has more than one state. Not all classes require a state diagram. (Section 5.4)

- ■ **Entry and exit activities**. When a state has multiple incoming transitions, and all transitions cause the same activity to occur, use an *entry* activity within the state rather than repeatedly listing the activity on transition arcs. Do likewise for *exit* activities. (Section 5.5.3)

- ■ **Guard conditions**. Be careful with guard conditions so that an object does not become "stuck" in a state. (Section 5.5.4)

- ■ **Race conditions**. Beware of unwanted race conditions in state diagrams. Race conditions may occur when a state can accept events from more than one object. (Section 5.5.5)

5.7 Chapter Summary

Event and state are the two elementary concepts in state modeling. An event is an occurrence at a point in time. A state is an abstraction of the values and links of an object. Events represent points in time; states represent intervals of time. An object may respond to certain events when it is in certain states. All events are ignored in a state, except those for which behavior is explicitly prescribed. The same event can have different effects (or no effect) in different states.

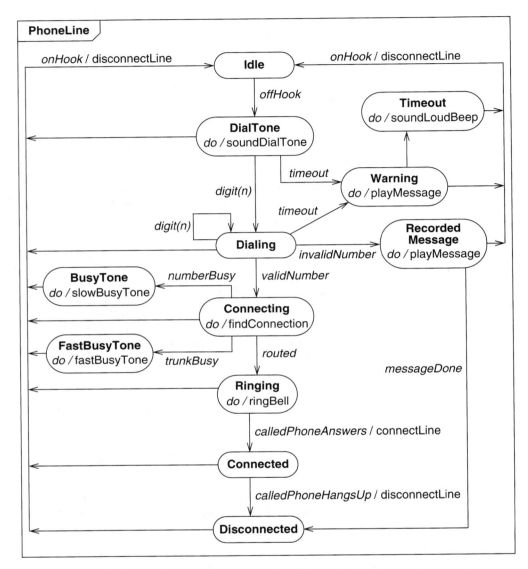

Figure 5.17 State diagram for phone line with activities. State diagrams let you express what objects do in response to events.

There are several kinds of events, such as a signal event, a change event, and a time event. A signal event is the sending or receipt of information communicated among objects. A change event is an event that is caused by the satisfaction of a boolean expression. A time event is an event caused by the occurrence of an absolute time or the elapse of a relative time.

A transition is an instantaneous change from one state to another and is caused by the occurrence of an event. An optional guard condition can cause the event to be ignored. A guard condition is a boolean expression that must be true in order for a transition to occur.

An effect is a reference to a behavior that is executed by objects in response to an event. An activity is the actual behavior that can be invoked by any number of effects. An activity may be performed upon a transition or upon an event within a state. A do-activity is an interruptible behavior that continues for an extended time. Consequently, a do-activity can occur only within a state and cannot be attached to a transition.

A state diagram is a graph whose nodes are states and whose directed arcs are transitions between states. A state diagram specifies the possible states, what transitions are allowed between states, what events cause the transitions to occur, and what behavior is executed in response to events. A state diagram describes the common behavior for the objects in a class; as each object has its own values and links, so too each object has its own state or position in the state diagram. The state model consists of multiple state diagrams, one state diagram for each class with important temporal behavior. The state diagrams must match on their interfaces—events and guard conditions.

activity	do-activity	race condition	state model
change event	effect	signal	time event
completion transition	event	signal event	transition
concurrency	fire (a transition)	state	
control	guard condition	state diagram	

Figure 5.18 Key concepts for Chapter 5

Bibliographic Notes

[Wieringa-98] has a thorough comparison of various ways for specifying software, including specification of the dynamic behavior of systems.

Finite state machines are a basic computer science concept and are described in any standard text on automata theory, such as [Hopcroft-01]. They are often described as recognizers or generators of formal languages. Basic finite state machines have limited expressive power. They have been extended with local variables and recursion as Augmented Transition Networks [Woods-70] and Recursive Transition Networks. These extensions expand the range of formal languages they can express but do little to address the combinatorial explosion that makes them unwieldy for practical control problems. (Chapter 6 addresses this.)

Traditional finite automata have been approached from a synchronous viewpoint. Petri nets [Reisig-92] formalize concurrency and synchronization of systems with distributed activity without resort to any notion of global time. Although they succeed well as an abstract conceptual model, they are too low-level and inexpressive to be useful for specifying large systems.

The need to specify interactive user interfaces has created several techniques for specifying control. This work is directed toward finding notations that clearly express powerful kinds of interactions while also being easily implementable. See [Green-86] for a comparison of some of these techniques.

The first edition of this book distinguished between *actions* (instantaneous behavior) and *activities* (lengthy behavior). UML2 has redefined both of these terms, and we have modified our explanation accordingly. UML2 now defines an activity as a specification of executable behavior and an action as a predefined primitive activity. In effect, the new definition of activity in UML2 subsumes the action and activity of the old book.

References

[Green-86] Mark Green. A survey of three dialogue models. *ACM Transactions on Graphics 5*, 3 (July 1986), 244–275.

[Hopcroft-01] J.E. Hopcroft, Rejeev Motwani, and J.D. Ullman. *Introduction to Automata Theory, Languages, and Computation., Second Edition,* Boston: Addison-Wesley, 2001.

[Reisig-92]. Wolfgang Reisig. *A Primer in Petri Net Design.* New York: Springer-Verlag, 1992.

[Wieringa-98] Roel Wieringa. A survey of structured and object-oriented software specification methods and techniques. *ACM Computing Surveys 30*, 4 (December 1998), 459–527.

[Woods-70] W.A. Woods. Transition network grammars for natural language analysis. *Communications of ACM 13,* 10 (October 1970), 591–606.

Exercises

5.1 (6) An extension ladder has a rope, pulley, and latch for raising, lowering, and locking the extension. When the latch is locked, the extension is mechanically supported and you may safely climb the ladder. To release the latch, you raise the extension slightly with the rope. You may then freely raise or lower the extension. The latch produces a clacking sound as it passes over rungs of the ladder. The latch may be reengaged while raising the extension by reversing direction just as the latch is passing a rung. Prepare a state diagram of an extension ladder.

5.2 (4) A simple digital watch has a display and two buttons to set it, the A button and the B button. The watch has two modes of operation, display time and set time. In the display time mode, the watch displays hours and minutes, separated by a flashing colon.

   The set time mode has two submodes, set hours and set minutes. The A button selects modes. Each time it is pressed, the mode advances in the sequence: display, set hours, set minutes, display, etc. Within the submodes, the B button advances the hours or minutes once each time it is pressed. Buttons must be released before they can generate another event. Prepare a state diagram of the watch.

5.3 (4) Figure E5.1 is a partially completed and simplified state diagram for the control of a telephone answering machine. The machine detects an incoming call on the first ring and answers the call with a prerecorded announcement. When the announcement is complete, the machine records the caller's message. When the caller hangs up, the machine hangs up and shuts off. Place the following in the diagram: call detected, answer call, play announcement, record message, caller hangs up, announcement complete.

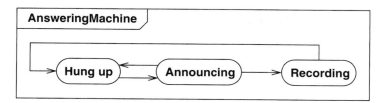

Figure E5.1 Partial state diagram for an answering machine

5.4   (7) The telephone answering machine in the previous exercise activates on the first ring. Revise the state diagram so that the machine answers after five rings. If someone answers the telephone before five rings, the machine should do nothing. Be careful to distinguish between five calls in which the telephone is answered on the first ring and one call that rings five times.

5.5   (3) In a personal computer, a disk controller is typically used to transfer a stream of bytes from a floppy disk drive to a memory buffer with the help of a host such as the central processing unit (CPU) or a direct memory access (DMA) controller. Figure E5.2 shows a partially completed and simplified state diagram for the control of the data transfer.

The controller signals the host each time a new byte is available. The data must then be read and stored before another byte is ready. When the disk controller senses the data has been read, it indicates that data is not available, in preparation for the next byte. If any byte is not read before the next one comes along, the disk controller asserts a data lost error signal until the disk controller is reset. Add the following to the diagram: reset, indicate data not available, indicate data available, data read by host, new data ready, indicate data lost.

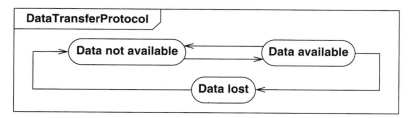

Figure E5.2 Partially completed state diagram of a data transfer protocol

5.6   (5) Figure E5.3 is a partially completed state diagram for one kind of motor control that is commonly used in household appliances. A separate appliance control determines when the motor should be on and continuously asserts *on* as an input to the motor control when the motor should be running.

When *on* is asserted, the motor control should start and run the motor. The motor starts by applying power to both the *start* and the *run* windings. A sensor, called a *starting relay*, determines when the motor has started, at which point the *start* winding is turned off, leaving only the *run* winding powered. Both windings are shut off when *on* is not asserted.

Appliance motors could be damaged by overheating if they are overloaded or fail to start. To protect against thermal damage, the motor control often includes an over-temperature sensor. If

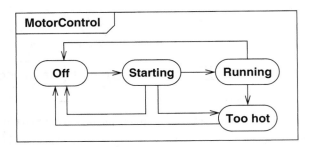

Figure E5.3 Partially completed state diagram for a motor control

the motor becomes too hot, the motor control removes power from both windings and ignores any *on* assertion until a reset button is pressed and the motor has cooled off.

Add the following to the diagram. Activities: apply power to run winding, apply power to start winding. Events: motor is overheated, on is asserted, on is no longer asserted, motor is running, reset. Condition: motor is not overheated.

5.7   (6) There was a single, continuously active input to the control in Exercise 5.6. In another common motor control, there are two pushbuttons, one for *start* and one for *stop*. To start the motor, the user presses the *start* button. The motor continues to run after the *start* button is released.To stop the motor, the user presses the *stop* button. The *stop* button takes precedence over the *start* button, so that the motor does not run while both buttons are pressed.

If both buttons are pressed and released, whether or not the motor starts depends on the order in which the buttons are released. If the *stop* button is released first, the motor starts. Otherwise the motor does not start. Modify the state diagram that you prepared in Exercise 5.6 to accommodate *start* and *stop* buttons.

5.8   (5) Prepare a state diagram for selecting and dragging objects with the diagram editor described in Exercise 4.2.

A cursor on the diagram tracks a two-button mouse. If the left button is pressed with the cursor on an object (a box or a line), the object is selected, replacing any previously selected object. If the left button is pressed with the cursor not on an object, the selection is set to null. Moving the mouse with the left button held down drags any selected object.

5.9   (6) Extend the diagram editor from Exercise 5.8. If the user left clicks on an object and holds the shift key, the object is added to the selection. Moving the mouse with the left button held down drags any selected objects.

5.10   (5) Figure E5.4 shows a state diagram for a copy machine. Initially the copy machine is off. When power is turned on, the machine reverts to a default state—one copy, automatic contrast, and normal size. While the machine is warming, it flashes the ready light. When the machine completes internal testing, the ready light stops flashing and remains on. Then the machine is ready for copying.

The operator may change any of the parameters when the machine is ready. The operator may increment or decrement the number of copies, change the size, toggle between automatic and manual contrast, and change the contrast when auto contrast is disabled. When the parameters are properly set, the operator pushes the start button to begin making copies. Ordinarily, copying proceeds until all copies are made. Occasionally the machine may jam or run out of

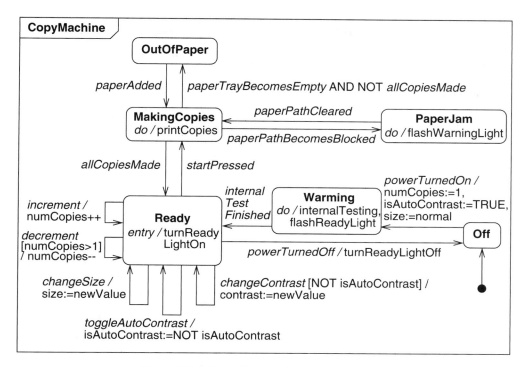

Figure E5.4 State diagram for a copy machine

paper. When the machine jams, the operator may clear the blockage and the machine will resume making copies. Adding paper allows the machine to proceed after running out of paper.

Extend the diagram for the following observations. The copy machine does not work quite right. When it jams, the operator must first remove the jammed paper and then turn the machine off and on before it will operate correctly again. If the machine is turned off and on without first removing the offending paper, the machine stays jammed.

5.11 (7) While exploring an old castle, you and a friend discovered a bookcase that you suspected to be the entrance to a secret passageway. While you examined the bookcase, your friend removed a candle from its holder, only to discover that the candle holder was the entrance control. The bookcase rotated a half turn, pushing you along, separating you from your friend. Your friend put the candle back. This time the bookcase rotated a full turn, still leaving you behind it.

Your friend took the candle out. The bookcase started to rotate a full turn again, but this time you stopped it just shy of a full turn by blocking it with your body. Your friend handed you the candle and together you managed to force the bookcase back a half turn, but this left your friend behind it and you in front of it. You put the candle back. As the bookcase began to rotate, you took out the candle, and the bookcase stopped after a quarter turn. You and your friend then entered to explore further.

Prepare a state diagram for the control of the bookcase that is consistent with the previous scenario. What should you have done at first to gain entry with the least fuss?

6

Advanced State Modeling

Conventional state diagrams are sufficient for describing simple systems but need additional power to handle large problems. You can more richly model complex systems by using nested state diagrams, nested states, signal generalization, and concurrency.

This is an advanced chapter and you can skip it upon a first reading of the book.

6.1 Nested State Diagrams

6.1.1 Problems with Flat State Diagrams

State diagrams have often been criticized because they allegedly are impractical for large problems. This problem is true of flat, unstructured state diagrams. Consider an object with n independent Boolean attributes that affect control. Representing such an object with a single flat state diagram would require 2^n states. By partitioning the state into n independent state diagrams, however, only $2n$ states are required.

Or consider the state diagram in Figure 6.1 in which n^2 transitions are needed to connect every state to every other state. If this model can be reformulated using structure, the number of transitions could be reduced as low as n. Complex systems typically contain much redundancy that structuring mechanisms can simplify.

6.1.2 Expanding States

One way to organize a model is by having a high-level diagram with subdiagrams expanding certain states. This is like a macro substitution in a programming language. Figure 6.2 shows such a state diagram for a vending machine. Initially, the vending machine is idle. When a person inserts coins, the machine adds the amount to the cumulative balance. After adding some coins, a person can select an item. If the item is empty or the balance is insufficient, the machine waits for another selection. Otherwise, the machine dispenses the item and returns the appropriate change.

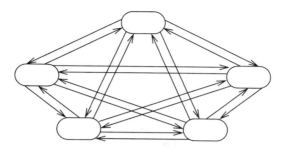

Figure 6.1 Combinatorial explosion of transitions in flat state diagrams.
Flat state diagrams are impractical for large problems.

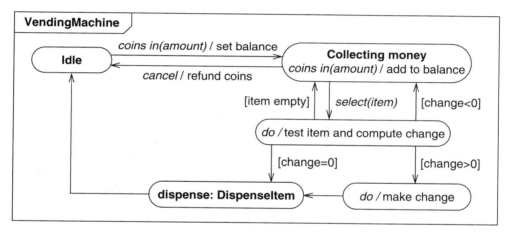

Figure 6.2 Vending machine state diagram. You can simplify state diagrams by using subdiagrams.

Figure 6.3 elaborates the *dispense* state with a lower-level state diagram called a submachine. A ***submachine*** is a state diagram that may be invoked as part of another state diagram.
The UML notation for invoking a submachine is to list a local state name followed by a colon
and the submachine name. Conceptually, the submachine state diagram replaces the local
state. Effectively, a submachine is a state diagram "subroutine."

6.2 Nested States

You can structure states more deeply than just replacing a state with a submachine. As a
deeper alternative, you can nest states to show their commonality and share behavior. (In accordance with UML2 we avoid using *generalization* in conjunction with states. See the *Bib-
liographic Notes* for an explanation.)

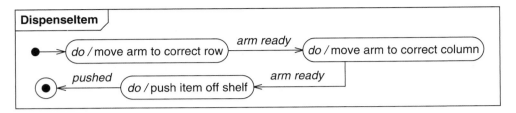

Figure 6.3 *Dispense item* **submachine of vending machine**. A lower-level
state diagram can elaborate a state.

Figure 6.4 simplifies the phone line model from Chapter 5; a single transition from *Active* to *Idle* replaces the transitions from each state to *Idle*. All the original states except *Idle* are nested states of *Active*. The occurrence of event *onHook* in any nested state causes a transition to state *Idle*.

The **composite state** name labels the outer contour that entirely encloses the nested states. Thus *Active* is a composite state with regard to nested states *DialTone, Timeout, Dialing*, and so forth. You may nest states to an arbitrary depth. A nested state receives the outgoing transitions of its composite state. (By necessity, only ingoing transitions with a specified nested state can be shared, or there would be ambiguity.)

Figure 6.5 shows a state diagram for an automobile automatic transmission. The transmission can be in reverse, neutral, or forward; if it is in forward, it can be in first, second, or third gear. States *First, Second,* and *Third* are nested states of state *Forward*.

Each of the nested states receives the outgoing transitions of its composite state. Selecting "N" in any forward gear shifts a transition to neutral. The transition from *Forward* to *Neutral* implies three transitions, one from each forward gear to neutral. Selecting "F" in neutral causes a transition to forward. Within state *Forward,* nested state *First* is the default initial state, shown by the unlabeled transition from the solid circle within the *Forward* contour. *Forward* is just an abstract state; control must be in a real state, such as *First*.

All three nested states share the transition on event *stop* from the *Forward* contour to state *First*. In any forward gear, stopping the car causes a transition to *First*.

It is possible to represent more complicated situations, such as an explicit transition from a nested state to a state outside the contour, or an explicit transition into the contour. In such cases, all the states must appear on one diagram. In simpler cases where there is no interaction except for initiation and termination, you can draw the nested states as separate diagrams and reference them by including a submachine, as in the vending machine example of Figure 6.2.

For simple problems you can implement nested states by degradation into "flat" state diagrams. Another option is to promote each state to a class, but then you must take special care to avoid loss of object identity. The *becomes* operation of Smalltalk lets an object change class without a loss of identity, facilitating promotion of a state to a class. However, the performance overhead of the *becomes* operation may become an issue with many state changes. Promotion of a state to a class is impractical with C++, unless you use advanced techniques, such as those discussed in [Coplien-92]. Java is similar to C++ in this regard.

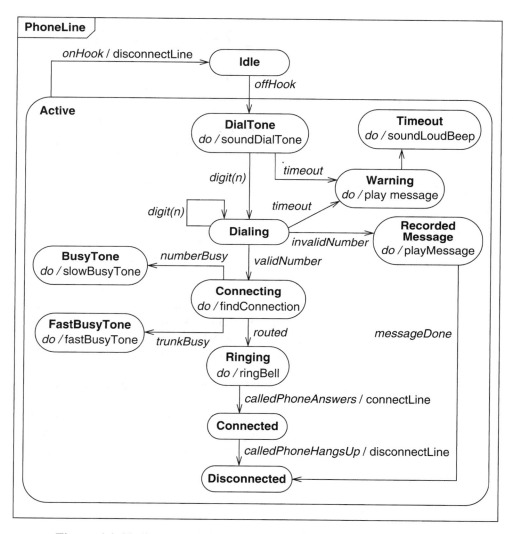

Figure 6.4 Nested states for a phone line. A nested state receives the
outgoing transitions of its enclosing state.

Entry and exit activities are particularly useful in nested state diagrams because they permit a state (possibly an entire subdiagram) to be expressed in terms of matched entry-exit activities without regard for what happens before or after the state is active. Transitioning into or out of a nested state can cause execution of several entry or exit activities, if the transition reaches across several levels of nesting. The entry activities are executed from the outside in and the exit activities from the inside out. This permits behavior similar to nested subroutine calls.

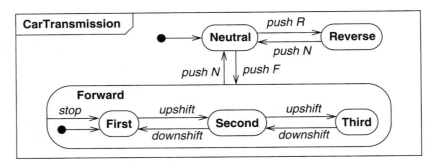

Figure 6.5 Nested states. You can nest states to an arbitrary depth.

6.3 Signal Generalization

You can organize signals into a generalization hierarchy with inheritance of signal attributes. Figure 6.6 shows part of a tree of input signals for a workstation. Signals *MouseButton* and *KeyboardCharacter* are two kinds of user input. Both signals inherit attribute *device* from signal *UserInput* (the root of the hierarchy). *MouseButtonDown* and *MouseButtonUp* inherit *location* from *MouseButton*. *KeyboardCharacters* can be divided into *Control* and *Graphic* characters. Ultimately you can view every actual signal as a leaf on a generalization tree of signals. In a state diagram, a received signal triggers transitions that are defined for any ancestor signal type. For example, typing an 'a' would trigger a transition on signal *Alphanumeric* as well as signal *KeyboardCharacter*. Analogous to generalization of classes, we recommend that all supersignals be abstract.

A signal hierarchy permits different levels of abstraction to be used in a model. For example, some states might handle all input characters the same; other states might treat control characters differently from printing characters; still others might have different activities on individual characters.

6.4 Concurrency

The state model implicitly supports concurrency among objects. In general, objects are autonomous entities that can act and change state independent of one another. However, objects need not be completely independent and may be subject to shared constraints that cause some correspondence among their state changes.

6.4.1 Aggregation Concurrency

A state diagram for an assembly is a collection of state diagrams, one for each part. The aggregate state corresponds to the combined states of all the parts. Aggregation is the "and-relationship." The aggregate state is one state from the first diagram, *and* a state from the second diagram, *and* a state from each other diagram. In the more interesting cases, the part

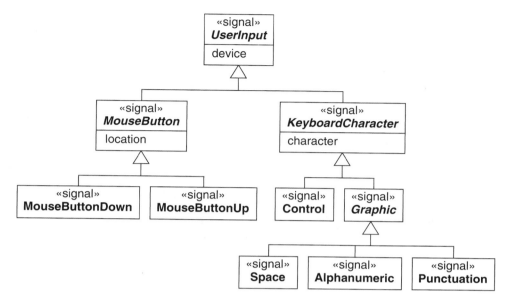

Figure 6.6 Partial hierarchy for keyboard signals. You can organize
signals using generalization.

states interact. Transitions for one object can depend on another object being in a given state. This allows interaction between the state diagrams, while preserving modularity.

Figure 6.7 shows the state of a *Car* as an aggregation of part states: *Ignition*, *Transmission*, *Accelerator,* and *Brake* (plus other unmentioned objects). The state of the car includes one state from each part. Each part undergoes transitions in parallel with all the others. The state diagrams of the parts are almost, but not quite, independent—the car will not start unless the transmission is in neutral. This is shown by the guard expression *Transmission in Neutral* on the transition from *Ignition-Off* to *Ignition-Starting*.

6.4.2 Concurrency within an Object

You can partition some objects into subsets of attributes or links, each of which has its own subdiagram. The state of the object comprises one state from each subdiagram. The subdiagrams need not be independent; the same event can cause transitions in more than one subdiagram. The UML shows concurrency within an object by partitioning the composite state into regions with dotted lines. You should place the name of the composite state in a separate tab so that it does not become confused with the concurrent regions.

Figure 6.8 shows the state diagram for the play of a bridge rubber. When a side wins a game, it becomes "vulnerable"; the first side to win two games wins the rubber. During the play of the rubber, the state of the rubber consists of one state from each subdiagram. When the *Playing rubber* composite state is entered, both regions are initially in their respective default states *Not vulnerable*. Each region can independently advance to state *Vulnerable*

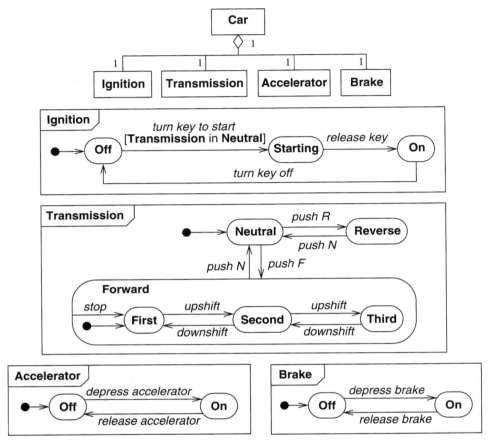

Figure 6.7 An aggregation and its concurrent state diagrams. The state diagram
for an assembly is a collection of state diagrams, one for each part.

when its side wins a game. When one side wins a second game, a transition occurs to the
corresponding *Wins rubber* state. This transition terminates both concurrent regions, because
they are part of the same composite state *Playing rubber* and are active only when the top-
level state diagram is in that state.

Most programming languages lack intrinsic support for concurrency. You can use a library, operating system primitives, or a DBMS to provide concurrency. During analysis you
should regard all objects as concurrent. During design you devise the best accommodation;
many implementations do not require concurrency, and a single thread of control suffices.

6.4.3 Synchronization of Concurrent Activities

Sometimes one object must perform two (or more) activities concurrently. The object does not
synchronize the internal steps of the activities but must complete both activities before it can

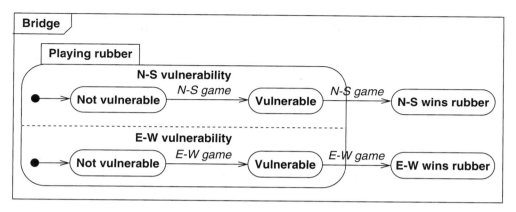

Figure 6.8   Bridge game with concurrent states. You can partition some objects into subsets of attributes or links, each of which has its own subdiagram.

progress to its next state. For example, a cash dispensing machine dispenses cash and returns the user's card at the end of a transaction. The machine must not reset itself until the user takes both the cash and the card, but the user may take them in either order or even simultaneously. The order in which they are taken is irrelevant, only the fact that both of them have been taken. This is an example of *splitting control* into concurrent activities and later *merging control*.

Figure 6.9 shows a concurrent state diagram for the emitting activity. The number of concurrently active states varies during execution from one to two and back to one again. The UML shows concurrent activities within a single composite activity by partitioning a state into regions with dotted lines, as explained previously. Each region is a subdiagram that represents a concurrent activity within the composite activity. The composite activity consists of exactly one state from each subdiagram.

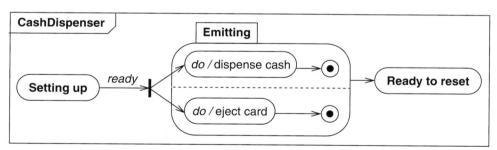

Figure 6.9   Synchronization of control. Control can split into concurrent activities that subsequently merge.

A transition that forks indicates splitting of control into concurrent parts. A small heavy bar with one input arrow and two or more output arrows denotes the fork. The event and an optional guard condition label the input arrow. The output arrows have no labels. Each output arrow selects a state from a different concurrent subdiagram. In the example, the transition on event *ready* splits into two concurrent parts, one to each concurrent subdiagram. When this transition fires, two concurrent **substates** become active and execute independently.

Any transition into a state with concurrent subdiagrams activates each of the subdiagrams. If the transition omits any subdiagrams, the subdiagrams start in their default initial states. In this example, a forked arrow is not actually necessary. You could draw a transition to the *Emitting* state, with each subdiagram having a default initial state.

The UML shows explicit merging of concurrent control by a transition with two or more input arrows and one output arrow, all connected to a small heavy bar (not shown in Figure 6.9). The trigger event and optional guard condition are placed near the bar. The target state becomes active when all of the source states are active and the trigger event occurs. Note that the transition involves a single event, not one event per input arrow. If any subdiagrams in the composite state are not part of the merge, they automatically terminate when the merge transition fires. As a consequence, a transition from a single concurrent substate to a state outside the composite state causes the other concurrent substates to terminate. You can regard this as a degenerate merge involving a single state.

An unlabeled (completion) transition from the outer composite state to another state indicates implicit merging of concurrent control (Figure 6.9). A completion transition fires when activity in the source state is complete. A composite concurrent state is complete when each of its concurrent substates is complete—that is, when each of them has reached its final state. All substates must complete before the completion transition fires and the composite state terminates. In the example, when both activities have been performed, both substates are in their final states, the merge transition fires, and state *Ready to reset* becomes active. Drawing a separate transition from each substate to the target state would have a different meaning; either transition would terminate the other subdiagram without waiting for the other. The firing of a merge transition causes a state diagram to perform the exit activities (if any) of all subdiagrams, in the case of both explicit and implicit merges.

6.5 A Sample State Model

We present a sample state model of a real device (a Sears "Weekender" Programmable Thermostat) to show how the various modeling constructs fit together. We constructed this model by reading the instruction manual and experimenting with the actual device. The device controls a furnace and air conditioner according to time-dependent attributes that the owner enters using a pad of buttons.

While running, the thermostat operates the furnace or air conditioner to keep the current temperature equal to the target temperature. The target temperature is taken from a table of values at the beginning of each program period. The table specifies the target temperature and start time for eight different time periods, four on weekdays and four on weekends. The user can override the target temperature.

The user programs the thermostat using a pad of ten pushbuttons and three switches and sees parameters on an alphanumeric display. Each pushbutton generates an event every time it is pushed. We assign one input event per button:

TEMP UP	raises target temperature or program temperature
TEMP DOWN	lowers target temperature or program temperature
TIME FWD	advances clock time or program time
TIME BACK	retards clock time or program time
SET CLOCK	sets current time of day
SET DAY	sets current day of the week
RUN PRGM	leaves setup or program mode and runs the program
VIEW PRGM	enters program mode to examine and modify eight program time and program temperature settings
HOLD TEMP	holds current target temperature in spite of the program
F-C BUTTON	alternates temperature display between Fahrenheit and Celsius

Each switch supplies a parameter value chosen from two or three possibilities. We model each switch as an independent concurrent subdiagram with one state per switch setting. Although we assign event names to a change in state, it is the state of each switch that is of interest. The switches and their settings are:

NIGHT LIGHT	Lights the alphanumeric display. Values: light off, light on.
SEASON	Specifies which device the thermostat controls. Values: heat (furnace), cool (air conditioner), off (none).
FAN	Specifies when the ventilation fan operates. Values: fan on (fan runs continuously), fan auto (fan runs only when furnace or air conditioner is operating).

The thermostat controls the furnace, air conditioner, and fan power relays. We model this control by activities *run furnace*, *run air conditioner*, and *run fan*.

The thermostat has a sensor for air temperature that it reads continuously, which we model by an external parameter *temp*. The thermostat also has an internal clock that it reads and displays continuously. We model the clock as another external parameter *time*, since we are not interested in building a state model of the clock. In building a state model, it is important to include only states that affect the flow of control and to model other information as parameters or variables. We introduce an internal state variable *target temp* to represent the current temperature that the thermostat is trying to maintain. Some activities read this state variable and others set it; the state variable permits communication among parts of the state model.

Figure 6.10 shows the top-level state diagram of the programmable thermostat. It contains seven concurrent subdiagrams. The user interface is too large to show and is expanded separately (Figure 6.11). The diagram includes trivial subdiagrams for the season switch and the fan switch. The other four subdiagrams show the output of the thermostat: the furnace, air conditioner, the run indicator light, and fan relays. Each of these subdiagrams contains an *Off* and an *On* substate. The state of each subdiagram is totally determined by input parameters and the state of other subdiagrams, such as the season switch or the fan switch. The state of the four subdiagrams on the right is totally derived and contains no additional information.

Figure 6.11 shows the subdiagram for the user interface. The diagram contains three concurrent subdiagrams, one for the interactive display, one for the temperature mode, and one for the night light. The night light is controlled by a physical switch, so the default initial state is irrelevant; its value can be determined directly. The temperature display mode is controlled by a single pushbutton that toggles the temperature units between Fahrenheit and Celsius. The default initial state is necessary; when the device is powered on, the initial temperature mode is Fahrenheit.

The subdiagram for the interactive display is more interesting. The device is either operating or being set up. State *Operate* has three concurrent substates—one includes *Run* and *Hold*, another controls the target temperature display, and the third controls the time and temperature display. Every two seconds the display alternates between the current time and current temperature. The target temperature is displayed continuously and is modified by the *temp up* and *temp down* buttons, as well as the *set target* event that is generated only in the *Run* state. Note that the *target temp* parameter set by this subdiagram is the same parameter that controls the output relays.

After every second in the *Run* state, the current time is compared to the stored program times in the program table; if they are equal, then the program advances to the next program period, and the *Run* state is reentered. The run state is also entered whenever the *run program* button is pressed in any state, as shown by the transition from the contour to the *Operate* state and the default initial transition to *Run*. Whenever the *Run* state is entered, the entry activity on the state resets the target temperature from the program table.

While the program is in the *Hold* state, the program temperature cannot be advanced automatically, but the temperature can still be modified directly by the *temp up* and *temp down* buttons. If the interface is in one of the setup states for 90 seconds without any input, the system enters the *Hold* state. Entering the *Hold* substate also forces entry to the default initial states of the other two concurrent subdiagrams of *Operate*. The *Setup* state was included in the model just to group the three setup nested states for the 90-second timeout transition. Note a small anomaly of the device: The *hold* button has no effect within the *Setup* state, although the *Hold* state can be entered by waiting for 90 seconds.

The three setup subdiagrams are shown in Figure 6.12. Pressing *set clock* enters the *Set minutes* nested state as initial default. Subsequent *set clock* presses toggle between the *Set hours* and the *Set minutes* nested states. The *time fwd* and *time back* buttons modify the program time. Pressing *set day* enters the *Set day* nested state and shows the day of the week. Subsequent presses increment the day directly.

Pressing *view program* enters the *Set program* nested state, which has three concurrent subdiagrams, one each controlling the display of the program time, program temperature, and program period. The *Set program* state always starts with the first program period, while subsequent *view program* events cycle through the 8 program periods. The *view program* event is shown on all three subdiagrams, each diagram advancing the setting that it controls. Note that the *time fwd* and *time back* events modify time in 15-minute increments, unlike the same events in the *set clock* state. Note also that the *temp up* and *temp down* transitions have guard conditions to keep the temperature in a fixed range.

None of the *Interactive display* nested states has an explicit exit transition. Each nested state is implicitly terminated by a transition into another nested state from the main *Interactive display* contour.

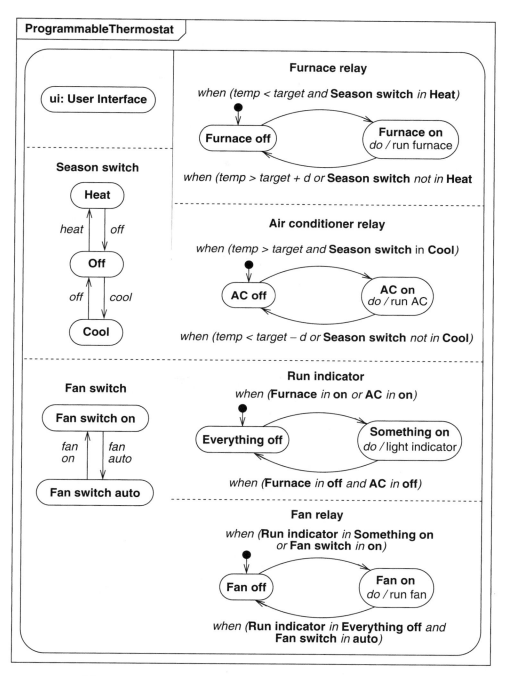

Figure 6.10 State diagram for programmable thermostat

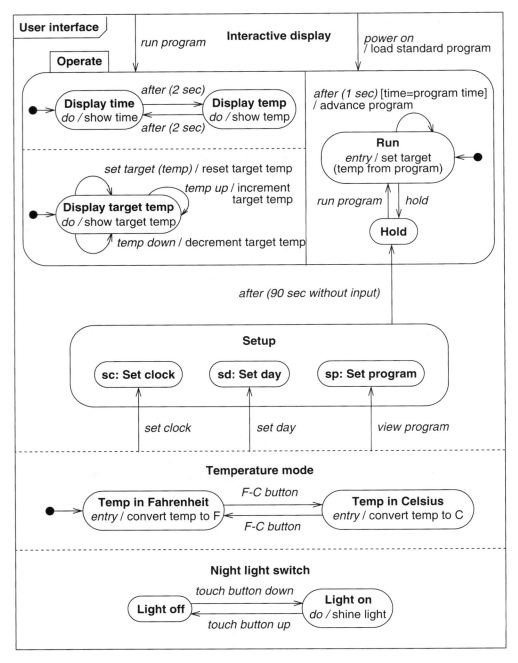

Figure 6.11 Subdiagram for thermostat user interface

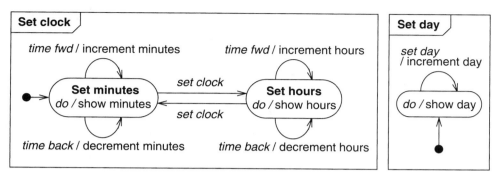

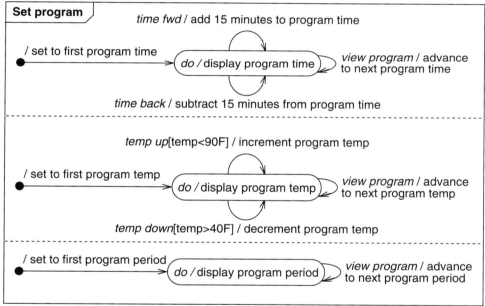

Figure 6.12 Subdiagrams for thermostat user interface setup

6.6 Relation of Class and State Models

The state model specifies allowable sequences of changes to objects from the class model. A state diagram describes all or part of the behavior of the objects of a given class. States are equivalence classes of values and links for an object.

State structure is related to and constrained by class structure. A nested state refines the values and links that an object can have. Both generalization of classes and nesting of states partition the set of possible object values. A single object can have different states over time—the object preserves its identity—but it cannot have different classes. Inherent differences among objects are therefore properly modeled as different classes, while temporary differences are properly modeled as different states of the same class.

A composite state is the aggregation of more than one concurrent substate. There are three sources of concurrency within the class model. The first is aggregation of objects: Each part of an aggregation has its own independent state, so the assembly can be considered to have a state that is the combination of the states of all its parts. The second source is aggregation within an object: The values and links of an object are its parts, and groups of them taken together define concurrent substates of the composite object state. The third source is concurrent behavior of an object, such as found in Figure 6.9. The three sources of concurrency are usually interchangeable. For example, an object could contain an attribute to indicate that it was performing a certain activity.

The state model of a class is inherited by its subclasses. The subclasses inherit both the states of the ancestor and the transitions. The subclasses can have their own state diagrams. But how do the state diagrams of the superclass and the subclass interact? If the superclass state diagrams and the subclass state diagrams deal with disjoint sets of attributes, there is no problem—the subclass has a composite state composed of concurrent state diagrams.

If, however, the state diagram of the subclass involves some of the same attributes as the state diagram of the superclass, a potential conflict exists. The state diagram of the subclass must be a refinement of the state diagram of the superclass. Any state from the parent state diagram can be elaborated with nesting or split into concurrent parts, but new states or transitions cannot be introduced into the parent diagram directly, because the parent diagram must be a projection of the child diagram. Although refinement of inherited state diagrams is possible, usually the state diagram of a subclass should be an independent, orthogonal, concurrent addition to the state diagram inherited from a superclass, defined on a different set of attributes (usually the ones added in the subclass).

The signal hierarchy is independent of the class hierarchy for the classes exchanging signals, in practice if not in theory. Signals can be defined across different classes of objects. Signals are more fundamental than states and more parallel to classes. States are defined by the interaction of objects and events. Transitions can often be implemented as operations on objects, with the operation name corresponding to the signal name. Signals are more expressive than operations, however, because the effect of a signal depends not only on the class of an object but also on its state.

6.7 Practical Tips

The following practical tips have been mentioned throughout the chapter but are summarized here for convenience.

- **Structured state diagrams**. Use structure to organize models with more than 10–15 states. (Section 6.1)
- **State nesting**. Use nesting when the same transition applies to many states. (Section 6.2)

- **Concrete supersignals**. Analogous to generalization of classes, it is best to avoid concrete supersignals. Then, abstract and concrete signals are readily apparent at a glance—all supersignals are abstract and all leaf subsignals are concrete. You can always eliminate concrete supersignals by introducing an *Other* subsignal. (Section 6.3)

- **Concurrency**. Most concurrency arises from object aggregation and need not be shown explicitly in the state diagram. Use composite states to show independent facets of the behavior of a single object. (Section 6.4)

- **Consistency of diagrams**. Check the various state diagrams for consistency on shared events so that the full state model will be correct. (Section 6.5)

- **State modeling and class inheritance**. Try to make the state diagrams of subclasses independent of the state diagrams of their superclasses. Subclass state diagrams should concentrate on attributes unique to the subclasses. (Section 6.6)

6.8 Chapter Summary

A class model describes the objects, values, and links that can exist in a system. The values and links held by an object are called its state. Over time, the objects stimulate each other, resulting in a series of changes to their states. Objects respond to events, which are occurrences at a point in time. The response to an event depends on the state of the object receiving it, and can include a change of state or the sending of a signal to the original sender or to a third object.

The combinations of events, states, and state transitions for a given class can be abstracted and represented as a state diagram. A state diagram is a network of states and events, just as a class diagram is a network of classes and relationships. The state model consists of multiple state diagrams, one state diagram for each class with important dynamic behavior, and shows the possible behavior for an entire system. Each object independently executes the state diagram for its class. The state diagrams for the various classes communicate via shared events.

States and events can both be expanded to show greater detail. Nested states share the transitions of their composite states. Signals can be organized into inheritance hierarchies. Subsignals trigger the same transitions as their supersignals.

Objects are inherently concurrent, and each object has its own state. State diagrams show concurrency as an aggregation of concurrent states, each operating independently. Concurrent objects interact by exchanging events and by testing conditions of other objects, including states. Transitions can split or merge flow of control.

Entry and exit activities permit activities to cover all the transitions entering or exiting the state. They make self-contained state diagrams possible for use in multiple contexts. Internal activities represent transitions that do not leave the state.

A subclass inherits the state diagrams of its ancestors, to be concurrent with any state diagram that it defines. It is also possible to refine an inherited state diagram by expanding states into nested states or concurrent subdiagrams.

A realistic model of a programmable thermostat takes three pages and illustrates subtleties of behavior that are not apparent from the instruction manual or from everyday operation.

composite state	nested state diagram	state model
concurrency	region	synchronization
control	signal generalization	submachine
nested state	state aggregation	

Figure 6.13 Key concepts for Chapter 6

Bibliographic Notes

Much of this chapter follows the work of David Harel, who has formalized his concepts in a notation called state charts [Harel-87]. Harel's treatment is the most successful attempt to date to structure finite state diagrams and avoid the combinatorial explosion that has plagued them. Harel describes a contour-based notation for state diagrams as a special case of a general diagram notation that he calls *higraphs* [Harel-88].

The first edition of this book included *state generalization*, but the second edition omits the concept in accordance with its omission in UML2. The UML2 metamodel restricts generalization to classifiers and a state is not a classifier. There are similarities between generalization of classes and nesting of states, but strictly speaking, in UML2 there is no state generalization.

There are many fine points of state modeling with UML2. See [Rumbaugh-05] for more information.

We thank Mikael Berndtsson for suggesting Exercise 6.12.

References

[Coplien-92] James O. Coplien. *Advanced C++: Programming Styles and Idioms*. Boston: Addison-Wesley, 1992.

[Harel-87] David Harel. Statecharts: a visual formalism for complex systems. *Science of Computer Programming 8* (1987), 231–274.

[Harel-88] David Harel. On visual formalisms. *Communications of ACM 31,* 5 (May 1988), 514–530.

[Rumbaugh-05] James Rumbaugh, Ivar Jacobson, Grady Booch. *The Unified Modeling Language Reference Manual, Second Edition*. Boston: Addison-Wesley, 2005.

Exercises

6.1   (3) The direction control for some of the first toy electric trains was accomplished by interrupting the power to the train. Prepare state diagrams for the headlight and wheels of the train, corresponding to the following sequence of events:

Power is off, train is not moving.
Power is turned on, train runs forward with its headlight shining.
Power is turned off, train stops and headlight goes out.
Power is turned on, headlight shines and train does not move.
Power is turned off, headlight goes out.
Power is turned on, train runs backward with its headlight shining.
Power is turned off, train stops and headlight goes out.
Power is turned on, headlight shines and train does not move.
Power is turned off, headlight goes out.
Power is turned on, train runs forward with its headlight shining.

6.2   (6) Revise the state diagram from Exercise 5.2 to provide for more rapid setting of the time by pressing and holding the B button. If the B button is pressed and held for more than 5 seconds in set time mode, the hours or minutes (depending on the submode) increment once every 1/2 second. (Instructor's note: You may want to give the students a copy of our answer to Exercise 5.2 as the basis for this exercise.)

6.3   (5) Revise the state diagram from your answer to Exercise 5.6 by noting the commonality of the starting and running states. There is a transition from either the starting or the running state to the off state when "on" is not wanted. (Instructor's note: You may want to give the students a copy of our answer to Exercise 5.6 as the basis for this exercise.)

6.4   (6) Three-phase induction motors will spin either clockwise or counterclockwise, depending on the connection to the power lines. In applications requiring motor operation in both directions, two separate contactors (power relays) might be used to make the connections, one for each direction. Also, in some applications of large motors, the motor starts through a transformer that reduces the impact on the power supply. The transformer is bypassed by a third contactor after the motor has been given enough time to come up to speed. There are three momentary control inputs: requests for forward, reverse, or off. When the motor is off, forward or reverse requests cause the motor to start up and run in the requested direction. A reverse request is ignored if the motor is starting or running in the forward direction. and vice versa. An off request at any time shuts the motor off.
      Figure E6.1 is a state diagram for one possible motor control. Convert it from a single state diagram into two concurrent state diagrams, one to control the direction of the motor and one for starting control.

6.5   (3) The control in the previous exercise does not provide for thermal protection.
       a. Modify the state diagram in Figure E6.1 to shut the motor off if an overheating condition is detected at any time.
       b. Modify the concurrent state diagrams that you produced in Exercise 6.4 to shut the motor off if an overheating condition is detected at any time.

6.6   (2) Place the following signal classes into a generalization hierarchy: pick, character input, line pick, circle pick, box pick, text pick, input signal.

6.7   (7) A gas-fired, forced hot-air, home heating system maintains room temperature and humidity in the winter using distributed controls. The comfort of separate rooms may be controlled somewhat independently. Heat is requested from the furnace for each room based on its measured temperature and the desired temperature for that room. When one or more rooms require heat, the furnace is turned on. When the temperature in the furnace is high enough, a blower on the

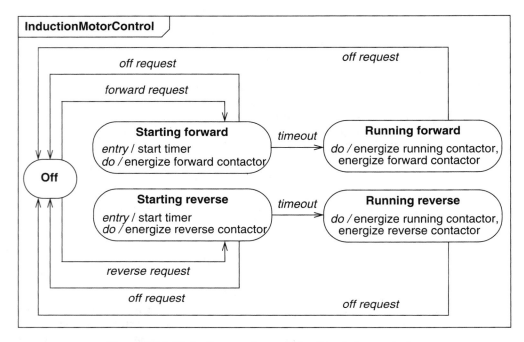

Figure E6.1 State diagram for an induction motor control

furnace is turned on to send hot air through heating ducts. If the temperature in the furnace exceeds a safety limit, the furnace is shut off and the blower continues to run. Flappers in the ducts are controlled by the system to deliver heat only to those rooms that need it. When the room(s) no longer require heat, the furnace is shut off, but the blower continues to deliver hot air until the furnace has cooled off.

Humidity is also maintained based on a strategy involving desired humidity, measured humidity, and outside temperature. The desired humidity is set by the user for the entire home. Humidity of the cool air returning to the blower is measured. When the system determines that the humidity is too low, a humidifier in the furnace is turned on, whenever the blower is on, to inject moisture into the air leaving the blower.

Partition the control of this system into concurrent state diagrams. Describe the functioning of each state diagram without actually going into the details of states or activities.

6.8   Figure E6.2 is a portion of the state diagram for the control of a video cassette recorder (VCR). The VCR has several buttons, including *select*, *on/off*, and *set* for setting the clock and automatic start–stop timers, *auto* for enabling automatic recording, *vcr* for bypassing the VCR, and *timed* for recording for 15-minute increments. Many of the events in Figure E6.2 correspond to pressing the button with the same name. Several buttons have a toggling behavior. For example, pressing *vcr* toggles between VCR and TV mode. Several buttons used for manual control of the VCR are not accounted for in Figure E6.2, such as *play*, *record*, *fast forward*, *rewind*, *pause*, and *eject*. These buttons are enabled only in the *Manual* state. Do the following:
a. (2) Prepare lists of events and activities along with a brief definition.
b. (7) Prepare a user's manual explaining how to operate the VCR.

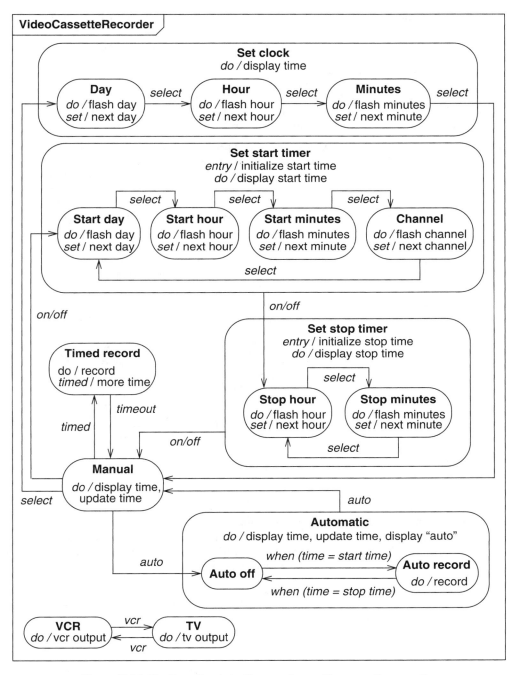

Figure E6.2 Portion of a state diagram for a video cassette recorder

   c. (7) By adding states, extend the state diagram to accommodate another start–stop timer for a second channel.

   d. (7) There is a great deal of commonality in your answer to the previous part. For example, setting the hour may be done in several contexts with similar results. Discuss how duplication of effort could be reduced.

6.9   (6) The diagram in Figure E5.4 has a major omission. The power can be turned off at any time, and the machine should transition to the off state. We could add a transition from each state to the off state, but this would clutter the diagram. Remedy this defect by using nested states.

6.10 (6) Figure E6.3 contains a class diagram for two persons playing a game of table tennis. Construct a state model corresponding to the class model.

   The rules of table tennis are as follows. At the beginning of a game, the two players 'ping' for serve—that is, they bounce the ball over the net and hit it back and forth several times. The winner of the 'ping' serves first.

   The winner of the 'ping' serves five times. Then the other player serves five times. Then the winner of the 'ping' serves five times again. This alternation of serve continues until either player wins the game.

   A game may be won upon shutout (11-0) or when a player reaches 21 with at least a 2-point margin. If the score becomes tied at 20-20, the players then begin alternating individual serves until a player has a 2-point margin of victory.

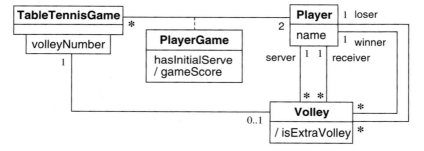

Figure E6.3 Class model for game of table tennis

6.11 (10) Sometimes it is helpful to use reification—to promote something that is not an object into an object. Reification is a helpful technique for meta applications because it lets you shift the level of abstraction. On occasion it is useful to promote attributes, methods, constraints, and control information into objects so you can describe and manipulate them as data.

   Construct a class model that reifies and supports the following state modeling concepts: event, state, transition, condition, activity, signal event, change event, and signal attribute.

6.12 (7) Take the model in Figure 6.5 and remove state nesting. That is, construct a flat state diagram with equivalent semantics.

7

Interaction Modeling

The interaction model is the third leg of the modeling tripod and describes interactions within a system. The class model describes the objects in a system and their relationships, the state model describes the life cycles of the objects, and the interaction model describes how the objects interact.

The interaction model describes how objects interact to produce useful results. It is a holistic view of behavior across many objects, whereas the state model is a reductionist view of behavior that examines each object individually. Both the state model and the interaction model are needed to describe behavior fully. They complement each other by viewing behavior from two different perspectives.

Interactions can be modeled at different levels of abstraction. At a high level, use cases describe how a system interacts with outside actors. Each use case represents a piece of functionality that a system provides to its users. Use cases are helpful for capturing informal requirements.

Sequence diagrams provide more detail and show the messages exchanged among a set of objects over time. Messages include both asynchronous signals and procedure calls. Sequence diagrams are good for showing the behavior sequences seen by users of a system.

And finally, activity diagrams provide further detail and show the flow of control among the steps of a computation. Activity diagrams can show data flows as well as control flows. Activity diagrams document the steps necessary to implement an operation or a business process referenced in a sequence diagram.

7.1 Use Case Models

7.1.1 Actors

An *actor* is a direct external user of a system—an object or set of objects that communicates directly with the system but that is not part of the system. Each actor represents those objects that behave in a particular way toward the system. For example, *customer* and *repair technician* are different actors of a vending machine. For a travel agency system, actors might include *traveler*, *agent*, and *airline*. For a computer database system, actors might include *user* and *administrator*. Actors can be persons, devices, and other systems—anything that interacts directly with the system.

An object can be bound to multiple actors if it has different facets to its behavior. For example, the objects Mary, Frank, and Paul may be customers of a vending machine. Paul may also be a repair technician for the vending machine.

An actor has a single well-defined purpose. In contrast, objects and classes often combine many different purposes. An actor represents a particular facet of objects in its interaction with a system. The same actor can represent objects of different classes that interact similarly toward a system. For example, even though many different individual persons use a vending machine, their behavior toward the vending machine can all be summarized by the actors *customer* and *repair technician*. Each actor represents a coherent set of capabilities for its objects.

Modeling the actors helps to define a system by identifying the objects within the system and those on its boundary. An actor is directly connected to the system—an indirectly connected object is not an actor and should not be included as part of the system model. Any interactions with an indirectly connected object must pass through the actors. For example, the dispatcher of repair technicians from a service bureau is not an actor of a vending machine—only the repair technician interacts directly with the machine. If it is necessary to model the interactions among such indirect objects, then a model should be constructed of the environment itself as a larger system. For example, it might be useful to build a model of a repair service that includes dispatchers, repair technicians, and vending machines as actors, but that is a different model from the vending machine model.

7.1.2 Use Cases

The various interactions of actors with a system are quantized into use cases. A **use case** is a coherent piece of functionality that a system can provide by interacting with actors. For example, a *customer* actor can *buy a beverage* from a vending machine. The customer inserts money into the machine, makes a selection, and ultimately receives a beverage. Similarly, a *repair technician* can *perform scheduled maintenance* on a vending machine. Figure 7.1 summarizes several use cases for a vending machine.

Each use case involves one or more actors as well as the system itself. The use case *buy a beverage* involves the *customer* actor and the use case *perform scheduled maintenance* involves the *repair technician* actor. In a telephone system, the use case *make a call* involves two actors, a *caller* and a *receiver*. The actors need not all be persons. The use case *make a trade* on an online stock broker involves a *customer* actor and a *stock exchange* actor. The stock broker system needs to communicate with both actors to execute a trade.

A use case involves a sequence of messages among the system and its actors. For example, in the *buy a beverage* use case, the customer first inserts a coin and the vending machine displays the amount deposited. This can be repeated several times. Then the customer pushes

- ■ **Buy a beverage**. The vending machine delivers a beverage after a customer selects and pays for it.

- ■ **Perform scheduled maintenance**. A repair technician performs the periodic service on the vending machine necessary to keep it in good working condition.

- ■ **Make repairs**. A repair technician performs the unexpected service on the vending machine necessary to repair a problem in its operation.

- ■ **Load items**. A stock clerk adds items into the vending machine to replenish its stock of beverages.

Figure 7.1 Use case summaries for a vending machine. A use case is a coherent piece of functionality that a system can provide by interacting with actors.

a button to indicate a selection; the vending machine dispenses the beverage and issues change, if necessary.

Some use cases have a fixed sequence of messages. More often, however, the message sequence may have some variations. For example, a customer can deposit a variable number of coins in the *buy a beverage* use case. Depending on the money inserted and the item selected, the machine may, or may not, return change. You can represent such variability by showing several examples of distinct behavior sequences. Typically you should first define a mainline behavior sequence, then define optional subsequences, repetitions, and other variations.

Error conditions are also part of a use case. For example, if the customer selects a beverage whose supply is exhausted, the vending machine displays a warning message. Similarly, the vending transaction can be cancelled. For example, the customer can push the coin return on the vending machine at any time before a selection has been accepted; the machine returns the coins, and the behavior sequence for the use case is complete. From the user's point of view, some kinds of behavior may be thought of as errors. The designer, however, should plan for all possible behavior sequences. From the system's point of view, user errors or resource failures are just additional kinds of behavior that a robust system can accommodate.

A use case brings together all of the behavior relevant to a slice of system functionality. This includes normal mainline behavior, variations on normal behavior, exception conditions, error conditions, and cancellations of a request. Figure 7.2 explains the *buy a beverage* use case in detail. Grouping normal and abnormal behavior under a single use case helps to ensure that all the consequences of an interaction are considered together.

In a complete model, the use cases partition the functionality of the system. They should preferably all be at a comparable level of abstraction. For example, the use cases *make telephone call* and *record voice mail message* are at comparable levels. The use case *set external speaker volume to high* is too narrow. It would be better as *set speaker volume* (with the volume level selection as part of the use case) or maybe even just *set telephone parameters*, under which we might group setting volume, display pad settings, setting the clock, and so on.

Use Case: Buy a beverage

Summary: The vending machine delivers a beverage after a customer selects and pays for it.

Actors: Customer

Preconditions: The machine is waiting for money to be inserted.

Description: The machine starts in the waiting state in which it displays the message "Enter coins." A customer inserts coins into the machine. The machine displays the total value of money entered and lights up the buttons for the items that can be purchased for the money inserted. The customer pushes a button. The machine dispenses the corresponding item and makes change, if the cost of the item is less than the money inserted.

Exceptions:

Canceled: If the customer presses the cancel button before an item has been selected, the customer's money is returned and the machine resets to the waiting state.

Out of stock: If the customer presses a button for an out-of-stock item, the message "That item is out of stock" is displayed. The machine continues to accept coins or a selection.

Insufficient money: If the customer presses a button for an item that costs more than the money inserted, the message "You must insert $*nn.nn* more for that item" is displayed, where *nn.nn* is the amount of additional money needed. The machine continues to accept coins or a selection.

No change: If the customer has inserted enough money to buy the item but the machine cannot make the correct change, the message "Cannot make correct change" is displayed and the machine continues to accept coins or a selection.

Postconditions: The machine is waiting for money to be inserted.

Figure 7.2 Use case description. A use case brings together all of the behavior relevant to a slice of system functionality.

7.1.3 Use Case Diagrams

A system involves a set of use cases and a set of actors. Each use case represents a slice of the functionality the system provides. The set of use cases shows the complete functionality of the system at some level of detail. Similarly, each actor represents one kind of object for which the system can perform behavior. The set of actors represents the complete set of objects that the system can serve. Objects accumulate behavior from all the systems with which they interact as actors.

The UML has a graphical notation for summarizing use cases and Figure 7.3 shows an example. A rectangle contains the use cases for a system with the actors listed on the outside. The name of the system may be written near a side of the rectangle. A name within an ellipse

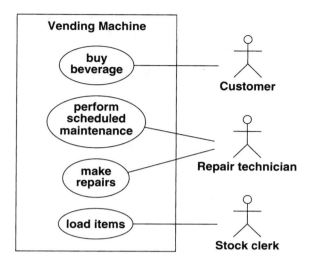

Figure 7.3 Use case diagram for a vending machine. A system involves a set of use cases and a set of actors.

denotes a use case. A "stick man" icon denotes an actor, with the name being placed below or adjacent to the icon. Solid lines connect use cases to participating actors.

In the figure, the actor *Repair technician* participates in two use cases, the others in one each. Multiple actors can participate in a use case, even though the example has only one actor per use case.

7.1.4 Guidelines for Use Case Models

Use cases identify the functionality of a system and organize it according to the perspective of users. In contrast, traditional requirements lists can include functionality that is vague to users, as well as overlook supporting functionality, such as initialization and termination. Use cases describe complete transactions and are therefore less likely to omit necessary steps. There is still a place for traditional requirements lists in describing global constraints and other nonlocalized functionality, such as mean time to failure and overall throughput, but you should capture most user interactions with use cases. The main purpose of a system is almost always found in the use cases, with requirements lists supplying additional implementation constraints. Here are some guidelines for constructing use case models.

■ **First determine the system boundary**. It is impossible to identify use cases or actors if the system boundary is unclear.

■ **Ensure that actors are focused**. Each actor should have a single, coherent purpose. If a real-world object embodies multiple purposes, capture them with separate actors. For example, the owner of a personal computer may install software, set up a database, and send email. These functions differ greatly in their impact on the computer system and the potential for system damage. They might be broken into three actors: *system admin-*

istrator, database administrator, and *computer user.* Remember that an actor is defined with respect to a system, not as a free-standing concept.

- **Each use case must provide value to users**. A use case should represent a complete transaction that provides value to users and should not be defined too narrowly. For example, *dial a telephone number* is not a good use case for a telephone system. It does not represent a complete transaction of value by itself; it is merely part of the use case *make telephone call*. The latter use case involves placing the call, talking, and terminating the call. By dealing with complete use cases, we focus on the purpose of the functionality provided by the system, rather than jumping into implementation decisions. The details come later. Often there is more than one way to implement desired functionality.

- **Relate use cases and actors**. Every use case should have at least one actor, and every actor should participate in at least one use case. A use case may involve several actors, and an actor may participate in several use cases.

- **Remember that use cases are informal**. It is important not to be obsessed by formalism in specifying use cases. They are not intended as a formal mechanism but as a way to identify and organize system functionality from a user-centered point of view. It is acceptable if use cases are a bit loose at first. Detail can come later as use cases are expanded and mapped into implementations.

- **Use cases can be structured**. For many applications, the individual use cases are completely distinct. For large systems, use cases can be built out of smaller fragments using relationships (see Chapter 8).

7.2 Sequence Models

The sequence model elaborates the themes of use cases. There are two kinds of sequence models: scenarios and a more structured format called sequence diagrams.

7.2.1 Scenarios

A *scenario* is a sequence of events that occurs during one particular execution of a system, such as for a use case. The scope of a scenario can vary; it may include all events in the system, or it may include only those events impinging on or generated by certain objects. A scenario can be the historical record of executing an actual system or a thought experiment of executing a proposed system.

A scenario can be displayed as a list of text statements, as Figure 7.4 illustrates. In this example, John Doe logs on with an online stock broker system, places an order for GE stock, and then logs off. Sometime later, after the order is executed, the securities exchange reports the results of the trade to the broker system. John Doe will see the results on the next login, but that is not part of this scenario.

The example expresses interaction at a high level. For example, the step *John Doe logs in* might require several messages between John Doe and the system. The essential purpose of the step, however, is the request to enter the system and providing the necessary identifi-

> John Doe logs in.
> System establishes secure communications.
> System displays portfolio information.
> John Doe enters a buy order for 100 shares of GE at the market price.
> System verifies sufficient funds for purchase.
> System displays confirmation screen with estimated cost.
> John Doe confirms purchase.
> System places order on securities exchange.
> System displays transaction tracking number.
> John Doe logs out.
> System establishes insecure communication.
> System displays good-bye screen.
> Securities exchange reports results of trade.

Figure 7.4 Scenario for a session with an online stock broker. A scenario is a sequence of events that occurs during one particular execution of a system.

cation—the details can be shown separately. At early stages of development, you should express scenarios at a high level. At later stages, you can show the exact messages. Determining the detailed messages is part of development.

A scenario contains messages between objects as well as activities performed by objects. Each message transmits information from one object to another. For example, *John Doe logs in* transmits a message from John Doe to the broker system. The first step of writing a scenario is to identify the objects exchanging messages. Then you must determine the sender and receiver of each message, as well as the sequence of the messages. Finally, you can add activities for internal computations as scenarios are reduced to code.

7.2.2 Sequence Diagrams

A text format is convenient for writing, but it does not clearly show the sender and receiver of each message, especially if there are more than two objects. A *sequence diagram* shows the participants in an interaction and the sequence of messages among them. A sequence diagram shows the interaction of a system with its actors to perform all or part of a use case.

Figure 7.5 shows a sequence diagram corresponding to the previous stock broker scenario. Each actor as well as the system is represented by a vertical line called a *lifeline* and each message by a horizontal arrow from the sender to the receiver. Time proceeds from top to bottom, but the spacing is irrelevant; the diagram shows only the sequence of messages, not their exact timing. (Real-time systems impose time constraints on event sequences, but that requires extra notation.) Note that sequence diagrams can show concurrent signals—*stock broker system* sends messages to *customer* and *securities exchange* concurrently—and signals between participants need not alternate—*stock broker system* sends *secure communication* followed by *display portfolio*.

Each use case requires one or more sequence diagrams to describe its behavior. Each sequence diagram shows a particular behavior sequence of the use case. It is best to show a specific portion of a use case and not attempt to be too general. Although it is possible to

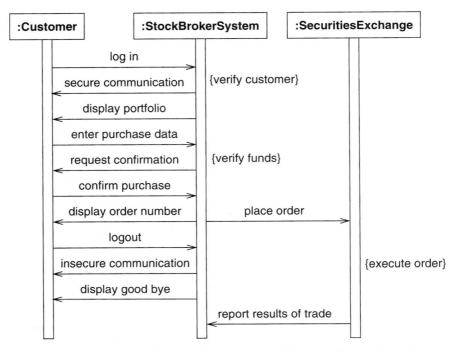

Figure 7.5 Sequence diagram for a session with an online stock broker.
A sequence diagram shows the participants in an interaction and
the sequence of messages among them.

show conditionals within a sequence diagram, usually it is clearer to prepare one sequence diagram for each major flow of control.

Sequence diagrams can show large-scale interactions, such as an entire session with the stock broker system, but often such interactions contain many independent tasks that can be combined in various ways. Rather than repeating information, you can draw a separate sequence diagram for each task. For example, Figure 7.6 and Figure 7.7 show an order to purchase a stock and a request for a quote on a stock. These and various other tasks (not shown) would fit within an entire stock trading session.

You should also prepare a sequence diagram for each exception condition within the use case. For example, Figure 7.8 shows a variation in which the customer does not have sufficient funds to place the order. In this example, the customer cancels the order. In another variation (not shown), the customer would reduce the number of shares purchased and the order would be accepted.

In most systems, there are an unlimited number of scenarios, so it is not possible to show them all. However, you should try to elaborate all the use cases and cover the basic kinds of behavior with sequence diagrams. For example, a stock broker system can interleave purchases, sales, and inquiries arbitrarily. It is unnecessary to show all combinations of activities, once the basic pattern is established.

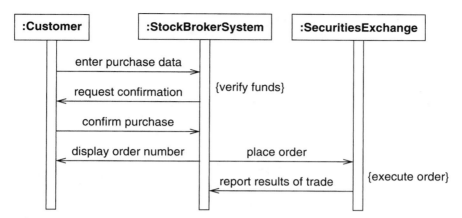

Figure 7.6 Sequence diagram for a stock purchase. Sequence diagrams can show large-scale interactions as well as smaller, constituent tasks.

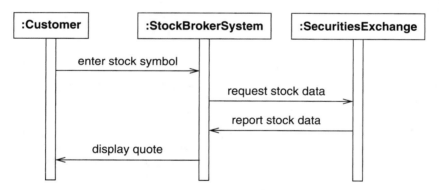

Figure 7.7 Sequence diagram for a stock quote

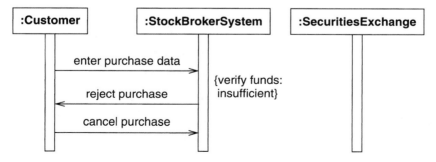

Figure 7.8 Sequence diagram for a stock purchase that fails

7.2.3 Guidelines for Sequence Models

The sequence model adds detail and elaborates the informal themes of use cases. There are two kinds of sequence models. Scenarios document a sequence of events with prose. Sequence diagrams also document the sequence of events but more clearly show the actors involved. The following guidelines will help you with sequence models.

- **Prepare at least one scenario per use case.** The steps in the scenario should be logical commands, not individual button clicks. Later, during implementation, you can specify the exact syntax of input. Start with the simplest mainline interaction—no repetitions, one main activity, and typical values for all parameters. If there are substantially different mainline interactions, write a scenario for each.

- **Abstract the scenarios into sequence diagrams.** The sequence diagrams clearly show the contribution of each actor. It is important to separate the contribution of each actor as a prelude to organizing behavior about objects.

- **Divide complex interactions.** Break large interactions into their constituent tasks and prepare a sequence diagram for each of them.

- **Prepare a sequence diagram for each error condition.** Show the system response to the error condition.

7.3 Activity Models

An *activity diagram* shows the sequence of steps that make up a complex process, such as an algorithm or workflow. An activity diagram shows flow of control, similar to a sequence diagram, but focuses on operations rather than on objects. Activity diagrams are most useful during the early stages of designing algorithms and workflows.

Figure 7.9 shows an activity diagram for the processing of a stock trade order that has been received by an online stock broker. The elongated ovals show activities and the arrows show their sequencing. The diamond shows a decision point and the heavy bar shows splitting or merging of concurrent threads.

The online stock broker first verifies the order against the customer's account, then executes it with the stock exchange. If the order executes successfully, the system does three things concurrently: mails trade confirmation to the customer, updates the online portfolio to reflect the results of the trade, and settles the trade with the other party by debiting the account and transferring cash or securities. When all three concurrent threads have been completed, the system merges control into a single thread and closes the order. If the order execution fails, then the system sends a failure notice to the customer and closes the order.

An activity diagram is like a traditional flowchart in that it shows the flow of control from step to step. Unlike a traditional flowchart, however, an activity diagram can show both sequential and concurrent flow of control. This distinction is important for a distributed system. Activity diagrams are often used for modeling human organizations because they involve many objects—persons and organizational units—that perform operations concurrently.

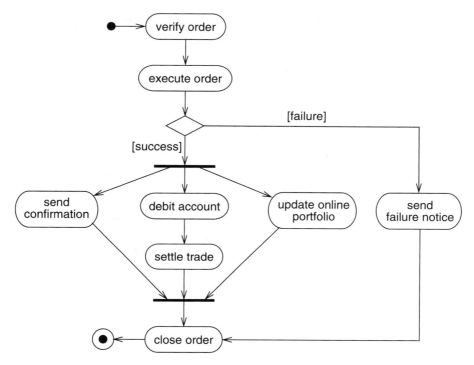

Figure 7.9 Activity diagram for stock trade processing. An activity diagram
shows the sequence of steps that make up a complex process.

7.3.1 *Activities*

The steps of an activity diagram are operations, specifically activities from the state model.
The purpose of an activity diagram is to show the steps within a complex process and the
sequencing constraints among them.

Some activities run forever until an outside event interrupts them, but most activities
eventually complete their work and terminate by themselves. The completion of an activity
is a completion event and usually indicates that the next activity can be started. An unlabeled
arrow from one activity to another in an activity diagram indicates that the first activity must
complete before the second activity can begin.

An activity may be decomposed into finer activities. For example, Figure 7.10 expands
the *execute order* activity of Figure 7.9. It is important that the activities on a diagram be at
the same level of detail. For example, in Figure 7.9 *execute order* and *settle trade* are similar
in detail; they both express a high-level operation without showing the underlying mechanisms. If one of these activities were replaced in the activity diagram by its more detailed
steps, the other activities should be replaced as well to maintain balance. Alternatively, balance can be preserved by elaborating the activities in separate diagrams.

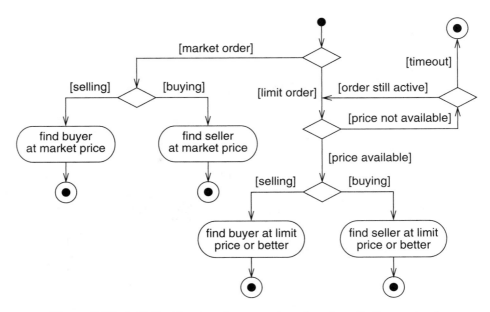

Figure 7.10 Activity diagram for *execute order*. An activity may be decomposed into finer activities.

7.3.2 Branches

If there is more than one successor to an activity, each arrow may be labeled with a condition in square brackets, for example, *[failure]*. All subsequent conditions are tested when an activity completes. If one condition is satisfied, its arrow indicates the next activity to perform. If no condition is satisfied, the diagram is badly formed and the system will hang unless it is interrupted at some higher level. To avoid this danger, you can use the *else* condition; it is satisfied in case no other condition is satisfied. If multiple conditions are satisfied, only one successor activity executes, but there is no guarantee which one it will be. Sometimes this kind of nondeterminism is desirable, but often it indicates an error, so the modeler should determine whether any overlap of conditions can occur and whether it is correct.

As a notational convenience, a diamond shows a branch into multiple successors, but it means the same thing as arrows leaving an activity symbol directly. In Figure 7.9 the diamond has one incoming arrow and two outgoing arrows, each with a condition. A particular execution chooses only one path of control.

If several arrows enter an activity, the alternate execution paths merge. Alternatively, several arrows may enter a diamond and one may exit to indicate a merge.

7.3.3 Initiation and Termination

A solid circle with an outgoing arrow shows the starting point of an activity diagram. When an activity diagram is activated, control starts at the solid circle and proceeds via the outgoing arrow toward the first activities. A bull's-eye (a solid circle surrounded by a hollow circle) shows the termination point—this symbol only has incoming arrows. When control reaches a bull's-eye, the overall activity is complete and execution of the activity diagram ends.

7.3.4 Concurrent Activities

Unlike traditional flow charts, organizations and computer systems can perform more than one activity at a time. The pace of activity can also change over time. For example, one activity may be followed by another activity (sequential control), then split into several concurrent activities (a fork of control), and finally be combined into a single activity (a merge of control). A fork or merge is shown by a synchronization bar—a heavy line with one or more input arrows and one or more output arrows. On a synchronization, control must be present on all of the incoming activities, and control passes to all of the outgoing activities.

Figure 7.9 illustrates both a fork and merge of control. Once an order is executed, there is a fork—several tasks need to occur and they can occur in any order. The stock trade system must send confirmation to the customer, debit the customer's account, and update the customer's online portfolio. After the three concurrent tasks complete and the trade is settled, there is a merge, and execution proceeds to the activity of closing the order.

7.3.5 Executable Activity Diagrams

Activity diagrams are not only useful for defining the steps in a complex process, but they can also be used to show the progression of control during execution. An *activity token* can be placed on an activity symbol to indicate that it is executing. When an activity completes, the token is removed and placed on the outgoing arrow. In the simplest case, the token then moves to the next activity.

If there are multiple outgoing arrows with conditions, the conditions are examined to determine the successor activity. Only one successor activity can receive the token, even if more than one condition is true. If no condition is satisfied, the activity diagram is ill formed.

Multiple tokens can arise through concurrency. If an executing activity is followed by a concurrent split of control, completion causes an increase in the number of tokens—a token is placed on each of the concurrent activities. Similarly, a merge of control causes a decrease in the number of tokens as tokens migrate from the input activities to the output activities. All the input activities must complete before the merge can actually occur.

7.3.6 Guidelines for Activity Models

Activity diagrams elaborate the details of computation, thus documenting the steps needed to implement an operation or a business process. In addition, activity diagrams can help developers understand complex computations by graphically displaying the progression through intermediate execution steps. Here is some advice for activity models.

■ **Don't misuse activity diagrams**. Activity diagrams are intended to elaborate use case and sequence models so that a developer can study algorithms and workflow. Activity diagrams supplement the object-oriented focus of UML models and should not be used as an excuse to develop software via flowcharts.

- **Level diagrams**. Activities on a diagram should be at a consistent level of detail. Place additional detail for an activity in a separate diagram.

- **Be careful with branches and conditions**. If there are conditions, at least one must be satisfied when an activity completes—consider using an *else* condition. In undeterministic models, it is possible for multiple conditions to be satisfied—otherwise this is an error condition.

- **Be careful with concurrent activities**. Concurrency means that the activities can complete in any order and still yield an acceptable result. Before a merge can happen, all inputs must first complete.

- **Consider executable activity diagrams**. Executable activity diagrams can help developers understand their systems better. Sometimes they can even be helpful for end users who want to follow the progression of a process.

7.4 Chapter Summary

The interaction model provides a holistic view of behavior—how objects interact and exchange messages. At a high level, use cases partition the functionality of a system into discrete pieces meaningful to external actors. You can elaborate the behavior of use cases with scenarios and sequence diagrams. Sequence diagrams clearly show the objects in an interaction and the messages among them. Activity diagrams specify the details of a computation.

The class, state, and interaction models all involve the same concepts, namely data, sequencing, and operations, but each model focuses on a particular aspect and leaves the other aspects uninterpreted. All three models are necessary for a full understanding of a problem, although the balance of importance among the models varies according to the kind of application. The three models come together in the implementation of methods, which involve data (target object, arguments, and variables), control (sequencing constructs), and interactions (messages, calls, and sequences).

activity	concurrency	scenario	use case
activity diagram	interaction model	sequence diagram	use case diagram
activity token	lifeline	system boundary	
actor	message	thread	

Figure 7.11 Key concepts for Chapter 7

Bibliographic Notes

Jacobson first introduced use cases [Jacobson-92]. The first edition of this book included scenarios and event trace diagrams. The latter are equivalent to simple sequence diagrams.

References

[Jacobson-92] Ivar Jacobson, Magnus Christerson, Patrik Jonsson, and Gunnar Övergaard. *Object-Oriented Software Engineering: A Use Case Driven Approach.* Wokingham, England: Addison-Wesley, 1992.

Exercises

7.1   Consider a physical bookstore, such as in a shopping mall.
   a. (2) List three actors that are involved in the design of a checkout system. Explain the relevance of each actor.
   b. (2) One use case is the purchase of items. Take the perspective of a customer and list another use case at a comparable level of abstraction. Summarize the purpose of each use case with a sentence.
   c. (4) Prepare a use case diagram for a physical bookstore checkout system.
   d. (3) Prepare a normal scenario for each use case. Remember that a scenario is an example, and need not exercise all functionality of the use case.
   e. (3) Prepare an exception scenario for each use case.
   f. (5) Prepare a sequence diagram corresponding to each scenario in (d).

7.2   Consider a computer email system.
   a. (2) List three actors. Explain the relevance of each actor.
   b. (2) One use case is to get email. List four additional use cases at a comparable level of abstraction. Summarize the purpose of each use case with a sentence.
   c. (4) Prepare a use case diagram for a computer email system.
   d. (3) Prepare a normal scenario for each use case. Remember that a scenario is an example, and need not exercise all functionality of the use case.
   e. (3) Prepare an exception scenario for each use case.
   f. (5) Prepare a sequence diagram corresponding to each scenario in (d).

7.3   Consider an online airline reservation system. You may want to check airline Web sites to give you ideas.
   a. (2) List two actors. Explain the relevance of each actor.
   b. (2) One use case is to make a flight reservation. List four additional use cases at a comparable level of abstraction. Summarize the purpose of each use case with a sentence.
   c. (4) Prepare a use case diagram for an online airline reservation system.

7.4   Consider a software system for supporting checkout of materials at a public library.
   a. (2) List four actors. Explain the relevance of each actor.
   b. (2) One use case is to borrow a library item. List three additional use cases at a comparable level of abstraction. Summarize the purpose of each use case with a sentence.
   c. (4) Prepare a use case diagram for a library checkout system.

7.5   (3) Identify at least 10 use cases for the Windows Explorer. Just list them textually and summarize the purpose of each use case in one or two sentences.

7.6   (3) Write scenarios for the following situations:
   a. Moving a bag of corn, a goose, and a fox across a river in a boat. Only one thing may be carried in the boat at a time. If the goose is left alone with the corn, the corn will be eaten. If

the goose is left alone with the fox, the goose will be eaten. Prepare two scenarios, one in which something gets eaten and one in which everything is safely transported across the river.

b. Getting ready to take a trip in your car. Assume an automatic transmission. Don't forget your seat belt and emergency brake.

c. An elevator ride to the top floor.

d. Operation of a car cruise control. Include an encounter with slow-moving traffic that requires you to disengage and then resume control.

7.7　(4) Some combined bath–showers have two faucets and a lever for controlling the flow of the water. The lever controls whether the water flows from the shower head or directly into the tub. When the water is first turned on, it flows directly into the tub. When the lever is pulled, a valve closes and latches, diverting the flow of water to the shower head. To switch from shower to bath with the water running, one must push the lever. Shutting off the water releases the lever, so that the next time the water is turned on, it flows directly into the tub. Write a scenario for a shower that is interrupted by a telephone call.

7.8　(4) Prepare an activity diagram for computing a restaurant bill. There should be a charge for each delivered item. The total amount should be subject to tax and a service charge of 18% for groups of six of more. For smaller groups, there should be a blank entry for a gratuity according to the customer's discretion. Any coupons or gift certificates submitted by the customer should be subtracted.

7.9　(4) Prepare an activity diagram for awarding frequent flyer credits. In the past, TWA awarded a minimum of 750 miles for each flight. Gold and red card holders received a minimum of 1000 miles per flight. Gold card holders received a 25% bonus for any flight. Red card holders received a 50% bonus for any flight.

7.10　(5) Prepare an activity diagram that elaborates the details of logging into an email system. Note that entry of the user name and the password can occur in any order.

8

Advanced Interaction Modeling

The interaction model has several advanced features that can be helpful. You can skip this chapter on a first reading of the book.

8.1 Use Case Relationships

Independent use cases suffice for simple applications. However, it can be helpful to structure use cases for large applications. Complex use cases can be built from smaller pieces with the *include*, *extend,* and *generalization* relationships.

8.1.1 Include Relationship

The *include* relationship incorporates one use case within the behavior sequence of another use case. An included use case is like a subroutine—it represents behavior that would otherwise have to be described repeatedly. Often the fragment is a meaningful unit of behavior for the actors, although this is not required. The included use case may or may not be usable on its own.

The UML notation for an include relationship is a dashed arrow from the source (including) use case to the target (included) use case. The keyword *«include»* annotates the arrow. Figure 8.1 shows an example from an online stock brokerage system. Part of establishing a secure session is validating the user password. In addition, the stock brokerage system validates the password for each stock trade. Use cases *secure session* and *make trade* both include use case *validate password.*

A use case can also be inserted within a textual description with the notation *include use-case-name.* An included use case is inserted at a specific location within the behavior sequence of the larger use case, just as a subroutine is called from a specific location within another subroutine.

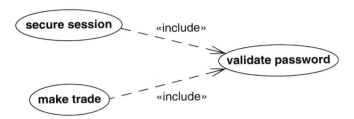

Figure 8.1 Use case inclusion. The *include* relationship lets a base use
case incorporate behavior from another use case.

You should not use include relationships to structure fine details of behavior. The purpose of use case modeling is to identify the functionality of the system and the general flow
of control among actors and the system. Factoring a use case into pieces is appropriate when
the pieces represent significant behavior units.

8.1.2 Extend Relationship

The *extend* relationship adds incremental behavior to a use case. It is like an include relationship looked at from the opposite direction, in which the extension adds itself to the base,
rather than the base explicitly incorporating the extension. It represents the frequent situation
in which some initial capability is defined, and later features are added modularly. The include and extend relationships both add behavior to a base use case.

For example, a stock brokerage system might have the base use case *trade stocks*, which
permits a customer to purchase stocks for cash on hand in the account. The extension use
case *margin trading* would add the ability to make a loan to purchase stocks when the account does not contain enough cash. It is still possible to buy stocks for cash, but if there is
insufficient cash, then the system offers to proceed with the transaction after verifying that
the customer is willing to make a margin purchase. The additional behavior is inserted at the
point where the purchase cost is checked against the account balance.

Figure 8.2 shows the base use case *trade stocks* for a stock brokerage system. The UML
notation for an extend relationship is a dashed arrow from the extension use case to the base
use case. The keyword *«extend»* annotates the arrow. The base use case permits simple purchases and sales of a stock at the market price. The brokerage system adds three capabilities:
buying a stock on margin, selling a stock short, and placing a limit on the transaction price.
The use case *trade options* also has an extension for placing a limit on the transaction price.

The extend relationship connects an extension use case to a base use case. The extension
use case often is a fragment—that is, it cannot appear alone as a behavior sequence. The base
use case, however, must be a valid use case in the absence of any extensions. The extend relationship can specify an insert location within the behavior sequence of the base use case;
the location can be a single step in the base sequence or a range of steps. The behavior sequence of the extension use case occurs at the given point in the sequence. In most cases, an
extend relationship has a condition attached. The extension behavior occurs only if the condition is true when control reaches the insert location.

Figure 8.2   Use case extension. The *extend* relationship is like an *include* relationship looked at from the opposite direction. The extension adds itself to the base.

8.1.3 Generalization

Generalization can show specific variations on a general use case, analogous to generalization among classes. A parent use case represents a general behavior sequence. Child use cases specialize the parent by inserting additional steps or by refining steps. The UML indicates generalization by an arrow with its tail on the child use case and a triangular arrowhead on the parent use case, the same notation that is used for classes.

For example, an online stock brokerage system (Figure 8.3) might specialize the general use case *make trade* into the child use cases *trade bonds, trade stocks,* and *trade options*. The parent use case contains steps that are performed for any kind of trade, such as entering the trading password. Each child use case contains the additional steps particular to a specific kind of trade, such as entering the expiration date of an option.

Figure 8.3   Use case generalization. A parent use case has common behavior and child use cases add variations, analogous to generalization among classes.

A parent use case may be abstract or concrete—an abstract use case cannot be used directly. As with the class model, we recommend that you consider only abstract parents and forego concrete ones. Then a model is more symmetric and a parent use case is not cluttered with the handling of special cases. Use cases also exhibit polymorphism—a child use case can freely substitute for a parent use case, for example, as an inclusion in another use case. In all these respects, generalization is the same for use cases and for classes.

In one respect, use case generalization is more complicated than class generalization. A subclass adds attributes to the parent class, but their order is unimportant. A child use case adds behavior steps, but they must appear in the proper locations within the behavior sequence of the parent. This is similar to overriding a method that is inherited by a subclass, in which new statements may be inserted at various locations in the parent's method. The simplest approach is to simply list the entire behavior sequence of the child use case, including the steps inherited from the parent. A more general approach is to assign symbolic locations within the parent's sequence and to indicate where additions and replacements go. In general, a child may revise behavior subsequences at several different points in the parent's sequence.

With classes there can be multiple inheritance, but we do not allow such complexity with use cases. In practice, the include and extend relationships obviate the need for multiple inheritance with use cases.

8.1.4 Combinations of Use Case Relationships

A single diagram may combine several kinds of use case relationships. Figure 8.4 shows a use case diagram from a stock brokerage system. The *secure session* use case includes the behavior of the *validate password*, *make trade*, and *manage account* use cases. *Make trade* is an abstract parent with the children—*trade bonds*, *trade stocks*, and *trade options*. Use case *make trade* also includes the behavior of *validate password*. The brokerage system validates the password once per session and additionally for every trade.

The use case *margin trading* extends both *trade bonds* and *trade stocks*—a customer may purchase stocks and bonds on margin, but not options. Use case *limit order* extends abstract use case *make trade*—limit orders apply to trading bonds, stocks, and options. We assume that a *short sale* is only permitted for stocks and not for bonds or options.

Note that the *Customer* actor connects only to the *secure session* use case. The brokerage system invokes all the other use cases indirectly by inclusion, specialization, or extension. The *Securities exchange* actor connects to the *make trade* use case. This actor does not initiate a use case but it is invoked during execution.

8.1.5 Guidelines for Use Case Relationships

Don't carry use case relationships to extremes and lapse into programming. Use cases are intended to clarify requirements. There can be many ways to implement requirements and you should not commit to an approach before you fully understand a problem. Here are some additional guidelines.

- **Use case generalization**. If a use case comes in several variations, model the common behavior with an abstract use case and then specialize each of the variations. Do not use generalization simply to share a behavior fragment; use the include relationship for that purpose.

- **Use case inclusion**. If a use case includes a well-defined behavior fragment that is likely to be useful in other situations, define a use case for the behavior fragment and include it in the original use case. In most cases, you should think of the included use case as a meaningful activity but not as an end in itself. For example, validating a password is meaningful to users but has a purpose only within a broader context.

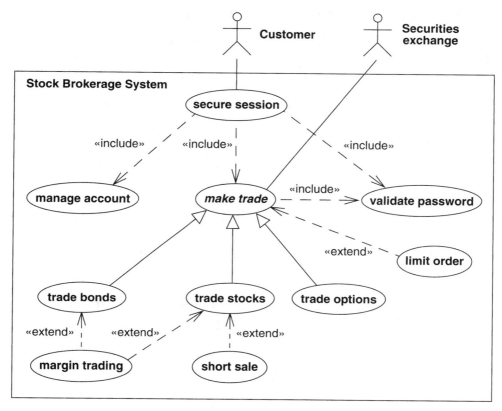

Figure 8.4 Use case relationships. A single use case diagram may combine
several kinds of relationships.

■ **Use case extension**. If you can define a meaningful use case with optional features, then
model the base behavior as a use case and add features with the extend relationship. This
permits the system to be tested and debugged without the extensions, which can be added later. Use the extend relationship when a system might be deployed in different configurations, some with the additional features and some without them.

■ **Include relationship vs. extend relationship**. The include relationship and the extend
relationship can both factor behavior into smaller pieces. The include relationship, however, implies that the included behavior is a necessary part of a configured system (even
if the behavior is not executed every time), whereas the extend relationship implies that
a system without the added behavior would be meaningful (even if there is no intention
to configure it that way).

8.2 Procedural Sequence Models

In Chapter 7, we saw sequence diagrams containing independent objects, all of which are active concurrently. An object remains active after sending a message and can respond to other messages without waiting for a response. This is appropriate for high-level models. However, most implementations are procedural and limit the number of objects that can execute at a time. The UML has elaborations for sequence diagrams to show procedure calls.

8.2.1 *Sequence Diagrams with Passive Objects*

With procedural code all objects are not constantly active. Most objects are passive and do not have their own threads of control. A passive object is not activated until it has been called. Once the execution of an operation completes and control returns to the caller, the passive object becomes inactive.

Figure 8.5 computes the commission for a stock brokerage transaction. The transaction object receives a request to compute its commission. It obtains the customer's service level from the customer table, then asks the rate table to compute the commission based on the service level, after which it returns the commission value to the caller.

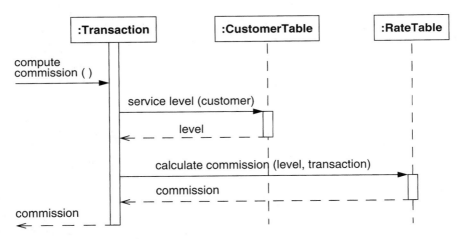

Figure 8.5   Sequence diagram with passive objects. Sequence diagrams can show the implementation of operations.

The UML shows the period of time for an object's execution as a thin rectangle. This is called the *activation* or *focus of control*. An activation shows the time period during which a call of a method is being processed, including the time when the called method has invoked another operation. The period of time when an object exists but is not active is shown as a dashed line. The entire period during which the object exists is called the *lifeline*, as it shows the lifetime of the object.

8.2.2 *Sequence Diagrams with Transient Objects*

Figure 8.6 shows further notation. *ObjectA* is an active object that initiates an operation. Because it is active, its activation rectangle spans the entire time shown in the diagram. *ObjectB* is a passive object that exists during the entire time shown in the diagram, but it is not active for the whole time. The UML shows its existence by the dashed line (the lifeline) that covers the entire time period. *ObjectB's* lifeline broadens into an activation rectangle when it is processing a call. During part of the time, it performs a recursive operation, as shown by the doubled activation rectangle between the call by *objectC* on *operationE* and the return of the result value. *ObjectC* is created and destroyed during the time shown on the diagram, so its lifeline does not span the whole diagram.

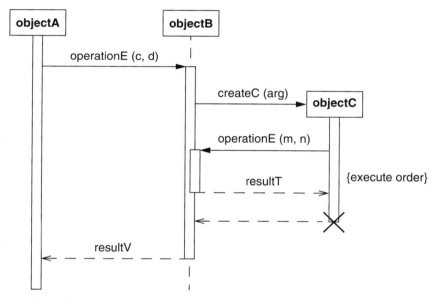

Figure 8.6   Sequence diagram with a transient object. Many applications have
a mix of active and passive objects. They create and destroy objects.

The notation for a call is an arrow from the calling activation to the activation created by the call. The tail of the arrow is somewhere along the rectangle of the calling activation. The arrowhead aligns with the top of the rectangle of the newly created activation, because the call creates the activation. The filled arrowhead indicates a call (as opposed to the stick arrowhead for an asynchronous signal in Chapter 7).

The UML shows a return by a dashed arrow from the bottom of the called activation to the calling activation. Not all return arrows have result values—for example, the return from *objectC* to *objectB*. An activation, therefore, has a call arrow coming into its top and a return arrow leaving its bottom. In between, it may have arrows to and from subordinate activations that it calls. You can suppress return arrows, because their location is implicit at the bottom of the activation, but for clarity it is better to show them.

If an object does not exist at the beginning of a sequence diagram, then it must be created during the sequence diagram. The UML shows creation by placing the object symbol at the head of the arrow for the call that creates the object. For example, the *createC* call creates *objectC*. The new object may or may not retain control after it is created. In the example, *objectC* does retain control, as shown by the activation rectangle that begins immediately below the object rectangle.

Similarly, a large 'X' marks the end of the life of an object that is destroyed during the sequence diagram. The 'X' is placed at the head of the call arrow that destroys the object. If the object destroys itself and returns control to another object, the 'X' is placed at the tail of the return arrow. In the example, *objectC* destroys itself and returns control to *objectB*. The lifeline of the object does not extend before its creation or after its destruction.

The UML shows a call to a second method on the same object (including a recursive call to the same method) with an arrow from the activation rectangle to the top of an additional rectangle superimposed on the first. For example, the second call to *operationE* on *objectB* is a recursive call nested within the first call to *operationE*. The second rectangle is shifted horizontally slightly so that both rectangles can be seen. The number of superimposed rectangles shows the number of activations of the same object.

You can also show conditionals on a sequence diagram, but this is more complex than we wish to include in this book. For further information, see [Rumbaugh-05].

8.2.3 Guidelines for Procedural Sequence Models

There are additional guidelines that apply to procedural sequence models beyond those mentioned in Chapter 7.

- **Active vs. passive objects**. Differentiate between active and passive objects. Most objects are passive and lack their own thread of control. By definition, active objects are always activated and have their own focus of control.

- **Advanced features**. Advanced features can show the implementation of sequence diagrams. Be selective in using these advanced features. Only show implementation details for difficult or especially important sequence diagrams.

8.3 Special Constructs for Activity Models

Activity diagrams have additional notation that is useful for large and complex applications.

8.3.1 Sending and Receiving Signals

Consider a workstation that is turned on. It goes through a boot sequence and then requests that the user log in. After entry of a name and password, the workstation queries the network to validate the user. Upon validation, the workstation then finishes its startup process. Figure 8.7 shows the corresponding activity diagram.

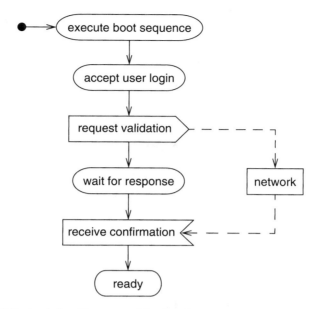

Figure 8.7 Activity diagram with signals. Activity diagrams can show
fine control via sending and receiving events.

The UML shows the sending of a signal as a convex pentagon. When the preceding activity completes, the signal is sent, then the next activity is started. The UML shows the receiving of a signal as a concave pentagon. When the preceding activity completes, the receipt construct waits until the signal is received, then the next activity starts.

8.3.2 Swimlanes

In a business model, it is often useful to know which human organization is responsible for an activity. Sales, finance, marketing, and purchasing are examples of organizations. When the design of the system is complete, the activity will be assigned to a person, but at a high level it is sufficient to partition the activities among organizations.

You can show such a partitioning with an activity diagram by dividing it into columns and lines. Each column is called a *swimlane* by analogy to a swimming pool. Placing an activity within a particular swimlane indicates that it is performed by a person or persons within the organization. Lines across swimlane boundaries indicate interactions among different organizations, which must usually be treated with more care than interactions within an organization. The horizontal arrangement of swimlanes has no inherent meaning, although there may be situations in which the order has meaning.

Figure 8.8 shows a simple example for servicing an airplane. The flight attendants must clean the trash, the ground crew must add fuel, and catering must load food and drink before a plane is serviced and ready for its next flight.

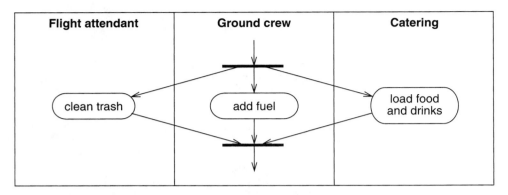

Figure 8.8 Activity diagram with swimlanes. Swimlanes can show organizational responsibility for activities.

8.3.3 Object Flows

Sometimes it is helpful to see the relationships between an operation and the objects that are its argument values or results. An activity diagram can show objects that are inputs to or outputs from the activities. An input or output arrow implies a control flow, therefore it is unnecessary to draw a control flow arrow where there is an object flow.

Frequently the same object goes through several states during the execution of an activity diagram. The same object may be an input to or an output from several activities, but on closer examination an activity usually produces or uses an object in a particular state. The UML shows an object value in a particular state by placing the state name in square brackets following the object name. If the objects have state names, the activity diagram shows both the flow of control and the progression of an object from state to state as activities act on it. In Figure 8.9 an airplane goes through several states as it leaves the gate, flies, and then lands again.

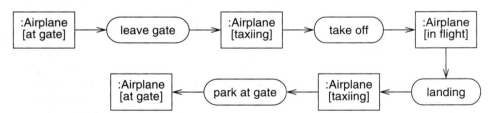

Figure 8.9 Activity diagram with object flows. An activity diagram can show the objects that are inputs or outputs of activities.

An activity diagram showing object flows among different object states has most of the advantages of a data flow diagram without most of their disadvantages. In particular, it unifies data flow and control flow, whereas data flow diagrams often separate them.

8.4 Chapter Summary

Independent use cases suffice for simple applications. However, it can be helpful to structure use cases for large applications using the include, extend, and generalization relationships. The include relationship incorporates one use case within the behavior sequence of another use case, like a subroutine call. The extend relationship adds incremental behavior to a base use case. Generalization can show specific variations on a general use case, analogous to generalization among classes. Don't use these relationships to excess. Remember that use cases are intended to be informal—use case relationships should only be used to structure major behavior units.

Sequence models are not only useful for fleshing out the interactions behind use cases, but they are also helpful for showing details of implementation. Not all objects in a sequence model need be active and exist for the entire computation. Some objects are passive and lack their own flow of control. Other objects are transient and may exist for only part of the duration of an operation.

Activity models also have additional notation that is helpful for large and complex applications. You can show fine controls via the sending and receiving of events that may interact with other objects that are not the focus of an activity diagram. You can augment activity diagrams with swimlanes to show the organizations that are responsible for different activities. And you can show the evolution of states of an object and how the states interleave with the flow of activities.

activation	passive object	use case extension
activity diagram	sequence diagram	use case generalization
focus of control	swimlane	use case inclusion
interaction model	transient object	
lifeline	use case	

Figure 8.10 Key concepts for Chapter 8

References

[Rumbaugh-05] James Rumbaugh, Ivar Jacobson, Grady Booch. *The Unified Modeling Language Reference Manual, Second Edition*. Boston: Addison-Wesley, 2005.

Exercises

8.1   Consider the purchase of gasoline from an electronic gasoline pump.
   a. (4) Prepare a use case diagram. Normally the customer pays cash for a gas purchase. Add
      extend relationships to handle the incremental behavior of paying by credit card outside or
      paying by credit card inside. Add an include relationship to represent the optional purchase
      of a car wash.
   b. (2) List and explain the relevance of each actor.
   c. (2) Summarize the purpose of each use case with a sentence.

8.2   (5) You are interacting with an online travel agent and encounter the following use cases. Pre-
       pare a use case diagram, using the generalization and include relationships.

   ■ **Purchase a flight**. Reserve a flight and provide payment and address information.

   ■ **Provide payment information**. Provide a credit card to pay for the incurred charges.

   ■ **Provide address**. Provide mailing and residence addresses.

   ■ **Purchase car rental**. Reserve a rental car and provide payment and address information.

   ■ **Purchase a hotel stay**. Reserve a hotel room and provide payment and address information.

   ■ **Make a purchase**. Make a travel purchase and provide payment and address information.

8.3   (7) Consider an online frequent flyer program. Some use cases are listed below. Prepare a use
       case diagram and include the appropriate relationships for the use cases. You can add an abstract
       parent for each use case generalization.

   ■ **View credits**. View the frequent flyer points currently available in the account.

   ■ **Submit missing credit**. Request credit for an activity that was not credited.

   ■ **Change address**. Submit a new mailing address.

   ■ **Change user name**. Change the user name for the account.

   ■ **Change password**. Change the password for the account.

   ■ **Book a free flight**. Use frequent flyer credits to obtain a free flight.

   ■ **Book a free hotel**. Use frequent flyer credits to obtain a free hotel.

   ■ **Book a free rental car**. Use frequent flyer credits to obtain a free rental car.

   ■ **Request a frequent flyer credit card**. Fill out an application for a credit card that gives fre-
     quent flyer points as a bonus for purchases.

   ■ **Check prices and routes**. Find possible routings and corresponding prices for a paid flight.

   ■ **Check availability for a free flight**. Check availability of free travel for a specified flight.

8.4   (8) Consider software that manages electronic music files. Some use cases are listed below. Pre-
       pare a use case diagram and include the appropriate relationships for the use cases. You can add
       an abstract parent for each use case generalization.

   ■ **Play a song**. Add the song to the end of the play queue.

   ■ **Play a library**. Add the songs in the library to the play queue.

   ■ **Randomize order**. Randomly reorder the songs in the play queue.

   ■ **Delete a song**. Delete a song from a music library.

   ■ **Destroy a song**. Delete a song from all music libraries and delete the underlying file.

   ■ **Add a song**. Add a music file to a music library.

- **Create a music library**. Create a new music library that contains no songs.
- **Delete a music library**. Delete the music library.
- **Destroy a music library**. Destroy all songs in the music library and then delete the music library.
- **Rip a CD**. Digitize the music on an analog CD.
- **Create a CD**. Burn an analog CD from a list of digital songs.
- **View songs by title**. Display the songs in a music library sorted by title.
- **View songs by artist**. Display the songs in a music library sorted by artist.
- **View songs by album**. Display the songs in a music library sorted by album.
- **View songs by genre**. Display the songs in a music library sorted by genre.
- **Start play**. Start playing songs from the queue. If previously stopped, resume playing from the last position, otherwise start playing at the start of the queue.
- **Stop play**. Suspend playing of music.

8.5 (8) Consider a simple payroll system. Prepare a use case diagram and include the appropriate relationships for the following use cases. You can add an abstract parent for each use case generalization.

- **Add deduction**. Add another deduction type for the employee and incorporate the deduction in subsequent paychecks.
- **Drop deduction**. Remove the deduction type for the employee.
- **Sum income**. Total all income for a paycheck.
- **Sum deductions**. Total all deductions for a paycheck.
- **Compute net take-home pay**. Compute the total income less the total deductions for a paycheck.
- **Compute charitable contributions**. Total all contributions to charity for a paycheck.
- **Compute taxes**. Compute all taxes paid for a paycheck.
- **Compute retirement savings**. Compute all contributions to retirement funds for a paycheck.
- **Compute other deductions**. Compute the total of all deductions, other than charity, taxes, and retirement for a paycheck.
- **Change employee name**. Change the name of the employee that is on record.
- **Change employee address**. Change the mailing address of the employee that is on record.
- **Compute base pay**. Compute the base pay of the employee for the paycheck.
- **Compute overtime pay**. Compute the overtime pay of the employee for the paycheck.
- **Compute other pay**. Compute all other income (other than base pay and overtime) of the employee for the paycheck.
- **Change method of payment**. Change the method of disbursing the paycheck, such as cash, direct deposit, and check.

8.6 (4) Consider stock management software that records all transactions that occur for a portfolio. For example, stocks may be purchased and sold. Dividend payments may be received. Complex situations can occur, such as stock splits.

The current contents of a portfolio can be determined by replaying the transaction log. The portfolio has some initial contents, and all subsequent changes are captured via the transaction log. The changes in the transaction log are then applied through the target date to determine the current contents.

Construct a procedural sequence diagram to show the calculation of the contents of a portfolio as of some date. Limit the detail in your diagram to four message flows.

8.7   (5) Compute the value of a stock portfolio as of a specified date. First compute the contents of the portfolio (the previous exercise) and then multiply the quantity of each stock by its value on the specified date to determine the overall value of the portfolio.

8.8   (7) Once again compute the value of a stock portfolio as of a specified date. However, for this exercise a portfolio may contain stock and lesser portfolios. For simplicity, assume that a portfolio is at most three levels deep.

For example, portfolio *net worth* may contain portfolios *retirement funds* and *taxable account*. Portfolios *retirement funds* and *taxable account* contain only stocks.

8.9   (6) A customer decides to upgrade her PC and purchase a DVD player. She begins by calling the sales department of the PC vendor and they tell her to talk to customer support. She then calls customer support and they put her on hold while talking to engineering. Finally, customer support tells the customer about several supported DVD options. The customer chooses a DVD and it is shipped by the mail department. The customer receives the DVD, installs it satisfactorily, and then mails her payment to accounting.

Construct an activity diagram for this process. Use swimlanes to show the various interactions.

8.10   (6) A company is manufacturing a new product and must coordinate several departments. The product starts out as a raw marketing idea that goes to engineering. Engineering simulates the function of the product and prepares a design. Manufacturing reviews the design and adjusts it to conform to existing machinery. Engineering approves the revisions and customer service then looks at the design—a good design must enable ready repair. Engineering approves the customer service proposals and ensures that the resulting design still meets the target functionality.

Construct an activity diagram for this process. Use swimlanes to show the various interactions. Show the changes in the state of the design as the activity diagram proceeds.

9

Concepts Summary

We find it useful to model a system from three related but different viewpoints: the *class model*, describing the objects in the system and their relationships; the *state model*, describing the life history of objects; and the *interaction model*, describing the interactions among objects. A complete description requires all three models, but different problems place different emphasis. Each model applies during all stages of development and acquires detail as development progresses.

9.1 Class Model

The *class model* describes the static structure of objects in a system—their identity, their relationships to other objects, their attributes, and their operations. The class model provides the essential framework into which the state and interaction models can be placed. Changes and interactions are meaningless unless there is something to be changed or with which to interact. Objects are the units into which we divide the world, the molecules of our models.

The most important concepts in class models are classes, associations, and generalizations. A class describes a group of similar objects. An association describes a group of similar connections between objects. Generalization structures the description of objects by organizing classes by their similarities and differences. Attributes and operations are secondary and serve to elaborate the fundamental structure provided by classes, associations, and generalizations.

9.2 State Model

The *state model* describes those aspects of an object concerned with time—events that mark changes and states that define the context for events. Events represent external stimuli and states represent values of objects. Over time, the objects stimulate each other, resulting in a series of changes to their states. The state model consists of multiple state diagrams, one state diagram for each class with important temporal behavior. The state diagrams must match on their interfaces—events and guard conditions. Each state diagram shows the state and event sequences permitted for one class of objects.

A state diagram specifies the possible states, which transitions are allowed between states, what stimuli cause the transitions to occur, and what operations are executed in response to stimuli. A state diagram describes the collective behavior for the objects in a class. As each object has its own values and links, so too each object has its own state or position in the state diagram.

9.3 Interaction Model

The *interaction model* describes how objects collaborate to achieve results. It is a holistic view of behavior across many objects, whereas the state model is a reductionist view of behavior that examines each object individually. Both the state model and the interaction model are needed to describe behavior fully. They complement each other by viewing behavior from two different perspectives.

Interactions can be modeled at different levels of abstraction. At a high level, use cases describe how a system interacts with outside actors. Use cases represent pieces of functionality and are helpful for capturing informal requirements. Sequence diagrams provide more detail and show the objects that interact and the time sequence of their interactions. Activity diagrams provide the finest detail and show the flow of control among the processing steps of a computation.

9.4 Relationship Among the Models

The class, state, and interaction models all involve the same concepts—data, sequencing, and operations—but each model focuses on a particular aspect and leaves the other aspects uninterpreted. All three models are necessary for a full understanding of a problem, although the balance of importance among the models varies according to the kind of application. The three models come together in the implementation of methods, which involve data (target object, arguments, and variables), control (sequencing constructs), and interactions (messages and calls).

Each model describes one aspect of the system but contains references to the other models. The class model describes data structure on which the state and interaction models operate. The operations in the class model correspond to events, conditions, and activities. The state model describes the control structure of objects. It shows decisions that depend on object values; the decisions cause changes in object values and subsequent states. The interaction model focuses on the exchanges between objects and provides a holistic overview of the operation of a system.

Generalization and aggregation are relationships that cut across the models, and we will now examine their usage.

9.4.1 *Generalization*

Generalization appears in all three models. Generalization is the "or-relationship" and can show specific variations on a general situation. In UML 2.0, inheritance applies to classifiers, and classes, signals, and use cases are all classifiers.

- **Class generalization**. Generalization organizes classes by their similarities and differences. A subclass inherits the attributes, operations, associations, and state diagrams of its superclasses. Subclasses can reuse inherited properties from a superclass or override them; subclasses can add new properties.

  A subclass inherits the state diagrams of its ancestors, to be concurrent with any state diagram that it defines. A subclass inherits both the states of its ancestors and the transitions. To avoid confusion, subclass state diagrams should normally be an orthogonal addition to the state diagram from the superclass.

  The class model supports multiple inheritance—a class may inherit from more than one superclass. For simplicity, we normally disallow multiple inheritance for signals and use cases.

- **Signal generalization**. A generalization hierarchy can also organize signals with inheritance of signal attributes. Ultimately you can regard every actual signal as a leaf on a generalization tree of signals. An input signal triggers transitions on any ancestor signal type.

- **Use case generalization**. Generalization also applies to use cases. A parent use case represents a general behavior sequence. Child use cases specialize the parent by inserting additional steps or by refining steps. In one respect, use case generalization is more complicated than class generalization. A subclass adds attributes to the parent class, but their order is unimportant. A child use case adds behavior steps, but they must appear in the proper locations within the behavior sequence of the parent.

With inheritance a parent classifier may be abstract or concrete. However, we recommend that you consider only abstract parents and forego concrete ones. Then abstract and concrete classifiers are readily apparent at a glance; all superclassifiers are abstract and all leaf subclassifiers are concrete. Classifiers also exhibit polymorphism—a child classifier can freely substitute for a parent classifier.

The first edition of this book also supported inheritance of states, but this has been disallowed in UML2 because a state is not a classifier. There are similarities between generalization of classifiers and nesting of states, but strictly speaking, in UML2 there is no state generalization.

9.4.24 *Aggregation*

Aggregation is the "and-relationship" and breaks an assembly into orthogonal parts that have limited interaction.

- **Object aggregation**. Aggregation is a special form of association with additional properties, most notably transitivity and antisymmetry. The UML has two forms of object aggregation: a general form called aggregation (a constituent part is reusable and may exist apart from an assembly) and a more restrictive form called composition (the constituent part can belong to at most one assembly and has a coincident lifetime).

A state diagram for an assembly is a collection of state diagrams, one for each part. The aggregate state corresponds to the combined states of all the parts. The aggregate state is one state from the first diagram, *and* a state from the second diagram, *and* a state from each other diagram. In the more interesting cases, the part states interact.

■ **State aggregation**. Some states can be partitioned into lesser states, each operating independently and each having its own subdiagram. The state of the object comprises one state from each subdiagram.

This completes our treatment of concepts and notation for object-oriented modeling.

Part 2

Analysis and Design

Part 1 covers *concepts*, specifically the concepts and notation for the class, state, and interaction models. We now shift our focus in Parts 2 and 3 and present a *process* for devising the models. Part 1 discusses *what* constitutes a model; Parts 2 and 3 explain *how to* formulate a model. Our treatment of process is language independent and applies equally well to OO languages, non-OO languages, and databases.

Chapter 10 provides an overview of the process for building models and emphasizes that development is normally iterative and seldom a rigid sequence of steps.

Chapter 11 presents the first stage of development—system conception—during which a visionary conceives an application and sells the idea to an organization.

Once you have a concept for an application, you elaborate and refine the concept by building models as Chapters 12 and 13 explain. First build a domain model that focuses on the real-world things that carry the semantics of the application. Then build an application model that addresses the computer aspects of the application that are visible to users.

The analysis models give you a thorough understanding of an application. The next stage is to address the practicalities of realizing the models. Chapter 14 covers system design, in which you devise a high-level strategy for building a solution. Chapter 15 covers class design, in which you flesh out the details for classes, associations, and operations.

Chapter 16 concludes Part 2 by summarizing the analysis and design portion of the development process.

After reading Part 2, you will understand the basics of how to prepare OO models. You will not be an expert, but you will have a good start on learning a valuable software development skill. You will be ready to study implementation and software engineering in the final two parts.

10

Process Overview

A *software development process* provides a basis for the organized production of software, using a collection of predefined techniques and notations. The process in this book starts with formulation of the problem, then continues through analysis, design, and implementation. The presentation of the stages is linear, but the actual process is seldom linear.

10.1 Development Stages

Software development has a sequence of well-defined stages, each with a distinct purpose, input, and output.

- **System conception**. Conceive an application and formulate tentative requirements.
- **Analysis**. Deeply understand the requirements by constructing models. The goal of analysis is to specify *what* needs to be done, not *how* it is done. You must understand a problem before attempting a solution.
- **System design**. Devise a high-level strategy—the architecture—for solving the application problem. Establish policies to guide the subsequent class design.
- **Class design**. Augment and adjust the real-world models from analysis so that they are amenable to computer implementation. Determine algorithms for realizing the operations.
- **Implementation**. Translate the design into programming code and database structures.
- **Testing**. Ensure that the application is suitable for actual use and that it truly satisfies the requirements.
- **Training**. Help users master the new application.
- **Deployment**. Place the application in the field and gracefully cut over from legacy applications.
- **Maintenance**. Preserve the long-term viability of the application.

The entire process is seamless. You continually elaborate and optimize models as your focus shifts from analysis to design to implementation. Throughout development the same concepts and notation apply; the only difference is the shift in perspective from the initial emphasis on business needs to the later emphasis on computer resources.

An OO approach moves much of the software development effort up to analysis and design. It is sometimes disconcerting to spend more time during analysis and design, but this extra effort is more than compensated by faster and simpler implementation. Because the resulting design is cleaner and more adaptable, future changes are much easier.

Part 2 covers the first four topics and Part 3 covers implementation. In this book we emphasize development and only briefly consider testing, training, deployment, and maintenance. These last four topics are important, but are not the focus of this book.

10.1.1 System Conception

System conception deals with the genesis of an application. Initially somebody thinks of an idea for an application, prepares a business case, and sells the idea to the organization. The innovator must understand both business needs and technological capabilities.

10.1.2 Analysis

Analysis focuses on creation of models. Analysts capture and scrutinize requirements by constructing models. They specify *what* must be done, not *how* it should be done. Analysis is a difficult task in its own right, and developers must fully understand the problem before addressing the additional complexities of design. Sound models are a prerequisite for an extensible, efficient, reliable, and correct application. No amount of implementation patches can repair an incoherent application and compensate for a lack of forethought.

During analysis, developers consider the available sources of information (documents, business interviews, related applications) and resolve ambiguities. Often business experts are not sure of the precise requirements and must refine them in tandem with software development. Modeling quickens the convergence between developers and business experts, because it is much faster to work with multiple iterations of models than with multiple implementations of code. Models highlight omissions and inconsistencies so that they can be resolved. As developers elaborate and refine a model, it gradually becomes coherent.

There are two substages of analysis: domain analysis and application analysis. ***Domain analysis*** focuses on real-world things whose semantics the application captures. For example, an airplane flight is a real-world object that a flight reservation system must represent. Domain objects exist independently of any application and are meaningful to business experts. You find them during domain analysis or by prior knowledge. Domain objects carry information about real-world objects and are generally passive—domain analysis emphasizes concepts and relationships, with much of the functionality being implicit in the class model. The job of constructing a domain model is mainly to decide which information to capture and how to represent it.

Domain analysis is then followed by ***application analysis*** that addresses the computer aspects of the application that are visible to users. For example, a flight reservation screen is part of a flight reservation system. Application objects do not exist in the problem domain and are meaningful only in the context of an application. Application objects, however, are not merely internal design decisions, because the users see them and must agree with them. The application model does not prescribe the implementation of the application. It describes how the application appears from the outside—the black-box view of it. You cannot find application classes with domain analysis, but you can often reuse them from previous applications. Otherwise, you must devise application objects during analysis as you think about interfaces with other systems and how your application interacts with users.

10.1.3 System Design

During *system design*, the developer makes strategic decisions with broad consequences. You must formulate an architecture and choose global strategies and policies to guide the subsequent, more detailed portion of design. The ***architecture*** is the high-level plan or strategy for solving the application problem. The choice of architecture is based on the requirements as well as past experience. If possible, the architecture should include an executable skeleton that can be tested. The system designer must understand how a new system interacts with other systems. The architecture must also support future modification of the application.

For straightforward problems, preparation of the architecture follows analysis. However, for large and complex problems their preparation must be interleaved. The architecture helps to establish a model's scope. In turn, modeling reveals important issues of strategy to resolve. For large and complex problems, there is much interplay between the construction of a model and the model's architecture, and they must be built together.

10.1.4 Class Design

During ***class design***, the developer expands and optimizes analysis models; there is a shift in emphasis from application concepts toward computer concepts. Developers choose algorithms to implement major system functions, but they should continue to defer the idiosyncrasies of particular programming languages.

10.1.5 Implementation

Implementation is the stage for writing the actual code. Developers map design elements to programming language and database code. Often, tools can generate some of the code from the design model.

10.1.6 Testing

After implementation, the system is complete, but it must be carefully tested before being commissioned for actual use. The ideas that inspired the original project should have been nurtured through the previous stages by the use of models. Testers once again revisit the original business requirements and verify that the system delivers the proper functionality. Testing can also uncover accidental errors (bugs) that have been introduced. If an application runs on multiple hardware and operating system platforms, it should be tested on all of them.

Developers should check a program at several levels. Unit tests exercise small portions of code, such as methods or possibly entire classes. Unit tests discover local problems and often require that extra instrumentation be built into the code. System tests exercise a major subsystem or the entire application. In contrast to unit tests, system tests can discover broad failures to meet specifications. Both unit and system tests are necessary. Testing should not wait until the entire application is coded. It must be planned from the beginning, and many tests can be performed during implementation.

10.1.7 Training

An organization must train users so that they can fully benefit from an application. Training accelerates users on the software learning curve. A separate team should prepare user documentation in parallel to the development effort. Quality control can then check the software against the user documentation to ensure that the software meets its original goals.

10.1.8 Deployment

The eventual system must work in the field, on various platforms and in various configurations. Unexpected interactions can occur when a system is deployed in a customer environment. Developers must tune the system under various loads and write scripts and install procedures. Some customers will require software customizations. Staff must also localize the product to different spoken languages and locales. The result is a usable product release.

10.1.9 Maintenance

Once development is complete and a system has been deployed, it must be maintained for continued success. There are several kinds of maintenance. Bugs that remain in the original system will gradually appear during use and must be fixed. A successful application will also lead to enhancement requests and a long-lived application will occasionally have to be restructured.

Models ease maintenance and transitions across staff changes. A model expresses the business intent for an application that has been driven into the programming code, user interface, and database structure.

10.2 Development Life Cycle

An OO approach to software development supports multiple life-cycle styles. You can use a waterfall approach performing the phases of analysis, design, and implementation in strict sequence for the entire system. However, we typically recommend an iterative development strategy. We summarize the distinction here and elaborate in Chapter 21.

10.2.1 Waterfall Development

The waterfall approach dictates that developers perform the software development stages in a rigid linear sequence with no backtracking. Developers first capture requirements, then construct an analysis model, then perform a system design, then prepare a class design, followed by implementation, testing, and deployment. Each stage is completed in its entirety before the next stage is begun.

The waterfall approach is suitable for well-understood applications with predictable outputs from analysis and design, but such applications seldom occur. Too many organizations attempt to follow a waterfall when requirements are fluid. This leads to the familiar situation where developers complain about changing requirements, and the business complains about inflexible software development. A waterfall approach also does not deliver a useful system until completion. This makes it difficult to assess progress and correct a project that has gone awry.

10.2.2 Iterative Development

Iterative development is more flexible. First you develop the nucleus of a system—analyzing, designing, implementing, and delivering working code. Then you grow the scope of the system, adding properties and behavior to existing objects, as well as adding new kinds of objects. There are multiple iterations as the system evolves to the final deliverable.

Each iteration includes a full complement of stages: analysis, design, implementation, and testing. Unlike the strict sequence of the waterfall method, iterative development can interleave the different stages and need not construct the entire system in lock step. Some parts may be completed early, while other, less crucial parts are completed later. Each iteration ultimately yields an executable system that can be integrated and tested. You can accurately gauge progress and make adjustments to your plans based on feedback from the early iterations. If there is a problem, you can move backward to an earlier stage for rework.

Iterative development is the best choice for most applications because it gracefully responds to change and minimizes risk of failure. Management and business users get early feedback about progress.

10.3 Chapter Summary

A software engineering process provides a basis for the organized production of software. There is a sequence of well-defined stages that you can apply to each of the pieces of a system. For example, parallel development teams might develop a database design, key algorithms, and a user interface. An iterative development of software is flexible and responsive to evolving requirements. First you prepare a nucleus of a system, and then you successively grow its scope until you realize the final desired software.

analysis	domain analysis	system conception
application analysis	implementation	system design
architecture	iterative development	testing
class design	life cycle	training
deployment	maintenance	waterfall development

Figure 10.1 Key concepts for Chapter 10

Bibliographic Notes

The *class design* stage is renamed from *object design* in the first edition of this book.

Exercises

10.1 (2) It seems there is never enough time to do a job right the first time, but there is always time to do it over. Discuss how the approach presented in this chapter overcomes this tendency of human behavior. What kinds of errors do you make if you rush into the implementation phase of a software project? Compare the effort required to prevent errors with that needed to detect and correct them.

10.2 (4) This book explains how to use OO techniques to implement programs and databases. Discuss how OO techniques could be applied in other areas, such as language design, knowledge representation, and hardware design.

11

System Conception

System conception deals with the genesis of an application. Initially some person, who understands both business needs and technology, thinks of an idea for an application. Developers must then explore the idea to understand the needs and devise possible solutions. The purpose of system conception is to defer details and understand the big picture—what need does the proposed system meet, can it be developed at a reasonable cost, and will the demand for the result justify the cost of building it?

This chapter introduces the automated teller machine (ATM) case study that threads throughout the remainder of the book.

11.1 Devising a System Concept

Most ideas for new systems are extensions of existing ideas. For example, a human relations department may have a database of employee benefit choices and require that a clerk enter changes. An obvious extension is to allow employees to view and enter their own changes. There are many issues to resolve (security, reliability, privacy, and so on), but the new idea is a straightforward extension of an existing concept.

Occasionally a new system is a radical departure from the past. For example, an online auction automates the ancient idea of buyers bidding against each other for products, but the first online auction systems were brand new software. The concept became feasible when several enabling technologies came into place: the Internet, widespread personal computer access, and reliable servers. The large customer base and low unit cost due to automation changed the nature of auctions—an online auction can sell inexpensive items and still make a profit. In addition, online systems have made the auction process concurrent and distributed.

Here are some ways to find new system concepts.

■ **New functionality**. Add functionality to an existing system.

- **Streamlining**. Remove restrictions or generalize the way a system works.

- **Simplification**. Let ordinary persons perform tasks previously assigned to specialists.

- **Automation**. Automate manual processes.

- **Integration**. Combine functionality from different systems.

- **Analogies**. Look for analogies in other problem domains and see if they have useful ideas.

- **Globalization**. Travel to other countries and observe their cultural and business practices.

11.2 Elaborating a Concept

Most systems start as vague ideas that need more substance. A good system concept must answer the following questions.

- **Who is the application for?** You should clearly understand which persons and organizations are stakeholders of the new system. Two of the most important kinds of stakeholders are the financial sponsors and the end users.

  The financial sponsor are important because they are paying for the new system. They expect the project to be on schedule and within budget. You should get the financial sponsors to agree to some measure of success. You need to know when the system is complete and meets their expectations.

  The users are also stakeholders, but in another sense. The users will ultimately determine the success of the new system by an increase (or decrease) in their productivity or effectiveness. Users can help you if they are receptive and provide critical comments. They can improve your system by telling you what is missing and what could be improved. In general, users will not consider new software unless they have a compelling interest—either personal or business. You should try to help them find a vested interest in your project so that you can obtain their buy-in. If you cannot get their buy-in, you should question the need for the project and reconsider doing it.

- **What problems will it solve?** You must clearly bound the size of the effort and establish its scope. You should determine which features will be in the new system and which will not. You must reach various kinds of users in different organizations with their own viewpoints and political motivations. You must not only decide which features are appropriate, but you must also obtain the agreement of influential persons.

- **Where will it be used?** At this early stage, it is helpful to get a general idea of where the new system might be used. You should determine if the new system is mission-critical software for the organization, experimental software, or a new capability that you can deploy without disrupting the workflow. You should have a rough idea about how the new system will complement the existing systems. It is important to know if the software will be used locally or will be distributed via a network. For a commercial product, you should characterize the customer base.

■ **When is it needed?** Two aspects of time are important. The first is the *feasible* time, the time in which the system can be developed within the constraints of cost and available resources. The other is the *required* time, when the system is needed to meet business goals. You must make sure that the timing expectations driven by technical feasibility are consistent with the timing the business requires. If there is a disconnect, you must initiate a dialogue between technologists and business experts to reach a solution.

■ **Why is it needed?** You may need to prepare a business case for the new system if someone has not already done so. The business case contains the financial justification for the new system, including the cost, tangible benefits, intangible benefits, risk, and alternatives. You must be sure that you clearly understand the motivation for the new system. The business case will give you insight into what stakeholders expect, roughly indicate the scope, and may even provide information for seeding your models. For a commercial product, you should estimate the number of units that can be sold and determine a reasonable selling price; the revenue must cover costs and a profit.

■ **How will it work?** You should brainstorm about the feasibility of the problem. For large systems you should consider the merits of different architectures. The purpose of this speculation is not to choose a solution, but to increase confidence that the problem can be solved reasonably. You might need some prototyping and experimentation.

11.2.1 The ATM Case Study

Figure 11.1 lists our original system concept for an Automated Teller Machine (ATM). We ask high-level questions to elaborate the initial concept.

Develop software so that customers can access a bank's computers and carry out their own financial transactions without the mediation of a bank employee.

Figure 11.1 System concept for an automated teller machine

■ **Who is the application for?** A number of companies provide ATM products. Consequently, only a vendor or a large financial company could possibly justify the cost and effort of building ATM software.

A vendor would be competing for customers in an established market. A large vendor could certainly enter such a market, but might find it advantageous to partner with or acquire an existing supplier. A small vendor would need some special feature to differentiate itself from the crowd and attract attention.

It is unlikely that a financial company could justify developing ATM software just for its own use, because it would probably be more expensive than purchasing a product. If a financial company wanted special features, it could partner with a vendor. Or it might decide to create a separate organization that would build the software, sell it to the sponsoring company, and then market it to others.

For the ATM case study, we will assume that we are a vendor building the software. We will assume that we are developing an ordinary product, since deep complexities of the ATM problem domain are beyond the scope of this book.

■ **What problems will it solve?** The ATM software is intended to serve both the bank and the customer. For the bank, ATM software increases automation and reduces manual handling of routine paperwork. For the customer, the ATM is ubiquitous and always available, handling routine transactions whenever and wherever the customer desires. ATM software must be easy to use and convenient so that customers will use it in preference to bank tellers. It must be reliable and secure since it will be handling money.

■ **Where will it be used?** ATM software has become essential to financial institutions. Customers take it for granted that a bank will have an ATM machine. ATM machines are available at many stores, sporting events, and other locations throughout the world.

■ **When is it needed?** Any software development effort is a financial proposition. The investment in development ultimately leads to a revenue stream. From an economic perspective, it is desirable to minimize the investment, maximize the revenue, and realize revenue as soon as possible. Thoughtful modeling and OO techniques are conducive to this goal.

■ **Why is it needed?** There are many reasons why a vendor might decide to build a software product. If other companies are making money with similar products, there is an economic incentive to participate. A novel product could outflank competitors and lead to premium pricing. Businesses commission internal efforts for technology that is difficult to buy and critical to them. We have no real motivation to develop ATM software, other than to demonstrate the techniques in this book.

■ **How will it work?** We will adopt a three-tier architecture to separate the user interface from programming logic, and programming logic from the database. In reality, the architecture is *n*-tier, because there can be any number of intermediate programming levels communicating with each other. We will discuss architecture further in the *System Design* chapter.

11.3 Preparing a Problem Statement

Once you have fleshed out the raw idea by answering the high-level questions, you are ready to write a requirements statement that outlines the goals and general approach of the desired system.

Throughout development, you should distinguish among requirements, design, and implementation. Requirements describe how a system behaves from the user's point of view. The system is considered as a black box—all we care about is its external behavior. For example, some requirements for a car are that when you press on the accelerator pedal, the car goes faster, and when you step on the brake, the car slows down. Design decisions are engineering choices that provide the behavior specified by the requirements. For example, some design decisions are how the internal linkages are routed, how the engine is controlled, and what kinds of brake pads are on the wheels. Implementation deals with the ultimate realization in programming code.

Frequently customers mix true requirements with design decisions. Usually this is a bad idea. If you separate requirements from design decisions, you preserve the freedom to change a design. Typically there are many possible ways to design a system, and you should defer a solution until you fully understand a problem.

A system concept document may include an example implementation. The purpose of the example is to show how the system could be implemented using current technology at a reasonable cost. It is a "proof of existence" statement. However, make it clear that the sample implementation could be done differently in the final system. The sample implementation is merely proposed as a possibility.

For example, when the Apollo program to put a man on the moon in the 1960s was first proposed, the plan was to place a rocket in earth orbit, then launch a landing vehicle directly to the moon's surface. In the final successful program, the rocket was launched directly into a lunar orbit, from which the lander was launched to the moon's surface. It was not a bad thing to make the first proposal, however, as this gave confidence that there was a feasible approach.

As Figure 11.2 shows, the problem statement should state what is to be done and not how it is to be implemented. It should be a statement of needs, not a proposal for a system architecture. The requestor should avoid describing system internals, as this restricts development flexibility. Performance specifications and protocols for interaction with external systems are legitimate requirements. Software engineering standards, such as modular construction, design for testability, and provision for future extensions, are also proper.

Requirements Statement	Design	Implementation
■ Problem scope	■ General approach	■ Platforms
■ What is needed	■ Algorithms	■ Hardware specs
■ Application context	■ Data structures	■ Software libraries
■ Assumptions	■ Architecture	■ Interface standards
■ Performance needs	■ Optimizations	
	■ Capacity planning	

Figure 11.2   Kinds of requirements. Do not make early design and implementation decisions or you will compromise development.

A problem statement may have more or less detail. A requirement for a conventional product, such as a payroll program or a billing system, may have considerable detail. A requirement for a research effort in a new area may lack details, but presumably the research has some objective that should be clearly stated.

Most problem statements are ambiguous, incomplete, or even inconsistent. Some requirements are just plain wrong. Some requirements, although precisely stated, have unpleasant consequences on the system behavior or impose unreasonable implementation costs. Some requirements do not work out as well as the requestor thought. The problem statement is just a starting point for understanding the problem, not an immutable document. The purpose of the subsequent analysis (next chapter) is to fully understand the problem and its implications. There is no reason to expect that a problem statement prepared without a full analysis will be correct.

11.3.1 The ATM Case Study

Figure 11.3 shows a problem statement for an automated teller machine (ATM) network.

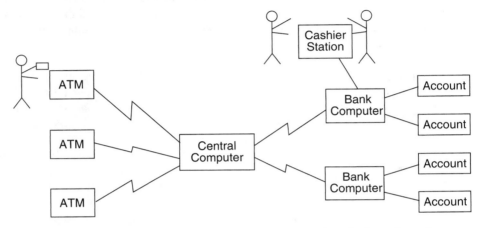

Figure 11.3 ATM network. The ATM case study threads throughout the remainder of this book.

Design the software to support a computerized banking network including both human cashiers and automatic teller machines (ATMs) to be shared by a consortium of banks. Each bank provides its own computer to maintain its own accounts and process transactions against them. Cashier stations are owned by individual banks and communicate directly with their own bank's computers. Human cashiers enter account and transaction data.

Automatic teller machines communicate with a central computer that clears transactions with the appropriate banks. An automatic teller machine accepts a cash card, interacts with the user, communicates with the central system to carry out the transaction, dispenses cash, and prints receipts. The system requires appropriate recordkeeping and security provisions. The system must handle concurrent accesses to the same account correctly.

The banks will provide their own software for their own computers; you are to design the software for the ATMs and the network. The cost of the shared system will be apportioned to the banks according to the number of customers with cash cards.

11.4 Chapter Summary

The first stage of a project is to devise a new idea. The idea can involve a new system or an improvement to an existing system. Before investing time and money into development, it is necessary to evaluate the feasibility of the system, the difficulty and risk of developing it, the demand for the system, and the cost-benefit ratio. This process should consider the viewpoints of all the stakeholders of the system and should make the trade-offs necessary to provide a good chance of success, not just technical success, but also business success. This process usually results in some adjustments to the original idea. When the system conception stage is complete, write a problem statement that serves as the starting point for analysis. The problem statement need not be complete, and it will change during development, but the writing of the statement helps to focus the attention of the project.

business case	problem statement
cost-benefit trade-off	requirement
design decision	stakeholder
implementation constraint	system conception

Figure 11.4 Key concepts for Chapter 11

Exercises

11.1   (3) Consider a new antilock braking system for crash avoidance in an automobile. Elaborate the following high-level questions and explain your answers.
   a. Who is the application for? Who are the stakeholders? Estimate how many persons in your country are potential customers.
   b. Identify three features that should be included and three features that should be omitted.
   c. Identify three systems with which it must work.
   d. What are two of the largest risks?

11.2   (3) Repeat Exercise 11.1 for software that supports Internet selling of books.

11.3   (3) Repeat Exercise 11.1 for software that supports the remodeling of kitchens.

11.4   (3) Repeat Exercise 11.1 for an online auction system.

11.5   (4) Prepare a problem statement, similar to that for the ATM system, for each of the following systems. You may limit the scope of the system, but be precise and avoid making implementation decisions. Use 75–150 words per specification.
   a. bridge player
   b. change-making machine
   c. car cruise control
   d. electronic typewriter
   e. spelling checker
   f. telephone answering machine

11.6   (3) Rephrase the following requirements to make them more precise. Remove any design decisions posing as requirements:
   a. A system to transfer data from one computer to another over a telecommunication line. The system should transmit data reliably over noisy channels. Data must not be lost if the receiv-

ing end cannot keep up or if the line drops out. Data should be transmitted in packets, using a master–slave protocol in which the receiving end acknowledges or negatively acknowledges all exchanges.

b. A system for automating the production of complex machined parts. The parts will be designed using a three–dimensional drafting editor that is part of the system. The system will produce tapes that can be used by numerical control (N/C) machines to actually produce the parts.

c. A desktop publishing system, based on a what-you-see-is-what-you-get philosophy. The system will support text and graphics. Graphics include lines, squares, rectangles, polygons, circles, and ellipses. Internally, a circle is represented as a special case of an ellipse and a square as a special case of a rectangle. The system should support interactive, graphical editing of documents.

d. A system for generating nonsense. The input is a sample document. The output is random text that mimics the input text by imitating the frequencies of combinations of letters of the input. The user specifies the order of the imitation and the length of the desired output. For order N, every output sequence of N characters is found in the input and at approximately the same frequency. As the order increases, the style of the output more closely matches the input.

The system should generate its output with the following method: Select a position at random in the document being imitated. Scan forward in the input text until a sequence of characters is found that exactly matches the last $N - 1$ characters of the output. If you reach the end of the input, continue scanning from the beginning. When a match is found, copy the letter that follows the matched sequence from the input to the output. Repeat until the desired amount of text is generated.

e. A system for distributing electronic mail over a network. Each user of the system should be able to send mail from any computer account and receive mail on one designated account. There should be provisions for answering or forwarding mail, as well as saving messages in files or printing them. Also, users should be able to send messages to several other users at once through distribution lists. Each computer on the net should hold any messages destined for computers that are down.

12

Domain Analysis

Domain analysis, the next stage of development, is concerned with devising a precise, concise, understandable, and correct model of the real world. Before building anything complex, the builder must understand the requirements. Requirements can be stated in words, but these are often imprecise and ambiguous. During analysis, we build models and begin to understand the requirements deeply.

To build a domain model, you must interview business experts, examine requirements statements, and scrutinize related artifacts. You must analyze the implications of the requirements and restate them rigorously. It is important to abstract important features first and defer small details until later. The successful analysis model states what must be done, without restricting how it is done, and avoids implementation decisions.

In this chapter you will learn how to take OO concepts and apply them to construct a domain model. The model serves several purposes: It clarifies the requirements, it provides a basis for agreement between the stakeholders and the developers, and it becomes the starting point for design and implementation.

12.1 Overview of Analysis

As Figure 12.1 shows, analysis begins with a problem statement generated during system conception. The statement may be incomplete or informal; analysis makes it more precise and exposes ambiguities and inconsistencies. The problem statement should not be taken as immutable but should serve as a basis for refining the real requirements.

Next, you must understand the real-world system described by the problem statement, and abstract its essential features into a model. Statements in natural language are often ambiguous, incomplete, and inconsistent. The analysis model is a precise, concise representation of the problem that permits answering questions and building a solution. Subsequent design steps refer to the analysis model, rather than the original vague problem statement.

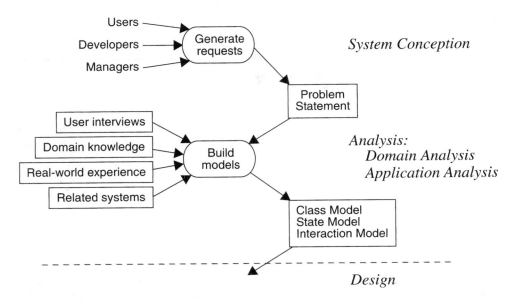

Figure 12.1 Overview of analysis. The problem statement should not be taken as immutable, but rather as a basis for refining the requirements.

Perhaps even more important, the process of constructing a rigorous model of the problem domain forces the developer to confront misunderstandings early in the development process while they are still easy to correct.

The analysis model addresses the three aspects of objects: static structure of objects (class model), interactions among objects (interaction model), and life-cycle histories of objects (state model). All three submodels are not equally important in every problem. Almost all problems have useful class models derived from real-world entities. Problems concerning reactive control and timing, such as user interfaces and process control, have important state models. Problems containing significant computation as well as systems that interact with other systems and different kinds of users have important interaction models.

Analysis is not a mechanical process. The exact representations involve judgment and in many regards are a matter of art. Most problem statements lack essential information, which must be obtained from the requestor or from the analyst's knowledge of the real-world problem domain. Also there is a choice in the level of abstraction for the model. The analyst must communicate with the requestor to clarify ambiguities and misconceptions. The analysis models enable precise communication.

We have divided analysis into two substages. The first, **domain analysis**, is covered in this chapter and focuses on understanding the real-world essence of a problem. The second, **application analysis**, is covered in the next chapter and builds on the domain model—incorporating major application artifacts that are seen by users and must be approved by them.

12.2 Domain Class Model

The first step in analyzing the requirements is to construct a domain model. The domain model shows the static structure of the real-world system and organizes it into workable pieces. The domain model describes real-world classes and their relationships to each other. During analysis, the class model precedes the state and interaction models because static structure tends to be better defined, less dependent on application details, and more stable as the solution evolves. Information for the domain model comes from the problem statement, artifacts from related systems, expert knowledge of the application domain, and general knowledge of the real world. Make sure you consider all information that is available and do not rely on a single source.

Find classes and associations first, as they provide the overall structure and approach to the problem. Next add attributes to describe the basic network of classes and associations. Then combine and organize classes using inheritance. Attempts to specify inheritance directly without first understanding classes and their attributes can distort the class structure to match preconceived notions. Operations are usually unimportant in a domain model. The main purpose of a domain model is to capture the information content of a domain.

It is best to get ideas down on paper before trying to organize them too much, even though they may be redundant and inconsistent, so as not to lose important details. An initial analysis model is likely to contain flaws that must be corrected by later iterations. The entire model need not be constructed uniformly. Some aspects of the problem can be analyzed in depth through several iterations while other aspects are still sketchy.

You must perform the following steps to construct a domain class model.

- Find classes. [12.2.1–12.2.2]
- Prepare a data dictionary. [12.2.3]
- Find associations. [12.2.4–12.2.5]
- Find attributes of objects and links. [12.2.6–12.2.7]
- Organize and simplify classes using inheritance. [12.2.8]
- Verify that access paths exist for likely queries. [12.2.9]
- Iterate and refine the model. [12.2.10]
- Reconsider the level of abstraction. [12.2.11]
- Group classes into packages. [12.2.12]

12.2.1 Finding Classes

The first step in constructing a class model is to find relevant classes for objects from the application domain. Objects include physical entities, such as houses, persons, and machines, as well as concepts, such as trajectories, seating assignments, and payment schedules. All classes must make sense in the application domain; avoid computer implementation constructs, such as linked lists and subroutines. Not all classes are explicit in the problem statement; some are implicit in the application domain or general knowledge.

As Figure 12.2 shows, begin by listing candidate classes found in the written description of the problem. Don't be too selective; write down every class that comes to mind. Classes often correspond to nouns. For example, in the statement "a reservation system to sell tickets to performances at various theaters" tentative classes would be *Reservation, System, Ticket, Performance,* and *Theater.* Don't operate blindly, however. The idea to is capture concepts; not all nouns are concepts, and concepts are also expressed in other parts of speech.

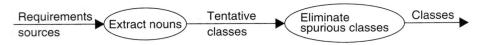

Figure 12.2 Finding classes. You can find many classes by considering nouns.

Don't worry much about inheritance or high-level classes; first get specific classes right so that you don't subconsciously suppress detail in an attempt to fit a preconceived structure. For example, if you are building a cataloging and checkout system for a library, identify different kinds of materials, such as books, magazines, newspapers, records, videos, and so on. You can organize them into broad categories later, by looking for similarities and differences.

   ATM example. Examination of the concepts in the ATM problem statement from Chapter 11 yields the tentative classes shown in Figure 12.3. Figure 12.4 shows additional classes that do not appear directly in the statement but can be identified from our knowledge of the problem domain.

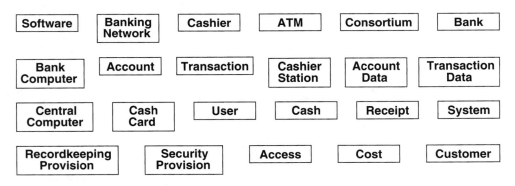

Figure 12.3 ATM classes extracted from problem statement nouns

Figure 12.4 ATM classes identified from knowledge of problem domain

12.2.2 Keeping the Right Classes

Now discard unnecessary and incorrect classes according to the following criteria. Figure 12.5 shows the classes eliminated from the ATM example.

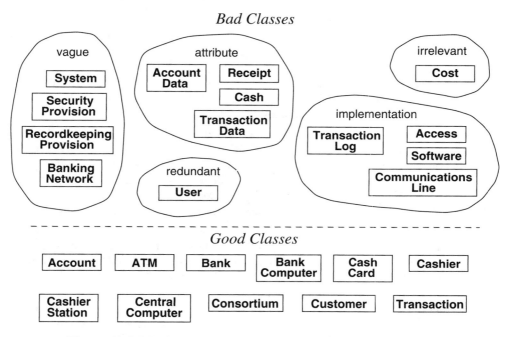

Figure 12.5 Eliminating unnecessary classes from ATM problem

■ **Redundant classes.** If two classes express the same concept, you should keep the most descriptive name. For example, although *Customer* might describe a person taking an airline flight, *Passenger* is more descriptive. On the other hand, if the problem concerns contracts for a charter airline, *Customer* is also an appropriate word, since a contract might involve several passengers.

   ATM example. *Customer* and *User* are redundant; we retain *Customer* because it is more descriptive.

■ **Irrelevant classes.** If a class has little or nothing to do with the problem, eliminate it. This involves judgment, because in another context the class could be important. For example, in a theater ticket reservation system, the occupations of the ticket holders are irrelevant, but the occupations of the theater personnel may be important.

   ATM example. Apportioning *Cost* is outside the scope of the ATM software.

■ **Vague classes.** A class should be specific. Some tentative classes may have ill-defined boundaries or be too broad in scope.

ATM example. *RecordkeepingProvision* is vague and is handled by *Transaction*. In other applications, this might be included in other classes, such as *StockSales, TelephoneCalls,* or *MachineFailures*.

■ **Attributes**. Names that primarily describe individual objects should be restated as attributes. For example, *name*, *birthdate*, and *weight* are usually attributes. If the independent existence of a property is important, then make it a class and not an attribute. For example, an employee's office would be a class in an application to reassign offices after a reorganization.

ATM example. *AccountData* is underspecified but in any case probably describes an account. An ATM dispenses cash and receipts, but beyond that cash and receipts are peripheral to the problem, so they should be treated as attributes.

■ **Operations**. If a name describes an operation that is applied to objects and not manipulated in its own right, then it is not a class. For example, a telephone call is a sequence of actions involving a caller and the telephone network. If we are simply building telephones, then *Call* is part of the state model and not a class.

An operation that has features of its own should be modeled as a class, however. For example, in a billing system for telephone calls a *Call* would be an important class with attributes such as *date*, *time*, *origin*, and *destination*.

■ **Roles**. The name of a class should reflect its intrinsic nature and not a role that it plays in an association. For example, *Owner* would be a poor name for a class in a car manufacturer's database. What if a list of drivers is added later? What about persons who lease cars? The proper class is *Person* (or possibly *Customer*), which assumes various different roles, such as *owner, driver,* and *lessee*.

One physical entity sometimes corresponds to several classes. For example, *Person* and *Employee* may be distinct classes in some circumstances and redundant in others. From the viewpoint of a company database of employees, the two may be identical. In a government tax database, a person may hold more than one job, so it is important to distinguish *Person* from *Employee;* each person can correspond to zero or more instances of employee information.

■ **Implementation constructs**. Eliminate constructs from the analysis model that are extraneous to the real world. You may need them later during design, but not now. For example, CPU, subroutine, process, algorithm, and interrupt are implementation constructs for most applications, although they are legitimate classes for an operating system. Data structures, such as linked lists, trees, arrays, and tables, are almost always implementation constructs.

ATM example. Some tentative classes are really implementation constructs. *TransactionLog* is simply the set of transactions; its exact representation is a design issue. Communication links can be shown as associations; *CommunicationsLine* is simply the physical implementation of such a link.

■ **Derived classes**. As a general rule, omit classes that can be derived from other classes. If a derived class is especially important, you can include it, but do so only sparingly. Mark all derived classes with a preceding slash ('/') in the class name.

12.2.3 *Preparing a Data Dictionary*

Isolated words have too many interpretations, so prepare a data dictionary for all modeling elements. Write a paragraph precisely describing each class. Describe the scope of the class within the current problem, including any assumptions or restrictions on its use. The data dictionary also describes associations, attributes, operations, and enumeration values. Figure 12.6 shows a data dictionary for the classes in the ATM problem.

12.2.4 *Finding Associations*

Next, find associations between classes. A structural relationship between two or more classes is an association. A reference from one class to another is an association. As we discussed in Chapter 3, attributes should not refer to classes; use an association instead. For example, class *Person* should not have an attribute *employer*; relate class *Person* and class *Company* with association *WorksFor*. Associations show relationships between classes at the same level of abstraction as the classes themselves, while object-valued attributes hide dependencies and obscure their two-way nature. Associations can be implemented in various ways, but such implementation decisions should be kept out of the analysis model to preserve design freedom.

Associations often correspond to stative verbs or verb phrases. These include physical location (*NextTo*, *PartOf*, *ContainedIn*), directed actions (*Drives*), communication (*TalksTo*), ownership (*Has*, *PartOf*), or satisfaction of some condition (*WorksFor*, *MarriedTo*, *Manages*). Extract all the candidates from the problem statement and get them down on paper first; don't try to refine things too early. Again, don't treat grammatical forms blindly; the idea is to capture relationships, however they are expressed in natural language.

ATM example. Figure 12.7 shows associations. The majority are taken directly from verb phrases in the problem statement. For some associations the verb phrase is implicit in the statement. Finally, some associations depend on real-world knowledge or assumptions. These must be verified with the requestor, as they are not in the problem statement.

12.2.5 *Keeping the Right Associations*

Now discard unnecessary and incorrect associations, using the following criteria.

■ **Associations between eliminated classes**. If you have eliminated one of the classes in the association, you must eliminate the association or restate it in terms of other classes.

   ATM example. We can eliminate *Banking network includes cashier stations and ATMs, ATM dispenses cash, ATM prints receipts, Banks provide software, Cost apportioned to banks, System provides recordkeeping,* and *System provides security.*

■ **Irrelevant or implementation associations**. Eliminate any associations that are outside the problem domain or deal with implementation constructs.

   ATM example. For example, *System handles concurrent access* is an implementation concept. Real-world objects are inherently concurrent; it is the implementation of the access algorithm that must be concurrent.

Account—a single account at a bank against which transactions can be applied. Accounts may be of various types, such as checking or savings. A customer can hold more than one account.

ATM—a station that allows customers to enter their own transactions using cash cards as identification. The ATM interacts with the customer to gather transaction information, sends the transaction information to the central computer for validation and processing, and dispenses cash to the user. We assume that an ATM need not operate independently of the network.

Bank—a financial institution that holds accounts for customers and issues cash cards authorizing access to accounts over the ATM network.

BankComputer—the computer owned by a bank that interfaces with the ATM network and the bank's own cashier stations. A bank may have its own internal computers to process accounts, but we are concerned only with the one that talks to the ATM network.

CashCard—a card assigned to a bank customer that authorizes access of accounts using an ATM machine. Each card contains a bank code and a card number. The bank code uniquely identifies the bank within the consortium. The card number determines the accounts that the card can access. A card does not necessarily access all of a customer's accounts. Each cash card is owned by a single customer, but multiple copies of it may exist, so the possibility of simultaneous use of the same card from different machines must be considered.

Cashier—an employee of a bank who is authorized to enter transactions into cashier stations and accept and dispense cash and checks to customers. Transactions, cash, and checks handled by each cashier must be logged and properly accounted for.

CashierStation—a station on which cashiers enter transactions for customers. Cashiers dispense and accept cash and checks; the station prints receipts. The cashier station communicates with the bank computer to validate and process the transactions.

CentralComputer—a computer operated by the consortium that dispatches transactions between the ATMs and the bank computers. The central computer validates bank codes but does not process transactions directly.

Consortium—an organization of banks that commissions and operates the ATM network. The network handles transactions only for banks in the consortium.

Customer—the holder of one or more accounts in a bank. A customer can consist of one or more persons or corporations; the correspondence is not relevant to this problem. The same person holding an account at a different bank is considered a different customer.

Transaction—a single integral request for operations on the accounts of a single customer. We specified only that ATMs must dispense cash, but we should not preclude the possibility of printing checks or accepting cash or checks. We may also want to provide the flexibility to operate on accounts of different customers, although it is not required yet.

Figure 12.6 Data dictionary for ATM classes. Prepare a data dictionary for all modeling elements.

Verb phrases
Banking network includes cashier stations and ATMs
Consortium shares ATMs
Bank provides bank computer
Bank computer maintains accounts
Bank computer processes transaction against account
Bank owns cashier station
Cashier station communicates with bank computer
Cashier enters transaction for account
ATMs communicate with central computer about transaction
Central computer clears transaction with bank
ATM accepts cash card
ATM interacts with user
ATM dispenses cash
ATM prints receipts
System handles concurrent access
Banks provide software
Cost apportioned to banks
Implicit verb phrases
Consortium consists of banks
Bank holds account
Consortium owns central computer
System provides recordkeeping
System provides security
Customers have cash cards
Knowledge of problem domain
Cash card accesses accounts
Bank employs cashiers

Figure 12.7 Associations from ATM problem statement

■ **Actions**. An association should describe a structural property of the application domain, not a transient event. Sometimes, a requirement expressed as an action implies an underlying structural relationship and you should rephrase it accordingly.

   ATM example. *ATM accepts cash card* describes part of the interaction cycle between an ATM and a customer, not a permanent relationship between ATMs and cash cards. We can also eliminate *ATM interacts with user*. *Central computer clears transaction with bank* describes an action that implies the structural relationship *Central computer communicates with bank*.

■ **Ternary associations**. You can decompose most associations among three or more classes into binary associations or phrase them as qualified associations. If a term in a ternary association is purely descriptive and has no identity of its own, then the term is an attribute on a binary association. Association *Company pays salary to person* can be rephrased as binary association *Company employs person* with a *salary* value for each *Company-Person* link.

   Occasionally, an application will require a general ternary association. *Professor teaches course in room* cannot be decomposed without losing information. We have not encountered associations with four or more classes in our work.

ATM example. *Bank computer processes transaction against account* can be broken into *Bank computer processes transaction* and *Transaction concerns account*. *Cashier enters transaction for account* can be broken similarly. *ATMs communicate with central computer about transaction* is really the binary associations *ATMs communicate with central computer* and *Transaction entered on ATM*.

■ **Derived associations**. Omit associations that can be defined in terms of other associations, because they are redundant. For example, *GrandparentOf* can be defined in terms of a pair of *ParentOf* associations. Also omit associations defined by conditions on attributes. For example, *youngerThan* expresses a condition on the birth dates of two persons, not additional information.

As much as possible, classes, attributes, and associations in the class model should represent independent information. Multiple paths between classes sometimes indicate derived associations that are compositions of primitive associations. *Consortium shares ATMs* is a composition of the associations *Consortium owns central computer* and *Central computer communicates with ATMs*.

Be careful, because not all associations that form multiple paths between classes indicate redundancy. Sometimes the existence of an association can be derived from two or more primitive associations and the multiplicity can not. Keep the extra association if the additional multiplicity constraint is important. For example, in Figure 12.8 a company employs many persons and owns many computers. Each employee is assigned zero or more computers for the employee's personal use; some computers are for public use and are not assigned to anyone. The multiplicity of the *AssignedTo* association cannot be deduced from the *Employs* and *Owns* associations.

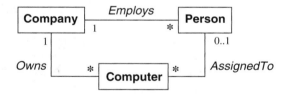

Figure 12.8 Nonredundant associations. Not all associations that form multiple paths between classes indicate redundancy.

Although derived associations do not add information, they are useful in the real world and in design. For example, kinship relationships such as *Uncle, MotherInLaw,* and *Cousin* have names because they describe common relationships considered important within our society. If they are especially important, you may show derived associations in class diagrams, but put a slash in front of their names to indicate their dependent status and to distinguish them from fundamental associations.

Further specify the semantics of associations as follows:

■ **Misnamed associations**. Don't say how or why a situation came about, say what it is. Names are important to understanding and should be chosen with great care.

ATM example. *Bank computer maintains accounts* is a statement of action; re-phrase as *Bank holds account*.

■ **Association end names**. Add association end names where appropriate. For example, in the *WorksFor* association a *Company* is an *employer* with respect to a *Person* and a *Person* is an *employee* with respect to a *Company*. If there is only one association between a pair of classes and the meaning of the association is clear, you may omit association end names. For example, the meaning of *ATMs communicate with central computer* is clear from the class names. An association between two instances of the same class requires association end names to distinguish the instances. For example, the association *Person manages person* would have the end names *boss* and *worker*.

■ **Qualified associations**. Usually a name identifies an object within some context; most names are not globally unique. The context combines with the name to uniquely identify the object. For example, the name of a company must be unique within the chartering state but may be duplicated in other states (there once was a Standard Oil Company in Ohio, Indiana, California, and New Jersey). The name of a company qualifies the association *State charters company*; *State* and *company name* uniquely identify *Company*. A qualifier distinguishes objects on the "many" side of an association.

 ATM example. The qualifier *bankCode* distinguishes the different banks in a consortium. Each cash card needs a bank code so that transactions can be directed to the appropriate bank.

■ **Multiplicity**. Specify multiplicity, but don't put too much effort into getting it right, as multiplicity often changes during analysis. Challenge multiplicity values of "one." For example, the association *one Manager manages many employees* precludes matrix management or an employee with divided responsibilities. For multiplicity values of "many" consider whether a qualifier is needed; also ask if the objects need to be ordered in some way.

■ **Missing associations**. Add any missing associations that are discovered.

 ATM example. We overlooked *Transaction entered on cashier station*, *Customers have accounts*, and *Transaction authorized by cash card*. If cashiers are restricted to specific stations, then the association *Cashier authorized on cashier station* would be needed.

■ **Aggregation**. Aggregation is important for certain kinds of applications, especially for those involving mechanical parts and bills of material. For other applications aggregation is relatively minor and it can be unclear whether to use aggregation or ordinary association. For these other applications, don't spend much time trying to distinguish between association and aggregation. Aggregation is just an association with extra connotations. Use whichever seems more natural at the time and move on.

 ATM example. We decide that a *Bank* is a part of a *Consortium* and indicate the relationship with aggregation.

ATM example. Figure 12.9 shows a class diagram with the remaining associations. We have included only significant association names. Note that we have split *Transaction* into *Re-*

moteTransaction and *CashierTransaction* to accommodate different associations. The diagram shows multiplicity values. We could have made some analysis decisions differently. Don't worry; there are many possible correct models of a problem. We have shown the analysis process in small steps; with practice, you can elide several steps together in your mind.

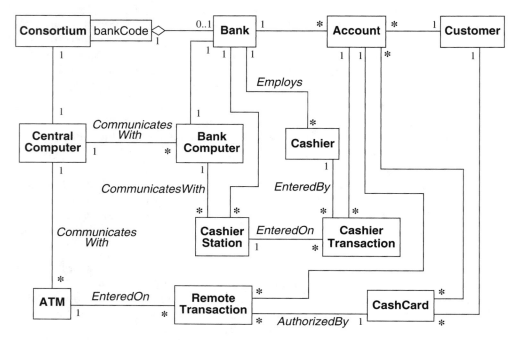

Figure 12.9 Initial class diagram for ATM system

12.2.6 Finding Attributes

Next find attributes. Attributes are data properties of individual objects, such as weight, velocity, or color. Attribute values should not be objects; use an association to show any relationship between two objects.

Attributes usually correspond to nouns followed by possessive phrases, such as "the color of the car" or "the position of the cursor." Adjectives often represent specific enumerated attribute values, such as *red, on,* or *expired.* Unlike classes and associations, attributes are less likely to be fully described in the problem statement. You must draw on your knowledge of the application domain and the real world to find them. You can also find attributes in the artifacts of related systems. Fortunately, attributes seldom affect the basic structure of the problem.

Do not carry discovery of attributes to excess. Only consider attributes directly relevant to the application. Get the most important attributes first; you can add fine details later. During analysis, avoid attributes that are solely for implementation. Be sure to give each attribute a meaningful name.

Normally, you should omit derived attributes. For example, *age* is derived from *birthdate* and *currentTime* (which is a property of the environment). Do not express derived attributes as operations, such as *getAge*, although you may eventually implement them that way.

Also look for attributes on associations. Such an attribute is a property of the link between two objects, rather than being a property of an individual object. For example, the many-to-many association between *Stockholder* and *Company* has an attribute of *numberOfShares*.

12.2.7 Keeping the Right Attributes

Eliminate unnecessary and incorrect attributes with the following criteria.

■   **Objects**. If the independent existence of an element is important, rather than just its value, then it is an object. For example, *boss* refers to a class and *salary* is an attribute. The distinction often depends on the application. For example, in a mailing list *city* might be considered as an attribute, while in a census *City* would be a class with many attributes and relationships of its own. An element that has features of its own within the given application is a class.

■   **Qualifiers**. If the value of an attribute depends on a particular context, then consider restating the attribute as a qualifier. For example, *employeeNumber* is not a unique property of a person with two jobs; it qualifies the association *Company employs person*.

■   **Names**. Names are often better modeled as qualifiers rather than attributes. Test: Does the name select unique objects from a set? Can an object in the set have more than one name? If so, the name qualifies a qualified association. If a name appears to be unique in the world, you may have missed the class that is being qualified. For example, *departmentName* may be unique within a company, but eventually the program may need to deal with more than one company. It is better to use a qualified association immediately.

A name is an attribute when its use does not depend on context, especially when it need not be unique within some set. Names of persons, unlike names of companies, may be duplicated and are therefore attributes.

■   **Identifiers**. OO languages incorporate the notion of an object identifier for unambiguously referencing an object. Do not include an attribute whose only purpose is to identify an object, as object identifiers are implicit in class models. Only list attributes that exist in the application domain. For example, *accountCode* is a genuine attribute; *Banks* assign *accountCodes* and customers see them. In contrast, you should not list an internal *transactionID* as an attribute, although it may be convenient to generate one during implementation.

■   **Attributes on associations**. If a value requires the presence of a link, then the property is an attribute of the association and not of a related class. Attributes are usually obvious on many-to-many associations; they cannot be attached to either class because of their multiplicity. For example, in an association between *Person* and *Club* the attribute *membershipDate* belongs to the association, because a person can belong to many clubs and a club can have many members. Attributes are more subtle on one-to-many associations because they could be attached to the "many" class without losing information. Resist the urge to attach them to classes, as they would be invalid if multiplicity changed. Attributes are also subtle on one-to-one associations.

■ **Internal values**. If an attribute describes the internal state of an object that is invisible outside the object, then eliminate it from the analysis.

■ **Fine detail**. Omit minor attributes that are unlikely to affect most operations.

■ **Discordant attributes**. An attribute that seems completely different from and unrelated to all other attributes may indicate a class that should be split into two distinct classes. A class should be simple and coherent. Mixing together distinct classes is one of the major causes of troublesome models. Unfocused classes frequently result from premature consideration of implementation decisions during analysis.

■ **Boolean attributes**. Reconsider all boolean attributes. Often you can broaden a boolean attribute and restate it as an enumeration [Coad-95].

ATM example. We apply these criteria to obtain attributes for each class (Figure 12.10). Some tentative attributes are actually qualifiers on associations. We consider several aspects of the model.

■ *BankCode* and *cardCode* are present on the card. Their format is an implementation detail, but we must add a new association *Bank issues CashCard*. *CardCode* is a qualifier on this association; *bankCode* is the qualifier of *Bank* with respect to *Consortium*.

■ The computers do not have state relevant to this problem. Whether the machine is up or down is a transient attribute that is part of implementation.

■ Avoid the temptation to omit *Consortium*, even though it is currently unique. It provides the context for the *bankCode* qualifier and may be useful for future expansion.

Keep in mind that the ATM problem is just an example. Real applications, when fleshed out, tend to have many more attributes per class than Figure 12.10 shows.

12.2.8 Refining with Inheritance

The next step is to organize classes by using inheritance to share common structure. Inheritance can be added in two directions: by generalizing common aspects of existing classes into a superclass (bottom up) or by specializing existing classes into multiple subclasses (top down).

■ **Bottom-up generalization**. You can discover inheritance from the bottom up by searching for classes with similar attributes, associations, and operations. For each generalization, define a superclass to share common features. You may have to slightly redefine some attributes or classes to fit in. This is acceptable, but don't push too hard if it doesn't fit; you may have the wrong generalization. Some generalizations will suggest themselves based on an existing taxonomy in the real world; use existing concepts whenever possible. Symmetry will suggest missing classes.

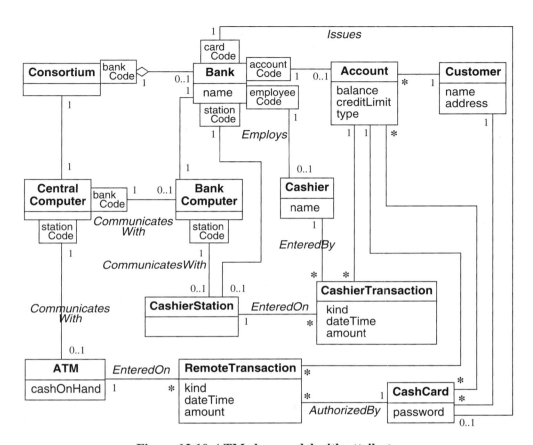

Figure 12.10 ATM class model with attributes

ATM example. *RemoteTransaction* and *CashierTransaction* are similar, except in their initiation, and can be generalized by *Transaction*. On the other hand, *CentralComputer* and *BankComputer* have little in common for purposes of the ATM example.

- **Top-down specialization**. Top-down specializations are often apparent from the application domain. Look for noun phrases composed of various adjectives on the class name: *fluorescent* lamp, *incandescent* lamp; *fixed* menu, *pop-up* menu, *sliding* menu. Avoid excessive refinement. If proposed specializations are incompatible with an existing class, the existing class may be improperly formulated.

- **Generalization vs. enumeration**. Enumerated subcases in the application domain are the most frequent source of specializations. Often, it is sufficient to note that a set of enumerated subcases exists, without actually listing them. For example, an ATM account could be refined into *CheckingAccount* and *SavingsAccount*. While undoubtedly useful in some banking applications, this distinction does not affect behavior within the ATM application; *type* can be made a simple attribute of *Account*.

■ **Multiple inheritance**. You can use multiple inheritance to increase sharing, but only if necessary, because it increases both conceptual and implementation complexity.

■ **Similar associations**. When the same association name appears more than once with substantially the same meaning, try to generalize the associated classes. Sometimes the classes have nothing in common but the association, but more often you will uncover an underlying generality that you have overlooked.

     ATM example. *Transaction* is entered on both *CashierStation* and *ATM; EntryStation* generalizes *CashierStation* and *ATM*.

■ **Adjusting the inheritance level**. You must assign attributes and associations to specific classes in the class hierarchy. Assign each one to the most general class for which it is appropriate. You may need some adjustment to get everything right. Symmetry may suggest additional attributes to distinguish among subclasses more clearly.

Figure 12.11 shows the ATM class model after adding inheritance.

12.2.9 Testing Access Paths

Trace access paths through the class model to see if they yield sensible results. Where a unique value is expected, is there a path yielding a unique result? For multiplicity "many" is there a way to pick out unique values when needed? Think of questions you might like to ask. Are there useful questions that cannot be answered? They indicate missing information. If something that seems simple in the real world appears complex in the model, you may have missed something (but make sure that the complexity is not inherent in the real world).

     It can be acceptable to have classes that are "disconnected" from other classes. This usually occurs when the relationship between a disconnected class and the remainder of the model is diffuse. However, check disconnected classes to make sure you have not overlooked any associations.

     ATM example. A cash card itself does not uniquely identify an account, so the user must choose an account somehow. If the user supplies an account type (savings or checking), each card can access at most one savings and one checking account. This is probably reasonable, and many cash cards actually work this way, but it limits the system. The alternative is to require customers to remember account numbers. If a cash card accesses a single account, then transfers between accounts are impossible.

     We have assumed that the ATM network serves a single consortium of banks. Real cash machines today often serve overlapping networks of banks and accept credit cards as well as cash cards. The model would have to be extended to handle that situation. We will assume that the customer is satisfied with this limitation on the system.

12.2.10 Iterating a Class Model

A class model is rarely correct after a single pass. The entire software development process is one of continual iteration; different parts of a model are often at different stages of completion. If you find a deficiency, go back to an earlier stage if necessary to correct it. Some refinements can come only after completing the state and interaction models.

     There are several signs of missing classes.

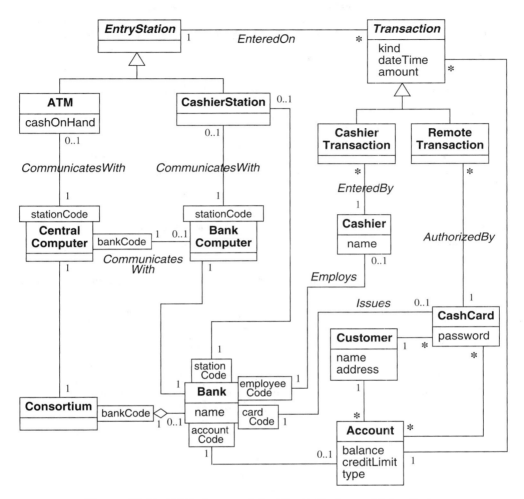

Figure 12.11 ATM class model with attributes and inheritance

■ **Asymmetries in associations and generalizations**. Add new classes by analogy.

■ **Disparate attributes and operations on a class**. Split a class so that each part is coherent.

■ **Difficulty in generalizing cleanly**. One class may be playing two roles. Split it up and one part may then fit in cleanly.

■ **Duplicate associations with the same name and purpose**. Generalize to create the missing superclass that unites them.

■ **A role that substantially shapes the semantics of a class**. Maybe it should be a separate class. This often means converting an association into a class. For example, a person can be employed by several companies with different conditions of employment at each; *Employee* is then a class denoting a person working for a particular company, in addition to class *Person* and *Company*.

Also look out for missing associations.

■ **Missing access paths for operations**. Add new associations so that you can answer queries.

Another concern is superfluous model elements.

■ **Lack of attributes, operations, and associations on a class**. Why is the class needed? Avoid inventing subclasses merely to indicate an enumeration. If proposed subclasses are otherwise identical, mark the distinction using an attribute.

■ **Redundant information**. Remove associations that do not add new information or mark them as derived.

And finally you may adjust the placement of attributes and associations.

■ **Association end names that are too broad or too narrow for their classes**. Move the association up or down in the class hierarchy.

■ **Need to access an object by one of its attribute values**. Consider a qualified association.

In practice, model building is not as rigidly ordered as we have shown. You can combine several steps, once you are experienced. For example, you can find candidate classes, reject the incorrect ones without writing them down, and add them to the class diagram together with their associations. You can take some parts of the model through several steps and develop them in some detail, while other parts are still sketchy. You can interchange the order of steps when appropriate. If you are just learning class modeling, however, we recommend that you follow the steps in full detail the first few times.

ATM example. *CashCard* really has a split personality—it is both an authorization unit within the bank allowing access to the customer's accounts and also a piece of plastic data that the ATM reads to obtain coded IDs. In this case, the codes are actually part of the real world, not just computer artifacts; the codes, not the cash card, are communicated to the central computer. We should split cash card into two classes: *CardAuthorization*, an access right to one or more customer accounts; and *CashCard*, a piece of plastic that contains a bank code and a cash card number meaningful to the bank. Each card authorization may have several cash cards, each containing a serial number for security reasons. The card code, present on the physical card, identifies the card authorization within the bank. Each card authorization identifies one or more accounts—for example, one checking account and one savings account.

Transaction is not general enough to permit transfers between accounts because it concerns only a single account. In general, a *Transaction* consists of one or more *updates* on individual accounts. An *update* is a single action (withdrawal, deposit, or query) on a single account. All updates in a single transaction must be processed together as an atomic unit; if any one fails, then they all are canceled.

The distinction between *Bank* and *BankComputer* and between *Consortium* and *CentralComputer* doesn't seem to affect the analysis. The fact that communications are processed by computers is actually an implementation artifact. Merge *BankComputer* into *Bank* and *CentralComputer* into *Consortium*.

Customer doesn't seem to enter into the analysis so far. However, when we consider operations to open new accounts, it may be an important concept, so leave it alone for now.

Figure 12.12 shows a revised class diagram that is simpler and cleaner.

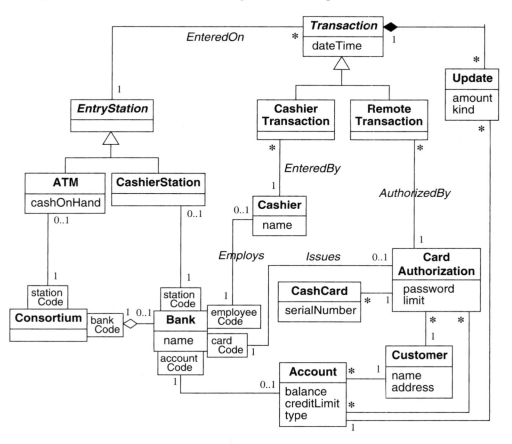

Figure 12.12 ATM class model after further revision

12.2.11 Shifting the Level of Abstraction

So far in analysis, we have taken the problem statement quite literally. We have regarded nouns and verbs in the problem description as direct analogs of classes and associations. This is a good way to begin analysis, but it does not always suffice. Sometimes you must raise the level of abstraction to solve a problem. You should be doing this throughout as you build a model, but we put in an explicit step to make sure you do not overlook abstraction.

For example, we encountered one application in which the developers had separate classes for *IndividualContributor*, *Supervisor*, and *Manager*. *IndividualContributors* report to *Supervisors* and *Supervisors* report to *Managers*. This model certainly is correct, but it suffers from some problems. There is much commonality between the three classes—the only difference is the reporting hierarchy. For example, they all have phone numbers and addresses. We could handle the commonality with a superclass, but that only makes the model larger. An additional problem arose when we talked to the developers and they said they wanted to add another class for the persons to whom managers reported.

Figure 12.13 shows the original model and an improved model that is more abstract. Instead of "hard coding" the management hierarchy in the model, we can "soft code" it with an association between boss and worker. A person who has an *employeeType* of "individual-Contributor" is a worker who reports to another person with an *employeeType* of "supervisor." Similarly, a person who is a supervisor reports to a person who is a manager. In the improved model a worker has an optional boss, because the reporting hierarchy eventually stops. The improved model is smaller and more flexible. An additional reporting level does not change the model's structure; it merely alters the data that is stored.

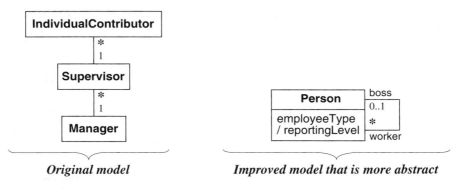

Original model   *Improved model that is more abstract*

Figure 12.13 Shifting the level of abstraction. Abstraction makes a model more
            complex but can increase flexibility and reduce the number of classes.

One way that you can take advantage of abstraction is by thinking in terms of patterns. Different kinds of patterns apply to the different development stages, but here we are interested in patterns for analysis. A *pattern* distills the knowledge of experts and provides a proven solution to a general problem. For example, the right side of Figure 12.13 is a pattern for modeling a management hierarchy. Whenever we encounter the need for a management hierarchy, we immediately think in terms of the pattern and place it in our application model. The use of tried and tested patterns gives us the confidence of a sound approach and boosts our productivity in building models.

ATM example. We have already included some abstractions in the ATM model. We distinguished between a *CashCard* and a *CardAuthorization*. Furthermore, we included the notion of transactions rather than trying to list each possible kind of interaction.

12.2.12 Grouping Classes into Packages

The last step of class modeling is to group classes into packages. A *package* is a group of elements (classes, associations, generalizations, and lesser packages) with a common theme. Packages organize a model for convenience in drawing, printing, and viewing. Furthermore, when you place classes and associations in a package, you are making a semantic statement. Generally speaking, classes in the same package are more closely related than classes in different packages.

Normally you should restrict each association to a single package, but you can repeat some classes in different packages. To assign classes to packages, look for cut points— a cut point is a class that is the sole connection between two otherwise disconnected parts of a model. Such a class forms the bridge between two packages. For example, in a file management system, a *File* is the cut point between the directory structure and the file contents. Try to choose packages to reduce the number of crossovers in the class diagrams. With a little care, you can draw most class diagrams as planar graphs, without crossing lines.

Reuse a package from a previous design if possible, but avoid forcing a fit. Reuse is easiest when part of the problem domain matches a previous problem. If the new problem is similar to a previous problem but different, you may have to extend the original model to encompass both problems. Use your judgment about whether this is better than building a new model.

ATM example. The current model is small and would not require breakdown into packages, but it could serve as a core for a more detailed model. The packages might be:

- tellers—cashier, entry station, cashier station, ATM
- accounts—account, cash card, card authorization, customer, transaction, update, cashier transaction, remote transaction
- banks—consortium, bank

Each package could add details. The account package could contain varieties of transactions, information about customers, interest payments, and fees. The bank package could contain information about branches, addresses, and cost allocations.

12.3 Domain State Model

Some domain objects pass through qualitatively distinct states during their lifetime. There may be different constraints on attribute values, different associations or multiplicities in the various states, different operations that may be invoked, different behavior of the operations, and so on. It is often useful to construct a state diagram of such a domain class. The state diagram describes the various states the object can assume, the properties and constraints of the object in various states, and the events that take an object from one state to another.

Most domain classes do not require state diagrams and can be adequately described by a list of operations. For the minority of classes that do exhibit distinct states, however, a state model can help in understanding their behavior.

First identify the domain classes with significant states and note the states of each class. Then determine the events that take an object from one state to another. Given the states and the events, you can build state diagrams for the affected objects. Finally, evaluate the state diagrams to make sure they are complete and correct.

The following steps are performed in constructing a domain state model.

- Identify domain classes with states. [12.3.1]
- Find states. [12.3.2]
- Find events. [12.3.3]
- Build state diagrams. [12.3.4]
- Evaluate state diagrams. [12.3.5]

12.3.1 Identifying Classes with States

Examine the list of domain classes for those that have a distinct life cycle. Look for classes that can be characterized by a progressive history or that exhibit cyclic behavior. Identify the significant states in the life cycle of an object. For example, a scientific paper for a journal goes from *Being written* to *Under consideration* to *Accepted* or *Rejected*. There can be some cycles, for example, if the reviewers ask for revisions, but basically the life of this object is progressive. On the other hand, an airplane owned by an airline cycles through the states of *Maintenance, Loading, Flying,* and *Unloading.* Not every state occurs in every cycle, and there are probably other states, but the life of this object is cyclic. There are also classes whose life cycle is chaotic, but most classes with states are either progressive or cyclic.

ATM example. *Account* is an important business concept, and the appropriate behavior for an ATM depends on the state of an *Account*. The life cycle for *Account* is a mix of progressive and cycling to and from problem states. No other ATM classes have a significant domain state model.

12.3.2 Finding States

List the states for each class. Characterize the objects in each class—the attribute values that an object may have, the associations that it may participate in and their multiplicities, attributes and associations that are meaningful only in certain states, and so on. Give each state a meaningful name. Avoid names that indicate how the state came about; try to directly describe the state.

Don't focus on fine distinctions among states, particularly quantitative differences, such as small, medium, or large. States should be based on qualitative differences in behavior, attributes, or associations.

It is unnecessary to determine all the states before examining events. By looking at events and considering transitions among states, missing states will become clear.

ATM example. Here are some states for an *Account*: *Normal* (ready for normal access), *Closed* (closed by the customer but still on file in the bank records), *Overdrawn* (customer withdrawals exceed the balance in the account), and *Suspended* (access to the account is blocked for some reason).

12.3.3 Finding Events

Once you have a preliminary set of states, find the events that cause transitions among states. Think about the stimuli that cause a state to change. In many cases, you can regard an event as completing a do-activity. For example, if a technical paper is in the state *Under consideration*, then the state terminates when a decision on the paper is reached. In this case, the decision can be positive (*Accept paper*) or negative (*Reject paper*). In cases of completing a do-activity, other possibilities are often possible and may be added in the future—for example, *Conditionally accept with revisions*.

You can find other events by thinking about taking the object into a specific state. For example, if you lift the receiver on a telephone, it enters the *Dialing* state. Many telephones have pushbuttons that invoke specific functions. If you press the *redial* button, the phone transmits the number and enters the *Calling* state. If you press the *program* button, it enters the *Programming* state.

There are additional events that occur within a state and do not cause a transition. For the domain state model you should focus on events that cause transitions among states. When you discover an event, capture any information that it conveys as a list of parameters.

ATM example. Important events include: *close account*, *withdraw excess funds*, *repeated incorrect PIN*, *suspected fraud*, and *administrative action*.

12.3.4 Building State Diagrams

Note the states to which each event applies. Add transitions to show the change in state caused by the occurrence of an event when an object is in a particular state. If an event terminates a state, it will usually have a single transition from that state to another state. If an event initiates a target state, then consider where it can occur, and add transitions from those states to the target state. Consider the possibility of using a transition on an enclosing state rather than adding a transition from each substate to the target state. If an event has different effects in different states, add a transition for each state.

Once you have specified the transitions, consider the meaning of an event in states for which there is no transition on the event. Is it ignored? Then everything is fine. Does it represent an error? Then add a transition to an error state. Does it have some effect that you forgot? Then add another transition. Sometimes you will discover new states.

It is usually not important to consider effects when building a state diagram for a domain class. If the objects in the class perform activities on transitions, however, add them to the state diagram.

ATM example. Figure 12.14 shows the domain state model for the *Account* class.

12.3.5 Evaluating State Diagrams

Examine each state model. Are all the states connected? Pay particular attention to paths through it. If it represents a progressive class, is there a path from the initial state to the final state? Are the expected variations present? If it represents a cyclic class, is the main loop present? Are there any dead states that terminate the cycle?

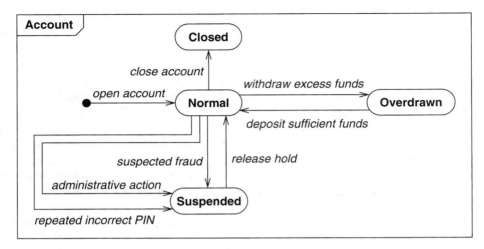

Figure 12.14 Domain state model. The domain state model documents important classes that change state in the real world.

Use your knowledge of the domain to look for missing paths. Sometimes missing paths indicate missing states. When a state model is complete, it should accurately represent the life cycle of the class.

ATM example. Our state model for *Account* is simplistic but we are satisfied with it. We would require substantial banking knowledge to construct a deeper model.

12.4 Domain Interaction Model

The interaction model is seldom important for domain analysis. During domain analysis the emphasis is on key concepts and deep structural relationships and not the users' view of them. The interaction model, however, is an important aspect of application modeling and we will cover it in the next chapter.

12.5 Iterating the Analysis

Most analysis models require more than one pass to complete. Problem statements often contain circularities, and most applications cannot be approached in a completely linear way, because different parts of the problem interact. To understand a problem with all its implications, you must attack the analysis iteratively, preparing a first approximation to the model and then iterating the analysis as your understanding increases. There is no firm line between analysis and design, so don't overdo it. Verify the final analysis with the requestor and application domain experts.

12.5.1 *Refining the Analysis Model*

The overall analysis model may show inconsistencies and imbalances within and across models. Iterate the different portions to produce a cleaner, more coherent model. Try to refine classes to increase sharing and improve structure. Add details that you glossed over during the first pass.

Some constructs will feel awkward and won't seem to fit in right. Reexamine them carefully; you may have the wrong concepts. Sometimes major restructuring in the model is needed as your understanding increases. It is easier to do now than it will ever be, so don't avoid changes just because you already have a model in place. When there are many constructs that appear similar but don't quite fit together, you have probably missed or miscast a more general concept. Watch out for generalizations factored on the wrong aspects.

A common difficulty is a physical object that has two logically distinct aspects. Each aspect should be modeled with a distinct object. An indication of this problem is a class that doesn't fit in cleanly and seems to have two sets of unrelated attributes, associations, and operations.

Other indications to watch for include exceptions, many special cases, and lack of expected symmetry. Consider restructuring your model to capture constraints better within its structure.

Be wary of codifying arbitrary business practices in your model. Software should facilitate operation of the business and not inhibit reasonable changes. Often you can introduce abstractions that increase business flexibility without substantially complicating a model.

Remove classes or associations that seemed useful at first but now appear extraneous. Often two classes in the analysis can be combined, because the distinction between them doesn't affect the rest of the model in any meaningful way. There is a tendency for models to grow as analysis proceeds. This is a concern, since the amount of development work escalates as a model becomes larger in size. Take a close look at your model for minor concepts to cut or abstractions that can simplify the model.

A good model feels right and does not appear to have extraneous detail. Don't worry if it doesn't seem perfect; even a good model will often have a few small areas where the design is adequate but never feels quite right.

12.5.2 *Restating the Requirements*

When the analysis is complete, the model serves as the basis for the requirements and defines the scope of future discourse. Most of the real requirements will be part of the model. In addition you may have some performance constraints; these should be stated clearly, together with optimization criteria. Other requirements specify the method of solution and should be separated and challenged, if possible.

You should verify the final model with the requestor. During analysis some requirements may appear to be incorrect or impractical; confirm corrections to the requirements. Also business experts should verify the analysis model to make sure that it correctly models the real world. We have found analysis models to be an effective means of communication with business experts who are not computer experts.

The final verified analysis model serves as the basis for system architecture, design, and implementation. You should revise the original problem statement to incorporate corrections and understanding discovered during analysis.

12.5.3 Analysis and Design

The goal of analysis is to specify the problem fully without introducing a bias to any particular implementation, but it is impossible in practice to avoid all taints of implementation. There is no absolute line between the various development stages, nor is there any such thing as a perfect analysis. Don't treat the rules we have given too rigidly. The purpose of the rules is to preserve flexibility and permit changes later, but remember that the goal of modeling is to accomplish the total job, and flexibility is just a means to an end.

ATM example. We have no further changes to the ATM model at this time. A true application is more likely to incur revision than a textbook example, because you have reviewers who are passionate about the application and have a vested interest in it.

12.6 Chapter Summary

The domain model captures general knowledge about an application—concepts and relationships known to experts in the domain. The domain model has class models and sometimes state models, but seldom has an interaction model. The purpose of analysis is to understand the problem and the application so that a correct design can be constructed. A good analysis captures the essential features of the problem without introducing implementation artifacts that prematurely restrict design decisions.

The domain class model shows the static structure of the real world. First find classes. Then find associations between classes. Note attributes, though you can defer minor ones. You can use generalization to organize and simplify the class structure. Group tightly coupled classes and associations into packages. Supplement the class models with a data dictionary—brief textual descriptions, including the purpose and scope of each element.

If a domain class has several qualitatively different states during its life cycle, make a state diagram for it, but most domain classes will not require state diagrams.

Methodologies are never as linear as they appear in books. This one is no exception. Any complex analysis is constructed by iteration on multiple levels. You need not prepare all parts of the model at the same pace. The result of analysis replaces the original problem statement and serves as the basis for design.

Bibliographic Notes

Abbott explains how to use nouns and verbs in the problem statement to seed thinking about an application [Abbott-83]. [Coad-95] is a good book with some examples of analysis patterns.

building the domain class model	finding classes
building the domain state model	finding events
data dictionary	finding states
domain analysis	refining a model with inheritance
finding associations	shifting the level of abstraction
finding attributes	testing the model

Figure 12.15 Key concepts for Chapter 12

References

[Abbott-83] Russell J. Abbott. Program Design by Informal English Descriptions. *Communications of the ACM 26*, 11 (November 1983), 882–894.

[Coad-95] Peter Coad, David North, and Mark Mayfield. *Object Models: Strategies, Patterns, and Applications*. Upper Saddle River, NJ: Yourdon Press, 1995.

Exercises

12.1 (3) For each of the following systems, identify the relative importance of the three aspects of modeling: 1) class modeling, 2) state modeling, 3) interaction modeling. Explain your answers. For example, for a compiler, the answer might be 3, 1, and 2. Interaction modeling is most important for a compiler because it is dominated by data transformation concerns.
  a. bridge player
  b. change-making machine
  c. car cruise control
  d. electronic typewriter
  e. spelling checker
  f. telephone answering machine

12.2 (7) Create a class diagram for each system from Exercise 11.6. Note that the requirements are incomplete, so your class models will also be incomplete.

Exercises 12.3–12.8 are related. Do the exercises in sequence. The following are tentative specifications for a simple diagram editor that could be used as the core of a variety of applications.

The editor will be used interactively to create and modify drawings. A drawing contains several sheets. Drawings are saved to and loaded from named ASCII files. Sheets contain boxes and links. Each box may optionally contain a single line of text. Text is allowed only in boxes. The editor must automatically adjust the size of a box to fit any enclosed text. The font size of the text is not adjustable. Any pair of boxes on the same sheet may be linked by a series of alternating horizontal and vertical lines. Figure E12.1 shows a simple, one sheet drawing.

The editor will be menu driven, with pop-up menus. A three-button mouse will be used for menu, object, and link selections. The following are some operations the editor should provide: create sheet, delete sheet, next sheet, previous sheet, create box, link boxes, enter text, group selection, cut selections, move selections, copy selections, paste, edit text, save drawing, and load drawing. Copy, cut,

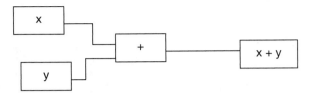

Figure E12.1 A sample drawing

and paste will work through a buffer. Copy will create a copy of selections from a sheet to the buffer. Cut will remove selections to the buffer. Paste will copy the contents of the buffer to the sheet. Each copy and cut operation overwrites the previous contents of the buffer. Pan and zoom will not be allowed; sheets will have fixed size. When boxes are moved, enclosed text should move with them and links should be stretched.

12.3   (3) The following is a list of candidate classes. Prepare a list of classes that should be eliminated for any of the reasons given in this chapter. Give a reason for each elimination. If there is more than one reason, give the main one.

character, line, x coordinate, y coordinate, link, position, length, width, collection, selection, menu, mouse, button, computer, drawing, drawing file, sheet, pop-up, point, menu item, selected object, selected line, selected box, selected text, file name, box, buffer, line segment coordinate, connection, text, name, origin, scale factor, corner point, end point, graphics object.

12.4   (3) Prepare a data dictionary for proper classes from the previous exercise.

12.5   (3) The following is a list of candidate associations and generalizations for the diagram editor. Prepare a list of associations and generalizations that should be eliminated or renamed for any of the reasons given in this chapter. Give a reason for each elimination or renaming. If there is more than one reason, give the main one.

a box has text, a box has a position, a link logically associates two boxes, a box is moved, a link has points, a link is defined by a sequence of points, a selection or a buffer or a sheet is a collection, a character string has a location, a box has a character string, a character string has characters, a line has length, a collection is composed of links and boxes, a link is deleted, a line is moved, a line is a graphical object, a point is a graphical object, a line has two points, a point has an x coordinate, a point has a y coordinate

12.6   Figure E12.2 is a partially completed class diagram for the diagram editor. Show how could it be used for each of the following queries. Use a combination of the OCL (see Chapter 3) and pseudocode to express your queries.

a. (2) Find all selected boxes and links.

b. (4) Given a box, determine all other boxes that are directly linked to it.

c. (8) Given a box, find all other boxes that are directly or indirectly linked to it.

d. (2) Given a box and a link, determine if the link involves the box.

e. (3) Given a box and a link, find the other box logically connected to the given box through the other end of the link.

f. (4) Given two boxes, determine all links between them.

g. (6) Given a selection, determine which links are "bridging" links. If a selection does not include all boxes on a sheet, "bridging" links may result. A "bridging" link is a link that con-

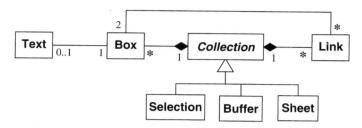

Figure E12.2 Partially completed class diagram for a diagram editor

nects a box that has been selected to a box that has not. A link that connects two boxes that are selected or two boxes that are not selected is not a "bridging" link. "Bridging" links require special handling during a *cut* or a *move* operation on a selection.

12.7   (6) Figure E12.3 is a variation of the class diagram in which the class *Connection* explicitly represents the connection of a link to a box. Redo the queries from the previous exercise using this representation.

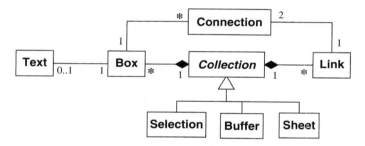

Figure E12.3 Alternative partially completed class diagram for a diagram editor

12.8   (5) What classes require state diagrams? Describe some relevant states and events.

Exercises 12.9–12.13 are related. Do the exercises in sequence. These exercises concern a computerized scoring system that you have volunteered to create for the benefit of a local children's synchronized swimming league. Teams get together for competitions called meets during which the children perform in two types of events: figures and routines. Figure events, which are performed individually, are particular water ballet maneuvers such as swimming on your back with one leg raised straight up. Routines, which are performed by the entire team, are water ballets. Both figures and routines are scored, but your system need only address figures.

   Each child must provide his or her name, age, address, and team name to register prior to the meet. To simplify scoring, each contestant is assigned a number.

   During a meet, figure events are held simultaneously at several stations that are set up around a swimming pool, usually one at each corner. There are volunteer judges and scorekeepers. Scorekeepers tend to tire, so there is often turnover in their ranks. Several judges and scorekeepers are assigned to each station during a meet. Over the course of a season each judge and scorekeeper may serve several stations. For scoring consistency, each figure is held at exactly one station with the same judges. A station may process several figure events in the course of a meet.

Contestants are organized into groups, with each group starting at a different station. When a child is finished at one station, he or she proceeds to another station for another event. When everyone has been processed at a station for a given event, the station switches to the next event assigned to it.

Each competitor gets one try at each event, called a trial. Just before a trial, the child's number is announced to the child and to the scorekeepers. Sometimes the children get out of order or the scorekeepers become confused and the station stops while the problem is fixed. Each judge indicates a raw score for each observed trial by holding up numbered cards. The raw scores are read to the scorekeepers, who record them and compute a net score for the trial. The highest and lowest raw scores are discarded, and the average of the remaining scores is multiplied by a difficulty factor for the figure.

Individual and team prizes are awarded at the conclusion of a meet based on top individual and team scores. There are several age categories, with separate prizes for each category. Individual prizes are based on figures only. Team prizes are based on figures and routines.

Your system will be used to store all information needed for scheduling, registering, and scoring. At the beginning of a season, all swimmers will be entered into the system and a season schedule will be prepared, including deciding which figures will be judged at which meets. Prior to a meet, the system will be used to process registrations. During a meet, it will record scores and determine winners.

12.9   (3) The following is a list of candidate classes for the scoring system. Prepare a list of classes that should be eliminated for any of the reasons given in this chapter. Give a reason for each elimination. If there is more than one reason, give the main one.

address, age, age category, average score, back, card, child, child's name, competitor, compute average, conclusion, contestant, corner, date, difficulty factor, event, figure, file of team member data, group, individual, individual prize, judge, league, leg, list of scheduled meets, meet, net score, number, person, pool, prize, register, registrant, raw score, routine, score, scorekeeper, season, station, team, team prize, team name, trial, try, water ballet.

12.10 (3) Prepare a data dictionary for proper classes from the previous exercise.

12.11 (4) The following is a list of candidate associations and generalizations for the scoring system. Prepare a list of associations and generalizations that should be eliminated or renamed for any of the reasons given in this chapter. Give a reason for each elimination or renaming. If there is more than one reason, give the main one.

a season consists of several meets, a competitor registers, a competitor is assigned a number, a number is announced, competitors are split into groups, a meet consists of several events, several stations are set up at a meet, several events are processed at a station, several judges are assigned to a station, routines and figures are events, raw scores are read, highest score is discarded, lowest score is discarded, figures are processed, a league consists of several teams, a team consists of several competitors, a trial of a figure is made by a competitor, a trial receives several scores from the judges, prizes are based on scores.

12.12 Figure E12.4 is a partially completed class diagram for the scoring system. The association between meet and event is not derived, because an event may be determined for a meet before a station is assigned to it. Show how it could be used for each of the following queries. Use a combination of the OCL (see Chapter 3) and pseudocode to express your queries.

a. (2) Find all the members of a given team.

b. (6) Find which figures were held more than once in a given season.

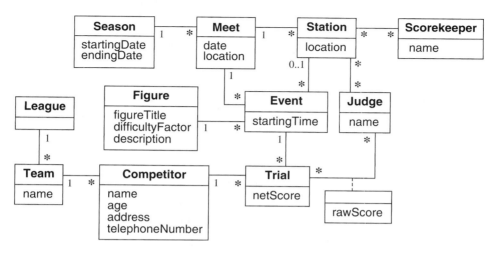

Figure E12.4 Partially completed class diagram for a scoring system

   c. (6) Find the net score of a competitor for a given figure at a given meet.
   d. (6) Find the team average over all figures in a given season.
   e. (6) Find the average score of a competitor over all figures in a given meet.
   f. (6) Find the team average in a given figure at a given meet.
   g. (4) Find the set of all individuals who competed in any events in a given season.
   h. (7) Find the set of all individuals who competed in all of the events held in a given season.
   i. (6) Find all the judges who judged a given figure in a given season.
   j. (6) Find the judge who awarded the lowest score during a given event.
   k. (6) Find the judge who awarded the lowest score for a given figure.
   l. (7) Modify the diagram so that the competitors registered for an event can be determined.

12.13 (5) What classes require state diagrams? Describe some relevant states and events.

12.14 (7) Revise the diagrams in Figure E12.5, Figure E12.6, Figure E12.7, and Figure E12.8 to elim-
      inate ternary associations. In some cases you will have to promote the association to a class.
         Figure E12.5 is a relationship between *Doctor*, *Patient,* and *DateTime* that might be encoun-
      tered in a system used by a clinic with several doctors on the staff. The combination of *DateTime*
      + *Patient* is unique as well as *DateTime* + *Doctor.*
         Figure E12.6 is a relationship between *Student*, *Professor*, and *University* that might be used
      to express the contacts between students attending and professors teaching at several universi-
      ties. There is one link in the relationship for a student that takes one or more classes from a pro-
      fessor at a university. The combination of *Student* + *Professor* + *University* is unique.
         Figure E12.7 shows the relationship expressing the seating arrangement at a concert.
      Concert + *Seat* is unique.
         Figure E12.8 expresses the connectivity of a directed graph. Each edge of a directed graph
      is connected in a specific order to exactly two vertices. More than one edge can be connected
      between a given pair of vertices. The attribute *Edge* is unique for the relationship.
         In each case, try to come as close as possible to the original intent and compare the merits of
      the original and the revised models.

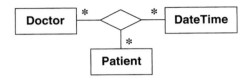

Figure E12.5 Ternary association for *Doctor***,** *Patient***, and** *DateTime*

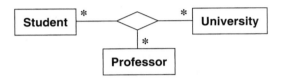

Figure E12.6 Ternary association for *Student***,** *Professor***, and** *University*

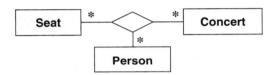

Figure E12.7 Ternary association for *Seat***,** *Person***, and** *Concert*

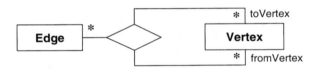

Figure E12.8 Ternary association for directed graphs

12.15 (9) Figure E12.9 lists requirements for a document manager. We then prepared the initial model in Figure E12.10. Note some flaws in the model.

Develop software for managing professional records of papers, books, journals, notes, and computer files. The system must be able to record authors of published works in the appropriate order, name of work, date of publication, publisher, publisher city, an abstract, as well as a comment. The software must be able to group published works into various categories that are defined by the user to facilitate searching. The user must be able to assign a quality indicator of the perceived value of each work.

Only some of the papers in each issue of a journal may be of interest. It would also be helpful to be able to attach comments to sections or even individual pages of a work.

Figure E12.9 Requirements for a document manager

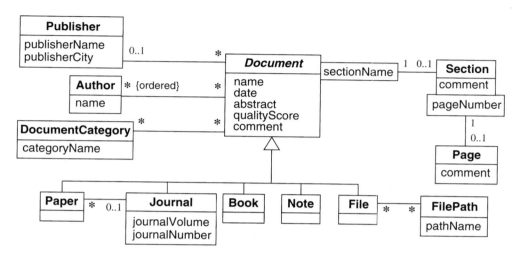

Figure E12.10 Initial model for a document manager

■ There is little difference between subclasses. Is an outline of a paper a "paper" or a "note"? How should we handle a paper that is in both an electronic file and a binder? How should we represent information about slides for talks?

■ We would like to handle both standard comments (applicable to many documents and chosen by point and click in a user interface) and custom comments (applicable to one document and specifically typed by the user).

■ We should be able to comment on a numbered page without having sections.

Improve the model by making it more abstract. (Hint: You should have generic classes for location, document properties, and comments. It is adequate to represent document composition with a hierarchy.)

Exercises 12.16–12.19 are related. Do the exercises in sequence. The following are tentative specifications for scheduling software.

The scheduling software must support the following functions: arranges meetings, schedules appointments, plans tasks, and tracks holidays (including vacations).

The scheduler runs on a network that many users share. Each user may have a schedule. A schedule contains multiple entries. Most entries belong to a single schedule; however, a meeting entry may appear in many schedules.

There are four kinds of entries: meetings, appointments, tasks, and holidays. Meetings and appointments both occur within a single day and have a start time and end time. In contrast, tasks and holidays may extend over several days and just have a start date and end date. Any entry may be repeated. Repeat information includes how often the entry should be repeated, when it starts, and when it ends.

12.16 (3) The following is a list of candidate classes. Prepare a list of classes that should be eliminated for any of the reasons given in this chapter. Give a reason for each elimination. If there is more than one reason, give the main one.

scheduling software, function, meeting, appointment, task, holiday, vacation, scheduler, network, user, schedule, entry, meeting entry, day, start time, end time, start date, end date, repeat information.

12.17 (3) Prepare a data dictionary for proper classes from the previous exercise.

12.18 (4) The following is a list of candidate associations and generalizations for the scoring system. Prepare a list of associations and generalizations that should be eliminated or renamed for any of the reasons given in this chapter. Give a reason for each elimination or renaming. If there is more than one reason, give the main one.

- scheduling software that supports the following functions
- the scheduler runs on a network that many users share
- user may have a schedule
- a schedule contains multiple entries
- entries pertain to a single schedule
- a meeting entry may appear in many schedules
- meetings and appointments both occur within a single day and have a start time and end time
- tasks and holidays may extend over several days and just have a start date and end date.

12.19 (5) Construct a class model for the scheduling software.

Exercises 12.20–12.23 are related. Do the exercises in sequence. The following provides requirements for meetings and extends the scheduling software from Exercises 12.16–12.19.

The scheduling software facilitates meetings. When a user (the chairperson) arranges a meeting, the software places a meeting entry in the schedule of each attendee. The chairperson uses the scheduler to reserve a room for the meeting, to identify the attendees, and to find time on their schedules when everyone is available. The chairperson can indicate whether the attendance for each attendee is required or optional. The system tracks the acceptance status for each attendee—whether an attendee has accepted or declined.

The scheduler manages meeting notices. When a meeting is set up, the scheduler sends invitations to all attendees, who are able to view meeting information. Each invitee can accept or refuse as well as possibly cancel later on. The system also manages notices in case the meeting is rescheduled or cancelled.

12.20 (3) The following is a list of candidate classes. Prepare a list of classes that should be eliminated for any of the reasons given in this chapter. Give a reason for each elimination. If there is more than one reason, give the main one.

scheduling software, meeting, user, chairperson, software, meeting entry, schedule, attendee, scheduler, room, time, everyone, attendance, acceptance status, meeting notice, invitation, meeting information, invitee, notice.

12.21 (3) Prepare a data dictionary for proper classes from the previous exercise.

12.22 (4) The following is a list of candidate associations and generalizations. Prepare a list of associations and generalizations that should be eliminated or renamed for any of the reasons given in this chapter. Give a reason for each elimination or renaming. If there is more than one reason, give the main one.

- scheduling software facilitates meetings

- user (the chairperson) arranges a meeting
- software places a meeting entry in the schedule of each attendee
- chairperson uses the scheduler to reserve a room for the meeting, to identify the attendees, and to find time on their schedules when everyone is available
- chairperson can indicate whether the attendance for each attendee is required or optional
- system tracks the acceptance status for each attendee—whether an attendee has accepted or declined
- scheduler manages meeting notices
- scheduler sends invitations to all attendees, who are able to view meeting information
- system also manages notices in case the meeting is rescheduled or cancelled.

12.23 (7) Construct a class model for the extension to the scheduling software. Your answer should resolve a problem from Exercise 12.19. In the class model for our answer to Exercise 12.19, we cannot tell which user owns an entry. (Hint: You should reconcile the chairperson and attendee associations from the extended requirements with the association between *Schedule* and *Entry* from the Exercise 12.16–12.19 requirements.)

13

Application Analysis

This chapter completes our treatment of analysis by adding major application artifacts to the domain model from the prior chapter. We include these application artifacts in analysis, because they are important, visible to users, and must be approved by them. In general, you cannot find the application classes in the domain itself, but must find them in use cases.

13.1 Application Interaction Model

Most domain models are static and operations are unimportant, because a domain as a whole usually doesn't *do* anything. The focus of domain modeling is on building a model of intrinsic concepts. After completing the domain model we then shift our attention to the details of an application and consider interaction.

Begin interaction modeling by determining the overall boundary of the system. Then identify use cases and flesh them out with scenarios and sequence diagrams. You should also prepare activity diagrams for use cases that are complex or have subtleties. Once you fully understand the use cases, you can organize them with relationships. And finally check against the domain class model to ensure that there are no inconsistencies.

You can construct an application interaction model with the following steps.

- Determine the system boundary. [13.1.1]
- Find actors. [13.1.2]
- Find use cases. [13.1.3]
- Find initial and final events. [13.1.4]
- Prepare normal scenarios. [13.1.5]
- Add variation and exception scenarios. [13.1.6]
- Find external events. [13.1.7]
- Prepare activity diagrams for complex use cases. [13.1.8]

■   Organize actors and use cases. [13.1.9]
■   Check against the domain class model. [13.1.10]

13.1.1 Determining the System Boundary

You must know the precise scope of an application—the boundary of the system—in order to specify functionality. This means that you must decide what the system includes and, more importantly, what it omits. If the system boundary is drawn correctly, you can treat the system as a black box in its interactions with the outside world—you can regard the system as a single object, whose internal details are hidden and changeable. During analysis, you determine the purpose of the system and the view that it presents to its actors. During design, you can change the internal implementation of the system as long as you maintain the external behavior.

Usually, you should not consider humans as part of a system, unless you are modeling a human organization, such as a business or a government department. Humans are actors that must interact with the system, but their actions are not under the control of the system. However, you must allow for human error in your system.

ATM example. The original problem statement from Chapter 11 says to "design the software to support a computerized banking network including both human cashiers and automatic teller machines..." Now it is important that cashier transactions and ATM transactions be seamless—from the customer's perspective either method of conducting business should yield the same effect on a bank account. However, in commercial practice an ATM application would be separate from a cashier application—an ATM application spans banks while a cashier application is internal to a bank. Both applications would share the same underlying domain model, but each would have its own distinct application model. For this chapter we focus on ATM behavior and ignore cashier details.

13.1.2 Finding Actors

Once you determine the system boundary, you must identify the external objects that interact directly with the system. These are its *actors*. Actors include humans, external devices, and other software systems. The important thing about actors is that they are not under control of the application, and you must consider them to be somewhat unpredictable. That is, even though there may be an expected sequence of behavior by the actors, an application's design should be robust so that it does not crash if an actor fails to behave as expected.

In finding actors, we are not searching for individuals but for archetypical behavior. Each actor represents an idealized user that exercises some subset of the system functionality. Examine each external object to see if it has several distinct faces. An actor is a coherent face presented to the system, and an external object may have more than one actor. It is also possible for different kinds of external objects to play the part of the same actor.

ATM example. A particular person may be both a bank teller and a customer of the same bank. This is an interesting but usually unimportant coincidence—a person approaches the bank in one or the other role at a time. For the ATM application, the actors are *Customer*, *Bank*, and *Consortium*.

13.1.3 Finding Use Cases

For each actor, list the fundamentally different ways in which the actor uses the system. Each of these ways is a *use case*. The use cases partition the functionality of a system into a small number of discrete units, and all system behavior must fall under some use case. You may have trouble deciding where to place some piece of marginal behavior. Keep in mind that there are always borderline cases when making partitions; just make a decision even if it is somewhat arbitrary.

Each use case should represent a kind of service that the system provides—something that provides value to the actor. Try to keep all of the use cases at a similar level of detail. For example, if one use case in a bank is "apply for loan," then another use case should not be "withdraw cash from savings account using ATM." The latter description is much more detailed than the former; a better match would be "make withdrawal." Try to focus on the main goal of the use case and defer implementation choices.

At this point you can draw a preliminary use case diagram. Show the actors and the use cases, and connect actors to use cases. Usually you can associate a use case with the actor that initiates it, but other actors may be involved as well. Don't worry if you overlook some participating actors. They will become apparent when you elaborate the use cases. You should also write a one or two sentence summary for each use case.

ATM example. Figure 13.1 shows the use cases, and the bullets summarize them.

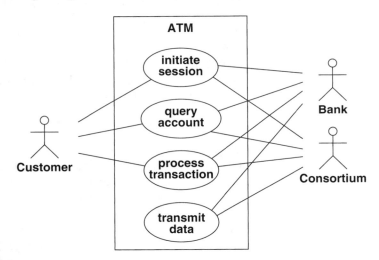

Figure 13.1 Use case diagram for the ATM. Use cases partition the functionality of a system into a small number of discrete units that cover its behavior.

- **Initiate session**. The ATM establishes the identity of the user and makes available a list of accounts and actions.
- **Query account**. The system provides general data for an account, such as the current balance, date of last transaction, and date of mailing for last statement.

- **Process transaction**. The ATM system performs an action that affects an account's balance, such as deposit, withdraw, and transfer. The ATM ensures that all completed transactions are ultimately written to the bank's database.

- **Transmit data**. The ATM uses the consortium's facilities to communicate with the appropriate bank computers.

13.1.4 Finding Initial and Final Events

Use cases partition system functionality into discrete pieces and show the actors that are involved with each piece, but they do not show the behavior clearly. To understand behavior, you must understand the execution sequences that cover each use case. You can start by finding the events that initiate each use case. Determine which actor initiates the use case and define the event that it sends to the system. In many cases, the initial event is a request for the service that the use case provides. In other cases, the initial event is an occurrence that triggers a chain of activity. Give this event a meaningful name, but don't try to determine its exact parameter list at this point.

You should also determine the final event or events and how much to include in each use case. For example, the use case of applying for a loan could continue until the application is submitted, until the loan is granted or rejected, until the money from the loan is delivered, or until the loan is finally paid off and closed. All of these could be reasonable choices. The modeler must define the scope of the use case by defining when it terminates.

ATM example. Here are initial and final events for each use case.

- **Initiate session**. The initial event is the customer's insertion of a cash card. There are two final events: the system keeps the cash card or the system returns the cash card.

- **Query account**. The initial event is a customer's request for account data. The final event is the system's delivery of account data to the customer.

- **Process transaction**. The initial event is the customer's initiation of a transaction. There are two final events: committing or aborting the transaction.

- **Transmit data**. The initial event could be triggered by a customer's request for account data. Another possible initial event could be recovery from a network, power, or another kind of failure. The final event is successful transmission of data.

13.1.5 Preparing Normal Scenarios

For each use case, prepare one or more typical dialogs to get a feel for expected system behavior. These scenarios illustrate the major interactions, external display formats, and information exchanges. A *scenario* is a sequence of events among a set of interacting objects. Think in terms of sample interactions, rather than trying to write down the general case directly. This will help you ensure that important steps are not overlooked and that the overall flow of interaction is smooth and correct.

For most problems, logical correctness depends on the sequences of interactions and not their exact times. (Real-time systems, however, do have specific timing requirements on interactions, but we do not address real-time systems in this book.)

Sometimes the problem statement describes the full interaction sequence, but most of the time you will have to invent (or at least flesh out) the interaction sequence. For example, the ATM problem statement indicates the need to obtain transaction data from the user but is vague about exactly what parameters are needed and in what order to ask for them. During analysis, try to avoid such details. For many applications, the order of gathering input is not crucial and can be deferred to design.

Prepare scenarios for "normal" cases—interactions without any unusual inputs or error conditions. An event occurs whenever information is exchanged between an object in the system and an outside agent, such as a user, a sensor, or another task. The information values exchanged are event parameters. For example, the event *password entered* has the password value as a parameter. Events with no parameters are meaningful and even common. The information in such an event is the fact that it has occurred. For each event, identify the actor (system, user, or other external agent) that caused the event and the parameters of the event.

ATM example. Figure 13.2 shows a normal scenario for each use case.

13.1.6 Adding Variation and Exception Scenarios

After you have prepared typical scenarios, consider "special" cases, such as omitted input, maximum and minimum values, and repeated values. Then consider error cases, including invalid values and failures to respond. For many interactive applications, error handling is the most difficult part of development. If possible, allow the user to abort an operation or roll back to a well-defined starting point at each step. Finally consider various other kinds of interactions that can be overlaid on basic interactions, such as help requests and status queries.

ATM example. Some variations and exceptions follow. We could prepare scenarios for each of these but will not go through the details here. (See the exercises.)

■ The ATM can't read the card.

■ The card has expired.

■ The ATM times out waiting for a response.

■ The amount is invalid.

■ The machine is out of cash or paper.

■ The communication lines are down.

■ The transaction is rejected because of suspicious patterns of card usage.

There are additional scenarios for administrative parts of the ATM system, such as authorizing new cards, adding banks to the consortium, and obtaining transaction logs. We will not explore these aspects.

13.1.7 Finding External Events

Examine the scenarios to find all external events—include all inputs, decisions, interrupts, and interactions to or from users or external devices. An event can trigger effects for a target object. Internal computation steps are not events, except for computations that interact with

Initiate session	The ATM asks the user to insert a card. The user inserts a cash card. The ATM accepts the card and reads its serial number. The ATM requests the password. The user enters "1234." The ATM verifies the password by contacting the consortium and bank. The ATM displays a menu of accounts and commands. . . . The user chooses the command to terminate the session. The ATM prints a receipt, ejects the card, and asks the user to take them. The user takes the receipt and the card. The ATM asks the user to insert a card
Query account	The ATM displays a menu of accounts and commands. The user chooses to query an account. The ATM contacts the consortium and bank which return the data. The ATM displays account data for the user. The ATM displays a menu of accounts and commands.
Process transaction	The ATM displays a menu of accounts and commands. The user selects an account withdrawal. The ATM asks for the amount of cash. The user enters $100. The ATM verifies that the withdrawal satisfies its policy limits. The ATM contacts the consortium and bank and verifies that the account has sufficient funds. The ATM dispenses the cash and asks the user to take it. The user takes the cash. The ATM displays a menu of accounts and commands.
Transmit data	The ATM requests account data from the consortium. The consortium accepts the request and forwards it to the appropriate bank. The bank receives the request and retrieves the desired data. The bank sends the data to the consortium. The consortium routes the data to the ATM.

Figure 13.2 Normal ATM scenarios. Prepare one or more scenarios for each use case.

the external world. Use scenarios to find normal events, but don't forget unusual events and error conditions.

A transmittal of information to an object is an event. For example, *enter password* is a message sent from external agent *User* to application object *ATM*. Some information flows are implicit. Many events have parameters.

Group together under a single name events that have the same effect on flow of control, even if their parameter values differ. For example, *enter password* should be an event, whose parameter is the password value. The choice of password value does not affect the flow of control; therefore events with different password values are all instances of the same kind of event. Similarly, *dispense cash* is also an event, since the amount of cash dispensed does not affect the flow of control. Event instances whose values affect the flow of control should be distinguished as different kinds of events. *Account OK, bad account,* and *bad password* are all different events; don't group them under *card status.*

You must decide when differences in quantitative values are important enough to distinguish as distinct events. For example, the different digits from a keyboard would usually be considered the same event, since the high-level control does not depend on numerical values. Pushing the "enter" key, however, might be considered a distinct event, since an application could treat it differently. The distinction among events depends on the application.

Prepare a sequence diagram for each scenario. A *sequence diagram* shows the participants in an interaction and the sequence of messages among them; each participant is assigned a column in a table. The sequence diagram clearly shows the sender and receiver of each event. If more than one object of the same class participates in the scenario, assign a separate column to each object. By scanning a particular column in the diagram, you can see the events that directly affect a particular object. From the sequence diagrams you can then summarize the events that each class sends and receives.

ATM example. Figure 13.3 shows a sequence diagram for the *process transaction* scenario. Figure 13.4 summarizes events with the arrows indicating the sender and receiver. For brevity, we do not show event parameters in Figure 13.4.

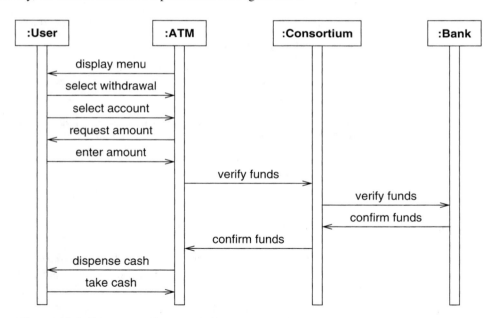

Figure 13.3 Sequence diagram for the *process transaction* scenario. A sequence diagram clearly shows the sender and receiver of each event.

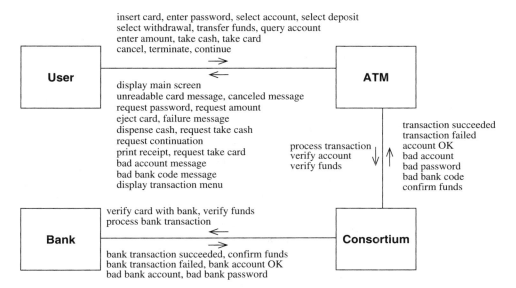

Figure 13.4 Events for the ATM case study. Tally the events in the scenarios and note the classes that send and receive each event.

13.1.8 Preparing Activity Diagrams for Complex Use Cases

Sequence diagrams capture the dialog and interplay between actors, but they do not clearly show alternatives and decisions. For example, you need one sequence diagram for the main flow of interaction and additional sequence diagrams for each error and decision point. Activity diagrams let you consolidate all this behavior by documenting forks and merges in the control flow. It is certainly appropriate to use activity diagrams to document business logic during analysis, but do not use them as an excuse to begin implementation.

ATM example. As Figure 13.5 shows, when the user inserts a card, there are many possible responses. Some responses indicate a possible problem with the card or account; hence the ATM retains the card. Only the successful completion of the tests allows ATM processing to proceed.

13.1.9 Organizing Actors and Use Cases

The next step is to organize use cases with relationships (include, extend, and generalization—see Chapter 8). This is especially helpful for large and complex systems. As with the class and state models, we defer organization until the base use cases are in place. Otherwise, there is too much of a risk of distorting the structure to match preconceived notions.

Similarly, you can also organize actors with generalization. For example, an *Administrator* might be an *Operator* with additional privileges.

ATM example. Figure 13.6 organizes the use cases with the include relationship.

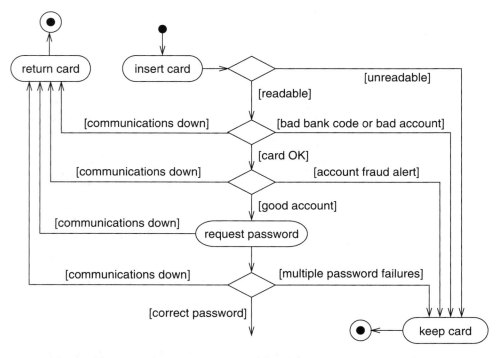

Figure 13.5 Activity diagram for card verification. You can use activity
diagrams to document business logic, but do not use them as
an excuse to begin premature implementation.

13.1.10 Checking Against the Domain Class Model

At this point, the application and domain models should be mostly consistent. The actors,
use cases, and scenarios are all based on classes and concepts from the domain model. Recall
that one of the steps in constructing the domain class model is to test access paths. In reality,
such testing is a first attempt at use cases.

Cross check the application and domain models to ensure that there are no inconsistencies. Examine the scenarios and make sure that the domain model has all the necessary data.
Also make sure that the domain model covers all event parameters.

13.2 Application Class Model

Application classes define the application itself, rather than the real-world objects that the application acts on. Most application classes are computer-oriented and define the way that users
perceive the application. You can construct an application class model with the following steps.

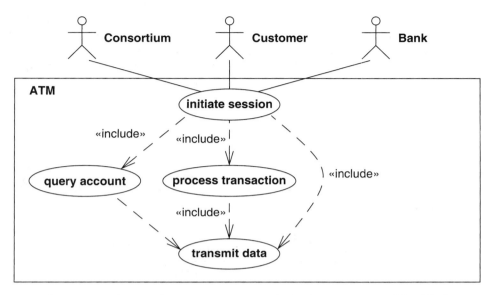

Figure 13.6 Organizing use cases. Once the basic use cases are identified, you can organize them with relationships.

- Specify user interfaces. [13.2.1]
- Define boundary classes. [13.2.2]
- Determine controllers. [13.2.3]
- Check against the interaction model. [13.2.4]

13.2.1 Specifying User Interfaces

Most interactions can be separated into two parts: application logic and the user interface. A *user interface* is an object or group of objects that provides the user of a system with a coherent way to access its domain objects, commands, and application options. During analysis the emphasis is on the information flow and control, rather than the presentation format. The same program logic can accept input from command lines, files, mouse buttons, touch panels, physical push buttons, or remote links, if the surface details are carefully isolated.

During analysis treat the user interface at a coarse level of detail. Don't worry about how to input individual pieces of data. Instead, try to determine the commands that the user can perform—a *command* is a large-scale request for a service. For example, "make a flight reservation" and "find matches for a phrase in a database" would be commands. The format of inputting the information for the commands and invoking them is relatively easy to change, so work on defining the commands first.

Nevertheless, it is acceptable to sketch out a sample interface to help you visualize the operation of an application and see if anything important has been forgotten. You may also want to mock up the interface so that users can try it. Dummy procedures can simulate application logic. Decoupling application logic from the user interface lets you evaluate the "look and feel" of the user interface while the application is under development.

ATM example. Figure 13.7 shows a possible ATM layout. Its exact details are not important at this point. The important thing is the information exchanged.

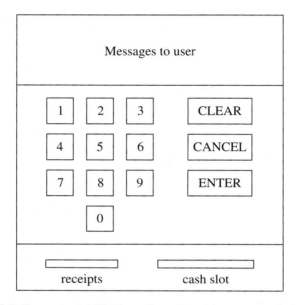

Figure 13.7 Format of ATM interface. Sometimes a sample interface
can help you visualize the operation of an application.

13.2.2 Defining Boundary Classes

A system must be able to operate with and accept information from external sources, but it should not have its internal structure dictated by them. It is often helpful to define boundary classes to isolate the inside of a system from the external world. A *boundary class* is a class that provides a staging area for communications between a system and an external source. A boundary class understands the format of one or more external sources and converts information for transmission to and from the internal system.

ATM example. It would be helpful to define boundary classes (*CashCardBoundary*, *AccountBoundary*) to encapsulate the communication between the ATM and the consortium. This interface will increase flexibility and make it easier to support additional consortiums.

13.2.3 Determining Controllers

A *controller* is an active object that manages control within an application. It receives signals from the outside world or from objects within the system, reacts to them, invokes operations on the objects in the system, and sends signals to the outside world. A controller is a piece of reified behavior captured in the form of an object—behavior that can be manipulated and transformed more easily than plain code. At the heart of most applications are one or more controllers that sequence the behavior of the application.

Most of the work in designing a controller is in modeling its state diagram. In the application class model, however, you should capture the existence of the controllers in a system, the control information that each one maintains, and the associations from the controllers to other objects in the system.

ATM example. It is apparent from the scenarios in Figure 13.2 that the ATM has two major control loops. The outer loop verifies customers and accounts. The inner loop services transactions. Each of these loops could most naturally be handled with a controller.

13.2.4 Checking Against the Interaction Model

As you build the application class model, go over the use cases and think about how they would work. For example, if a user sends a command to the application, the parameters of the command must come from some user-interface object. The requesting of the command itself must come from some controller object. When the domain and application class models are in place, you should be able to simulate a use case with the classes. Think in terms of navigation of the models, as we discussed in Chapter 3. This manual simulation helps to establish that all the pieces are in place.

ATM example. Figure 13.8 shows a preliminary application class model and the domain classes with which it interacts. There are two interfaces—one for users and the other for communicating with the consortium. The application model just has stubs for these classes, because it is not clear how to elaborate them at this time.

Note that the boundary classes "flatten" the data structure and combine information from multiple domain classes. For simplicity, it is desirable to minimize the number of boundary classes and their relationships.

The *TransactionController* handles both queries on accounts and the processing of transactions. The *SessionController* manages *ATMsessions*, each of which services a customer. Each *ATMsession* may or may not have a valid *CashCard* and *Account*. The *SessionController* has a status of *ready*, *impaired* (such as out of paper or cash but still able to operate for some functions), or *down* (such as a communications failure). There is a log of *ControllerProblems* and the specific problem type (bad card reader, out of paper, out of cash, communication lines down, etc.).

13.3 Application State Model

The application state model focuses on application classes and augments the domain state model. Application classes are more likely to have important temporal behavior than domain classes.

First identify application classes with multiple states and use the interaction model to find events for these classes. Then organize permissible event sequences for each class with

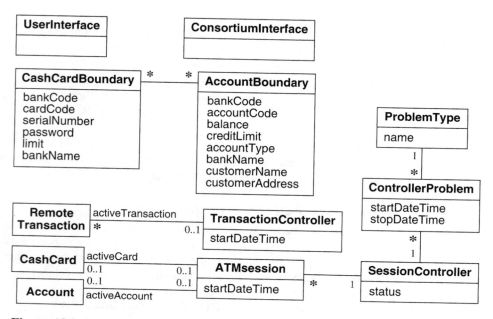

Figure 13.8 ATM application class model. Application classes augment the domain
classes and are necessary for development.

a state diagram. Next, check the various state diagrams to make sure that common events
match. And finally check the state diagrams against the class and interaction models to ensure consistency.

You can construct an application state model with the following steps.

- Determine application classes with states. [13.3.1]
- Find events. [13.3.2]
- Build state diagrams. [13.3.3]
- Check against other state diagrams. [13.3.4]
- Check against the class model. [13.3.5]
- Check against the interaction model. [13.3.6]

13.3.1 Determining Application Classes with States

The application class model adds computer-oriented classes that are prominent to users and
important to the operation of an application. Consider each application class and determine
which ones have multiple states. User interface classes and controller classes are good candidates for state models. In contrast, boundary classes tend to be static and used for staging
data import and export—consequently they are less likely to involve a state model.

ATM example. The user interface classes do not seem to have any substance. This is
probably because our understanding of the user interface is incomplete at this point in devel-

opment. The boundary classes also lack state behavior. However, the controllers do have important states that we will elaborate.

13.3.2 Finding Events

For the application interaction model, you prepared a number of scenarios. Now study those scenarios and extract events. Even though the scenarios may not cover every contingency, they ensure that you do not overlook common interactions and they highlight the major events.

Note the contrast between the domain and application processes for state models. With the domain model, first we find states and then we find events. That is because the domain model focuses on data—significant groupings of data form states that are subject to events. With the application model, in contrast, first we find events and then we determine states. The application model's early attention to events is a consequence of the emphasis on behavior— use cases are elaborated with scenarios that reveal events.

ATM example. We revisit the scenarios from the application interaction model. Some events are: *insert card*, *enter password*, *end session*, and *take card*.

13.3.3 Building State Diagrams

The next step is to build a state diagram for each application class with temporal behavior. Choose one of these classes and consider a sequence diagram. Arrange the events involving the class into a path whose arcs are labeled by the events. The interval between any two events is a state. Give each state a name, if a name is meaningful, but don't bother if it is not. Now merge other sequence diagrams into the state diagram. The initial state diagram will be a sequence of events and states. Every scenario or sequence diagram corresponds to a path through the state diagram.

Now find loops within the diagram. If a sequence of events can be repeated indefinitely, then they form a loop. In a loop, the first state and the last state are identical. If the object "remembers" that it has traversed a loop, then the two states are not really identical, and a simple loop is incorrect. At least one state in a loop must have multiple transactions leaving it or the loop will never terminate.

Once you have found the loops, merge other sequence diagrams into the state diagram. Find the point in each sequence diagram where it diverges from previous ones. This point corresponds to an existing state in the diagram. Attach the new event sequence to the existing state as an alternative path. While examining sequence diagrams, you may think of other possible events that can occur at each state; add them to the state diagram as well.

The hardest thing is deciding at which state an alternate path rejoins the existing diagram. Two paths join at a state if the object "forgets" which one was taken. In many cases, it is obvious from knowledge of the application that two states are identical. For example, inserting two nickels into a vending machine is equivalent to inserting one dime.

Beware of two paths that appear identical but can be distinguished under some circumstances. For example, some systems repeat the input sequence if the user makes an error entering information but give up after a certain number of failures. The repeat sequence is almost the same except that it remembers the past failures. The difference can be glossed over by adding a parameter, such as *number of failures,* to remember information. At least one transition must depend on the parameter.

The judicious use of parameters and conditional transitions can simplify state diagrams considerably but at the cost of mixing together state information and data. State diagrams with too much data dependency can be confusing and counterintuitive. Another alternative is to partition a state diagram into two concurrent subdiagrams, using one subdiagram for the main line and the other for the distinguishing information. For example, a subdiagram to allow for one user failure might have states *No error* and *One error.*

After normal events have been considered, add variation and exception cases. Consider events that occur at awkward times—for example, a request to cancel a transaction after it has been submitted for processing. In cases when the user (or other external agent) may fail to respond promptly and some resource must be reclaimed, a *time-out* event can be generated after a given interval. Handling user errors cleanly often requires more thought and code than the normal case. Error handling often complicates an otherwise clean and compact program structure, but it must be done.

You are finished with the state diagram of a class when the diagram covers all scenarios and the diagram handles all events that can affect a state. You can use the state diagram to suggest new scenarios by considering how some event not already handled should affect a state. Posing "what if" questions is a good way to test for completeness and error-handling capabilities.

If there are complex interactions with independent inputs, you can use a nested state diagram, as Chapter 6 describes. Otherwise a flat state diagram suffices. Repeat the above process of building state diagrams for each class that has time-dependent behavior.

ATM example. Figure 13.9 shows the state diagram for the *SessionController*. The middle of the diagram has the main behavior of processing the card and password. A communications failure can interrupt processing at any time. The ATM returns the card upon a communications failure, but keeps it if there are any suspicious circumstances. After finishing transactions, receipt printing occurs in parallel to card ejection, and the user can take the receipt and card in any order.

Figure 13.10 and Figure 13.11 show the state diagram for the *TransactionController* that is spawned by the *SessionController*. (See the exercises for the other subdiagrams of Figure 13.10.) We have separated the *TransactionController* and the *SessionController* because their purposes are much different—the *SessionController* focuses on verifying users, while the *TransactionController* services account inquiries and balance changes.

13.3.4 Checking Against Other State Diagrams

Check the state diagrams of each class for completeness and consistency. Every event should have a sender and a receiver, occasionally the same object. States without predecessors or successors are suspicious; make sure they represent starting or termination points of the interaction sequence. Follow the effects of an input event from object to object through the system to make sure that they match the scenarios. Objects are inherently concurrent; beware of synchronization errors where an input occurs at an awkward time. Make sure that corresponding events on different state diagrams are consistent.

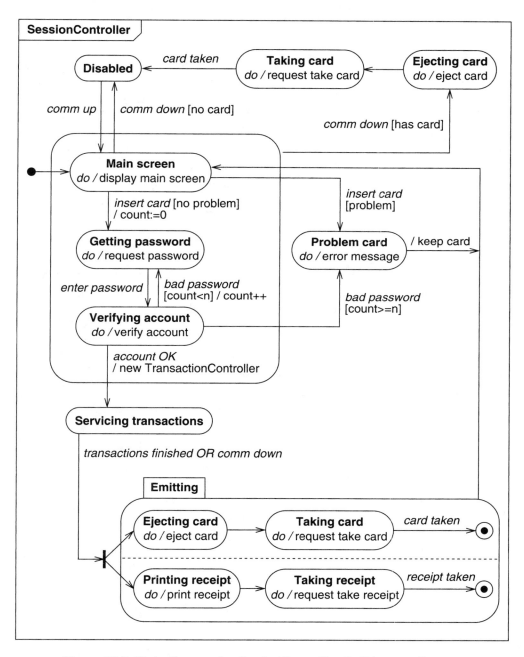

Figure 13.9 State diagram for *SessionController*. Build a state diagram for each application class with temporal behavior.

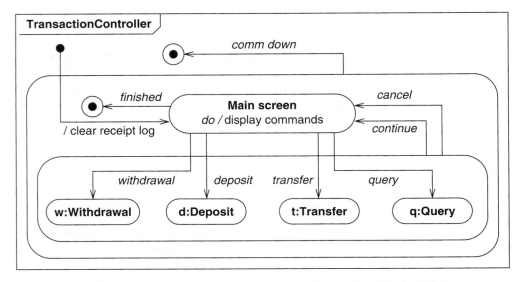

Figure 13.10 State diagram for *TransactionController*. Obtain information from the scenarios of the interaction model.

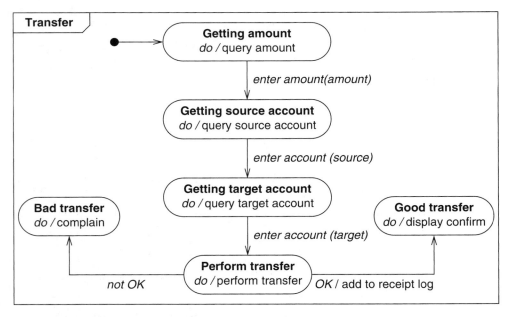

Figure 13.11 State diagram for *Transfer*. This diagram elaborates the *Transfer* state in Figure 13.10.

ATM example. The *SessionController* initiates the *TransactionController*, and the termination of the *TransactionController* causes the *SessionController* to resume.

13.3.5 Checking Against the Class Model

Similarly, make sure that the state diagrams are consistent with the domain and application class models.

      ATM example. Multiple ATMs can potentially concurrently access an account. Account access needs to be controlled to ensure that only one update at a time is applied. We will not resolve the details here.

13.3.6 Checking Against the Interaction Model

When the state model is ready, go back and check it against the scenarios of the interaction model. Simulate each behavior sequence by hand and verify that the state diagram gives the correct behavior. If an error is discovered, change either the state diagram or the scenarios. Sometimes a state diagram will uncover irregularities in the scenarios, so don't assume that the scenarios are always correct.

      Then take the state model and trace out legitimate paths. These represent additional scenarios. Ask yourself whether they make sense. If not, then modify the state diagram. Often, however, you will discover useful behavior that you had not considered before. The mark of a good design is the discovery of unexpected information that follows from the design, properties that appear meaningful (and often seem obvious) once they are observed.

      ATM example. As best as we can tell right now, the state diagrams are sound and consistent with the scenarios.

13.4 Adding Operations

Our style of object-oriented analysis places much less emphasis on defining operations than the traditional programming-based methodologies. We de-emphasize operations because the list of potentially useful operations is open-ended and it is difficult to know when to stop adding them. Operations arise from the following sources, and you should add major operations now. Chapter 15 discusses detailed operations.

13.4.1 Operations from the Class Model

The reading and writing of attribute values and association links are implied by the class model, and you need not show them explicitly. During analysis all attributes and associations are assumed to be accessible.

13.4.2 Operations from Use Cases

Most of the complex functionality of a system comes from its use cases. During the construction of the interaction model, use cases lead to activities. Many of these correspond to operations on the class model.

ATM example. *Consortium* has the activity *verifyBankCode,* and *Bank* has the activity *verifyPassword.* You could implement Figure 13.5 with the operation *verifyCashCard* on class *ATM*.

13.4.3 Shopping-List Operations

Sometimes the real-world behavior of classes suggests operations. Meyer [Meyer-97] calls this a "shopping list," because the operations are not dependent on a particular application but are meaningful in their own right. Shopping-list operations provide an opportunity to broaden a class definition beyond the narrow needs of the immediate problem.

ATM example. Shopping-list operations include:

■ account.close()

■ bank.createSavingsAccount(customer): account

■ bank.createCheckingAccount(customer): account

■ bank.createCashCardAuth(customer): cashCardAuthorization

■ cashCardAuthorization.addAccount (account)

■ cashCardAuthorization.removeAccount (account)

■ cashCardAuthorization.close()

13.4.4 Simplifying Operations

Examine the class model for similar operations and variations in form on a single operation. Try to broaden the definition of an operation to encompass such variations and special cases. Use inheritance where possible to reduce the number of distinct operations. Introduce new superclasses as needed to simplify the operations, provided that the new superclasses are not forced and unnatural. Locate each operation at the correct level within the class hierarchy. A result of this refinement is often fewer, more powerful operations that are nevertheless simpler to specify than the original operations, because they are more uniform and general.

ATM example. The ATM example does not require simplification. Figure 13.12 adds some operations to the ATM domain class model from Chapter 12.

13.5 Chapter Summary

The purpose of analysis is to understand the problem so that a correct design can be constructed. A good analysis captures the essential features of the problem without introducing implementation artifacts that prematurely restrict design decisions.

There are two phases of analysis—domain and application. Domain analysis captures general knowledge about an application. Domain analysis involves class models and sometimes state models but seldom has an interaction model. In contrast, application analysis focuses on major application artifacts that are important, visible to users, and must be approved by them. The interaction model dominates application analysis, but the class and state models are also important.

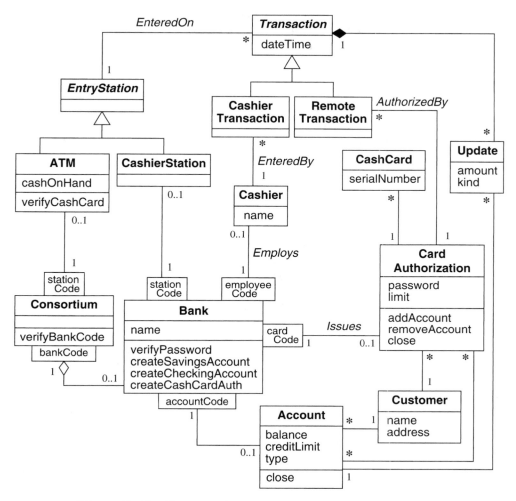

Figure 13.12 ATM domain class model with some operations

The application interaction model shows the interactions between the system and the outside world. First determine the precise scope—the system boundary. Then, define actors for external objects that communicate directly with the system. Also, define use cases for externally visible functionality. For each use case, make up scenarios for normal cases, variations, extreme cases, and exceptions. You can clarify complex use cases with activity diagrams and organize the use cases and actors with relationships. Finally, check the use cases against the domain class model to ensure that there are no inconsistencies.

Next augment the domain classes with application classes. Application classes arise from user interfaces, boundary classes, and controllers. Carefully check the use cases and scenarios to find them.

The last phase of application analysis is to build an application state model. This state model tends to be richer and reveals more behavior than does the domain state model. First identify application classes with multiple states and study the interaction scenarios to find events for these classes. The most difficult aspect is to reconcile the various scenarios and detect overlap and closure of loops. As you complete the state model, check the state diagrams for consistency with each other, as well as the class and interaction models.

We emphasized the need for abstraction during domain analysis, and it is also important for application analysis. Try to think expansively as you construct your models. Do not commit an application to arbitrary business practices that may change over time. Instead, try to build in flexibility that will anticipate and accommodate future changes.

activity diagram	controller
actor	scenario
application analysis	sequence diagram
boundary class	shopping-list operation
building the application class model	system boundary
building the application interaction model	use case
building the application state model	user interface

Figure 13.13 Key concepts for Chapter 13

Bibliographic Notes

Meyer [Meyer-97] provides many useful insights into the principles underlying a good design. He advocates the use of data-directed bottom-up design, discovery of "shopping-list operations," and the lack of any "main program" in a system. He makes effective use of assertions, preconditions, and postconditions for specifying operations.

References

[Meyer-97] Bertrand Meyer. *Object-Oriented Software Construction, Second Edition*. Upper Saddle River, NJ: Prentice Hall, 1997.

Exercises

13.1   (4) Prepare scenarios for the variations and exception bullets in Section 13.1.6.

13.2   (6) Complete the *Deposit*, *Withdrawal*, and *Query* subdiagrams from Figure 13.10.

13.3   (4) Figure E13.1 is a class diagram for Exercise 11.6a. *Sender* and *Receiver* are the only classes with important temporal behavior. Construct a sequence diagram for the following scenario: Sender tries to establish a connection to the receiver by sending a start-of-transaction packet.

The receiver successfully reads the packet and replies with an acknowledgment. The sender then transmits a start-of-file packet, which is acknowledged. Then, the file data is transmitted in three acknowledged packets, followed by end of file and end of transaction, which are also acknowledged.

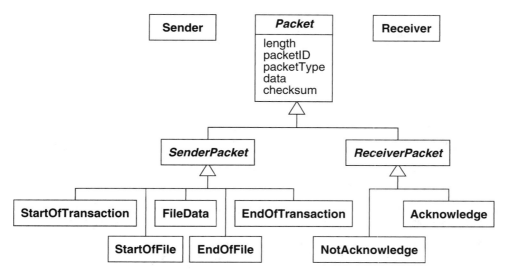

Figure E13.1 A class diagram for a file transfer system

13.4 (3) Prepare additional sequence diagrams for the previous example to include errors caused by noise corruption of each type of sender packet. Revise your previous answer.

13.5 (5) Prepare a state diagram for a file transfer system from the sequence diagrams prepared in Exercises 13.3 and 13.4.

13.6 (8) Prepare a state diagram for a bike odometer from the given scenarios.

■ The user turns on the odometer on a bike that is moving.
The odometer displays the current time. The user presses the mode button.
The odometer displays the distance biked today. The user presses the mode button.
The odometer displays the high speed since reset. The user presses the mode button.
The odometer displays the riding time since reset. The user presses the mode button.
The odometer displays the distance since reset. The user presses the mode button.
The odometer displays the average speed since reset. The user presses the mode button.
The odometer displays the current time...

■ The user turns on the odometer on a bike that is stationary.
The odometer displays the current time. The user presses the mode button.
The odometer displays the total distance biked. The user presses the mode button.
The odometer displays the total time biked. The user presses the mode button.
The odometer displays the distance biked today. The user presses the mode button.
The odometer displays the high speed since reset. The user presses the mode button.
The odometer displays the riding time since reset. The user presses the mode button.
The odometer displays the distance since reset. The user presses the mode button.

The odometer displays the average speed since reset. The user presses the mode button.
The odometer displays the current time...

■ The odometer displays the distance biked today.
The clock rolls over past midnight and begins a new day.
The odometer sets the distance biked today to zero.

■ The user stops biking.
Four minutes elapse.
The odometer display dims.
The user presses the mode button.
The odometer lights up.

■ The user holds the mode button.
The odometer sets all variables computed since reset to zero.

Consider the simple diagram editor from Exercises 12.3–12.8.

13.7   (2) Describe the system boundary for this application in a few sentences.

13.8   (2) Identify two actors for the application.

13.9   (4) List at least four use cases and define them with a one- or two-sentence bullet. Construct a use case diagram.

13.10 (6) Organize commonality in the use cases with use case relationships. You can create new use cases for common behavior. (Instructor's note: You should give the students the answer to the previous exercise.)

13.11 (4) Prepare a normal scenario for making the drawing in Figure E12.1. Include at least ten editor operations from the problem description in Chapter 12. Do not worry about error conditions.

13.12 (3) Prepare three error scenarios, starting from the previous exercise.

13.13 (4) Prepare sequence diagrams for the scenarios you prepared in the previous exercise.

Consider the computerized scoring system from Exercises 12.9–12.13.

13.14 (2) Describe the system boundary for this application in a few sentences.

13.15 (2) Identify four actors for the application.

13.16 (5) Here are some use cases: register child, schedule meet, schedule season, score figure, judge figure, and compute statistics. Define each one with a one- or two-sentence bullet. Construct a use case diagram.

13.17 (3) Prepare a scenario for setting up the scoring system at the beginning of a season. Enter data on teams, competitors, and judges. Prepare a schedule of meets for the season and select events for each meet. Enter difficulty factors for figures. Include at least 2 teams, 6 competitors, 3 judges, 3 meets, and 12 events. Do not worry about error conditions.

13.18 (3) Prepare three error scenarios, starting from Exercise 13.17.

13.19 (3) Prepare a scenario for printing and processing preregistration forms for the scoring system. In the scenario two children should change their address and another two children should indicate that they are unable to attend. Assign a number to each contestant.

13.20 (6) Prepare an activity diagram for the following computation. Show swim lanes for competitor, computer operator, judge, and scorekeeper.

The computer operator calls the competitor's number as it appears on the display. The competitor verifies her number and then performs the figure. The three judges hold up their scores. A scorekeeper reads the scores. As they are read, the computer operator enters them into the computer.

13.21 (3) Prepare a shopping list of operations for the scoring system and place them in a class diagram.

13.22 (5) For each method listed in the previous exercise, summarize what the method should do.

14

System Design

After you have analyzed a problem, you must decide how to approach the design. During system design you devise the high-level strategy—the *system architecture*—for solving the problem and building a solution. You make decisions about the organization of the system into subsystems, the allocation of subsystems to hardware and software, and major policy decisions that form the basis for class design.

In this chapter you will learn about the many aspects that you should consider when formulating a system design. We also list several common architectural styles that you can use as a starting point. This list is not meant to be complete; new architectures can always be invented. The treatment in this chapter is intended for small to medium software development efforts; large complex systems, involving more than about ten developers, are limited by human communication issues and require a much greater emphasis on logistics. Most of the suggestions in this chapter are suitable for non-OO as well as OO systems.

14.1 Overview of System Design

During analysis, the focus is on *what* needs to be done, independent of *how* it is done. During design, developers make decisions about how the problem will be solved, first at a high level and then with more detail.

System design is the first design stage for devising the basic approach to solving the problem. During system design, developers decide the overall structure and style. The system architecture determines the organization of the system into subsystems. In addition, the architecture provides the context for the detailed decisions that are made in later stages. You must make the following decisions.

■   Estimate system performance. [14.2]

■   Make a reuse plan. [14.3]

- Organize the system into subsystems. [14.4]
- Identify concurrency inherent in the problem. [14.5]
- Allocate subsystems to hardware. [14.6]
- Manage data stores. [14.7]
- Handle global resources. [14.8]
- Choose a software control strategy. [14.9]
- Handle boundary conditions. [14.10]
- Set trade-off priorities. [14.11]
- Select an architectural style. [14.12]

You can often choose the architecture of a system by analogy to previous systems. Certain kinds of architecture pertain to broad classes of problems. Section 14.12 surveys several common architectures and describes their corresponding problems. Not all problems can be solved by one of these architectures, but many can. You can construct additional architectures by combining these forms.

14.2 Estimating Performance

Early in the planning for a new system you should prepare a rough performance estimate. Engineers call this a "back of the envelope" calculation. The purpose is not to achieve high accuracy, but merely to determine if the system is feasible. Getting within a factor of two is usually sufficient, although what you can achieve depends on the problem. The calculation should be fast and involve common sense. You will have to make simplifying assumptions. Don't worry about details—just approximate, estimate, and guess, if necessary.

ATM example. Suppose we are planning an ATM network for a bank. We might proceed as follows. The bank has 40 branches. Suppose there are an equal number of terminals in supermarkets and other stores. Suppose on a busy day half the terminals are busy at once. (We could assume all of the terminals are busy without changing the results much. The point is to establish reasonable performance limits.) Suppose that each customer takes one minute to perform a session, and that most transactions involve a single deposit or withdrawal. So we estimate a peak requirement of about 40 transactions a minute, or about one per second. This may not be precise, but it shows that we do not require unusually fast computer hardware. The situation would be much different if we were estimating for an online bookseller or stockbroker, in which case the computer hardware would become a big issue.

You can perform similar estimates for data storage. Count the number of customers, estimate the amount of data for each one, and multiply. In the case of a bank, the requirements for data storage are more severe than for ATM computing power, but they are hardly enormous. Again, the situation would be different for a satellite-based ground imaging system, in which both data storage and access bandwidth would be key architectural issues.

14.3 Making a Reuse Plan

Reuse is often cited as an advantage of OO technology, but reuse does not happen automatically. There are two very different aspects of reuse—using existing things and creating reusable new things. It is much easier to reuse existing things than to design new things for uncertain uses to come. Of course, someone must have designed things in the past in order for us to reuse them now. The point is that most developers reuse existing things, and only a small fraction of developers create new things. Don't feel that you should start with OO technology by building reusable things—that takes a great deal of experience.

Reusable things include models, libraries, frameworks, and patterns. Reuse of models is often the most practical form of reuse. The logic in a model can apply to multiple problems.

14.3.1 Libraries

A *library* is a collection of classes that are useful in many contexts. The collection of classes must be carefully organized, so that users can find them. Good organization takes a lot of work, and it can be difficult to decide where to place everything. Online searching can help, but is no substitute for careful organization. In addition, the classes must have accurate and thorough descriptions to help users determine their relevance. [Korson-92] notes several qualities of "good" class libraries.

■ **Coherence**. A class library should be organized about a few, well-focused themes.

■ **Completeness**. A class library should provide complete behavior for the chosen themes.

■ **Consistency**. Polymorphic operations should have consistent names and signatures across classes.

■ **Efficiency**. A library should provide alternative implementations of algorithms (such as various sort algorithms) that trade time and space.

■ **Extensibility**. The user should be able to define subclasses for library classes.

■ **Genericity**. A library should use parameterized class definitions where appropriate.

Unfortunately, problems can arise when integrating class libraries from multiple sources, as shown below [Berlin-90]. Developers often disperse pragmatic decisions across classes and inheritance hierarchies. Class libraries may adopt policies that are individually sensible, but fundamentally incompatible with those of other class libraries. You cannot fix such pragmatic inconsistencies by specializing a class or adding code. Instead, you must break encapsulation and rework the source code. These problems are so severe that they will effectively limit your ability to reuse code from class libraries.

■ **Argument validation**. An application may validate arguments as a collection or individually as entered. Collective validation is appropriate for command interfaces; the user enters all arguments, and only then are they checked. In contrast, responsive user interfaces validate each argument or interdependent group of arguments as it is entered. A combination of class libraries, some that validate by collection and others that validate by individual, would yield an awkward user interface.

- **Error handling**. Class libraries use different error-handling techniques. Methods in one library may return error codes to the calling routine, for example, while methods in another library may directly deal with errors.

- **Control paradigms**. Applications may adopt event-driven or procedure-driven control. With event-driven control the user interface invokes application methods. With procedure-driven control the application calls user interface methods. It is difficult to combine both kinds of user interface within an application.

- **Group operations**. Group operations are often inefficient and incomplete. For example, an object-delete primitive may acquire database locks, make the deletion, and then commit the transaction. If you want to delete a group of objects as a transaction, the class library must have a group-delete function.

- **Garbage collection**. Class libraries use different strategies to manage memory allocation and avoid memory leaks. A library may manage memory for strings by returning a pointer to the actual string, returning a copy of the string, or returning a pointer with read-only access. Garbage collection strategies may also differ: mark and sweep, reference counting, or letting the application handle garbage collection (in C++, for example).

- **Name collisions**. Class names, public attributes, and public methods lie within a global name space, so you must hope they do not collide for different class libraries. Most class libraries add a distinguishing prefix to names to reduce the likelihood of collisions.

14.3.2 Frameworks

A *framework* [Johnson-88] is a skeletal structure of a program that must be elaborated to build a complete application. This elaboration often consists of specializing abstract classes with behavior specific to an individual application. A class library may accompany a framework, so that the user can perform much of the specialization by choosing the appropriate subclasses rather than programming subclass behavior from scratch. Frameworks consist of more than just the classes involved and include a paradigm for flow of control and shared invariants. Frameworks tend to be specific to a category of applications; framework class libraries are typically application specific and not suitable for general use.

14.3.3 Patterns

A *pattern* is a proven solution to a general problem. Various patterns target different phases of the software development lifecycle. There are patterns for analysis, architecture, design, and implementation. You can achieve reuse by using existing patterns, rather than reinventing solutions from scratch. A pattern comes with guidelines on when to use it, as well as trade-offs on its use.

There are many benefits of patterns. One advantage is that a pattern has been carefully considered by others and has already been applied to past problems. Consequently, a pattern is more likely to be correct and robust than an untested, custom solution. Also when you use patterns, you tap into a language that is familiar to many developers. A body of literature is available that documents patterns, explaining their subtleties and nuances. You can regard patterns as extending a modeling language—you need not think only in terms of primitives; you can also think in terms of recurring combinations. Patterns are prototypical model fragments that distill some of the knowledge of experts.

A pattern is different from a framework. A pattern is typically a small number of classes and relationships. In contrast, a framework is much broader in scope (typically at least an order of magnitude larger) and covers an entire subsystem or application.

ATM example. The notion of a transaction offers some possibility of reuse—transactions are a frequent occurrence in computer systems, and there is commercial software to support them. There may also be an opportunity for reuse with the communications infrastructure that connects the consortium to ATMs and bank computers.

14.4 Breaking a System into Subsystems

For all but the smallest applications, the first step in system design is to divide the system into pieces. Each major piece of a system is called a subsystem. Each subsystem is based on some common theme, such as similar functionality, the same physical location, or execution on the same kind of hardware. For example, a spaceship computer might include subsystems for life support, navigation, engine control, and running scientific experiments.

A *subsystem* is not an object nor a function but a group of classes, associations, operations, events, and constraints that are interrelated and have a well-defined and (hopefully) small interface with other subsystems. A subsystem is usually identified by the services it provides. A *service* is a group of related functions that share some common purpose, such as processing I/O, drawing pictures, or performing arithmetic. A subsystem defines a coherent way of looking at part of the problem. For example, the file system within an operating system is a subsystem; it comprises a set of related abstractions that are largely independent of abstractions in other subsystems, such as memory management and process control.

Each subsystem has a well-defined interface to the rest of the system. The interface specifies the form of all interactions and the information flow across subsystem boundaries but does not specify how the subsystem is implemented internally. Each subsystem can then be designed independently without affecting the others.

You should define subsystems so that most interactions are internal, rather than across subsystem boundaries. This reduces the dependencies among subsystems. A system should be divided into a small number of subsystems; 20 is probably too many. Each subsystem may in turn be decomposed into smaller subsystems of its own.

The relationship between two subsystems can be client-server or peer-to-peer. In a *client-server relationship*, the client calls on the server, which performs some service and replies with a result. The client must know the server's interface, but the server need not know its clients' interfaces because clients initiate all interactions.

In a *peer-to-peer relationship*, each subsystem may call on the others. A communication from one subsystem to another is not necessarily followed by an immediate response. Peer-to-peer interactions are more complicated, because the subsystems must know each other's interfaces. Communications cycles can occur that are hard to understand and liable to subtle design errors. Look for client-server decompositions whenever possible, because a one-way interaction is much easier to build, understand, and change than a two-way interaction.

The decomposition of systems into subsystems may be organized as a sequence of horizontal layers or vertical partitions.

14.4.1 Layers

A *layered system* is an ordered set of virtual worlds (a set of *tiers*), each built in terms of the ones below it and providing the implementation basis for the ones above it. The objects in each layer can be independent, although there is often some correspondence between objects in different layers. Knowledge is one-way only—a subsystem knows about the layers below it, but has no knowledge of the layers above it. A client-server relationship exists between upper layers (users of services) and lower layers (providers of services).

In an interactive graphics system, for example, windows are made from screen operations, which are implemented using pixel operations, which execute as device I/O operations. Each layer may have its own set of classes and operations. Each layer is implemented in terms of the classes and operations of lower layers.

Layered architectures come in two forms: closed and open. In a *closed architecture*, each layer is built only in terms of the immediate lower layer. This reduces the dependencies between layers and allows changes to be made most easily, because a layer's interface affects only the next layer. In an *open architecture*, a layer can use features of any lower layer to any depth. This reduces the need to redefine operations at each level, which can result in a more efficient and compact code. However, an open architecture does not observe the principle of information hiding. Changes to a subsystem can affect any higher subsystem, so an open architecture is less robust than a closed architecture. Both kinds of architectures are useful; the designer must weigh the relative value of efficiency and modularity.

Usually the problem statement specifies only the top and bottom layers: The top is the desired system and the bottom is the available resources (hardware, operating system, existing libraries). If the disparity between the two is too great (as it often is), then you must introduce intermediate layers to reduce the conceptual gap between adjoining layers.

You can port a system constructed in layers to other hardware/software platforms by rewriting one layer. It is a good practice to introduce at least one layer of abstraction between the application and any services provided by the operating system or hardware. Define a layer of interface classes providing logical services and map them onto the concrete services that are system dependent.

14.4.2 Partitions

Partitions vertically divide a system into several independent or weakly coupled subsystems, each providing one kind of service. For example, a computer operating system includes a file system, process control, virtual memory management, and device control. The subsystems may have some knowledge of each other, but this knowledge is not deep and avoids major design dependencies.

One difference between layers and partitions is that layers vary in their level of abstraction. In contrast, partitions merely divide a system into pieces, all of which have a similar level of abstraction. Another difference is that layers ultimately depend on each other, usually in a client-server relationship through an open or closed architecture. In contrast, partitions are peers that are independent or mutually dependent (peer-to-peer relationship).

14.4.3 Combining Layers and Partitions

You can decompose a system into subsystems by combining layers and partitions. Layers can be partitioned, and partitions can be layered. Figure 14.1 shows a block diagram of a typical application, which involves simulation and interactive graphics. Most large systems require a mixture of layers and partitions.

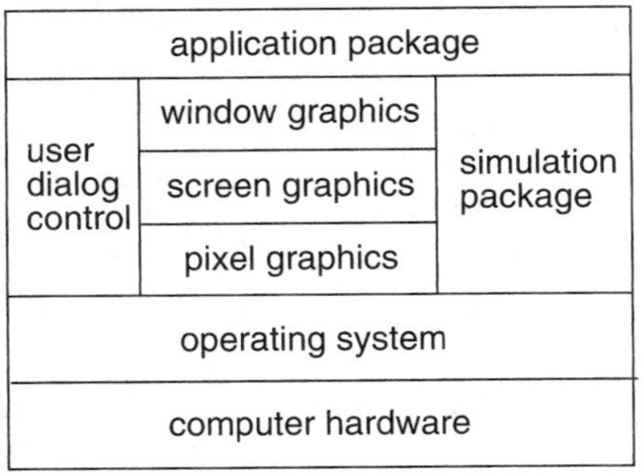

Figure 14.1 Block diagram of a typical application. Most large systems mix layers and partitions.

Once you have identified the top-level subsystems, you should show their information flow. Sometimes, all subsystems interact with all other subsystems, but often the flow is simpler. For example, many computations have the form of a pipeline; a compiler is an example. Other systems are arranged as a star, in which a master subsystem controls all interactions with other subsystems. Use simple topologies when possible to reduce the number of interactions among subsystems.

ATM example. Figure 14.2 shows the architecture of the ATM system. There are three major subsystems: the ATM stations, the consortium computer, and the bank computers. The topology is a simple star; the consortium computer communicates with all the ATM stations and with all the bank computers (comm links). The architecture uses the station code and the bank code to distinguish the phone lines to the consortium computer.

14.5 Identifying Concurrency

In the analysis model, as in the real world and in hardware, all objects are concurrent. In an implementation, however, not all software objects are concurrent, because one processor

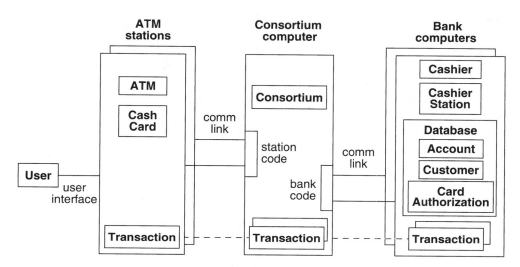

Figure 14.2 Architecture of ATM system. It is often helpful to make an informal diagram showing the organization of a system into subsystems.

may support many objects. In practice, you can implement many objects on a single processor if the objects cannot be active together. One important goal of system design is to identify the objects that must be active concurrently and the objects that have mutually exclusive activity. You can fold the latter objects onto a single thread of control, or task.

14.5.1 Identifying Inherent Concurrency

The state model is the guide to identifying concurrency. Two objects are inherently concurrent if they can receive events at the same time without interacting. If the events are unsynchronized, you cannot fold the objects onto a single thread of control. For example, the engine and the wing controls on an airplane must operate concurrently (if not completely independently). Independent subsystems are desirable, because you can assign them to different hardware units without any communication cost.

You need not implement two subsystems that are inherently concurrent as separate hardware units. The purpose of hardware interrupts, operating systems, and tasking mechanisms is to simulate logical concurrency in a uniprocessor. Separate sensors must, of course, process physically concurrent input, but if there are no timing constraints on response, then a multitasking operating system can handle the computation. Often the problem statement specifies that distinct hardware units must implement the objects.

ATM example. If the ATM statement from Chapter 11 contained the requirement that each machine should continue to operate locally in the event of a central system failure (perhaps with reduced transaction limits), then we would have no choice but to include a CPU in each ATM machine with a full control program.

14.5.2 Defining Concurrent Tasks

Although all objects are conceptually concurrent, in practice many objects in a system are interdependent. By examining the state diagrams of individual objects and the exchange of events among them, you can often fold many objects onto a single thread of control. A *thread of control* is a path through a set of state diagrams on which only a single object at a time is active. A thread remains within a state diagram until an object sends an event to another object and waits for another event. The thread passes to the receiver of the event until it eventually returns to the original object. The thread splits if the object sends an event and continues executing.

On each thread of control, only a single object at a time is active. You can implement threads of control as tasks in computer systems.

ATM example. While the bank is verifying an account or processing a bank transaction, the ATM machine is idle. If a central computer directly controls the ATM, we can combine the ATM object with the bank transaction object as a single task.

14.6 Allocation of Subsystems

You must allocate each concurrent subsystem to a hardware unit, either a general-purpose processor or a specialized functional unit as follows.

■ Estimate performance needs and the resources needed to satisfy them.

■ Choose hardware or software implementation for subsystems.

■ Allocate software subsystems to processors to satisfy performance needs and minimize interprocessor communication.

■ Determine the connectivity of the physical units that implement the subsystems.

14.6.1 Estimating Hardware Resource Requirements

The decision to use multiple processors or hardware functional units is based on a need for higher performance than a single CPU can provide. The number of processors required depends on the volume of computations and the speed of the machine. For example, a military radar system generates too much data in too short a time to handle in a single CPU, even a very large one. Many parallel machines must digest the data before analyzing a threat.

The system designer must estimate the required CPU processing power by computing the steady-state load as the product of the number of transactions per second and the time required to process a transaction. The estimate will usually be imprecise. Often some experimentation is useful. You should increase the estimate to allow for transient effects, due to random variations in load as well as to synchronized bursts of activity. The amount of excess capacity needed depends on the acceptable rate of failure due to insufficient resources. Both the steady-state load and the peak load are important.

ATM example. The ATM machine itself is relatively simple—all it must do is to provide a user interface and, possibly some local processing. At most a single CPU would suffice for each ATM. The consortium computer is essentially just a routing machine—it receives ATM requests and dispatches them to the appropriate bank computer. A large network might need to be partitioned in some way and involve multiple CPUs, so that the consortium computer does not become a bottleneck. The bank computers perform data processing and involve relatively straightforward database applications. The database vendors have single-processor and multiprocessor versions of their products, and the appropriate choice depends on the needed throughput and reliability.

14.6.2 Making Hardware-Software Trade-offs

Object orientation provides a good way for thinking about hardware. Each device is an object that operates concurrently with other objects (other devices or software). You must decide which subsystems will be implemented in hardware and which in software. There are two main reasons for implementing subsystems in hardware.

- **Cost**. Existing hardware provides exactly the functionality required. Today it is easier to buy a floating-point chip than to implement floating point in software. Sensors and actuators must be hardware, of course.

- **Performance**. The system requires a higher performance than a general-purpose CPU can provide, and more efficient hardware is available. For example, chips that perform the fast Fourier transform (FFT) are widely used in signal-processing applications.

Much of the difficulty of designing a system comes from meeting externally imposed hardware and software constraints. OO design provides no magic solution, but the external packages can be modeled nicely as objects. You must consider compatibility, cost, and performance issues. You should also think about flexibility for future changes, both design changes and future product enhancements. Providing flexibility costs something; the architect must decide how much it is worth.

   ATM example. There are no pressing performance issues for the ATM application. Hence general-purpose computers should suffice for the ATMs, consortium, and banks.

14.6.3 Allocating Tasks to Processors

The system design must allocate tasks for the various software subsystems to processors. There are several reasons for assigning tasks to processors.

- **Logistics**. Certain tasks are required at specific physical locations, to control hardware, or to permit independent operation. For example, an engineering workstation needs its own operating system to permit operation when the interprocessor network is down.

- **Communication limits**. The response time or data flow rate exceeds the available communication bandwidth between a task and a piece of hardware. For example, high performance graphics devices require tightly coupled controllers because of their high internal data generation rates.

- **Computation limits**. Computation rates are too great for a single processor, so several processors must support the tasks. You can minimize communication costs by assigning highly interactive subsystems to the same processor. You should assign independent subsystems to separate processors.

ATM example. The ATM does not have any issues with communication and computation limits. The communication traffic and computation that an ATM user initiates are relatively minor. However, there may be an issue with logistics. If the ATM must have autonomy and operate when the communications network is down, then it must have its own CPU and programming. Otherwise, if the ATM is just a dumb terminal that accesses the network and performs all computation via the network, we can simplify ATM logic.

14.6.4 Determining Physical Connectivity

After determining the kinds and relative numbers of physical units, you must determine the arrangement and form of the connections among the physical units.

- ■ **Connection topology**. Choose the topology for connecting the physical units. Associations in the class model often correspond to physical connections. Client-server relationships also correspond to physical connections. Some connections may be indirect; you should try to minimize the connection cost of important relationships.

- ■ **Repeated units**. Choose the topology of repeated units. If you have boosted performance by including several copies of a particular kind of unit or group of units, you must specify their topology. The class model is not a useful guide, because the use of multiple units is primarily a design optimization not required by analysis. The topology of repeated units usually has a regular pattern, such as a linear sequence, a matrix, a tree, or a star. You must consider the expected arrival patterns of data and the proposed parallel algorithm for processing it.

- ■ **Communications**. Choose the form of the connection channels and the communication protocols. The system design phase may be too soon to specify the exact interfaces among units, but often it is appropriate to choose the general interaction mechanisms and protocols. For example, interactions may be asynchronous, synchronous, or blocking. You must estimate the bandwidth and latency of the communication channels and choose the correct kind of connection channels.

Even when the connections are logical and not physical, you must consider them. For example, the units may be tasks within a single operating system connected by interprocess communication (IPC) calls. On most operating systems, such IPC calls are much slower than subroutine calls within the same program and may be impractical for certain time-critical connections. In that case, you must combine the tightly linked tasks into a single task and make the connections by simple subroutine calls.

ATM example. Figure 14.2 summarizes physical connectivity. Multiple ATMs connect to the consortium computer and then are routed to the appropriate bank computer. The topology is a star where the consortium computer mediates communication.

14.7 Management of Data Storage

There are several alternatives for data storage that you can use separately or in combination: data structures, files, and databases. Different kinds of data stores provide trade-offs among cost, access time, capacity, and reliability. For example, a personal computer application may use memory data structures and files. An accounting system may use a database to connect subsystems.

Files are cheap, simple, and permanent. However, file operations are low level, and applications must include additional code to provide a suitable level of abstraction. File implementations vary for different computer systems, so portable applications must carefully isolate file-system dependencies. Implementations for sequential files are mostly standard, but commands and storage formats for random-access files and indexed files vary. Figure 14.3 characterizes the kind of data that belongs in files.

- Data with high volume and low information density (such as archival files or historical records).
- Modest quantities of data with simple structure.
- Data that are accessed sequentially.
- Data that can be fully read into memory.

Figure 14.3 Data suitable for files. Files provide a low-tech solution to data management and should not be overlooked.

Databases, managed by database management systems (DBMSs), are another kind of data store. Various types of DBMSs are available from vendors, including relational and OO. DBMSs cache frequently accessed data in memory in order to achieve the best combination of cost and performance from memory and disk storage. Databases make applications easier to port to different hardware and operating system platforms, since the vendor ports the DBMS code. One disadvantage of DBMSs is their complex interface—many database languages integrate awkwardly with programming languages. Figure 14.4 characterizes the kinds of data that belong in a database.

- Data that require updates at fine levels of detail by multiple users.
- Data that must be accessed by multiple application programs.
- Data that require coordinated updates via transactions.
- Large quantities of data that must be handled efficiently.
- Data that are long-lived and highly valuable to an organization.
- Data that must be secured against unauthorized and malicious access.

Figure 14.4 Data suitable for databases. Databases provide heavyweight data management and are used for most important business applications.

OO-DBMSs have not become popular in the mass market. Consequently you should consider them only for specialty applications that have a wide variety of data types or that must access low-level data management primitives. These applications include engineering applications, multimedia applications, knowledge bases, and electronic devices with embedded software. For most applications that need a database, you should use a relational DBMS (RDBMS). RDBMSs dominate the marketplace, and their features are sufficient for most applications. RDBMSs can also provide a very good implementation of an OO model, *if* they are used properly—Chapter 19 presents the details.

ATM example. The typical bank computer would use a relational DBMS—they are fast, readily available, and cost-effective for these kinds of financial applications.

The ATM might also use a database, but the paradigm for that is less obvious. Relational and OO-DBMSs would both be possibilities. Many OO-DBMSs permit access to low-level primitives, and a stripped-down database might enable mass production of ATM software at a low cost. A stripped-down database might also simplify ATM operation. Alternatively, RDBMSs are mature products with many features that might reduce development effort.

14.8 Handling Global Resources

The system designer must identify global resources and determine mechanisms for controlling access to them. There are several kinds of global resources.

■ **Physical units**. Examples include processors, tape drives, and communication satellites.

■ **Space**. Examples include disk space, a workstation screen, and the buttons on a mouse.

■ **Logical names**. Examples include object IDs, filenames, and class names.

■ **Access to shared data**. Databases are an example.

If the resource is a physical object, then it can control itself by establishing a protocol for obtaining access. If the resource is a logical entity, such as an object ID or a database, then there is danger of conflicting access in a shared environment. Independent tasks could simultaneously use the same object ID, for example.

You can avoid conflict by having a "guardian object" own each global resource and control access to it. One guardian object can control several resources. All access to the resource must pass through the guardian object. Allocating each shared global resource to a single object is a recognition that the resource has identity.

You can also partition a resource logically, assigning subsets to different guardian objects for independent control. For example, one strategy for object ID generation in a parallel distributed environment is to preallocate a range of possible IDs to each processor in a network; each processor allocates the IDs within its preallocated range without the need for global synchronization.

In a time-critical application, the cost of passing all access to a resource through a guardian object is sometimes too high, and clients must access the resource directly. In this case, locks can be placed on subsets of the resource. A *lock* is a logical object associated with some defined subset of a resource that gives the lock holder the right to access the resource directly. A guardian object must still exist to allocate the locks, but after one interaction with the guardian to obtain a lock the user of the resource can access the resource directly. This approach is more dangerous, because each resource user must be trusted to behave itself in its access to the resource. Do not use direct access to shared resources unless it is absolutely necessary.

ATM example. Bank codes and account numbers are global resources. Bank codes must be unique within the context of a consortium. Account codes must be unique within the context of a bank.

14.9 Choosing a Software Control Strategy

The analysis model shows interactions as events between objects. Hardware control closely matches the analysis model, but there are several ways for implementing control in software. Although all subsystems need not use the same implementation, it is best to choose a single control style for the whole system. There are two kinds of control flows in a software system: external control and internal control.

External control concerns the flow of externally visible events among the objects in the system. There are three kinds of control for external events: procedure-driven sequential, event-driven sequential, and concurrent. The appropriate control style depends on the available resources (language, operating system) and on the kind of interactions in the application.

Internal control refers to the flow of control within a process. It exists only in the implementation and therefore is neither inherently concurrent nor sequential. The designer may choose to decompose a process into several tasks for logical clarity or for performance (if multiple processors are available). Unlike external events, internal transfers of control, such as procedure calls or intertask calls, are under the direction of the program and can be structured for convenience. Three kinds of control flow are common: procedure calls, quasi-concurrent intertask calls, and concurrent intertask calls. Quasi-concurrent intertask calls, such as coroutines or lightweight processes, are programming conveniences in which multiple address spaces or call stacks exist but only a single thread of control can be active at once.

14.9.1 Procedure-driven Control

In a procedure-driven sequential system, control resides within the program code. Procedures request external input and then wait for it; when input arrives, control resumes within the procedure that made the call. The location of the program counter and the stack of procedure calls and local variables define the system state.

The major advantage of procedure-driven control is that it is easy to implement with conventional languages; the disadvantage is that it requires the concurrency inherent in objects to be mapped into a sequential flow of control. The designer must convert events into operations between objects. A typical operation corresponds to a pair of events: an output event that performs output and requests input and an input event that delivers the new values. This paradigm cannot easily accommodate asynchronous input, because the program must explicitly request input. The procedure-driven paradigm is suitable only if the state model shows a regular alternation of input and output events. Flexible user interfaces and control systems are hard to build with this style.

Note that all major OO languages, such as C++ and Java, are procedural languages. Do not be fooled by the OO phrase *message passing*. A message *is* a procedure call with a built-in case statement that depends on the class of the target object. A major drawback of conventional OO languages is that they fail to support the concurrency inherent in objects. Some concurrent OO languages have been designed, but they are not yet widely used.

14.9.2 Event-driven Control

In an event-driven sequential system, control resides within a dispatcher or monitor that the language, subsystem, or operating system provides. Developers attach application procedures to events, and the dispatcher calls the procedures when the corresponding events occur ("callback"). Procedure calls to the dispatcher send output or enable input but do not wait for it in-line. All procedures return control to the dispatcher, rather than retaining control until input arrives. Consequently, the program counter and stack cannot preserve state. Procedures must use global variables to maintain state, or the dispatcher must maintain local state for them. Event-driven control is more difficult to implement with standard languages than procedure-driven control but is often worth the extra effort.

Event-driven systems permit more flexible control than procedure-driven systems. Event-driven systems simulate cooperating processes within a single multithreaded task; an errant procedure can block the entire application, so you must be careful. Event-driven user interface subsystems are particularly useful.

Use an event-driven system for external control in preference to a procedure-driven system whenever possible, because the mapping from events to program constructs is simpler and more powerful. Event-driven systems are also more modular and can handle error conditions better than procedure-driven systems.

14.9.3 Concurrent Control

In a concurrent system, control resides concurrently in several independent objects, each a separate task. Such a system implements events directly as one-way messages (*not* OO language "messages") between objects. A task can wait for input, but other tasks continue execution. The operating system resolves scheduling conflicts among tasks and usually supplies a queuing mechanism, so that events are not lost if a task is executing when they arrive. If there are multiple CPUs, then different tasks can actually execute concurrently.

14.9.4 Internal Control

During design, the developer expands operations on objects into lower-level operations on the same or other objects. Internal object interactions are similar to external object interactions, because you can use the same implementation mechanisms. However, there is an important difference—external interactions inherently involve waiting for events, because objects are independent and cannot force other objects to respond; objects generate internal operations as part of the implementation algorithm, so their form of response is predictable. Consequently, you can think of most internal operations as procedure calls, in which the caller issues a request and waits for the response. There are algorithms for parallel processing, but many computations are well represented sequentially and can easily be folded onto a single thread of control.

14.9.5 Other Paradigms

We assume that the reader is primarily interested in procedural programming, but other paradigms are possible, such as rule-based systems, logic programming systems, and other forms of nonprocedural programs. These constitute another control style in which explicit control is replaced by declarative specification with implicit evaluation rules, possibly nondeterministic or highly convoluted. Developers currently use such languages in limited areas, such as artificial intelligence and knowledge-based programming, but we expect their use to grow in the future. Because these languages are totally different from procedural languages (including OO languages), the remainder of this book has little to say about them.

   ATM example. Event-driven control is the appropriate paradigm for the ATM station. The ATM services a single user, so there is little need for concurrent control. The ATM must be responsive in its user interactions, and event-driven control is much better at that than procedure-driven control.

14.10 Handling Boundary Conditions

Although most of system design concerns steady-state behavior, you must consider boundary conditions as well and address the following kinds of issues.

- ■ **Initialization**. The system must proceed from a quiescent initial state to a sustainable steady state. The system must initialize constant data, parameters, global variables, tasks, guardian objects, and possibly the class hierarchy itself. During initialization only a subset of the functionality of the system is usually available. Initializing a system containing concurrent tasks is most difficult, because independent objects must not get either too far ahead or too far behind other independent objects during initialization.

- ■ **Termination**. Termination is usually simpler than initialization, because many internal objects can simply be abandoned. The task must release any external resources that it had reserved. In a concurrent system, one task must notify other tasks of its termination.

- ■ **Failure**. Failure is the unplanned termination of a system. Failure can arise from user errors, from the exhaustion of system resources, or from an external breakdown. The good system designer plans for orderly failure. Failure can also arise from bugs in the system and is often detected as an "impossible" inconsistency. In a perfect design, such errors would never happen, but the good designer plans for a graceful exit on fatal bugs by leaving the remaining environment as clean as possible and recording or printing as much information about the failure as possible before terminating.

14.11 Setting Trade-off Priorities

The system designer must set priorities that will be used to guide trade-offs for the rest of design. These priorities reconcile desirable but incompatible goals. For example, a system can often be made faster by using extra memory, but that increases power consumption and costs more. Design trade-offs involve not only the software itself but also the process of developing it. Sometimes it is necessary to sacrifice complete functionality to get a piece of software into use (or into the marketplace) earlier. Sometimes the problem statement specifies priority, but often the burden falls on the designer to reconcile the incompatible desires of the client and decide how to make trade-offs.

The system designer must determine the relative importance of the various criteria as a guide to making design trade-offs. The system designer does not *make* all the trade-offs, but establishes the priorities for making them. For example, the first video games ran on processors with limited memory. Conserving memory was the highest priority, followed by fast execution. Designers had to use every programming trick in the book, at the expense of maintainability, portability, and understandability. As another example, mathematical subroutine packages run on a wide range of machines. Well-conditioned numerical behavior is crucial to such packages, as well as portability and understandability. These cannot be sacrificed for fast development.

Design trade-offs affect the entire character of a system. The success or failure of the final product may depend on how well its goals are chosen. Even worse, if no system-wide priorities are established, then the various parts of the system may optimize opposing goals ("suboptimization"), resulting in a system that wastes resources. Even on small projects, programmers often forget the real goals and become obsessed with "efficiency" when it is really unimportant.

Setting trade-off priorities is at best vague. You cannot expect numerical accuracy ("speed 53%, memory 31%, portability 15%, cost 1%"). Priorities are rarely absolute; for example, trading memory for speed does not mean that any increase in speed, no matter how small, is worth any increase in memory, no matter how large. We cannot even give a full list of design criteria that might be subject to trade-offs. Instead, the priorities are a statement of design philosophy. Subsequent design will still require judgment and interpretation when trade-offs are actually made.

ATM example. The ATM station is a mass-market product. Consequently, the manufacturing cost is a concern, and the resulting product must have a polished user interface. The software must be robust and resilient in the face of failure. Development cost is a lesser concern, since the cost can be amortized across numerous copies.

14.12 Common Architectural Styles

Several prototypical architectural styles are common in existing systems. Each of these is well suited to a certain kind of system. If you have an application with similar characteristics, you can save effort by using the corresponding architecture, or at least using it as a starting point for your design. Some kinds of systems are listed below.

- **Batch transformation**—a data transformation executed once on an entire input set. [14.12.1]

- **Continuous transformation**—a data transformation performed continuously as inputs change. [14.12.2]

- **Interactive interface**—a system dominated by external interactions. [14.12.3]

- **Dynamic simulation**—a system that simulates evolving real-world objects. [14.12.4]
- **Real-time system**—a system dominated by strict timing constraints. [14.12.5]
- **Transaction manager**—a system concerned with storing and updating data, often including concurrent access from different physical locations. [14.12.6]

This is not meant to be a complete list of known systems and architectures but a list of common forms. Some problems require a new kind of architecture, but most can use an existing style or at least a variation on it. Many problems combine aspects of these architectures.

14.12.1 Batch Transformation

A *batch transformation* performs sequential computations. The application receives the inputs, and the goal is to compute an answer; there is no ongoing interaction with the outside world. Examples include standard computational problems such as compilers, payroll processing, VLSI automatic layout, stress analysis of a bridge, and many others. The state model is trivial or nonexistent for batch transformation problems. The class model is important—there are class models for the input, output, and the intervening stages. The interaction model documents the computation and couples the class models. The most important aspect of a batch transformation is to define a clean series of steps.

In the past, when we worked at GE R&D, one of our colleagues (Bill Premerlani) built a compiler that received an ASCII file of graphical pictures as input and generated relational database definition code as output. This work preceded the availability of commercial OO modeling tools. Figure 14.5 shows the sequence of steps. The compiler had five class models—one for the input, one for the output, and three for intermediate representations.

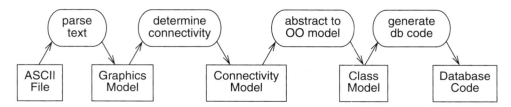

Figure 14.5 Sequence of steps for a compiler. A batch transformation is a sequential input-to-output transformation that does not interact with the outside world.

The steps in designing a batch transformation are as follows.

- Break the overall transformation into stages, with each stage performing one part of the transformation.
- Prepare class models for the input, output, and between each pair of successive stages. Each stage knows only about the models on either side of it.
- Expand each stage in turn until the operations are straightforward to implement.
- Restructure the final pipeline for optimization.

14.12.2 *Continuous Transformation*

A *continuous transformation* is a system in which the outputs actively depend on changing inputs. Unlike a batch transformation that computes the outputs only once, a continuous transformation updates outputs frequently (in theory continuously, although in practice they are computed discretely at a fine time scale). Because of severe time constraints, the system cannot recompute the entire set of outputs each time an input changes (otherwise the application would be a batch transformation). Instead, the system must compute outputs incrementally. Typical applications include signal processing, windowing systems, incremental compilers, and process monitoring systems. The class, state, and interaction models have similar purposes as with the batch transformation.

One way to implement a continuous transformation is with a pipeline of functions. The pipeline propagates the effect of each input change. Developers can define intermediate and redundant objects to improve the performance of the pipeline. Some high-performance systems, such as signal processing, need to synchronize values within the pipeline. Such systems perform operations at well-defined times and carefully balance the flow path of operations so that values arrive at the right place at the right time without bottlenecks.

Figure 14.6 shows the example of a graphics application. The application first maps geometric figures in user-defined coordinates to window coordinates. Then it clips the figures to fit the window bounds. Finally it offsets each figure by its window position to yield its screen position.

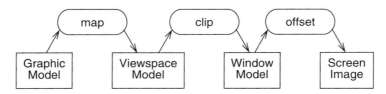

Figure 14.6 Sequence of steps for a graphics application. A continuous
transformation repeatedly propagates input changes to the output.

The steps in designing a pipeline for a continuous transformation are as follows.

■ Break the overall transformation into stages, with each stage performing one part of the transformation.

■ Define input, output, and intermediate models between each pair of successive stages, as for the batch transformation.

■ Differentiate each operation to obtain incremental changes to each stage. That is, propagate the incremental effects of each change to an input through the pipeline as a series of incremental updates.

■ Add additional intermediate objects for optimization.

14.12.3 Interactive Interface

An *interactive interface* is a system that is dominated by interactions between the system and external agents, such as humans or devices. The external agents are independent of the system, so the system cannot control the agents, although it may solicit responses from them. An interactive interface usually includes only part of an entire application, one that can often be handled independently from computations. Examples of interactive systems include a forms-based query interface, a workstation windowing system, and the control panel for a simulation.

The major concerns of an interactive interface are the communications protocol between the system and the external agents, the syntax of possible interactions, the presentation of output (the appearance on the screen, for instance), the flow of control within the system, performance, and error handling. Interactive interfaces are dominated by the state model. The class model represents interaction elements, such as input and output tokens and presentation formats. The interaction model shows how the state diagrams interact.

The steps in designing an interactive interface are as follows.

- Isolate interface classes from the application classes.

- Use predefined classes to interact with external agents, if possible. For example, windowing systems have extensive collections of predefined windows, menus, buttons, forms, and other kinds of classes ready to be adapted to applications.

- Use the state model as the structure of the program. Interactive interfaces are best implemented using concurrent control (multitasking) or event-driven control (interrupts or call-backs). Procedure-driven control (writing output and then waiting for input in-line) is awkward for anything but rigid control sequences.

- Isolate physical events from logical events. Often a logical event corresponds to multiple physical events. For example, a graphical interface can take input from a form, from a pop-up menu, from a function button on the keyboard, from a typed-in command sequence, or from an indirect command file.

- Fully specify the application functions that are invoked by the interface. Make sure that the information to implement them is present.

14.12.4 Dynamic Simulation

A *dynamic simulation* models or tracks real-world objects. Examples include molecular motion modeling, spacecraft trajectory computation, economic models, and video games. Simulations are perhaps the simplest system to design using an OO approach. The objects and operations come directly from the application. There are two ways for implementing control: an explicit controller external to the application objects can simulate a state machine, or objects can exchange messages among themselves, similar to the real-world situation.

Unlike an interactive system, the internal objects in a dynamic simulation do correspond to real-world objects, so the class model is usually important and often complex. Like an interactive system, the state and interaction models are also important.

The steps in designing a dynamic simulation are as follows.

- Identify active real-world objects from the class model. These objects have attributes that are periodically updated.

- Identify discrete events. Discrete events correspond to discrete interactions with the object, such as turning power on or applying the brakes. Discrete events can be implemented as operations on the object.

- Identify continuous dependencies. Real-world attributes may be dependent on other real-world attributes or vary continuously with time, altitude, velocity, or steering wheel position, for example. These attributes must be updated at periodic intervals, using numerical approximation techniques to minimize quantization error.

- Generally a simulation is driven by a timing loop at a fine time scale. Discrete events between objects can often be exchanged as part of the timing loop.

Usually, the hardest problem with simulations is providing adequate performance. In an ideal world, an arbitrary number of parallel processors would execute the simulation in an exact analogy to the real-world situation. In practice, the system designer must estimate the computational cost of each update cycle and provide adequate resources. Discrete steps must approximate continuous processes.

14.12.5 Real-time System

A *real-time system* is an interactive system with tight time constraints on actions. Hard real-time software involves critical applications that require a guaranteed response within the time constraints. In contrast, soft real-time software must also be highly reliable, but can occasionally violate time constraints. Typical real-time applications include process control, data acquisition, communications devices, device control, and overload relays.

Real-time design is complex and involves issues such as interrupt handling, prioritization of tasks, and coordinating multiple CPUs. Unfortunately, real-time systems are frequently designed to operate close to their resource limits, so that severe, nonlogical restructuring of the design is often needed to achieve the necessary performance. Such contortions come at the cost of portability and maintainability. Real-time design is a specialized topic that we do not cover in this book.

14.12.6 Transaction Manager

A *transaction manager* is a system whose main function is to store and retrieve data. Most transaction managers deal with multiple users who read and write data at the same time. They also must secure their data to protect it from unauthorized access as well as accidental loss. Transaction managers are often built on top of a database management system (DBMS)—this is a form of reuse. A DBMS has generic functionality for managing data that you can reuse and need not implement. Examples of transaction managers include airline reservations, inventory control, and order fulfillment.

The class model is dominant. The state model is occasionally important, especially for specifying the evolution of an object as well as constraints and methods that apply at different points in time. The interaction model is seldom significant.

The steps in designing an information system are as follows.

- Map the class model to database structures. See Chapter 19 for advice.

- Determine the units of concurrency—that is, the resources that inherently or by specification cannot be shared. Introduce new classes as needed.

- Determine the unit of transaction—that is, the set of resources that must be accessed together during a transaction. A transaction succeeds or fails in its entirety.

- Design concurrency control for transactions. Most database management systems provide this. The system may need to retry failed transactions several times before giving up.

14.13 Architecture of the ATM System

The ATM system is a hybrid of an interactive interface and a transaction management system. The entry stations are interactive interfaces—their purpose is to interact with a human to gather information needed to formulate a transaction. Specifying the entry stations consists of constructing a class model and a state model. The consortium and banks are primarily a distributed transaction management system. Their purpose is to maintain data and allow it to be updated over a distributed network under controlled conditions. Specifying the transaction management part of the system consists primarily of constructing a class model. Figure 14.2 shows the architecture of the ATM system.

The only permanent data stores are in the bank computers. A database ensures that data is consistent and available for concurrent access. The ATM system processes each transaction as a single batch operation, locking an account until the transaction is complete.

Concurrency arises because there are many ATM stations, each of which can be active at any time. There can be only one transaction per ATM station, but each transaction requires the assistance of the consortium computer and a bank computer. As Figure 14.2 shows, a transaction cuts across physical units; the diagram shows each transaction as three connected pieces. During design, each piece will become a separate implementation class. Although there is only one transaction per ATM station, there may be many concurrent transactions per consortium computer or bank computer. This does not pose any special problem, because the database synchronizes access to any one account.

The consortium computer and bank computers will be event driven. Each of them queues input events but processes them one at a time in the order received. The consortium computer has minimal functionality. It simply forwards a message from an ATM station to a bank computer and from a bank computer to an ATM station. The consortium computer must be large enough to handle the transaction load. It may be acceptable to block an occasional transaction, provided the user receives an appropriate message.

The bank computer is the only unit with any nontrivial procedures, but even those are mostly just database updates. The only complexity might come from failure handling. The bank computers must have capacity to handle the expected worst-case load, and they must have enough disk storage to record all transactions.

The system must contain operations for adding and deleting ATM stations and bank computers. Each physical unit must protect itself against the failure or disconnection from the rest of the network. A database protects against loss of data. However, special attention must be paid to failure during a transaction so that neither the user nor the bank loses money—this may require a complicated acknowledgment protocol before committing the transaction. The ATM station should display an appropriate message if the connection is down. The ATM must handle other kinds of failure as well, such as exhaustion of cash or paper for receipts.

On a financial system such as this, fail-safe transactions are the highest priority. If there is any doubt about the integrity of a transaction, then the ATM must abort the transaction with an appropriate message to the user.

14.14 Chapter Summary

After analyzing an application and before beginning the class design, the system designer must decide on the basic approach to the solution. The form of the high-level strategy for building the system is called the system architecture.

Early in the planning for a new system you should estimate the performance. The intention is to have a rough idea of what to expect. You want to make sure that it is reasonable and that there are no big surprises as development proceeds.

Next, prepare a reuse plan. Reuse is often cited as a benefit of OO technology, but it does not happen automatically. There are two different aspects of reuse. Most developers should focus on reusing existing models, libraries, frameworks, and patterns that are relevant to their applications. In addition, elite developers can create artifacts for reuse by others.

A system can be divided into horizontal layers and vertical partitions. Each layer defines a different abstract world that may differ completely from other layers. Each layer is a client of services of the layer or layers below it and a server of services for the layer or layers above it. Systems can also have partitions, each performing a general kind of service. Simple system topologies, such as pipelines or stars, reduce complexity. Most systems are a mixture of layers and partitions.

Inherently concurrent objects execute in parallel, and a single thread of control cannot combine them; they require separate hardware devices or separate tasks in a processor. You can combine nonconcurrent objects onto a single thread of control and implement them as a single task.

A system must have enough processors and special-purpose hardware units to meet performance goals. You should assign objects to hardware so that hardware use is balanced and meets concurrency constraints. You can do this by estimating computational throughput and allowing for queuing effects in configuring the hardware. You may want to use special-purpose hardware for compute-intensive computations. One goal in partitioning a hardware network is to minimize communications traffic between physically distinct modules.

Data stores can cleanly separate subsystems within an architecture and give application data some degree of permanence. In general, memory data structures, files, and databases can implement data stores. Files are simple, cheap, and permanent but may provide too low a level of abstraction for an application and necessitate much additional programming. Databases provide a higher level of abstraction than files, but they too involve compromises in terms of overhead costs and complexity.

The system designer must identify global resources and determine mechanisms for controlling access to them. Some common mechanisms are: establishing a "guardian" object that serializes all access, partitioning global resources into disjoint subsets which are managed at a lower level, and locking.

Hardware control is inherently concurrent, but software control can be procedure driven, event driven, and concurrent. Control for a procedure-driven system resides within the program code; the location of the program counter and the stack of procedure calls and local variables define the system state. In an event-driven system control resides within a dispatcher or monitor; application procedures are attached to events and are called by the dispatcher when the corresponding events occur. In a concurrent system, control resides concurrently in multiple independent objects. Event-driven and concurrent implementations are much more flexible than procedure-driven control.

Most of system design is concerned with steady-state behavior, but boundary conditions (initialization, termination, and failure) are also important.

An essential aspect of system architecture is making trade-offs between time and space, hardware and software, simplicity and generality, and efficiency and maintainability. These trade-offs depend on the goals of the application. The system designer must state the priorities, so that trade-off decisions during subsequent design will be consistent.

Several kinds of systems are frequently encountered for which standard architectural styles exist. These include two kinds of functional transformations: batch computation and continuous transformation; three kinds of time-dependent systems: interactive interface, dynamic simulation, and real-time; and a database system: transaction manager. Most application systems are usually a hybrid of several forms, possibly one for each major subsystem. Other kinds of architecture are possible.

architecture	hardware requirements	service
client-server	inherent concurrency	subsystem
concurrency	layer	system design
data management	partition	system topology
event-driven system	peer-to-peer	thread of control
framework	reuse plan	trade-off priorities

Figure 14.7 Key concepts for Chapter 14

Bibliographic Notes

Simple software applications do not require much systems engineering, but complex systems must be decomposed and the parts assigned to the appropriate specialists. [Clements-02] presents a process for evaluating software architectures. Essentially a group of stakeholders meet and prioritize criteria that the architecture should satisfy; they quantify the criteria with specific scenarios. Then they analyze the architecture to determine its compliance with the high-priority scenarios.

Patterns are a popular topic in the literature and the subject of a number of books. There are patterns for analysis [Coad-95], architecture [Buschmann-96] [Shaw-96], design [Gamma-95], and implementation [Coplien-92]. There have also been a number of conferences over the years that have focused on patterns, many of which have been sponsored by the Pattern Languages of Programming [PLoP].

References

[Berlin-90] Lucy Berlin. When objects collide: Experiences with reusing multiple class hierarchies. *ECOOP/OOPSLA 1990 Proceedings*, October 21–25, 1990, Ottawa, Ontario, Canada, 181–193.

[Buschmann-96] Frank Buschmann, Regine Meunier, Hans Rohnert, Peter Sommerlad, and Michael Stal. *Pattern-Oriented Software Architecture: A System of Patterns*. Chichester, UK: Wiley, 1996.

[Clements-02] Paul Clements, Rick Kazman, and Mark Klein. *Evaluating Software Architectures*. Boston: Addison-Wesley, 2002.

[Coad-95] Peter Coad, David North, and Mark Mayfield. *Object Models: Strategies, Patterns, and Applications*. Upper Saddle River, NJ: Yourdon Press, 1995.

[Coplien-92] James O. Coplien. *Advanced C++ Programming Styles and Idioms*. Boston: Addison-Wesley, 1992.

[Gamma-95] Erich Gamma, Richard Helm, Ralph Johnson, and John Vlissides. *Design patterns: Elements of Reusable Object-Oriented Software*. Boston: Addison-Wesley, 1995.

[Johnson-88] Ralph E. Johnson and Brian Foote. Designing reusable classes. *Journal of Object-Oriented Programming 1*, 3 (June/July 1988), 22–35.

[Korson-92] Tim Korson and John D. McGregor. Technical criteria for the specification and evaluation of object-oriented libraries. *Software Engineering Journal* (March 1992), 85–94.

[PLoP] jerry.cs.uiuc.edu/~plop

[Shaw-96] Mary Shaw and David Garlan. *Software Architecture*. Upper Saddle River, NJ: Prentice Hall, 1996.

Exercises

14.1 (4) For each of the following systems, list the applicable style(s) of system architecture: batch transformation, continuous transformation, interactive interface, dynamic simulation, real-time system, and transaction manager. Explain your selection(s). For systems that fit more than one style, group features of the system by style.

   a. **An electronic chess companion**. The system consists of a chess board with a built-in computer, lights, and membrane switches. The human player registers moves by pressing chess pieces on the board, activating membrane switches mounted under each square. The computer indicates moves through lights also mounted under each square. The human moves the chess pieces for the computer. The computer should make only legal moves, should reject attempted illegal human moves, and should try to win.

   b. **An airplane flight simulator for a video game system**. The video game system has already been implemented and consists of a computer with joystick and pushbutton inputs and an output interface for a color television. Your job is to develop the software for the computer to display the view from the cockpit of an airplane. The joystick and pushbutton control the airplane. The display should be based on a terrain description stored in memory. When your program is complete, it will be sold on cartridges that plug into the video game system.

c. **A floppy disk controller chip.** The chip is going to use a microprogram for internal control. You are concerned with the microprogram. The chip bridges the gap between a computer and a floppy disk drive. Your portion of the control will be responsible for positioning the read/write head and reading the data. Information on the diskette is organized into tracks and sectors. Tracks are equally spaced circles of data on the diskette. Data within a track is organized into sectors. Your architecture will need to support the following operations: Find track 0, find a given track, read a track, read a sector, write a track, and write a sector.

d. **A sonar system.** You are concerned with the portion of the system that detects undersea objects and computes how far away they are (range). This is done by transmitting an acoustic pulse and analyzing any resulting echo. A technique called correlation is used to perform the analysis, in which a time-delayed copy of the transmitted pulse is multiplied by the returned echo and integrated for many values of time delay. If the result is large for a particular value of time delay, it is an indication that there is an object with a range that corresponds to that delay.

14.2 (3) Discuss how you would implement control for the applications described in the previous exercise.

14.3 (7) As the system architect for a new signal-processing product, you must decide how to store data in real time. The product uses analog to digital convertors to sample an analog input signal at the rate of 16,000 bytes/second (128,000 bits/second) for 10 seconds. Unfortunately, the needed calculations are too time consuming to do as the samples are received, so you are going to have to store the samples temporarily. The decision has already been made to limit the amount of memory used for buffers to 64,000 bytes. The system has a floppy disk drive that uses diskettes organized into 77 tracks for a total of 243,000 bytes of storage per diskette. It takes 10 milliseconds to move the disk drive read/write head from one track to another and 83 milliseconds, on average, to find the beginning of a track once the head is positioned. The disk drive will be positioned at the correct track prior to the start of data acquisition.

Two solutions to the problem are being considered: (1) Simply write the data samples on the diskette as they become available. Why doesn't this work? (2) Use memory as a buffer. Data samples are placed in memory as they are acquired and written to the floppy disk as fast as possible on sequential tracks. Will this method work? Describe the method in more detail. How much memory is needed for the buffer? How many tracks will be used on the diskette? Prepare a few scenarios. Describe how the control might work.

14.4 (6) Consider a system for automating the drilling of holes in rectangular metal plates. The size and location of holes are described interactively, using a graphical editor on a personal computer. When the user is satisfied with a particular drawing, a peripheral device on the personal computer punches a numerical control (N/C) tape. The tape can then be used on a variety of commercially available N/C drilling machines that have moving drill heads and can change drill sizes.

You are concerned only with the editing of the drawings and the punching of the N/C tapes. The tapes contain sequences of instructions to move the drill head, change drills, and drill. Since it takes some time to move the drill between holes, and even longer to change drills, the system should determine a reasonably efficient drilling sequence. It is not necessary to achieve the absolute minimum time, but the system should not be grossly inefficient either. The drill head is controlled independently in the x and y directions, so the time it takes to move between holes is proportional to the larger of the required displacements in the x and the y direction. Prepare a system architecture. How would you characterize the style of the system?

14.5   (5) Consider a system for interactive symbolic manipulation of polynomials. The basic idea is to allow a mathematician to be more accurate and productive in developing formulas. The user enters mathematical expressions and commands a line at a time. Expressions are ratios of polynomials, which are constructed from constants and variables. Intermediate expressions may be assigned to variables for later recall. Operations include addition, subtraction, multiplication, division, and differentiation with respect to a variable.

Develop an architecture for the system. How would you characterize the style of the system? How would you save work in progress to resume at a future time?

14.6   (4) An architecture for the system described in the previous exercise could involve the following subsystems. Organize them into partitions and layers.
a. line syntax—scan a line of user input for tokens
b. line semantics—determine the meaning of a line of input
c. command processing—execute user input, error checking
d. construct expression—build an internal representation of an input expression
e. apply operation—carry out an operation on one or more expressions
f. save work—save the current context
g. load work—read in previously saved context
h. substitute—substitute one expression for a variable in another expression
i. rationalize—convert an expression to canonical form
j. evaluate—replace a variable in an expression with a constant and simplify the expression

14.7   (6) Consider a system for editing, saving, and printing class diagrams and generating relational database schema. The system supports only a limited subset of the class modeling notation—classes with attributes and binary associations with multiplicity. The system also includes editing functions such as create class, create association, cut, copy, and paste. The editor must understand the semantics of class diagrams. For example, when a class rectangle is moved, the lines representing any attached associations are stretched. If a class is deleted, attached associations are also deleted. When the user is satisfied with the diagram, the system will generate the corresponding relational database schema. Discuss the relative advantages of a single program that performs all functions versus two programs, one that edits class diagrams and the other that generates database schema from class diagrams.

14.8   (6) In the previous exercise, both physical and logical aspects of class diagrams must be considered. Physical aspects include location and sizes of lines, boxes, and text. Logical aspects include connectivity, classes, attributes, and associations. Discuss basing your architecture on the following strategies. Consider the issues involved in editing and saving class diagrams as well as generating database schema.
a. Model only the geometrical aspects of class diagrams. Treat logical aspects as derived.
b. Model both the geometrical and logical aspects of class diagrams.

14.9   (5) Another approach to the system described in Exercise 14.7 is to use a commercially available desktop publishing system for class diagram preparation instead of implementing your own class diagram editor. The desktop editor can dump its output in an ASCII markup language. The vendor supplies the grammar for the markup language.

Compare the two approaches. One approach is to build your own editor that understands the semantics of class diagrams. The other is to use a commercially available desktop publishing system to edit class diagrams. What happens if new versions of the desktop publishing system become available? Can you assume that the user prepares a diagram using a notation that your database generator will understand? Is it worth the effort to implement functions such as cut, copy, and paste that commercial systems already do so well? Who is going to help the users if they run into problems? How is your system going to be supported and maintained? How soon can you get the system completed?

14.10 (6) A common issue in many systems is how to store data so it is preserved in the event of power loss or hardware failure. The ideal solution should be reliable, low-cost, small, fast, maintenance free, and simple to incorporate into a system. Also, it should be immune to heat, dirt, and humidity. Compromises in the available technology often influence the functional requirements. Compare each of the following solutions in terms of the ideal. Note that this is not an exhaustive list of solutions.

    a. Do not worry about it at all. Reset all data every time the system is turned on.

    b. Never turn the power off if it can be helped. Use a special power supply, including backup generators, if necessary.

    c. Keep critical information on a magnetic disk drive. Periodically make full and/or incremental copies on magnetic tape.

    d. Use a battery to maintain power to the system memory when the rest of the system is off. It might even be possible to continue to provide limited functionality.

    e. Use a special memory component, such as a magnetic bubble memory or an electronically erasable programmable read-only memory.

    f. Critical parameters are entered by the user through switches. Several types of switches are commercially available for this use, including several toggle switches in a package that connects the same way as an integrated circuit.

14.11 (7) For each of the following systems, select one or more of the strategies for data storage from the previous exercise. In each case explain your reasoning and give an estimate (order of magnitude) of how much memory, in bytes, is required:

    a. **Four-function pocket calculator**. Main source of power is light. Performs basic arithmetic.

    b. **Electronic typewriter**. Main source of power is either rechargeable batteries or alternating current. Operates in two modes. In one mode, documents are typed a line at a time. Editing may be performed on a line before it is typed. A liquid crystal display will display up to 16 characters for editing purposes. In the other mode, an entire document can be entered and edited before printing. The typewriter should be able to save the working document for up to a year with the main power off.

    c. **System clock for a personal computer**. Main power is direct current supplied by the personal computer when it is on. Provides time and date information to the computer. Must maintain the correct date and time for at least five years with the main power off.

    d. **Airline reservation system**. Main power is alternating current. Used to reserve seats on airline flights. The system must be kept running at all times, at all costs. If, for some reason, the system must be shut off, no data should be lost.

    e. **Digital control and thermal protection unit for a motor**. The device provides thermal protection for motors over a wide range of horsepower ratings by calculating motor temperature based on measured current and a simulation of motor heat dissipation. If the calculated motor temperature exceeds safe limits, the motor is shut off and not allowed to be restarted until it cools down. The main source of power is alternating current, which may be interrupted. The system must provide protection as soon as it is turned on. Parameters needed for thermal simulation are initially set at the factory, but provision must be made to change them, if necessary, after the system is installed. Because the motor temperature is not measured directly, it is necessary to continue to simulate the motor temperature for at least an hour after loss of main power, in case power is restored before the motor cools.

14.12 (9) The design of file formats is a common task for system design. A BNF diagram is a convenient way to express file formats. Figure E14.1 is a portion of a BNF diagram of a language for describing classes and binary associations. Nonterminal symbols are shown in rectangles, and terminal symbols are shown in circles or rectangles with rounded corners. With the exception of *character*, the diagram defines all nonterminals. A diagram consists of classes and associations. A class has a unique name and many attributes. An association has an optional name and two ends. An association end contains the name one of the classes being associated and multiplicity information. Textual information is described by quoted strings. A character is any ASCII character except quote.

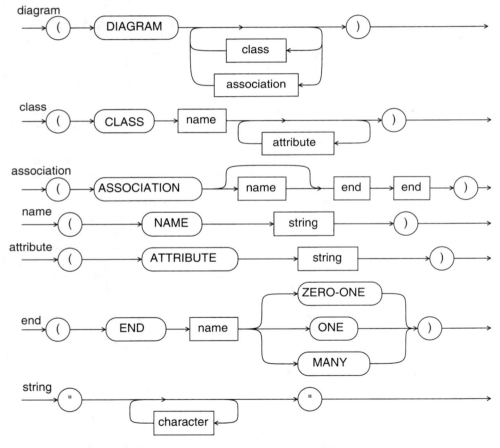

Figure E14.1 BNF diagram for a language that describes classes and associations

a. Use the language in Figure E14.1 to describe the class diagram in Figure E14.2.
b. Discuss similarities and differences between data in storage and data in motion. For example, the description you prepared in the previous part could be used to store a class diagram in a file or to transmit a diagram from one location to another.
c. The language in this problem is used to describe the structure of class diagrams. Invent a language to describe two-dimensional polygons. Use BNF to describe your language. Describe a square and a triangle in your language.

Figure E14.2 Class diagram of polygons

14.13 (6) A common problem encountered in digital systems is data corruption due to noise or hardware failure. One solution is to use a cyclic redundancy code (CRC). When data is stored or transmitted, a code is computed from the data and appended to it. When data is retrieved or received, the code is recomputed and compared with the value that was appended to the data. A match is necessary but not sufficient to indicate that the data is correct. The probability that errors will be detected depends on the sophistication of the function used to compute the CRC. Some functions can be used for error correction as well as detection. Parity is an example of a simple function that detects single-bit errors.

The function to compute a CRC can be implemented in hardware or software. The choice for a given problem is a compromise involving speed, cost, flexibility, and complexity. The hardware solution is fast, but may add unnecessary complexity and cost to the system hardware. The software solution is cheaper and more flexible, but may not be fast enough and may make the system software more complex.

For each of the following subsystems, decide whether or not a CRC is needed. If so, decide whether to implement the CRC in hardware or software. Explain your choices.
a. floppy disk controller
b. system to transmit data files from one computer to another over telephone lines
c. memory board on a computer board in the space shuttle
d. magnetic tape drive
e. validation of an account number (a CRC can be used to distinguish between valid accounts and those generated at random)

14.14 (6) Consider the scheduler software in Exercises 12.16–12.19 and 12.20–12.23.

With scheduling software it is also important to manage security—that is, the schedules that each user is permitted to read and write.

An obvious way to maintain security is to maintain a list of access permissions for each combination of user and schedule. However, this can become tedious to monitor and maintain.

Another solution is to allow permissions to be entered also for a group. A user can belong to multiple groups; each group may have multiple users and lesser groups. The users may access schedules for which they have permission or for which their groups have permission.

Extend the class models from Exercises 12.19 and 12.23 for this model of security. (Instructor's note: You should give the students our answers to Exercises 12.19 and 12.23.)

15

Class Design

The analysis phase determines what the implementation must do, and the system design phase determines the plan of attack. The purpose of class design is to complete the definitions of the classes and associations and choose algorithms for operations.

This chapter shows how to take the analysis model and flesh it out to provide a basis for implementation. The system design strategy guides your decisions, but during class design, you must now resolve the details. There is no need to change from one model to another, as the OO paradigm spans analysis, design, and implementation. The OO paradigm applies equally well in describing the real-world specification and computer-based implementation.

15.1 Overview of Class Design

The analysis model describes the information that the system must contain and the high-level operations that it must perform. You *could* prepare the design model in a completely different manner, with entirely new classes. Most of the time, however, the simplest and best approach is to carry the analysis classes directly into design. Class design then becomes a process of adding detail and making fine decisions. Moreover, if you incorporate the analysis model during design, it is easier to keep the analysis and design models consistent as they evolve.

During design, you choose among different ways to realize the analysis classes with an eye toward minimizing execution time, memory, and other cost measures. In particular, you must flesh out operations, choosing algorithms and breaking complex operations into simpler operations. This decomposition is an iterative process that is repeated at successively lower levels of abstraction. You may decide to introduce new classes to store intermediate results during program execution and avoid recomputation. However, it is important to avoid overoptimization, as ease of implementation, maintainability, and extensibility are also important concerns.

OO design is an iterative process. When you think that the class design is complete at one level of abstraction, you should consider the next lower level of abstraction. For each level, you may need to add new operations, attributes, and classes. You may even need to revise the relationships between objects (including changes to the inheritance hierarchy). Do not be surprised if you find yourself iterating several times.

Class design involves the following steps.

- Bridge the gap from high-level requirements to low-level services. [15.2]
- Realize use cases with operations. [15.3]
- Formulate an algorithm for each operation. [15.4]
- Recurse downward to design operations that support higher-level operations. [15.5]
- Refactor the model for a cleaner design. [15.6]
- Optimize access paths to data. [15.7]
- Reify behavior that must be manipulated. [15.8]
- Adjust class structure to increase inheritance. [15.9]
- Organize classes and associations. [15.10]

15.2 Bridging the Gap

Figure 15.1 summarizes the essence of design. There is a set of features that you want your system to achieve. You have a set of available resources. Think of the distance between them as a gap. Your job is to build a bridge across the gap. There are several sources of high-level needs: use cases, application commands, and system operations and services. Resources include the operating system infrastructure, class libraries, and previous applications.

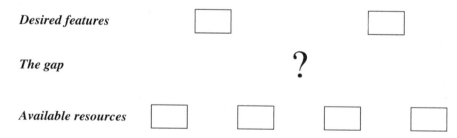

Figure 15.1 The design gap. There is often a disconnect between the desired features and the available resources.

If you can directly construct each feature from the resources, you are done. For example, a salesman can use a spreadsheet to construct a formula for his commission based on various assumptions. The resources are a good match for the task.

But usually it's not so easy. Suppose you want to build a Web-based ordering system. Now you cannot readily build the system from a spreadsheet or a programming language, because there is too big a gap between the features and the resources. You must invent some intermediate elements, so that each element can be expressed in terms of a few elements at the next lower level (Figure 15.2). Furthermore, if the gap is large you will need to organize the intermediate elements into multiple levels. The intermediate elements may be operations, classes, or other UML constructs. Inventing good intermediate elements is the essence of successful design.

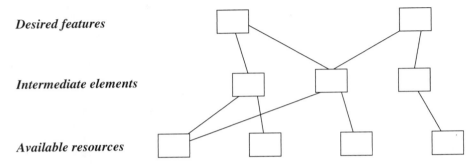

Desired features

Intermediate elements

Available resources

Figure 15.2 Bridging the gap. You must invent intermediate elements to bridge the gap between the desired features and the available resources.

Often the intermediate elements are not obvious. There can be many ways to decompose a high-level operation. You must guess at a likely set of intermediate operations, then try to build them. Be alert to intermediate operations that are similar but not identical. You can reduce the size of your code and increase its clarity by folding these similar operations into a smaller number of common operations. These reworked operations may be less than ideal for some of the higher-level operations. You may have to compromise, because a good design optimizes an entire system and not each separate decision.

If the intermediate elements have already been built, you can just use them, but the principle of bridging the gap is the same. You still have to find the elements in a framework or a class library, select them, and fit them together. The problem isn't making up individual elements—anybody can do that well. The problem is to fit the entire system together cleanly.

Design is difficult because it is not a pure analytic task. You cannot merely study system requirements and derive the ideal system. There are far too many choices of intermediate elements to try them all, so you must apply heuristics. Design requires synthesis: You have to invent new intermediate elements and try to fit them together. It is a creative task, like solving puzzles, proving theorems, playing chess, building bridges, or writing symphonies. You can't expect to push a button or follow a recipe and automatically get a design. A development process provides guidance, just as chess books and engineering handbooks and music theory courses help, but eventually it takes an act of creativity to produce a design.

15.3 Realizing Use Cases

In Chapter 13 we added major operations to the class model. Now during class design we elaborate the complex operations, most of which come from use cases.

Use cases define the required behavior, but they do not define its realization. That is the purpose of design—to choose among the options and prepare for implementation. Each choice has advantages and disadvantages. It is not sufficient merely to deliver the behavior, although that is a primary goal. You must also consider the consequences of each choice on performance, reliability, ease of future enhancement, and many other "ilities". Design is the process of realizing functionality while balancing conflicting needs.

Use cases define system-level behavior. During design you must invent new operations and new objects that provide this behavior. Then, in turn, you must define each of these new operations in terms of lower-level operations involving more objects. Eventually you can implement operations directly in terms of existing operations. Inventing the right intermediate operations is what we have called "bridging the gap."

To start, list the responsibilities of a use case or operation. A **responsibility** is something that an object knows or something it must do [Wirfs-Brock-90]. A responsibility is not a precise concept; it is meant to get the thought process going. For example, in an online theater ticket system, making a reservation has the responsibility of finding unoccupied seats to the desired show, marking the seats as occupied, obtaining payment from the customer, arranging delivery of the tickets, and crediting payment to the proper account. The theater system itself must track which seats are occupied, know the prices of various seats, and so on.

Each operation will have various responsibilities. Some of these may be shared by other operations, and others may be reused in the future. Group the responsibilities into clusters and try to make each cluster coherent. That is, each cluster should consist of related responsibilities that can be serviced by a single lower-level operation. Sometimes, if the responsibilities are broad and independent, each responsibility is in its own cluster.

Now define an operation for each responsibility cluster. Define the operation so that is not restricted to special circumstances, but don't make it so general that it is unfocused. The goal is to anticipate future uses of the new operation. If the operation can be used in several different places in the current design, you probably don't have to make it more general, except to cover the existing uses.

Finally, assign the new lower-level operations to classes. If there is no good class to hold an operation, you may need to invent a new lower-level class.

ATM example. One of the use cases from Chapter 13 is *process transaction*. Recall that a *Transaction* is a set of *Updates* and that the logic varies according to withdrawal, deposit, and transfer.

- **Withdrawal**. A withdrawal involves a number of responsibilities: get amount from customer, verify that amount is covered by the account balance, verify that amount is within the bank's policies, verify that ATM has sufficient cash, disburse funds, debit bank account, and post entry on the customer's receipt. Note that some of these responsibilities must be performed within the context of a database transaction. A database transaction ensures all-or-nothing behavior—all operations within the scope of a transaction happen or none of the operations happen. For example, the disbursement of funds and debiting of the bank account must both happen together.

- **Deposit**. A deposit involves several responsibilities: get amount from customer, accept funds envelope from customer, time-stamp envelope, credit bank account, and post entry on the customer's receipt. Some of these responsibilities must also be performed within the context of a database transaction.

- **Transfer**. Responsibilities include: get source account, get target account, get amount, verify that source account covers amount, verify that the amount is within the bank's policies, debit the source account, credit the target account, and post an entry on the customer's receipt. Once again some of the responsibilities must happen within a database transaction.

You can see that there is some overlap between the operations. For example, *withdrawal*, *deposit*, and *transfer* all request the amount from the customer. *Transfer* and *withdrawal* both verify that the source account has sufficient funds. A reasonable design would coalesce this behavior and build it once.

15.4 Designing Algorithms

Now formulate an ***algorithm*** for each operation. The analysis specification tells *what* the operation does for its clients, but the algorithm shows *how* it is done. Perform the following steps to design algorithms.

- Choose algorithms that minimize the cost of implementing operations.
- Select data structures appropriate to the algorithms.
- Define new internal classes and operations as necessary.
- Assign operations to appropriate classes.

15.4.1 Choosing Algorithms

Many operations are straightforward because they simply traverse the class model to retrieve or change attributes or links. The OCL (see Chapter 3) provides a convenient notation for expressing such traversals.

However, a class-model traversal cannot fully express some operations. We often use pseudocode to handle these situations. Pseudocode helps us think about the algorithm while deferring programming details. For example, many applications involve graphs and the use of transitive closure. (The transitive closure is the set of nodes that can be reached, directly or indirectly, from some starting node.) Figure 15.3 shows a simple model for an undirected graph and pseudocode for computing the transitive closure.

When efficiency is not an issue, you should use simple algorithms. In practice, only a few operations tend to be application bottlenecks. Typically, 20% of the operations consume 80% of execution time. For the remaining operations, it is better to have a design that is simple, understandable, and easy to program than to wring out minor improvements. You can focus your creativity on the algorithms for the operations that are a bottleneck. For example, scanning a set of size n for a value requires an average of $n/2$ operations, whereas a binary search takes $log n$ operations and a hash search takes less than 2 operations on average. Here are some considerations for choosing among alternative algorithms.

```
Node::computeTransitiveClosure () returns NodeSet
    nodes:= createEmptySet;
    return self.TCloop (nodes);
Node::TCloop (nodes:NodeSet) returns NodeSet
    add self to nodes;
    for each edge in self.Edge
        for each node in edge.Node
            /* 2 nodes are associated with an edge */
            if node is not in nodes then node.TCloop(nodes);
            end if
        end for each node
    end for each edge
```

Figure 15.3 Pseudocode example. You can express difficult algorithms with pseudocode. The top method initiates computation and the bottom method recurses for nodes that are one edge away and have not been visited before.

- **Computational complexity**. How does processor time increase as a function of data structure size? Don't worry about small factors in efficiency. For example, an extra level of indirection is insignificant if it improves clarity. It is essential, however, to think about algorithm complexity—that is, how the execution time (or memory) grows with the number of input values: constant time, linear, quadratic, or exponential. For example, the infamous "bubble sort" algorithm requires time proportional to n^2, where n is the size of the list, while most alternative sort algorithms require time proportional to $n \log n$.

- **Ease of implementation and understandability**. It is worth giving up some performance on noncritical operations if you can use a simple algorithm. For precisely this reason you should try to carry the analysis class model forward to design and make minimal adjustments. Unless you have a performance problem, it is not worth doing a lot of optimizing, because you make a model harder to understand and more difficult to program against.

- **Flexibility**. You will find yourself extending most programs, sooner or later. A highly optimized algorithm often sacrifices ease of change. One possibility is to provide two versions of critical operations—a simple but inefficient algorithm that you can implement quickly and use to validate the system, and a complicated but efficient algorithm, that you can check against the simple one.

ATM example. Interactions between the consortium computer and bank computers could be complex. One issue is distributed computing; the consortium computer is at one location and the bank computers are at many other locations. Also it would be important for the consortium computer to be scalable; the ATM system cannot afford the cost of an oversized consortium computer, but the consortium computer must be able to service new banks as they join the network. A third concern is that the bank systems are separate applications from the ATM system; there would be the inevitable conversions and compromises in coordinating the various data formats. All these issues make the choice of algorithms for coordinating the consortium and the banks important.

Many banks have sophisticated systems for reducing losses. Then a decision to approve or reject an ATM withdrawal may not be a simple formula, but could involve elaborate logic. The decision may depend on the customer's credit rating, past activity patterns, and account balance relative to the withdrawal amount. Good algorithms could reduce bank losses, much in excess of the development cost.

15.4.2 Choosing Data Structures

Algorithms require data structures on which to work. During analysis, you focused on the logical structure of system information, but during design you must devise data structures that will permit efficient algorithms. The data structures do not add information to the analysis model, but they organize it in a form convenient for algorithms. Many of these data structures are instances of *container classes*. Such data structures include arrays, lists, queues, stacks, sets, bags, dictionaries, trees, and many variations, such as priority queues and binary trees. Most OO languages provide an assortment of generic data structures as part of their predefined class libraries.

ATM example. A *Transaction* consists of a set of *Updates*. We should revise the class model—there is a sequence of updates that occurs within a transaction. Hence a *Transaction* should have an ordered list of *Updates*. By thinking about algorithms and working through the logic of an application, you can find flaws and improve a class model.

15.4.3 Defining Internal Classes and Operations

You may need to invent new, low-level operations during the decomposition of high-level operations. Some of the low-level operations may be in the "shopping list" of operations (see Chapter 13) from analysis. But usually you will need to add new internal operations as you expand high-level operations.

The expansion of algorithms may lead you to create new classes of objects to hold intermediate results. Typically, the client's description of the problem will not mention these low-level classes because they are artifacts.

ATM example. The design details for the *process transaction* use case involves a customer receipt. The ATM should post each update to a receipt so that customers can remember what they did. The analysis class model did not include a *Receipt* class, so we will add it.

15.4.4 Assigning Operations to Classes

When a class is meaningful in the real world, the operations on it are usually clear. During design, however, you introduce internal classes that do not correspond to real-world objects but merely some aspect of them. Since the internal classes are invented, they are somewhat arbitrary, and their boundaries are more a matter of convenience than of logical necessity.

How do you decide what class owns an operation? When only one object is involved in the operation, the decision is easy: Ask (or tell) that object to perform the operation. The decision is more difficult when more than one object is involved in an operation. You must decide which object plays the lead role in the operation. Ask yourself the following questions.

- **Receiver of action**. Is one object acted on while the other object performs the action? In general, it is best to associate the operation with the *target* of the operation, rather than the *initiator*.

- **Query vs. update**. Is one object modified by the operation, while other objects are only queried for their information? The object that is changed is the target of the operation.

- **Focal class**. Looking at the classes and associations that are involved in the operation, which class is the most centrally located in this subnetwork of the class model? If the classes and associations form a star about a single central class, it is the operation's target.

- **Analogy to real world**. If the objects were not software, but were the real-world objects, what real object would you push, move, activate, or otherwise manipulate to initiate the operation?

Sometimes it is difficult to assign an operation to a class within a generalization hierarchy. It is common to move operations up and down in the hierarchy during design, as their scope is adjusted. Furthermore, the definitions of the subclasses within the hierarchy are often fluid and can be adjusted during design.

ATM example. Let us consider the internal operations for *process transaction* from Section 15.3 and assign a class for each of them.

- *Customer.getAmount( )*—get amount from customer. Eventually *amount* will be stored as an attribute of *Update* objects, but we presume that these objects are not available when the customer specifies the amount and are created after some checking. We will store the amount for a customer in a temporary attribute.

- *Account.verifyAmount(amount)*—verify that amount is covered by the account balance.

- *Bank.verifyAmount(amount)*—verify that amount is within the bank's policies.

- *ATM.verifyAmount(amount)*—verify that the ATM has sufficient cash. Note that there are several *verifyAmount* methods, each belonging to a different class. This is a convenient way to organize the various ways of checking an amount. These methods should all have the same signature.

- *ATM.disburseFunds(amount)*—disburse funds.

- *Account.debit(amount)*—debit bank account.

- *Receipt.postTransaction( )*—add a transaction to a customer's receipt. It might seem that we should relate *Customer* to *Receipt*, but the model will be more precise if we instead relate *CashCard* to *Receipt*. By traversing the model, a *CashCard* does imply one *Customer*, but now we can also track the precise *CardAuthorization* and *CashCard* used for the ATM session.

- *ATM.receiveFunds(amount)*—accept funds envelope from the customer. The proper class for this method is not obvious. We could assign it to *ATM* or to *Customer*. We decided to assign it to *ATM* for symmetry with *ATM.disburseFunds*. We will consider time-stamping the envelope to be part of receiving the funds.

- *Account.credit(amount)*—credit bank account.
- *Customer.getAccount( )*—handles both *get source account* and *get target account*. There is an implicit constraint that this method must satisfy. A customer owns many accounts and the customer can provide only an account that he or she owns. A user interface would typically satisfy this constraint by providing a list of the accounts that a customer owns and letting the customer pick one of them.

Figure 15.4 elaborates the ATM domain class model from Chapter 13 with our progress.

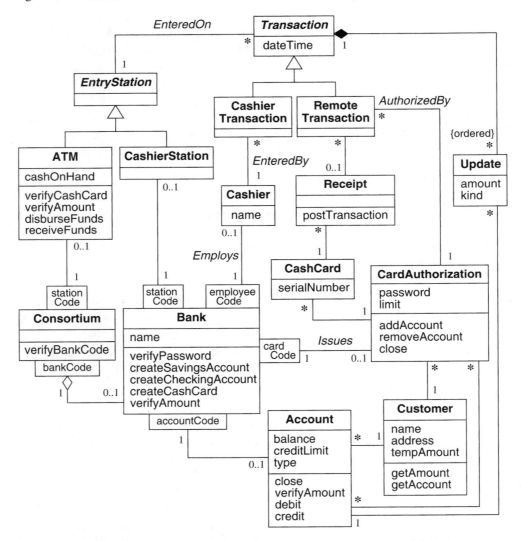

Figure 15.4 ATM domain class model with some class design elaborations

15.5 Recursing Downward

We recommend that you organize operations as layers—operations in higher layers invoke operations in lower layers. The design process generally works top down—you start with the higher-level operations and proceed to define lower-level operations. You can also work bottom up, but you risk designing operations that are never needed. Downward recursion proceeds in two main ways: by functionality and by mechanism.

15.5.1 Functionality Layers

Functionality recursion means that you take the required high-level functionality and break it into lesser operations. This is a natural way to proceed, but you can get into trouble if you perform the decomposition arbitrarily and the pieces do not relate well to classes. To avoid this, make sure you combine similar operations and attach the operations to classes.

The other danger of functionality recursion is that it may depend too much on the exact statement of top-level functionality. Then a small change can radically change the decomposition. To guard against this, you must attach operations to classes and broaden them for reuse. An operation should be coherent, meaningful, and not an arbitrary portion of code. Operations that are carefully attached to classes have much less risk than free-floating functionality. This approach to functionality makes sense, because you must implement the responsibilities of the system somewhere.

ATM example. In Section 15.3 we took a use case and decomposed it into responsibilities. In Section 15.4.4 we assigned the resulting operations to classes. We are satisfied with our operations, but would have had to rework them if they did not fit against the class model.

15.5.2 Mechanism Layers

Mechanism recursion means that you build the system out of layers of needed support mechanisms. In providing functionality, you need various mechanisms to store information, sequence control, coordinate objects, transmit information, perform computations, and provide other kinds of computing infrastructure. These mechanisms don't show up explicitly in the high-level responsibilities of a system, but they are needed to make it all work. For example, in constructing a tall building you need an infrastructure of support girders, utility conduits, and building control devices. These are not directly part of the users' needs for space, but they are needed to enable the chosen architecture. Similarly, computing architecture includes various kinds of general-purpose mechanisms, such as data structures, algorithms, and control patterns. These are not particular to a single application domain, but they may be associated with a particular software architectural style.

For example, a subject-view pattern associates many views with each subject object. A subject object contains the semantic information about some entity, and a view presents it to the user in a particular format. There are mechanisms to update subjects and broadcast the changes to all the views, and to update a view and propagate its changes into the subject. This infrastructure can serve many kinds of applications. However, as a piece of software, it is built in terms of other, more primitive mechanisms than itself.

Any large system mixes functionality layers and mechanism layers. A system designed entirely with functionality recursion is brittle and supersensitive to changes in requirements. A system designed entirely with mechanisms doesn't actually *do* anything useful. Part of the design process is to select the appropriate mix of the two approaches.

ATM example. We have already noted some important mechanisms. There is a need for both communications and distribution infrastructure. The bank and ATM computers are at different locations and must quickly and efficiently communicate with each other. Furthermore, the architecture must be resistant to errors and communications outages.

15.6 Refactoring

The initial design of a set of operations will contain inconsistencies, redundancies, and inefficiencies. This is natural, because it is impossible to get a large design correct in one pass. You must make decisions that are ultimately linked to other decisions. No matter in which order you make the decisions, some of them will be suboptimal.

Furthermore, as a design evolves, it also degrades. It is good to use an operation or class for multiple purposes. But it is inevitable that an operation or class conceived for one purpose will not fully fit additional purposes. You must revisit your design and rework the classes and operations so that they cleanly satisfy all their uses and are conceptually sound. Otherwise your application will become brittle, difficult to understand, and awkward to extend and maintain, and eventually it will collapse under its own weight.

Martin Fowler [Fowler-99] defines *refactoring* as changes to the internal structure of software to improve its design without altering its external functionality. It means that you step back, look across many different classes and operations, and reorganize them to support further development better. Refactoring may seem like a waste of time, but it is an essential part of any good engineering process. It is not enough to deliver functionality. If you expect to maintain a design, then you must keep the design clean, modular, and understandable. Refactoring keeps a design viable for continued development.

ATM example. In Section 15.4.4 we considered operations of the *process transaction* use case. An obvious revision is to combine *Account.credit(amount)* and *Account.debit(amount)* into a single operation *Account.post(amount)*. We would expect more opportunities for refactoring as we flesh out operations for additional use cases.

15.7 Design Optimization

A good way to design a system is to first get the logic correct and then optimize it. That is because it is difficult to optimize a design at the same time as you create it. Furthermore, a premature concern with efficiency often leads to a contorted and inferior design. Once you have the logic in place, you can run the application, measure its performance, and then fine tune it. Often a small part of the code is responsible for most of the time or space costs. It is better to focus optimization on the critical areas, than to spread effort evenly.

This does not mean that you should totally ignore efficiency during initial design. Some approaches are so obviously inefficient that you would not consider them. If there is a clean, simple, efficient way to design something, use it. But don't do something in a complicated, unnatural way just because of fears about performance. First get a clean design working. Then you can optimize it. You might find that your concern was misplaced.

The design model builds on the analysis model. The analysis model captures the logic of a system, while the design model adds development details. You can optimize the inefficient but semantically correct analysis model to improve performance, but an optimized system is more obscure and less likely to be reusable. You must strike an appropriate balance between efficiency and clarity. Design optimization involves the following tasks.

- Provide efficient access paths.

- Rearrange the computation for greater efficiency.

- Save intermediate results to avoid recomputation.

15.7.1 Adding Redundant Associations for Efficient Access

Redundant associations are undesirable during analysis because they do not add information. Design, however, has different motivations and focuses on the viability of a model for implementation. Can the associations be rearranged to optimize critical aspects of the system? Should new associations be added? Can existing associations be omitted? The associations from analysis may not form the most efficient network, when you consider access patterns and relative frequencies.

For an example, consider the design of a company's employee skills database. Figure 15.5 shows a portion of the analysis class model. The operation *Company.findSkill()* returns a set of persons in the company with a given skill. For example, an application might need all the employees who speak Japanese.

Figure 15.5 Analysis model for person skills. Derived data is undesirable during analysis because it does not add information.

For this example, suppose that the company has 1000 employees, each of whom has 10 skills on average. A simple nested loop would traverse *Employs* 1000 times and *HasSkill* 10,000 times. If only 5 employees actually speak Japanese, then the test-to-hit ratio is 2000.

Several improvements are possible. First, you could use a hashed set for *HasSkill* rather than an unordered list. An operation can perform hashing in constant time, so the cost of testing whether a person speaks Japanese is constant, provided that there is a unique *Skill* object for *speaks Japanese*. This rearrangement reduces the number of tests from 10,000 to 1000— one per employee.

In cases where the number of hits from a query is low because few objects satisfy the test, an ***index*** can improve access to frequently retrieved objects. For example, Figure 15.6

adds the derived association *SpeaksLanguage* from *Company* to *Person,* where the qualifier is the language spoken. The derived association does not add any information but permits fast access to employees who speak a particular language. Indexes incur a cost: They require additional memory and must be updated whenever the base associations are updated. As the designer, you decide when it is worthwhile to build indexes. Note that if most queries return a high fraction of the objects in the search path, then an index really does not save much.

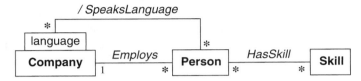

Figure 15.6 Design model for person skills. Derived data is acceptable during design for operations that are significant performance bottlenecks.

Start by examining each operation and see what associations it must traverse to obtain its information. Next, for each operation, note the following.

- **Frequency of access**. How often is the operation called?
- **Fan-out**. What is the "fan-out" along a path through the model? Estimate the average count of each "many" association encountered along the path. Multiply the individual fan-outs to obtain the fan-out of the entire path, which represents the number of accesses on the last class in the path. "One" links do not increase the fan-out, although they increase the cost of each operation slightly; don't worry about such small effects.
- **Selectivity**. What is the fraction of "hits" on the final class—that is, objects that meet selection criteria and are operated on? If the traversal rejects most objects, then a simple nested loop may be inefficient at finding target objects.

You should provide indexes for frequent operations with a low hit ratio, because such operations are inefficient when using nested loops to traverse a path in the network.

ATM example. In our discussion of the *postTransaction( )* operation in Section 15.4.4 we decided to relate *Receipt* to *CashCard* for precision. However, we may still need to quickly find the customer for a receipt. Given that the tracing from *CashCard* to *CardAuthorization* to *Customer* has no fan-out, traversal will be fast and a derived association is not needed.

In the United States, banks must report cash deposits and withdrawals greater than $10,000 to the government. We could traverse from *Bank* to *Account*, then from *Account* to *Update*, and then filter out the *Updates* that are cash and greater than $10,000. Note that we would need to elaborate the class model; we could extend *kind* to distinguish between cash and noncash. A derived association from *Bank* to *Update* would speed this operation.

15.7.2 Rearranging Execution Order for Efficiency

After adjusting the structure of the class model to optimize frequent traversals, the next thing to optimize is the algorithm itself. One key to algorithm optimization is to eliminate dead paths as early as possible. For example, suppose an application must find all employees who speak both Japanese and French. Suppose 5 employees speak Japanese and 100 speak French; it is better to test and find the Japanese speakers first, then test if they speak French. In general, it pays to narrow the search as soon as possible. Sometimes you must invert the execution order of a loop from the original specification.

ATM example. U.S. law requires that a bank not only report individual updates that are greater than $10,000 but also report "suspicious" activities that appear to be an attempt to evade the limit. For example, two withdrawals of $5000 in quick succession would be suspicious.

Suppose we not only check for large cash deposits and withdrawals, but also treat commercial and individual customers differently. We might trust individuals less and have a lower threshold for suspicious activities. We could get all suspicious *Updates* from a derived association ("suspicious" replaces "greater than $10,000" in the derived association in Section 15.7.1) and then traverse back to *Account* to distinguish between commercial and individual accounts. Special logic could then study the updates and determine the ones to report.

Alternately we could maintain two different derived associations between *Bank* and *Update*, one for individuals and the other for businesses. Then would not need to traverse back to *Account* to differentiate them.

15.7.3 Saving Derived Values to Avoid Recomputation

Sometimes it is helpful to define new classes to cache derived attributes and avoid recomputation. You must update the cache if any of the objects on which it depends are changed. There are three ways to handle updates.

- **Explicit update.** The designer inserts code into the update operation of source attributes to explicitly update the derived attributes that depend on it.

- **Periodic recomputation.** Applications often update values in bunches. You could recompute all the derived attributes periodically, instead of after each source change. Periodic recomputation is simpler than explicit update and less prone to bugs. On the other hand, if the data changes incrementally a few objects at a time, full recomputation can be inefficient.

- **Active values.** An *active value* is a value that is automatically kept consistent with its source values. A special registration mechanism records the dependency of derived attributes on source attributes. The mechanism monitors the values of source attributes and updates the values of the derived attributes whenever there is a change. Some programming languages provide active values.

ATM example. For convenience, we might add the class *SuspiciousUpdateGroup*. A *SuspiciousUpdateGroup* could have many *Updates* and an *Update* could belong to many *SuspiciousUpdateGroups*. This new class would store derived attributes to facilitate the study of suspicious behavior. In addition it would provide a convenient place to store comments and observations. A *SuspiciousUpdateGroup* would be a set of *Update* records that were suspected of trying to circumvent the $10,000 reporting limit.

15.8 Reification of Behavior

Behavior written in code is rigid. You can execute it, but cannot manipulate it at run time. Most of the time this is fine, because all you want to do is execute it. But if you need to store, pass, or modify the behavior at run time, you should reify it.

Reification is the promotion of something that is not an object into an object. Behavior usually meets this description. It isn't usually something that you would normally manipulate. If you reify behavior, you can store it, pass it to other operations, and transform it. Reification adds complexity but can dramatically expand the flexibility of a system.

You reify behavior by encoding it into an object and decoding it when it is run. The resulting run-time cost may or may not be significant. If the encoding invokes high-level procedures, the cost is only a few indirections. If the entire behavior is encoded in a different language, however, it must be interpreted, which can be an order of magnitude slower than direct execution of code. If the encoded behavior constitutes a small part of the run-time execution time, the performance overhead may not matter.

Exercise 4.16 in Chapter 4 illustrates reification. In one sense you can regard the tasks of a recipe as operations; in another sense they could be data in a class model.

[Gamma-95] lists a number of behavioral patterns that reify behavior. These include encoding a state machine as a table with a run-time interpreter (*State*), encoding a sequence of requests as parameterized command objects (*Command*), and parameterizing a procedure in terms of an operation that it uses (*Strategy*). These techniques have been around for a long time, but the language of patterns is convenient for describing them and weighing their benefits and costs. For example, the *Strategy* pattern was used in Fortran days for purposes such as passing a function to a mathematical integration routine. However, in Fortran there was no way to ensure correct matching of passed functions, and errors were easy to make. By encoding the passed function as an instance of a function class, you get extensibility via polymorphism, yet can enforce the signatures of an entire family of functions. In this case, OO technology permits a cleaner solution than previous techniques.

ATM example. We have already used reification in the case study. In one sense a transaction is an action—withdrawing, depositing, and transferring funds. We promoted transaction to a class so that we could describe it. The functionality that we need is routine and can readily be obtained by traversing the class model.

15.9 Adjustment of Inheritance

As class design progresses, you can often adjust the definitions of classes and operations to increase inheritance by performing the following steps.

- Rearrange classes and operations to increase inheritance.
- Abstract common behavior out of groups of classes.
- Use delegation to share behavior when inheritance is semantically invalid.

15.9.1 Rearranging Classes and Operations

Sometimes several classes define the same operation and can easily inherit it from a common ancestor, but more often operations in different classes are similar but not identical. By adjusting the definitions of the operations, you may be able to cover them with a single inherited operation.

Before using inheritance, the operations must match. All operations must have the same signature—that is, the same number and types of arguments and results. In addition, the operations must have the same semantics. You can use the following kinds of adjustments to increase the chance of inheritance.

- **Operations with optional arguments**. You may be able to align signatures by adding optional arguments that can be ignored. For example, a draw operation on a monochromatic display does not need a color parameter, but it can accept the parameter and ignore it for consistency with color displays.

- **Operations that are special cases**. Some operations may have fewer arguments because they are special cases of more general operations. Implement the special operations by calling the general operation with appropriate parameter values. For example, appending an element to a list is a special case of inserting an element into list; the insert point simply follows the last element.

- **Inconsistent names**. Similar attributes in different classes may have different names. Give the attributes the same name and move them to a common ancestor class. Then operations that access the attributes will match better. Also watch for similar operations with different names. A consistent naming strategy is important.

- **Irrelevant operations**. Several classes in a group may define an operation, but some others may not. Define the operation on the common ancestor class and declare it as a no-op on the classes that don't care about it. For example, rotation is meaningful for geometric figures, but is unimportant for circles.

ATM example. An ATM can post remote transactions on a receipt. It would seem that we should also be able to issue a receipt for cashier transactions. However, a receipt for a *RemoteTransaction* involves a *CashCard*, while a receipt for a *CashierTransaction* directly involves a *Customer*. Furthermore, the cashier software is apart from the ATM software. We will have two different kinds of receipts, a *RemoteReceipt* and a *CashierReceipt*.

15.9.2 Abstracting Out Common Behavior

You will not recognize all opportunities for inheritance during analysis, so it is worthwhile to reexamine the class model looking for commonality. In addition, you will be adding new classes and operations during design. If two classes seem to repeat several operations and attributes, it is possible that the two classes are really specializations of the same thing, when viewed at a higher level of abstraction.

When there is common behavior, you can create a common superclass for the shared features, leaving only the specialized features in the subclasses. This transformation of the class model is called ***abstracting out*** a common superclass or common behavior. We advise you to make only abstract superclasses, meaning that there are no direct instances of it, but the behavior it defines belongs to all instances of its subclasses. (You can always do this by adding an *Other* subclass.) For example, a *draw()* operation of a geometric figure on a display screen requires setup and rendering of the geometry. The rendering varies among different figures, such as circles, lines, and splines, but the figures can inherit the setup, such as setting the color, line thickness, and other parameters, from the abstract class *Figure*.

Sometimes it is worthwhile to abstract out a superclass even when your application has only one subclass that inherits from it. Although this does not yield any immediate sharing of behavior, the abstract superclass may be reusable in future projects. It may even be a worthwhile addition to your class library. When you complete a project, you should consider the potentially reusable classes for future applications.

Abstract superclasses have benefits beyond sharing and reuse. The splitting of a class into two classes that separate the specific aspects from the more general aspects is a form of modularity. Each class is a separately maintained component with a well-documented interface.

The creation of abstract superclasses also improves the extensibility of a software product. Imagine that you are developing a temperature-sensing module for a large computerized control system. You must use a specific type of sensor (Model J55) with a particular way of reading the temperature, and a formula for converting the raw numeric reading into degrees Celsius. You could place all this behavior in a single class, with one instance for each sensor in the system. But realizing that the J55 sensor is not the only type available, you create an abstract *Sensor* superclass that defines the general behavior common to all sensors. A particular subclass called *SensorJ55* provides reading and conversion that is particular to J55.

Now, when your control system converts to a new sensor model, you need only prepare a subclass that has the specialized behavior for the new model. The superclass already has the common behavior. Perhaps best of all, you will not have to change a single line of code in the large control system that uses these sensors, because the interface is the same, as defined by the *Sensor* superclass.

There is a subtle but important way that abstract superclasses improve configuration management for software maintenance and distribution. Suppose that you must distribute your control system software to many plants throughout the country, each having a different configuration that involves (among other things) a different mix of temperature sensors. Some plants still use the old J55 model, while others have converted to the newer K99 model, and some plants may have a mixture of both types. Generating customized versions of your software to match each different configuration could be tedious.

Instead, you distribute one version of software that contains a subclass for each known sensor model. When the software starts up, it reads the customer's configuration file that tells it which sensor model is used in which location and creates instances of the particular subclasses for the relevant sensors. All the rest of the code treats the sensors as if they were all the same as defined by the *Sensor* superclass. It is even possible to change from one type of sensor to another on-the-fly (while the system is running) if the software creates a new object for the new type of sensor.

ATM example. We did pay attention to inheritance during analysis when we constructed the class model. We do not see any additional inheritance at this time. In a full-fledged application there would be much more design detail and increased opportunities for inheritance.

15.9.3 Using Delegation to Share Behavior

Inheritance is a mechanism for implementing generalization, in which the behavior of a superclass is shared by all its subclasses. Sharing of behavior is justifiable only when a true generalization relationship occurs—that is, only when it can be said that the subclass *is* a form of the superclass. Operations of the subclass that override the corresponding operation of the superclass must provide the same services as the superclass. When class *B* inherits the specification of class *A*, you can assume that every instance of class *B is* an instance of class *A* because it behaves the same.

Sometimes programmers use inheritance as an implementation technique with no intention of guaranteeing the same behavior. It often happens that an existing class already implements some of the behavior that you want to provide in a newly defined class, although in other respects the two classes differ. The programmer is then tempted to inherit from the existing class to achieve part of the implementation of the new class. This can lead to problems if other inherited operations provide unwanted behavior. We discourage this ***inheritance of implementation*** because it can lead to incorrect behavior.

As an example of implementation inheritance, suppose that you need a *Stack* class and a *List* class is available. You may be tempted to make *Stack* inherit from *List*. You can push an element onto a stack by adding an element to the end of the list. Similarly, you can pop an element from a stack by removing an element from the end of the list. But you will also inherit unwanted operations that add or remove elements from arbitrary positions in the list. If these are ever used (by mistake or as a "short-cut"), then the *Stack* class will not behave as expected.

Often when you are tempted to use inheritance as an implementation technique, you could achieve the same goal in a safer way by making one class an associate of the other class. Then, one object can selectively invoke the desired operations of another class, using delegation rather than inheritance. ***Delegation*** consists of catching an operation on one object and sending it to a related object. You delegate only meaningful operations, so there is no danger of inheriting meaningless operations by accident.

A safer design of *Stack* would delegate to *List,* as Figure 15.7 shows. Every *Stack* instance contains a private *List* instance. (You could optimize the actual implementation of the aggregation by using an embedded object or a pointer attribute.) The *Stack.push()* operation delegates to *List* by calling its *last()* and *add()* operations to add an element at the end. The *pop()* operation has a similar implementation using the *last()* and *remove()* operations. The ability to corrupt the stack by adding or removing arbitrary elements is hidden from the client of the *Stack* class.

Some languages, such as C++ and Java, permit a subclass to inherit the form of a superclass but to selectively inherit operations from ancestors and selectively export operations to clients. This is tantamount to the use of delegation, because the subclass *is not* a form of the superclass in all respects and is not confused with it.

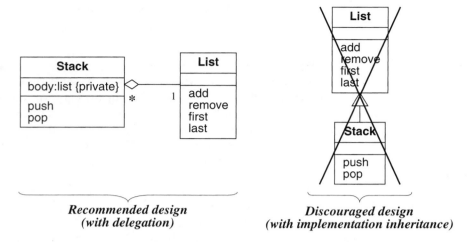

Recommended design   Discouraged design
(with delegation)   (with implementation inheritance)

Figure 15.7 Alternative designs. Do not use implementation inheritance.

ATM example. Our use of inheritance is deep and structural. That is the only way we ever use inheritance.

15.10 Organizing a Class Design

Programs consist of discrete physical units that can be edited, compiled, imported, or otherwise manipulated. In some languages, such as C and Fortran, the units are source files. In Ada and Java, the package is an explicit language construct. [Coplien-92] shows how to use a C++ class to group static member functions, lesser classes, enumerations, and constants. You can improve the organization of a class design with the following steps.

- ■ Hide internal information from outside view.
- ■ Maintain coherence of entities.
- ■ Fine-tune definition of packages.

15.10.1 Information Hiding

During analysis we did not consider information visibility—rather our focus was on understanding the application. The goals of design are different. During design we adjust the analysis model so that it is practical to implement and maintain. One way to improve the viability of a design is by carefully separating external specification from internal implementation. This is called *information hiding*. Then you can change the implementation of a class without requiring that clients of the class modify code. In addition, the resulting "firewalls" around classes limit the effects of changes so that you can better understand them.

There are several ways to hide information.

■ **Limit the scope of class-model traversals**. Taken to an extreme, a method could traverse all associations of the class model to locate and access an object. Such unconstrained visibility is appropriate during analysis, when you are trying to understand a problem, but methods that know too much about a model are fragile and easily invalidated by changes. During design you should try to limit the scope of any one method [Lieberherr-88]. An object should access only objects that are directly related (directly connected by an association). An object can access indirectly related objects via the methods of intervening objects.

■ **Do not directly access foreign attributes**. Generally speaking, it is acceptable for subclasses to access the attributes of their superclasses. However, classes should not access the attributes of an associated class. Instead, call an operation to access the attributes of an associated class.

■ **Define interfaces at a high a level of abstraction**. It is desirable to minimize class couplings. One way to do this is by raising the level of abstraction of interfaces. It is fine to call a method on another class for a meaningful task, but you should avoid doing so for minutia.

■ **Hide external objects**. Use boundary objects to isolate the interior of a system from its external environment. A ***boundary object*** is an object whose purpose is to mediate requests and responses between the inside and the outside. It accepts external requests in a client-friendly form and transforms them into a form convenient for the internal implementation.

■ **Avoid cascading method calls**. Avoid applying a method to the result of another method, unless the result class is already a supplier of methods to the caller. Instead consider writing a method to combine the two operations.

15.10.2 Coherence of Entities

Coherence is another important design principle. An entity, such as a class, an operation, or a package, is coherent if it is organized on a consistent plan and all its parts fit together toward a common goal. An entity should have a single major theme; it should not be a collection of unrelated parts.

A method should do one thing well. A single method should not contain both policy and implementation. ***Policy*** is the making of context-dependent decisions. ***Implementation*** is the execution of fully-specified algorithms. Policy involves making decisions, gathering global information, interacting with the outside world, and interpreting special cases. A policy method contains I/O statements, conditionals, and accesses data stores. A policy method does not contain complicated algorithms but instead calls the appropriate implementation methods. An implementation method encodes exactly one algorithm, without making any decisions, assumptions, defaults, or deviations. All its information is supplied as arguments, so the argument list may be long.

Separating policy and implementation greatly increases the possibility of reuse. The implementation methods do not contain any context dependencies, so they are likely to be reusable. Usually you must rewrite policy methods in a new application, but they are often simple and consist mostly of high-level decisions and low-level calls.

For example, consider an operation to credit interest on a checking account. Interest is compounded daily based on the balance, but all interest for a month is lost if the account is closed. The interest logic consists of two parts: an implementation method that computes the interest due between a pair of days, without regard to any forfeitures or other provisions; and a policy method that decides whether and for what interval the implementation method is called. The implementation method is complex, but likely to be reused. Policy methods are less likely to be reusable, but simpler to write.

A class should not serve too many purposes at once. If it is too complicated, you can break it up using either generalization or aggregation. Smaller pieces are more likely to be reusable than large complicated pieces. Exact numbers are somewhat risky, but as a rule of thumb consider breaking up a class if it contains more than about 10 attributes, 10 associations, or 20 operations. Always break a class if the attributes, associations, or operations sharply divide into two or more unrelated groups.

15.10.3 Fine-Tuning Packages

During analysis you partitioned the class model into packages. This initial organization may not be suitable or optimal for implementation. You should define packages so that their interfaces are minimal and well defined. The interface between two packages consists of the associations that relate classes in one package to classes in the other and operations that access classes across package boundaries.

You can use the connectivity of the class model as a guide for forming packages. As a rough rule of thumb, classes that are closely connected by associations should be in the same package, while classes that are unconnected, or loosely connected, may be in separate packages. Of course there are other aspects to consider. Packages should have some theme, functional cohesiveness, or unity of purpose.

The number of different operations that traverse a given association is a good measure of its coupling strength. We are referring to the number of different ways that the association is used, not the frequency of traversal. Try to keep strong coupling within a single package.

15.11 ATM Example

Figure 15.8 shows our final ATM domain class model after class design. (Keep in mind that the full class model also includes the application class model from Figure 13.8.)

15.12 Chapter Summary

Class design does not begin from scratch but rather elaborates the previous stages of analysis and system design. Class design adds details, such as designing algorithms, refactoring operations, optimizing classes, adjusting inheritance, and refining packages.

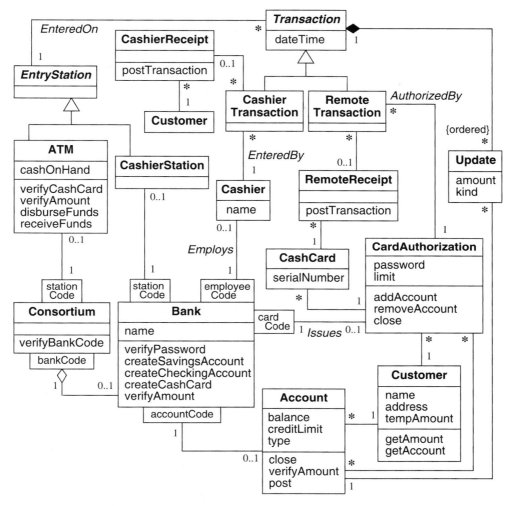

Figure 15.8 Final ATM domain class model after class design

The first step of class design is to add operations according to the use cases. Use cases define the required behavior but not its realization. The class designer invents operations that will deliver the behavior specified by the use cases.

Next, you must devise an algorithm for each operation. Class design focuses on computational complexity, but you should sacrifice small amounts of performance for greater clarity. You will need to recurse to define low-level operations to realize high-level operations. Recursion stops when you have operations that are already available or that are straightforward to implement.

The initial design of a set of operations will contain inconsistencies, redundancies, and inefficiencies. This is natural, because it is impossible to get a large design correct in one pass. Furthermore, as a design evolves, it also degrades. It is inevitable that an operation or class conceived for one purpose will not fully fit additional purposes. As you proceed with a design, you should occasionally refactor operations to improve their clarity and resilience.

During design, you may need to rework the analysis model for efficiency. Optimization does not discard the original information but adds new redundant information to speed access paths and preserve intermediate results. It can be helpful to rearrange algorithms and reduce the number of operations that need to be executed.

You should consider reification—the promotion of something that is not an object into an object. For example, a deposit, withdrawal, or transfer of funds would normally be an operation—it is something that someone *does*. However, for the ATM case study we promoted transaction to a class so that we could describe it.

As class design progresses, you can often adjust the definitions of classes and operations to increase inheritance. These adjustments include modifying the argument list of a method, moving attributes and operations from a class into a superclass, defining an abstract superclass to cover the shared behavior of several classes, and splitting an operation into an inherited part and a specific part. You should use delegation rather than inheritance when a class is similar to another class but not truly a subclass.

You must organize programs into physical units for editors and compilers as well as for the convenience of programming teams. Information hiding is a primary goal to ensure that future changes affect limited amounts of code. Packages should be coherent and organized about a common theme.

abstracting out a superclass	derived attributes	policy vs. implementation
adjusting inheritance	implementation inheritance	recursing
algorithm	index	refactoring
data structure	information hiding	reification
delegation	optimization	responsibility
derived associations	package	use case

Figure 15.9 Key concepts for Chapter 15

Bibliographic Notes

Algorithms and data structures are part of the basic computer science curriculum. [Aho-83] and [Sedgewick-95] are well-written books about algorithms.

Adding indexes and rearranging access order to improve performance is a mature technique in database optimization. See [Ullman-02] for examples.

[Lieberherr-88] is an early attempt to provide visibility guidelines (the law of Demeter) that preserve OO modularity. [Meyer-97] suggests style rules for using classes and operations.

The *class design* stage is renamed from *object design* in the first edition of this book.

References

[Aho-83] Alfred Aho, John Hopcroft, and Jeffrey Ullman. *Data Structures and Algorithms.* Boston: Addison-Wesley, 1983.

[Coplien-92] James O. Coplien. *Advanced C++: Programming Styles and Idiom.* Boston: Addison-Wesley, 1992.

[Fowler-99] Martin Fowler. *Refactoring: Improving the Design of Existing Code.* Boston: Addison-Wesley, 1999.

[Gamma-95] Erich Gamma, Richard Helm, Ralph Johnson, and John Vlissides. *Design Patterns: Elements of Reusable Object-Oriented Software.* Boston: Addison-Wesley, 1995.

[Lieberherr-88] K. Lieberherr, I. Holland, A. Riel. Object-oriented programming: an objective sense of style. *OOPSLA'88* as *ACM SIGPLAN 23,* 11 (November 1988), 323–334.

[Meyer-97] Bertrand Meyer. *Object-Oriented Software Construction, Second Edition.* Upper Saddle River, NJ: Prentice Hall, 1997.

[Sedgewick-95] Robert Sedgewick, Philippe Flajolet, and Peter Gordon. *An Introduction to the Analysis of Algorithms.* Boston: Addison-Wesley, 1995.

[Ullman-02] Jeffrey Ullman and Jennifer Widom. *A First Course in Database Systems.* Upper Saddle River, NJ: Prentice Hall, 2002.

[Wirfs-Brock-90] Rebecca Wirfs-Brock, Brian Wilkerson, and Lauren Wiener. *Designing Object-Oriented Software.* Upper Saddle River, NJ: Prentice Hall, 1990.

Exercises

15.1   (6) Take the use cases from Exercise 13.9 and list at least four responsibilities for each one. [Instructor's note: You may want to give the students our answer to Exercise 13.9.]

15.2   (6) Take the first three use cases from Exercise 13.16 and list at least four responsibilities for each one. [Instructor's note: You may want to give the students our answer to Exercise 13.16.]

15.3   (4) Write algorithms to draw the following figures on a graphics terminal. The figures are not filled. Assume pixel-based graphics. State any assumptions that you make.
   a. circle
   b. ellipse
   c. square
   d. rectangle

15.4   (3) Discuss whether or not the algorithm that you wrote in the previous exercise to draw an ellipse is suitable for drawing circles and whether or not the rectangle algorithm is suitable for squares.

15.5   (3) By careful ordering of multiplications and additions, the total number of arithmetic steps needed to evaluate a polynomial can be minimized. For example, one way to evaluate the polynomial $a_4x^4 + a_3x^3 + a_2x^2 + a_1x + a_0$ is to compute each term separately, adding each term to the total as it is computed, which requires 10 multiplications and 4 additions. Another way is to rearrange the order of the arithmetic to $x \cdot (x \cdot (x \cdot (x \cdot a_4 + a_3) + a_2) + a_1) + a_0$, which requires only 4 multiplications and 4 additions. How many multiplications and additions are required by each method for an nth-order polynomial? Discuss the relative merits of each approach.

15.6   (4) Improve the class diagram in Figure E15.1 by generalizing the classes *Ellipse* and *Rectangle* to the class *GraphicsPrimitive*, transforming the class diagram so that there is only a single one-to-one association to the object class *BoundingBox*. In effect, you will be changing the 0..1 multiplicity to exactly-one multiplicity. As it stands, the class *BoundingBox* is shared between *Ellipse* and *Rectangle*. A *BoundingBox* is the smallest rectangular region that will contain the associated *Ellipse* or *Rectangle*.

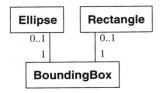

Figure E15.1 Portion of a class diagram with a shared class

15.7   (5) Which class(es) for the previous exercise must supply a delete operation visible to the outside world? To delete means to destroy an object and remove it from the application. Explain your answer.

15.8   (4) Modify the class diagram in Figure E15.2 so that a separate class provides margins. Different categories of pages may have a default margin, and specific pages may override the default.

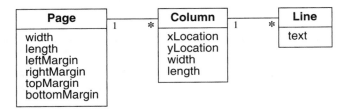

Figure E15.2 Portion of a class diagram of a newspaper

15.9   (3) Modify Figure E15.2 to make it possible to be able to determine what *Page* a *Line* is on without first determining the *Column*.

15.10 (7) Write pseudocode for each method in Figure E15.3. *Initialize* causes a deck to start with 52 cards and anything else to become empty. *Insert* and *delete* take a card as a single argument and insert or delete the card into a collection, forcing the collection to redisplay itself. *Delete* is allowed only on the top card of a pile. *Sort* is used to sort a hand by suit and rank.

       Pile is an abstract class. *TopOfPile* and *bottomOfPile* are queries. *Draw* deletes the top card from a pile and inserts the card into a hand, which is passed as an argument.

       Shuffle mixes a deck. *Deal* selects cards from the top of the deck one at a time, deleting them from the deck and inserting them into hands that are created and returned as an array of hands. *Display* displays a card. *Compare* determines which of two cards has the largest value. *Discard* deletes a card from the collection that contains it and places it on top of the draw pile that is passed as an argument.

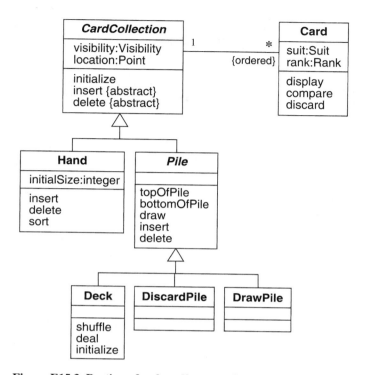

Figure E15.3 Portion of a class diagram of a card-playing program

15.11 (5) Write pseudocode for computing the net score for a trial in Figure E12.4.

Each attempt of a competitor in an event (a *Trial*) is observed by several judges. Each judge rates the attempt and holds up a score. A reader assigned to the group of judges announces the scores one at a time to a panel of scorekeepers. Three scorekeepers write the scores down, cross off the highest and the lowest scores, and total the rest. They check each other's total to detect recording and arithmetic errors. In some cases, they may ask the reader to repeat the scores. When they are satisfied, they hand their figures to three other scorekeepers, who multiply the total score by a difficulty factor for the event and take the average to determine a net score. The net scores are compared to detect and correct scoring errors.

15.12 Prepare pseudocode for the following operations to classes in Figure E12.4. You will need to add a many-to-many association *RegisteredFor* between a set of *Events* and an ordered list of *Competitors* to track who is registered for which *Events*. Use the registration order in scheduling trials.

   a. (3) Find the event for a figure and meet.

   b. (3) Register a competitor for an event.

   c. (3) Register a competitor for all events at a meet.

   d. (5) Select and schedule events for a meet.

   e. (3) Schedule meets in a season.

   f. (4) Assign judges and scorekeepers to stations.

15.13 (8) Figure E15.4 is a portion of a class diagram metamodel that might be used in a compiler of an OO language. Write pseudocode for the *traceInheritancePath* method that traces an inheritance hierarchy as follows. Input to the method is a pair of classes. The method returns an ordered list of classes on the path from the more general class to the more specific class. Tracing is only through generalizations; aggregations and associations are ignored. If tracing fails, an empty list is returned. You may assume that multiple inheritance is not allowed.

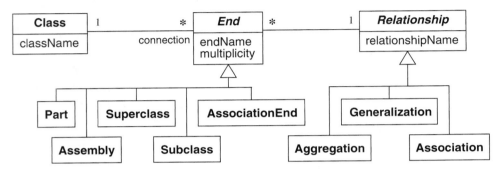

Figure E15.4 Portion of a class diagram metamodel

15.14 (8) Refine Figure E15.4 by eliminating the associations to the classes *End* and *Relationship*, replacing them with associations to the subclasses of *End* and *Relationship*. This is an example of a transformation on a class diagram. Write pseudocode for the *traceInheritancePath* method for the new diagram.

15.15 (7) Referring to Figure E15.4, prepare an algorithm for an operation that will generate a name for an association that does not already have one. Input to the operation is an instance of *Association*. The operation must return a globally unique *relationshipName*. If the association already has a name, the operation should return it. Otherwise the operation should generate a name using a strategy that you must devise.

The precise strategy is not critical, but the generated names must be unique, and anyone reading the names should be able to determine which association the name refers to. Assume all associations are binary. You may assume that a similar operation on the class *End* already has been designed that will return an *endName* unique within the context of a relationship. If the name that would be formed collides with an existing name, modify the name in some way to make it unique. If you feel you need to modify the diagram or use additional data structures, go ahead, but be sure to describe them.

15.16 (7) Improve the class diagram in Figure E15.5 by transforming it, adding the class *PoliticalParty*. Associate *Voter* with a party. Discuss why the transformation is an improvement.

15.17 (7) Sometimes an airline will substitute a smaller aircraft for a larger one for a flight with few passengers. Write an algorithm for reassigning seats so that passengers with low row numbers do not have to be reassigned. Assume both aircraft have the same number of seats per row.

15.18 (8) The need for implementation efficiency may force you to create classes that are not in the original problem statement. For example, a two-dimensional CAD system may use specialized data structures to determine which points fall within a rectangular window specified by the user.

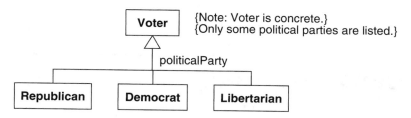

Figure E15.5 Class diagram representing voter membership in a political party

One technique is to maintain a collection of points sorted on x and then y. Points that fall within a rectangular window can usually be found without having to check all points.

Prepare a class diagram that describes collections of points sorted on x and y. Write pseudocode for the operations *search, add*, and *delete*. The input to *search* is a description of a rectangular region and a collection of points. The output of *search* is a set of points from the input collection that fall within the region. Inputs to both *add* and *delete* are a point and a collection of points. The input point is added or deleted from the collection.

15.19 (8) Determine how the time required by the search operation in the previous exercise depends on the number of points in a collection. Explicitly state any assumptions you make.

15.20 (3) In selecting an algorithm, it may be important to evaluate its resource requirements. How does the time required to execute the following algorithms depend on the following parameters?
   a. The algorithm in Exercise 15.13 on the depth of the inheritance hierarchy.
   b. The algorithm in Exercise 15.17 on the number of passengers.

16

Process Summary

As Figure 16.1 shows, a development process provides a basis for the organized production of software. We advocate that a process be based on OO concepts and the UML notation.

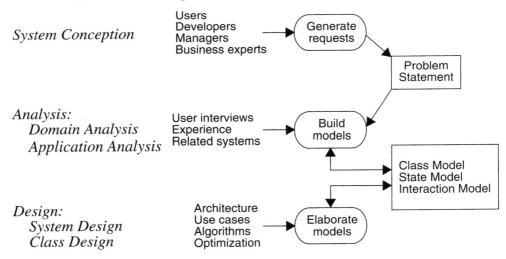

Figure 16.1 Summary of development process. A development process provides a basis for the organized production of software.

Note that there is no need to change from one model to another, as the OO paradigm spans analysis, design, and implementation. The OO paradigm applies equally well in describing the real-world specification and computer-based implementation.

This book's presentation of the stages is linear (an artifact of presentation), but in practice OO development is an iterative process, as Figure 16.1 emphasizes. When you think that a model is complete at one level of abstraction, you should consider the next lower level of abstraction. For each level, you may need to add new operations, attributes, and classes. You may even need to revise the relationships between objects (including changes to the inheritance hierarchy). Do not be surprised if you find yourself iterating several times. Chapter 21 explains more about iterative development.

16.1 System Conception

System conception deals with the genesis of an application. Initially some person, who understands both technology and business needs, thinks of an idea for an application. The purpose of system conception is to understand the big picture—what need does the proposed system meet, can it be developed at a reasonable cost, and will the demand for the result justify the cost of building it? The input to system conception is the raw idea for a new application. The output is a problem statement that is the starting point for careful analysis.

16.2 Analysis

Analysis focuses on preparing models to get a deep understanding of the requirements. The goal of analysis is to specify what needs to be done, not how it is done. You must understand a problem before attempting a solution. It is important to consider all available inputs, including requirements statements, user interviews, real-world experience, and artifacts from related systems. The output from analysis is a set of models that specify a system in a rigorous and complete manner. There are two substages to analysis: domain analysis and application analysis.

16.2.1 Domain Analysis

Domain analysis captures general knowledge about an application—concepts and relationships known to experts in the domain. The concern is with devising a precise, concise, understandable, and correct model of the real world. Before building anything complex, the builder must understand the requirements. Domain analysis leads to class models and sometimes state models, but seldom interaction models. The job of constructing a domain model is mainly to decide which information to capture (determine the application's scope) and how to represent it (the level of abstraction).

16.2.2 Application Analysis

Application analysis follows and addresses the computer aspects of the application (application objects) that are visible to users. Application objects are not merely internal design decisions, because the users see them and must agree with them. Application classes include controllers, devices, and boundary objects. The interaction model dominates application analysis, but the class and state models are also important.

16.3 Design

Analysis addresses the *what* of an application; design addresses the *how*. Once you have a thorough understanding of an application from analysis, you are ready to deal with the details of building a practical and maintainable solution. You could prepare the design model in a completely different manner than analysis, but most of the time, the simplest and best approach is to carry the analysis classes forward into design. Design then becomes a process of adding detail and making fine decisions. There are two substages to design: system design and class design.

16.3.1 System Design

The purpose of system design is to devise a high-level strategy—the architecture—for solving the application problem. The choice of architecture is an important decision with broad consequences and is based on the requirements as well as past experience. The system designer must also establish policies to guide the subsequent class design.

16.3.2 Class Design

Class design augments and adjusts the real-world models from analysis so that they are ready for implementation. Class designers complete the definitions of the classes and associations and choose algorithms for operations.

Part 3

Implementation

Parts 1 and 2 have presented OO concepts and an analysis and design process for applying the concepts. Part 3 covers the remainder of software development and discusses the specific details for implementing a system with C++, Java, and databases. OO models are also helpful with non-OO languages, but we do not cover non-OO languages in this book, because most developers now days are using OO languages.

Chapter 17 discusses implementation issues that transcend the choice of language. The focus is on techniques for realizing associations, since few languages have intrinsic support.

Chapter 18 explains the principles of how to implement an OO design with C++ and Java. We cover C++ and Java because they are the most popular OO programming languages.

Chapter 19 shows how to implement an OO design with a database. Our focus is on relational databases, because they dominate the marketplace. As you would expect, OO designs can also be implemented with OO databases, but OO databases have but a small market share and are only used in specialty situations.

Chapter 20 concludes with style recommendations for programming in any language or database. The programming code is the ultimate embodiment of the solution to the problem, so the way in which it is written is important for maintainability and extensibility.

Part 3 completes our explanation of how to take OO concepts and use them to develop applications. Part 4 deals with software engineering issues that are especially important for large and complex applications.

17

Implementation Modeling

Implementation is the final development stage that addresses the specifics of programming languages. Implementation should be straightforward and almost mechanical, because you should have made all the difficult decisions during design. To a large extent, your programming code should simply translate design decisions. You must add details while writing code, but each one should affect only a small part of the program.

17.1 Overview of Implementation

It is now, during implementation, that you finally capitalize on your careful preparation from analysis and design. First you should address implementation issues that transcend languages. This is what we call *implementation modeling* and involves the following steps.

- Fine-tune classes. [17.2]
- Fine-tune generalizations. [17.3]
- Realize associations. [17.4]
- Prepare for testing [17.5]

The first two steps are motivated by the theory of transformations. A *transformation* is a mapping from the domain of models to the range of models. When modeling, it is important not only to focus on customer requirements, but to also take an abstract mathematical perspective.

17.2 Fine-tuning Classes

Sometimes it is helpful to fine-tune classes before writing code in order to simplify development or to improve performance. Keep in mind that the purpose of implementation is to realize the models from analysis and design. Do not alter the design model unless there is a compelling reason. If there is, consider the following possibilities.

- **Partition a class**. In Figure 17.1, we can represent home and office information for a person with a single class or we can split the information into two classes. Both approaches are correct. If we have much home and office data, it would be better to separate them. If we have a modest amount of data, it may be easier to combine them.

  The partitioning of a class can be complicated by generalization and association. For example, if *Person* was a superclass and we split it into home and office classes, it would be less convenient for the subclasses to obtain both kinds of information. The subclasses would have to multiply inherit, or we would have to introduce an association between the home and office classes. Furthermore, if there were associations to *Person*, you would need to decide how to associate to the partitioned classes.

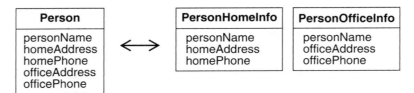

Figure 17.1 Partitioning a class. Sometimes it is helpful to fine-tune a model by partitioning or merging classes.

- **Merge classes**. The converse to partitioning a class is to merge classes. If we had started with *PersonHomeInfo* and *PersonOfficeInfo* in Figure 17.1, we could combine them. Figure 17.2 shows another example with intervening associations. Neither representation is inherently superior, because both are mathematically correct. Once again, you must consider the effects of generalization and association in your decisions.

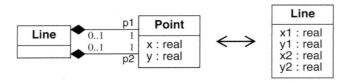

Figure 17.2 Merging classes. It is acceptable to rework your definitions of classes, but only do so for compelling development or performance reasons.

- **Partition / merge attributes**. You can also adjust attributes by partitioning and merging, as Figure 17.3 illustrates.
- **Promote an attribute / demote a class**. As Figure 17.4 shows, we can represent address as an attribute, as one class, or as several related classes. The bottom model would be helpful if we were preloading address data for an application.

ATM example. We may want to split *Customer address* into several classes if we are pre-populating address data. For example, we may preload *city*, *stateProvice*, and *postalCode*

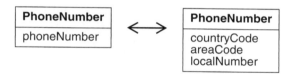

Figure 17.3 Partitioning / merging attributes

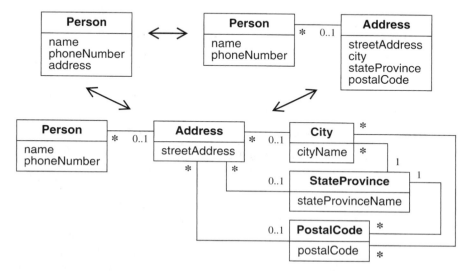

Figure 17.4 Promoting an attribute / demoting a class

data for the convenience of customer service representatives when creating a new *Customer* record.

We may also want to place *Account type* in its own class. Then it would be easier to program special behavior. For example, the screens may look different for checking accounts than for savings accounts.

All in all, the ATM model is small in size and carefully prepared, so we are not inclined to make many changes.

17.3 Fine-tuning Generalizations

As you can reconsider classes, so too you can reconsider generalizations. Sometimes it is helpful to remove a generalization or to add one prior to coding.

Figure 17.5 shows a translation model from one of our recent applications. A language translation service converts a *TranslationConcept* into a *Phrase* in the desired language. A *MajorLanguage* is a language such as English, French, or Japanese. A *MinorLanguage* is a dialect such as American English, British English, or Australian English. All entries in the application database that must be translated store a *translationConceptID*. The translator first tries to find the phrase for a concept in the specified *MinorLanguage* and then, if that is not found, looks for the concept in the corresponding *MajorLanguage*.

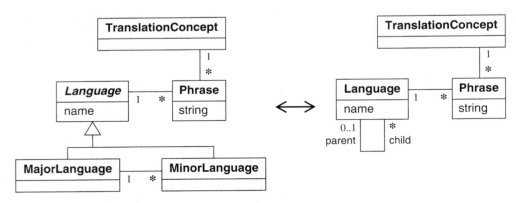

Figure 17.5 Removing / adding generalization. Sometimes it can simplify implementation to remove or add a generalization.

For implementation simplicity, we removed the generalization and used the right model. Since the translation service is separate from the application model, there were no additional generalizations or associations to consider, and it was easy to make the simplification.

ATM example. Back in Section 13.1.1 we mentioned that the ATM domain class model encompassed two applications—ATM and cashier. We did not concern ourselves with this during analysis—the purpose of analysis is to understand business requirements, and the eventual customer does not care how services are structured. Furthermore, we wanted to make sure that both applications had similar behavior. However, now that we are implementing, we must separate the applications and limit the scope to what we will actually build. Figure 17.6 deletes cashier information from the domain class model, leading to a removal of both generalizations.

Figure 17.6 is the full ATM class model. The top half (*Account* and above) presents the domain class model; the bottom half (*UserInterface*, *ConsortiumInterface*, and below) presents the application class model. The operations are representative, but only some are listed.

17.4 Realizing Associations

Associations are the "glue" of the class model, providing access paths between objects. Now we must formulate a strategy for implementing them. Either we can choose a global strategy for implementing all associations uniformly, or we can select a particular technique for each association, taking into account the way the application will use it. We will start by analyzing how associations are traversed.

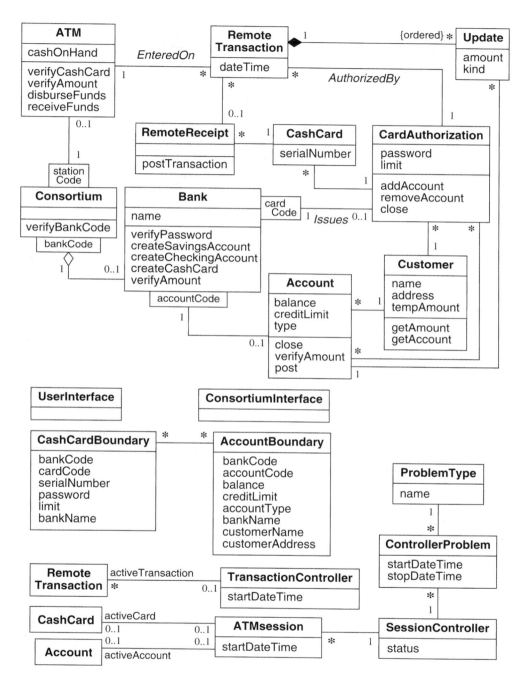

Figure 17.6 Full ATM implementation class model

17.4.1 Analyzing Association Traversal

We have assumed until now that associations are inherently bidirectional, which is certainly true in an abstract sense. But if your application has some associations that are traversed in only one direction, their implementation can be simplified. Be aware, however, that future requirements may change, and you may need to add a new operation later that traverses the association in the reverse direction.

For prototype work we always use bidirectional associations, so that we can add new behavior and modify the application quickly. For production work we optimize some associations. In any case, you should hide the implementation, using access methods to traverse and update the association. Then you can change your decision more easily.

17.4.2 One-way Associations

If an association is traversed only in one direction, you can implement it as a **pointer**—an attribute that contains an object reference. (Note that this chapter uses the word *pointer* in the logical sense. The actual implementation could be a programming-language pointer, a programming-language reference, or even a database foreign key.) If the multiplicity is "one," as Figure 17.7 shows, then it is a simple pointer; if the multiplicity is "many," then it is a set of pointers.

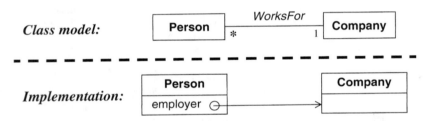

Figure 17.7 Implementing a one-way association with pointers. If an association is traversed only in one direction, you can implement it as a pointer.

17.4.3 Two-way Associations

Many associations are traversed in both directions, although not usually with equal frequency. There are three approaches to their implementation.

- **Implement one-way.** Implement as a pointer in one direction only and perform a search when backward traversal is required. This approach is useful only if there is a great disparity in traversal frequency in the two directions and minimizing both the storage and update costs is important. The rare backward traversal will be expensive.

- **Implement two-way.** Implement with pointers in both directions as Figure 17.8 shows. This approach permits fast access, but if either direction is updated, then the other must also be updated to keep the link consistent. This approach is useful if accesses outnumber updates.

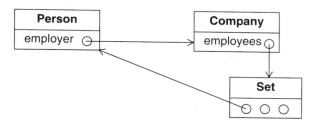

Figure 17.8 Implementing a two-way association with pointers. Dual pointers enable fast traversal of an association in either direction, but introduce redundancy, complicating maintenance.

■ **Implement with an association object**. Implement with a distinct association object, independent of either class, as Figure 17.9 shows [Rumbaugh-87]. An association object is a set of pairs of associated objects (triples for qualified associations) stored in a single variable-size object. For efficiency, you can implement an association object using two dictionary objects, one for the forward direction and one for the backward direction. Access is slightly slower than with pointers, but if hashing is used, then access is still constant time. This approach is useful for extending predefined classes from a library that cannot be modified, because the association object does not add any attributes to the original classes. Distinct association objects are also useful for sparse associations, in which most objects of the classes do not participate, because space is used only for actual links.

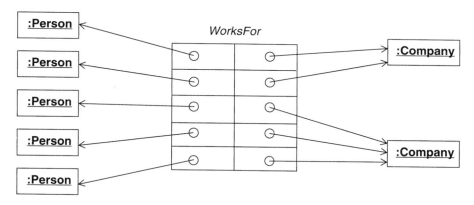

Figure 17.9 Implementing an association as an object. This is the most general approach for implementing associations but requires the most programming skill.

17.4.4 Advanced Associations

The appropriate techniques for implementing advanced associations vary.

- **Association classes**. The usual approach is to promote the association to a class. This handles any attributes of the association as well as associations of the association class. Note that promotion changes the meaning of the model; the promoted association has identity of its own, and methods must compensate to enforce the dependency of the association class on the constituent classes.

  Alternatively, if the association is one-to-one and has no further associations, you can implement the association with pointers and store any attributes for the association as attributes of either class. Similarly, if the association is one-to-many and has no further associations, you can implement the association with pointers and store attributes for the association as attributes of the "many" class, since each "many" class appears only once for the association.

- **Ordered associations**. Use an ordered set of pointers similar to Figure 17.8 or a dictionary with an ordered set of pairs similar to Figure 17.9.

- **Sequences**. Same as ordered association, but use a list of pointers.

- **Bags**. Same as ordered association, but use an array of pointers.

- **Qualified associations**. Implement a qualified association with multiplicity "one" as a dictionary object. using the techniques of Figure 17.9. Qualified associations with multiplicity "many" are rare, but you can implement them as a dictionary of object sets.

- **N-ary associations**. Promote the association to a class. Note that there is a change in identity and that you must compensate with additional programming, similar to that for association classes.

- **Aggregation**. Treat aggregation like an ordinary association.

- **Composition**. You can treat composition like an ordinary association. You will need to do some additional programming to enforce the dependency of the part on the assembly.

17.4.5 ATM Example

Exercise 17.1 addresses the implementation of associations from the ATM model.

17.5 Testing

If you have carefully modeled your application, as we advise, you will reduce errors in your software and need less testing. Nevertheless, testing is still important. Testing is a quality-assurance mechanism for catching residual errors. Furthermore, testing provides an independent measure of the quality of your software. The number of bugs found for a given testing effort is an indicator of software quality, and you should find fewer bugs as you become proficient at modeling. You should keep careful records of the bugs that you find, as well as customer complaints.

If your software is sound, the primary difficulty for developers is in finding the occasional, odd error. Fixing the errors is a much easier problem. (In contrast, if your software is haphazard, it can also be difficult to fix the errors.)

You need to test at every stage of development, not just during implementation. The nature of the testing changes, however, as you proceed. During analysis, you test the model against user expectations by asking questions and seeing if the model answers them. During design, you test the architecture and can simulate its performance. During implementation, you test the actual code—the model serves as a guide for paths to traverse.

Testing should progress from small pieces to ultimately the entire application. Developers should begin by testing their own code, their classes and methods—this is called *unit testing*. The next step is *integration testing*—that is, how the classes and methods fit together. You do integration testing in successive waves, putting code together in increasing chunks of scope and behavior. It is important to do integration testing early and often to ensure that the pieces of code cleanly fit together (see Chapter 21). The final step is *system testing*, where you check the entire application.

17.5.1 Unit Testing

Developers normally check their own code and do the unit and integration testing, because they understand the detailed logic and likely sources of error. Unit testing follows the same principles as in pre-OO days: developers should try to cover all paths and cases, use special values of arguments, and try extreme and "off-by-one" values for arguments. If your methods and classes are simple and focused, it will be easier to prepare unit tests.

It is a good idea to instrument objects and methods. You can place assertions (preconditions, postconditions, invariants) in your code to trap errors. You should try to detect problems near the source (where they are easier to understand) rather than downstream (where they can be confusing).

We agree with the use of paired programmers and aggressive code inspection that is part of the agile programming movement. Along the same lines, we also recommend formal software reviews (see Chapter 22), where developers present their work to others and receive comments.

17.5.2 System Testing

Ideally, a separate team apart from the developers should carry out system testing—this is a natural role for a quality assurance (QA) organization. QA should derive their testing from the analysis model of the original requirements and prepare their test suite in parallel to other development activities. Then the system testers are not distracted by the details of development and can provide an independent assessment of an application, reducing the chance of oversights. Once alpha testing is complete, customers perform beta tests, and then if the software looks good, it is ready for general release.

The scenarios of the interaction model define system-level test cases. You can generate additional scenarios from the use cases or state machines. Pick some typical test cases, but also consider atypical situations: zero iterations, the maximum number of iterations, coincidence of events if permitted by the model, and so on. Strange paths though the state machine make good test cases, because they check default assumptions. Also pay attention to performance and stress the software with multiuser and distributed access, if that is appropriate.

As much as possible, use a test suite. The test suite is helpful for rechecking code after bug fixes and detecting errors that creep into future software releases. It can be difficult to automate testing when you have an application with an interactive user interface, but even then you can still document your test scripts for later use.

ATM example. We have carefully and methodically prepared the ATM model. Consequently we would be in a good position for testing, if we were to build a production application.

17.6 Chapter Summary

Implementation is the final development stage that addresses the specifics of programming languages. First you should address implementation issues that transcend languages—we call this implementation modeling. Sometimes it is helpful to fine-tune classes and generalizations before writing code in order to simplify development or to improve performance. Do this only if you have a compelling reason.

Associations are a key concept in UML class modeling, but are poorly supported by most programming languages. Nevertheless, you should keep your thinking clear by using associations as you study requirements and then necessarily degrade them once you reach implementation. There are two primary ways of implementing associations with programming languages—with pointers (for one or both directions) or with association objects. An association object is a pair of dictionary objects, one for the forward direction and one for the backward direction.

Even though careful modeling reduces errors, it does not eliminate the need for testing. You will need unit, integration, and system tests. For unit testing, developers check the classes and methods of their own code. Integration testing combines multiple classes and methods and subjects them to additional tests. System testing exercises the overall application and ensures that it actually delivers the requirements originally uncovered during analysis.

association object	implementation modeling	transformation
association traversal	integration testing	two-way association
dictionary object	one-way association	unit testing
fine-tuning classes	pointer	
fine-tuning generalizations	system testing	

Figure 17.10 Key concepts for Chapter 17

Bibliographic Notes

Transformations provide the motivation for Section 17.2 and Section 17.3. [Batini-92] presents a comprehensive list of transformations. [Blaha-96] and [Blaha-98] present additional transformations.

References

[Batini-92] Carlo Batini, Stefano Ceri, and Shamkant B. Navathe. *Conceptual Database Design: An Entity-Relationship Approach*. Redwood City, CA: Benjamin Cummings, 1992.

[Blaha-96] Michael Blaha and William Premerlani. A catalog of object model transformations. *Third Working Conference on Reverse Engineering*, November 1996, Monterey, CA, 87–96.

[Blaha-98] Michael Blaha and William Premerlani. *Object-Oriented Modeling and Design for Database Applications*. Upper Saddle River, NJ: Prentice Hall, 1998.

[Rumbaugh-87] James E. Rumbaugh. Relations as semantic constructs in an object-oriented language. *OOPSLA'87 as ACM SIGPLAN 22*, 12 (December1987), 466–481.

Exercises

17.1 (7) Implement each association in Figure 17.6. Use one-way or two-way pointers as the semantics of the problem dictates. Explain your answers.

17.2 (5) Implement each association in Figure E12.3. Use one-way pointers wherever possible. Should any of the association ends be ordered? Explain your answers.

17.3 (4) Implement each association in Figure E15.2. Use one-way or two-way pointers as the semantics of the problem dictates. Should any of the association ends be ordered? Explain your answers.

17.4 (3) Implement the association in Figure E15.3. Use one-way or two-way pointers as the semantics of the problem dictates. Explain your answer.

17.5 (7) Implement each association in Figure E12.4. Use one-way or two-way pointers as the semantics of the problem dictates. Should any of the association ends be ordered? Explain your answers.

18

OO Languages

This chapter discusses how to take a generic design and make the final implementation decisions that are required to realize the design in C++ or Java. These are the two dominant languages used in OO implementation. The goal of this chapter is to produce code for a program. We do not intend to give a C++ or Java tutorial, but to highlight language features and explain their use with models.

Chris Kelsey was the primary author of this chapter and we thank her for her help.

18.1 Introduction

It is relatively easy to implement an OO design with an OO language, since language constructs are similar to design constructs. In this book we will focus on C++ and Java, since they are the dominant OO languages. Even if you are using another language, many of the principles will be the same and the discussion here will be relevant.

C++ and Java have much in common. Java is younger than C++ and borrows heavily from C++ syntax. Both are strongly typed languages, where variables and values must be known to belong to a particular native or user-defined type. Strong typing can improve reliability by detecting mismatched method arguments and assignments, and it increases opportunities for optimization.

18.1.1 Introduction to C++

C++ was developed by Bjarne Stroustrup at AT&T Bell Laboratories in the 1980s, with the intent of extending the widely used, procedural C language to include OO capabilities. It retains the "close to the machine" characteristics that are the hallmark of its C heritage, while adding the "close to the problem" capabilities of more direct expression of OO concepts.

Bell Labs originally implemented C++ as a preprocessor that translated C++ into standard C. As C++ came into mainstream use in the 1990s, direct compilers with symbolic debuggers and other development tools appeared. ISO/ANSI standardized the language and its libraries in 1998. C++ compilers for various operating systems are widely available from several major vendors, as well as from the Free Software Foundation.

C++ language syntax is a superset of C. Thus, C++ is a hybrid language, in which some entities are object types and some are traditional primitive types. Because of its origins, it retains features that are inconsistent with "pure" OO programming, such as free-standing functions that are not methods of a class. However, syntax and semantics remain consistent across native and object data types.

C++ supports generalization with inheritance and run-time method resolution (*polymorphism*). Classes may include a mix of polymorphic and nonpolymorphic methods. To enable run-time resolution for a method, a superclass must explicitly declare that method as *virtual*. The implementation is efficient, typically achieved by having each object contain a pointer to a table of methods for its class. There is no shared basic *Object* type as characterizes other OO languages. C++ permits multiple inheritance.

In addition to overriding methods via inheritance, C++ allows *overloading*—methods and functions may share the same name but have parameters that vary in number or type. Upon invocation, the language chooses the method or function with the appropriate parameters. Similarly, C++ operators may be overloaded, allowing a method to be expressed intuitively [such as $a + b$ instead of $a.add(b)$, where a and b are of type *ComplexNumber*].

Access specifiers promote encapsulation by restricting the availability of class members (methods or data) to methods of the class itself (*private*), the class and its subclasses (*protected*), or any class/method/function (*public*). A class may grant selective access to otherwise private members with a *friend* declaration. C++ performs all access restriction on a class, not object, basis—which means there is no access restriction among same-class objects. C++ *namespaces* provide a semantic scope for symbols but do not affect accessibility of visible entities. Namespaces were introduced in part to alleviate name conflicts among external libraries.

C++ exposes its memory management to the programmer, who may customize memory allocation strategies. The compiler statically allocates storage for objects (primitive or class types) declared at compile time. An application may also dynamically obtain storage from the heap at run time by using the *new* operation. A dynamically created object persists in memory until a *delete* operation explicitly destroys it.

Memory addresses remain fixed for the lifetime of an object and identify it. The programmer can get the address of a statically allocated object (using operator $\&$), as well as obtain an address as a handle for a dynamically allocated one. To access the target of a pointer, the pointer is *dereferenced* with the operator $*$, such that for any object O at address A, it is true that $\&O == A$ and $*A == O$. As with C, the programmer is generally not protected from memory-based errors at compile time or run time. C++ offers no run-time error-detection facilities; errors generally result in undefined program behavior.

In addition to the C-style pointers used as operands in memory operations, C++ includes *references* that syntactically appear as object aliases. References must be bound to an existing object at their creation. They are constant in their binding and so cannot be null. Otherwise, references behave much as permanently dereferenced pointers.

Classes have *constructors* and *destructors*, methods that C++ automatically invokes upon creation and destruction of objects. These are typically used for initialization and any operations that must occur upon termination (often deallocation), respectively.

In summary, C++ is a flexible language characterized by a concern for run-time efficiency, the ability to form broad type hierarchies, and uniform semantics. It provides a platform for fine granularity of expression and control at the expense of some simplicity.

18.1.2 Introduction to Java

Java came into being as a by-product of an early 1990s Sun Microsystems, Inc. exploration into programming consumer devices, a project that required a portable and device-independent language. It made its public debut in 1995 as a download on the then-infant World Wide Web, and the ability to run restricted Java programs was soon thereafter incorporated into Web browsers to allow dynamic and interactive content on Web pages. Within a few years, with the explosion of the Internet and distributed application architectures, Java became a staple of commercial development. Commercial, shareware, and free Java tools are widely available, as the language continues to evolve and its libraries grow. Sun maintains control over language releases and makes basic tools available at no charge for most computing platforms.

Java's popularity comes not so much from the core language itself as from its portability and its huge library of associated classes. Java source code compiles to an intermediate bytecode, which in turn runs on a platform-specific Java Virtual Machine. JVMs are available for nearly all operating systems and are readily substitutable with JVMs from other vendors. Native Java compilers are also available.

Just as C++ leveraged the experience of large numbers of C programmers, so Java leveraged the large base of C/C++ speakers. Java syntax is quite similar to C++, although its object and memory models differ significantly.

Java is a strongly typed language, with distinct primitive and object types. The usage of the two differs significantly: Java statically allocates primitives and treats them as value-based variables ($i = j$ assigns *j's* value to variable *i*), but dynamically allocates object types at run time and manipulates them only through reference variables ($i = j$ assigns the physical object referred to by *j* to an alternative reference *i*). Java has no reference syntax for primitives but does provide tools for conversion between primitives and corresponding object types, such as *int* and *Integer*. Java version 1.5 adds *autoboxing*, the automatic conversion between primitives and their corresponding wrappers in common circumstances such as parameter passing and use in collections.

All Java object types share a single *Object* ancestor and so are, at the most abstract level, type compatible. Run-time type checking throws exceptions if invalid downcasts (treating an object as a subtype) are used. Polymorphism is automatic, and a programmer can prevent it only by explicitly prohibiting the definition of overriding methods. Java supports only single inheritance, although *interfaces* (uninstantiable class specifications containing only constants and method declarations) can emulate multiple superclasses.

Packages organize classes and provide a scope for identifiers. Each source-code compilation unit (file) in Java can contain at most one public class and must bear the name of that class, although the file may define other supporting classes. A declaration at the top of the file identifies the package. Files using public symbols from a different package use an *import* directive to access the public elements of that package (such as *import java.io.** to use classes in Java's i/o package/library).

Similar to C++'s access specifiers, Java's access modifiers restrict the availability of attributes and methods. Without explicit specification, an attribute or method has by default *package* accessibility and may be used by all other methods defined within the package. Explicit options are *private* (intraclass access), *public* (universal access) and *protected* (extends access to subclasses defined outside their parent class's package). Thus the Java meaning of *protected* is a bit different than C++.

Memory management is the province of the JVM. All Java code—data and methods— exists within the context of a class. The system loads and unloads classes as needed and relocates code within memory during run time. The programmer need not, and cannot, know the location of objects—they must be addressed through their corresponding references that syntactically appear as object variables.

Object deallocation is done through garbage collection—when all references to an object have been retired, the system will return object memory to its pool. Although the programmer can suggest object destruction, the system cannot be forced to collect garbage on demand. Java also offers run-time memory error detection (such as array out of bounds and attempted use of null references) and throws appropriate exceptions on detection.

In summary, Java emphasizes run-time portability and code safety at the cost of some efficiency and flexibility. Java provides abstract interfaces to emulate multiple inheritance, distinguishes between object and primitive type semantics, and offers a rich library of objects for both general implementation and for system-level integration on distributed platforms.

18.1.3 Comparison of C++ and Java
Table 18.1 compares C++ and Java.

18.2 Abbreviated ATM Model

Figure 18.1 shows a portion of the ATM model that we will use as an example. We have added *CheckingAccount* and *SavingsAccount* so that we can discuss generalization.

18.3 Implementing Structure

The first step in implementing an OO design is to implement the structure specified by the class model. You should perform the following tasks.

■ Implement data types. [18.3.1]

■ Implement classes. [18.3.2]

■ Implement access control. [18.3.3]

■ Implement generalizations. [18.3.4]

■ Implement associations [18.3.5]

	C++	Java
Memory management	Accessible to programmer. Objects at fixed address.	System controlled. Objects relocatable in memory.
Inheritance model	Single and multiple inheritance. Polymorphism explicit per method. No universal base class. Encourages mix-in hierarchies.	Single inheritance with abstract interfaces. Polymorphism automatic. Universal *Object* ancestor.
Access control and object protection	Thorough and flexible model with *const* protection available.	Cumbersome model encourages weak encapsulation.
Type semantics	Consistent between primitive and object types	Differs for primitive and object types.
Program organization	Functions and data may exist external to any class. Global (file) and namespace scopes available.	All functions and data exist within classes. Package scope available.
Libraries	Predominantly low-level functionality. Rich generic (template) container (data structures) and algorithm library.	Massive. Classes for high-level services and system integration included.
Run-time error detection	Programmer responsibility. Results in undefined behavior at run time.	System responsibility. Results in compile-time or run-time termination.
Portability	Source must be recompiled for platform. Native code runs on CPU.	Bytecode classes portable to platform-specific JVMs. JVM must be available.
Efficiency	Excellent.	Good. Can vary with JVM implementation.

Table 18.1   C++ vs. Java. Both are powerful languages with different trade-offs.

18.3.1 Data Types

If you have not already assigned data types to attributes, you must do so now. Certain data types merit special consideration.

Primitives

Floating-point numbers, integer types, characters, and booleans can express simple values. Where possible, use numeric values instead of strings. Numeric types typically allow better storage and processing efficiency, as well as easier maintenance of attribute integrity. (See subsequent section on enumerations.)

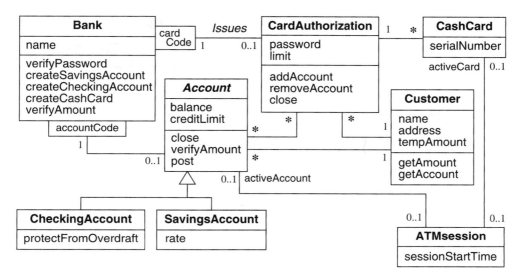

Figure 18.1 Abbreviated ATM implementation class model used in this chapter

Object Types

You can use objects to collect and organize attribute values into richer types. C++ supports the physical nesting of objects, where an instance of one object is physically created within the memory space of another during object construction. Java supports only the referencing of objects as members, so a Java object within another object is analogous to a C++ pointer or reference member that must be explicitly bound to another object.

C++ structs are technically no different than classes except that all members are public by default. They are conventionally used as "POD"—that is, "Plain Old Data"—to bind values together in a logical grouping with no methods. A constructor may be added to initialize data members. Although all members are public, the host object encapsulates access to the struct members.

```
struct address {
    string street;
    string city;
    string state;
    address() : street(""), city(""),state("") {}
};

class Customer {
    string name;
    address addr; // object attribute
    float tempAmount;
public :
    // ...
```

```
    string City() { return addr.city; } // use
};
```

You can follow a similar strategy with Java, although the host object's initialization or constructor must explicitly create the object-attribute instance. Default package access yields access to object-attribute members within the using class.

```
class Address {
    String street = "";
    String city = "";
    String state = "";
}

public class Customer {
    private String name;
        // note explicit construction of attribute
    private address addr = new Address(); // object attribute
    private float tempAmount;
    // ...
    String city() { return addr.city; } // use
}
```

Reference Types

You can use Java object references, and C++ pointers and references, to implement associations. In Java, all class-type variables represent references to objects, while in C++ a variable may directly represent an object. C++ requires extra care that objects are not mistakenly used where a reference type is intended.

Object Identifiers

OO languages have built-in mechanisms for identifying objects, and ways to test object identity. There is typically no need to create explicit object identifier types. If you need a unique object identifier, you can obtain it at run time from the system.

In C++ an object's actual memory address serves as a unique identifier and can be obtained by applying the & (address of) operator to an object or object reference. Object identity can be tested by pointer (address) comparison. Java's == operator provides run-time identity comparison. If a run-time identifier is needed, the universal *Object* superclass contains *hashCode*() and *toString*() methods that, if not indiscriminately overridden, yield unique integer and string identifiers. Although memory addresses are not available in Java, most systems implement these methods based on internal object location.

Do not confuse a unique domain identifier, such as a bank account code or taxpayer number, with an object identifier. A domain identifier describes a domain-dependent property, while an object identifier describes a system-based attribute.

Enumerations

Enumerations provide two advantages—a value domain constraint and symbolic representation of values. For example, CLUB, DIAMOND, HEART, SPADE can express the range of playing-card suits.

C++ can directly implement enumerations. Each enumeration is a discrete type, for which you can define methods and operators. Members that are not explicitly assigned a value take on sequential integral values, starting at 0 if not otherwise specified.

```
enum Card = { CLUB, DIAMOND, HEART, SPADE };
```

There is an implicit conversion from an enumerated type value to integral type, but not vice versa. C++ guarantees that the sizes of objects of enumerated type are large enough to hold the domain's largest value. For example, a variable of the enum {FALSE,TRUE} could be sized as a single bit. Enumerations may appear at global scope or may be class members.

In practice, it can be cumbersome to use C++ enumerations, owing to conversion issues and the burden of redefining operations that are natively available for *ints*. Enums are best used to clarify code by providing symbolic constants. Encapsulated attribute values may be internally stored and manipulated as *ints*, while the public interface uses the constants to restrict parameter values, and method implementations may use the constants as bounds.

```
class Car {
public: // make enum public so clients can use it
    enum direction {N,E,S,W};
private:
    int mph;     // car speed
    int nesw;    // car direction
public:
        // require enum type parameter
    Car(int speed,direction dir) : mph(speed), nesw(dir) {}
        // int allows ++, -- without overloading for enum type
    Car& TurnRight() {if (++nesw >W) nesw = N; return *this;}
    Car& TurnLeft()  {if (--nesw <N) nesw = W; return *this;}
        // ...
};

int main()
{
    Car (15,Car::E): // client uses public enum value
    // ...
}
```

Java versions prior to 1.5 do not include the ability to create enumerated types. Java enums are similar to those in C++. In the absence of enumerations, you can use interfaces (see Section 18.3.4) to group and share constants. The explicit field modifiers *public*, *static*, and *final* are optional here, as they apply by default to all *int* fields specified within an interface. (Note that the "Enumeration" found in the Java class library is a deprecated interface providing rudimentary iteration operations and is unrelated to enumerated types.)

```
public interface Card {
    public static final int CLUB = 0;
    public static final int DIAMOND = 1;
    public static final int HEART = 2;
    public static final int SPADE = 3;
```

```
    . . .
}
```

18.3.2 Classes

OO programming languages provide direct support for implementing objects. You must declare each attribute and method in a class model as part of its corresponding C++ or Java class. You will also need to add attributes and methods for implementing associations (see Section 18.3.5). It is good practice to carry forward the names from the design model.

You can regard objects as entities that provide service to client objects that make requests. Services appear as public methods of a class. Methods provide the protocol for obtaining services. In general, method parameters represent information that an object needs to perform a service, and the return value of the method represents the object's response to the client requesting the service.

Because the public interface describes the class's services, it is best to work "outside in" when defining classes. Start with the public interface—methods intended to provide services to others—and add internal methods and attributes as needed to support the public interface methods.

Because the public methods document class behavior, they typically appear at the beginning of a class declaration for easy visibility, although there is no requirement that they do so. Both C++ and Java resolve symbols only after reading an entire class definition, so members can refer to each other in any order.

18.3.3 Access Control

A class should define public methods for services that clients can request or invoke. A class may also specify data that is immutable as public. All other members of the class—attributes and methods used internally to implement public functionality—should be rendered invisible and inaccessible to other objects and functions.

Both Java and C++ rely on *access specifiers* (called *access modifiers* in Java) to control clients' access to methods and data. The most basic specifiers, applied to attributes and methods, are the same for both languages. Only methods of the class can access *private* attributes or methods. Any client can access *public* members of the class.

Access Control in Java

Strong encapsulation in Java requires detailed attention to packages as well as access specifiers. A Java package provides a scope that extends access privileges to other entities within that scope. Packages are indicated by a package declaration at the top of a source file; multiple files can thus be grouped into the same package. Unless the *private* access specifier explicitly qualifies an attribute or method, other methods of classes defined in the same package can freely access it. If no package is specified, a class is considered to be in a global default package where all but its explicitly private members are available to all other clients residing in any other source file without package specification.

We recommend that you avoid the default package and instead name packages to manage access control. Furthermore, you should declare all attributes and nonpublic methods as *private*—package access alone provides only weak encapsulation. You should guard access to all attributes by wrapping them with appropriate methods.

In addition to attributes and methods, Java classes have explicit access control. A Java class itself must be declared *public* to allow its public methods to be accessed by clients outside its package. See *Visibility and access to classes* below.

Access Control in C++

C++ access specifiers apply to sections of the class declaration. All members are assumed private until the compiler encounters an access specifier. Specifiers can appear anywhere in the declaration and apply until another specifier is encountered. Again, you should guard all attributes and methods other than the known public interface as private and relax access only with sound justification. Access specification within C++ structs is the same, with the exception that members are by default *public* until a more restrictive specifier is encountered (see Section 18.3.1).

C++ allows selective access to private members through a ***friend*** declaration. The class containing the declaration grants access to a named function, method, or class and in doing so allows the named entity full access to its private members. Friendship is best used sparingly, as it provides additional paths to encapsulated members.

Visibility and Access to Classes

For a class type to be recognized and its public members available, it must be visible to its potential clients. For both C++ and Java, the basic compilation unit is the file. Classes in a single file are visible to each other, but in practice it is best to place no more than a single class, along with incidental support classes, in a single file. Thus, class types from outside the file must explicitly be made visible to the compilation unit.

In Java, the package structure governs visibility and access. Classes in files declared to be in the same package are always visible to one another. Packages are dependent on disk file structure—all files declared to be in a package must reside in a directory named with the package name in order to be located by the Java system. For both compilation and execution, Java uses the environmental variable CLASSPATH, which gives a relative starting point for the system to search for packages and classes.

Although a package can contain many classes, each Java source file can have at most one *public* class, and the file must have the same name as the sole public class within. Classes outside the package can use only public methods of public classes. For a public class to be visible to a class in a different package, the client class's source file must include an import directive: *import packagename.classname* or *import packagename.**. The system locates classes by prepending the classpath to the package and optional file name.

For the ATM case study, we would place each of the classes in a separate file. For example, the source file Bank.java would contain:

```
package bankInfo
public class Bank { ... }
```

and the file Customer.java would contain:

```
package bankInfo
public class Customer { ... }
```

The files Bank.java, Customer.java, and other classes in the *bankInfo* package must reside in a disk directory named *bankInfo*. For *Bank* and *Customer* to be visible to the *ATMsession* class, which is not part of the *bankInfo* package, the ATMsession.java source file must first declare:

```
import bankInfo.*
public class ATMsession { ... }
```

The import statement lets the ATMsession implementation see and use the public methods of the public classes found in the *bankInfo* package.

The rules and naming requirements of packages are somewhat onerous, but do not be tempted to simplify by using a global package. Without controlling the visibility and access of the classes themselves, you abandon much of access control. Although private attributes are still respected as private, without packages, methods designed for internal access to those private attributes effectively become public, and nonpublic classes intended for restricted use also become publicly available.

C++ has no language-specified dependence on the location of source code or compiled code. C++ programs divide code into header files, which contain declarations (including classes), and implementation files, which contain the actual code for all but the most simple methods (very small methods are typically implemented within class declarations). To introduce symbols from one file that are needed in another, the *#include<filename>* (when the source resides on a system-specified search path) or *#include "filename"* (when the full path is specified within the quotes) directive is placed at the top of the client file. The directive incorporates the header file containing the declarations of the desired class into the client's compilation unit by substitution, so that the symbols contained in the header are effectively placed into the file at the directive's location.

C++ has a *namespace* feature that serves as a scoping mechanism for program names but does not affect access control. A class is placed into a namespace if it is declared within a namespace declaration in a file and has the fully qualified name of namespace::classname. A namespace can span source files, and a source file can contain multiple namespaces. To avoid cumbersome syntax, the symbols of one namespace can be introduced into another with a *using* directive. C++ standard library names exist within the namespace *std*.

When no namespace is specified, symbols are in the global namespace. Because namespaces impact visibility but not access control, they are used primarily to prevent or disambiguate coincident symbol names as might be found when utilizing multiple libraries.

Access Control in Inheritance Hierarchies

Both languages include the *protected* access specifier, but it works differently in C++ and Java. In C++, a protected member is accessible only by methods of the class and its subclasses.

In Java, protected attributes and methods have package access, which is further extended to methods of subclasses that are defined outside the package where the superclass is defined. Java does not have the equivalent of C++'s more restrictive protected access.

Applying Access Control

A UML model may have annotations—{public}, {private}, {protected}, {package} or +, −, #, ~—indicating access specifiers for class members (called *visibility* in the UML). The lack of an explicit indication implies that a method is part of the public interface. A thorough implementation should include access specifiers and make attributes private.

18.3.4 Generalization

OO languages provide robust support for generalization through **inheritance**. A class can serve as the parent **superclass** to one or more child **subclasses**. A subclass inherits all the members of its parent and may add attributes and methods of its own. The subclass may also **override** superclass methods to let the child express a behavior of the same name and signature (parameters and return) differently. Subclasses in turn may act as superclasses to successive generations of subclasses, allowing the creation of hierarchies of classes, with each level expressing extended and/or more specific behaviors.

Beyond the convenience of making subclasses easy to specify, the inheritance mechanism lets objects be utilized more abstractly. Inheritance enables **polymorphism** (from the Greek "many faces"), where a child type can be addressed as if it were any of its ancestral types. At run time, the system resolves which kind of child is in use, and invokes that subclass's variation of a behavior specified more generally by the ancestor. In a sound hierarchy, each subclass should be able to sensibly perform all superclass behaviors, such that anywhere the parent type might appear, the child type can fulfill the parent's behavioral expectations. [Liskov-88]

You need not fully specify all classes in an inheritance hierarchy. You can simply declare higher-level abstractions, deferring implementation detail to subclasses. These are **abstract classes**—classes that are described but remain partially or wholly unimplemented. Abstract classes describe types at a level where there is insufficient knowledge to implement a concrete behavior, but the general specification is known. For example, any *Shape* may be drawn, but until the type of *Shape* is specified, it is impossible to know *how* it is drawn.

Because they are incompletely implemented, you cannot create objects of abstract types. Instead, you create **concrete** objects of their subclass types—ones that fully implement the parent's specified behavior—and assign a superclass-type reference. The subclass objects are referred to as if they were of the more generic type. For example, a *Square* or *Circle*—concrete subclasses of an abstract *Shape*—might be assigned to a *Shape*-type reference variable. Although both would appear as *Shapes*, when their *draw()* method is invoked, each will polymorphically manifest its proper behavior. In Java,

```
Shape s1 = new Circle();
Shape s2 = new Square();
s1.draw(); s2.draw();
```

will result in drawings of different shapes.

C++ and Java implement somewhat different models of inheritance.

Inheritance in Java

All Java objects share a common ancestor, the *Object* class. *Object* contains minimal methods and fields to support programming concerns such as object identity, equivalence, and concurrency. The common basis also allows the manipulation of objects at an entirely generic level, such as forming collections of otherwise unrelated types. Using objects at an "un-

typed" level of abstraction avoids some of the constraints imposed by a strongly typed
language.

Inheritance is implemented with the *extends* keyword.

```
class Account {
    private float balance;
    public void Post(float amount) { ... }
    public float Balance() { return balance; }
}
class SavingsAccount extends Account {
    private float rate; // add interest rate attribute
    float CalcInterest() {
        // calculate unpaid interest due
    }
}
```

A Java class can extend at most one class. However, Java provides some of the benefits of
multiple inheritance through interfaces. A Java *interface* is a class specification with no implementation. It consists of method declarations without implementations and may also contain constant fields that are allocated per class, not per object. Like classes, interfaces can be
extended to create subinterfaces.

To use an interface, a class must declare that it implements the interface, and provide
code for all of the interface's methods. A class may extend at most one class and in addition
may implement any number of interfaces, allowing a simulation of multiple inheritance.
When multiple interfaces are implemented, an object may be referred to through the type of
any of its interfaces. Here, methods required for interest-bearing accounts are abstracted into
a separate interface, which in turn is implemented by a *SavingsAccount*. This can ensure a
uniformity of interest-bearing methods across all classes that implement the interface, be
they *SavingsAccount*, *InterestBearingCheckingAccount*, or some other type.

```
interface InterestBearingAcct {
    float CalcInterest();
}
class SavingsAccount extends Account
    implements InterestBearingAcct {
    private float rate;
    public float CalcInterest() {
        // implement interest calculation
    }
}
```

A *SavingsAccount* can now participate in programs as an *Account*, a *SavingsAccount*, or an
InterestBearingAcct.

Besides concrete classes and interfaces, Java allows abstract classes—incompletely implemented classes that cannot be instantiated, but serve as parents to concrete subtypes. Both
the class itself and any unimplemented methods must be specified as *abstract*.

```
public abstract class AbstractExample {
    void method1() { /* ... */ }
```

```
    abstract void method2 ();
}
```

A *public* class, because it is accessible to any client that has imported the package in which it resides, can serve as a superclass to a subclass defined in a different package. Subclasses defined outside their superclass's package can access protected, as well as public, members of their parent. Private members of a superclass are not visible to subclasses. (See Section 18.3.3.)

To prevent further subclassing of a type, a class can be declared *final*. Similarly, a *final* qualifier applied to a method prevents that method from being overridden.

Inheritance in C++

C++ classes share no common parent; class hierarchies can start arbitrarily with any class. A superclass is called a *base*, and a subclass is called a *derived* class. A *direct base* is an immediate parent of a derived class, while an *indirect base* is a more remote ancestor.

In C++, unlike Java, polymorphism is not automatic. A class may mix methods that are automatically resolved by type at run time with those that are not. To activate polymorphism, a method must be declared as *virtual*. Those that are not declared as *virtual* will be invoked according to the type by which the object is referenced, not the actual type of the derived class, even if the derived class overrides the method.

```
class Hello { //...
    public:
        void method1() { cout << "hello\n"; }
        virtual void method2() { cout << "hello\n"; }
};

class Goodbye : public Hello { //...
    public:
        void method1() { cout << "goodbye\n" ; }
        void method2() { cout << "goodbye\n"; }
};

int main() {
    Goodbye g;
    Hello& h = g; // same object through base type

    g.method1(); g.method2(); h.method1(); h.method2();
}
```

The output is:

```
goodbye   // method1 not virtual; called via derived
goodbye   // method2 is virtual; called via derived
hello     // method1 -- not virtual! -- via base
goodbye   // method2 via base
```

C++ does not provide a way to prohibit overriding of methods, but in a hierarchy where some methods are overridden and others are not, a nonvirtual method may indicate the authors' intent that the base implementation should be inherited intact and left unmodified.

C++ incorporates access specification in inheritance syntax. A derived class may be specified as *public*, *protected*, or *private*. Public inheritance specifies that all public methods inherited from the base remain public in the derived class.

```
class SavingsAccount : public Account { ...}
```

In private inheritance, all methods become private to the derived class. Private inheritance is used to indicate that a derived class is implemented in terms of its base, but it is not intended to describe a logical *is-a* relationship where the base should be considered an abstraction of the derived class. In practice, encapsulating the base type as a member of the (would-be) derived class (using delegation, see Section 15.9.3) is often the better strategy. Protected inheritance dictates that public methods in the base become accessible only to further derivations. In practice, this is rarely used.

Abstract classes are created by the inclusion of at least one pure virtual method, which is a virtual method that uses "initialization to 0" syntax at declaration: *void fn() = 0*. Such classes cannot be instantiated, and their derived classes are inherently abstract unless they implement all pure virtual functions inherited from their base.

C++ supports multiple inheritance, although in practice the best combinations of parent classes are mixes of concrete types and predominantly abstract classes that represent behavior specifications. The latter perform somewhat like Java interfaces, with the significant convenience that default implementations for methods may be written where appropriate and be maintained at a base level instead of requiring maintenance across derivations.

```
class Account { // nonabstract
    public:
            // assume Post implementation may be
            // specific to derived account types;
            // base implementation is default way.
        virtual void Post(float amount) { ... }
        float Balance() { return balance; }
    private:
        float balance;
};

class InterestBearingAcct { // abstract class
    public:
        virtual float CalcInterest() = 0; // "pure virtual"
        float Rate() { return rate; }
    private:
        float rate;
};

class SavingsAccount : public Account,
        public InterestBearingAcct {
    public:
        virtual float CalcInterest() {
        // calculate unpaid interest
```

```
        }
    };
```

18.3.5 Associations

OO languages lack direct support for associations. However, you can readily implement links with object references or distinct association objects. (See Section 17.4.) You should promote the association to a class if there are attributes describing the association itself. We also recommend promotion for n-ary and qualified associations.

One-Way Associations

One-way associations reduce interdependencies among classes. When one class references another, the referenced class must be visible and accessible to the hosting class. The referencing class must enforce and maintain the association, and typically utilizes the interface of the referenced class. To the extent these dependencies can be reduced to one side of an association, maintenance is reduced and reusability may be enhanced.

For example, in Figure 17.7, if we do not need to retrieve the collection of employees for a company, a pointer from *Person* to *Company* will suffice. In Java, the *Person* class can simply contain a *Company* field.

```
public class Company { ... }
public class Person {
    private Company employer;
    ...
}
```

C++ offers two options for implementing referencing attributes. Most commonly, a pointer may be used, which allows a link to be changed. Assuming a *Person* may change employers leads to the following C++ code. (This C++ code also permits a *null* employer, which is inconsistent with the multiplicity in Figure 17.7. Update methods would have to prevent a *null* employer to enforce the multiplicity.)

```
class Company { ... }
class Person {
    Company* employer;
    ...
}
```

A C++ reference member implies a permanent link in which the containing object has a dependency on the attribute object. References must be bound at initialization. They cannot be null, nor can they be assigned (changed), so the language enforces the preexistence of the link target. Assuming that an *Account* is issued for a particular *Bank* and is not transferable, and that no *Account* may be issued without a *Bank*,

```
class Bank { ... }
class Account {
    Bank& bank;
    ...
}
```

This reference-binding requirement of C++ necessitates the existence of a *Bank* prior to the construction of an *Account* (see Section 18.4.1). You can achieve a partial constraint in Java by declaring an object-type attribute as *final*, which ensures that a reference variable cannot be reassigned to a different object, although it does not entail the preexistence requirement.

When implementing associations through referencing attributes, take care not to subject the objects involved to inadvertent changes. An object that hosts a referencing attribute can potentially open a back door by inappropriately exposing the referenced object itself or its attributes. It is particularly important that attributes representing links should be well encapsulated and be modified or reported only through intentional and safe methods. C++ offers an added level of security with the ability to apply the *const* qualifier to referenced objects in situations where they may be intentionally exposed, but are not intended to be modified in the context of the association. Java does not distinguish between constant and mutable objects.

Two-Way Associations

Two-way associations entail link maintenance for both association ends. You can implement a one-to-one association with either a single reference on each end or an association object. Similarly, a one-to-many association requires a single reference on one end and a collection of pointers on the other end or an association object. For example, a customer may have several accounts and we want to be able to navigate this association in both directions. Both Java and C++ have collection object types available from their libraries that can represent the "many" side of the link. In Java,

```
public class Account {
        private Customer customer; // the 1 side of one-to-many
    ...
}

import java.util.* // to access HashSet class
public class Customer {
        // list of account ref's
        private HashSet accounts = new HashSet();
    ...
}
```

Association Classes

Association classes can increase independence of the objects involved by removing direct references to related classes, but they do so at some loss of efficiency and increase in complexity of implementing operations. Independent association classes decouple linked objects but require the overhead of navigating through the link.

An explicit association object is conceptually a set of tuples, each tuple containing one value from each associated class. A binary association object can be implemented as two dictionary objects, each dictionary mapping in one direction across the association. Both Java and C++ have library support for map objects. To encapsulate links and make link maintenance more intuitive, the maps may be wrapped into an application class that serves as a manager for construction or use of the objects involved.

Choosing an Implementation

If the model has not already prescribed implementation of an association, your choice may depend more on the scale, architecture, or enterprise environment of an application than on the nature of the association itself. If you are constrained from modifying existing classes, an association class may be preferable. Association classes often best implement one-to-many associations where the "many" side can be quite large, or is sparse, and can provide independent and extensible management operations where required.

For simple associations, referencing attributes provide navigation across links. Where possible, one-way associations provide more efficient and safer implementations. Care should be taken to encapsulate links and to prevent inadvertent exposure of a referent's information or interface through a host object.

18.4 Implementing Functionality

Once you have the structure in place, you can start implementing methods. For each class, specify methods by signature (method name, parameters, return type). The class model implies many methods. Obviously, you can create and destroy objects and links as well as access attribute values. More subtly, you can traverse a class model leading to additional methods. Methods also arise from derived attributes, the state model, and the interaction model.

- Object creation. [18.4.1]
- Object lifetime. [18.4.2]
- Object destruction. [18.4.3]
- Link creation. [18.4.4]
- Link destruction. [18.4.5]
- Derived attributes. [18.4.6]

Objects have state, behavior, and identity. This is reflected in the object life cycle. Objects are created by the system and should be initialized in a valid state. C++ has facilities for destruction of objects on demand, while Java can only suggest destruction to its garbage collector. Both have special methods that run at object creation, and both can specify behavior at the termination of an object's lifetime.

Object can request services or information from one another. They do so by invoking other objects' methods. In both Java and C++, object behaviors are invoked using a *membership operator* '.' to indicate that the right-hand operand—a method of the object's class—should be invoked on the named target object. The same membership syntax accesses attributes—$X.y$ names the y attribute of the object X, though normally attributes are encapsulated and so not reachable from another object.

Within the context of a class, objects have an implicit reference to self, called ***this*** in both Java and C++. You need not explicitly qualify member names within class definitions: In Java, *fn( )* means *this.fn( )* and *y=10* means *this.y=10*. In C++, *this* is a pointer, and so the pointer membership operator "->" would be used, *this->fn( )*.

For an object to call upon another object for services or information, it must have a name by which it can access its target. This handle may be provided in the form of a link, where the requesting object has a pointer or reference to another, or through a parameter, where one object receives a handle to another at method call. Any invocation of the target objects' methods (or, rarely, the use of target objects' attributes) takes place through the target handle and is governed by the target's members' access specifications.

Both C++ and Java allow *static* class members that are shared by all objects of a class type. Although they are subject to access specification, as any other data or method of a class might be, these static elements have entirely different life cycles than conventional objects and can be accessed through the class itself, apart from any particular instances that may exist. (See Section 18.4.2.)

18.4.1 Object Creation

In OO languages, objects are typically created dynamically (during run time), through a request to the system to create an object of a particular type. In Java, this is a requirement for nonprimitive types, while primitive types are statically (at compile time) allocated simply by declaration. In C++, both object and primitive types can be either statically or dynamically allocated, and the results are considered as objects in either case. Both Java and C++ use the *new* operator to create objects. In C++,

```
// static allocation -- creates a single account
Account acct1;

    // statically allocate an array of 10 accounts;
Account accounts1[10];

    // dynamic allocation: define a pointer,
    // initialize with result of new operation
Account* acct2 = new Account;

    // dynamically create array of 10 accounts
Account* accounts2 = new Account[10];
```

In Java,

```
    // create a reference variable,
    // initialize with result of new operation
Account acct = new Account();

    // create array of 10 references -- no accounts are made!
Account accounts = new Account[10];

    // now create the accounts for the array:
for (int i = 0; i < 10; i++) accounts[i] = new Account();
```

When a new object is created, the system allocates storage for its attribute values and performs other chores involved with the start of the object life cycle. OO languages free the programmer from having to understand technical details of object implementation such as object layout and internal identifiers. Java and C++ also let the programmer specify operations to occur at the time of object creation, so that you can ensure that objects come into existence in a valid logical state. Once the system has completed its creation chores, a special method, called a **constructor**, is automatically invoked. The constructor takes the form of a method, with no return value, that shares the class name. It may have any number of parameters and may be overloaded. For example, in Java, the following code specifies that *Account* has two constructors, one requiring an opening balance and one that takes no arguments.

```java
public class Account {
    ...
    public Account(float OpeningBalance) {
        balance = OpeningBalance;
    }
    public Account() { balance = 0; }
    ...
}
```

Constructors may be used to assign values to members, to create member objects, or perform other start-of-life processing on an object. Constructors run after the object is fully formed, so they may call other methods and in general have the same capabilities, privileges, and constraints of other methods. If no constructor is defined for an object, a constructor of the form *X(){}* is presumed to exist. Though it performs nothing, it allows creation expressions matching its imaginary declaration. Once you create a parameterized constructor, the system will no longer provide the no-argument form for you. If you need one, you will have to overload *X(...)* with *X()* , as done above for *Account*.

Understanding constructors in subclasses is not difficult, if you consider object construction. Subclass-type objects inherit their attributes and methods because they contain their parent type, plus any members they add at the subclass level. You can think of it as if their parent type is created, and then their own piece is added on, and so while constructors are not inherited, they run sequentially from the most general through the most specific level. In the case of C++, where objects can be statically allocated, member objects get constructed recursively—including the invocation of their respective constructors—before the host object can be fully constructed. Only after the host object is complete does its own constructor run. You can see this in action (here in C++).

```cpp
class X {
    public:
        X() { cout << "X!"; }
};

class Y : public X {
    public:
        Y() { cout << "Y!"; }
};

class Z : public Y {
    public:
```

```
        Z() { cout << "Z!"; }
};

int main() {
    Z z; // simply make a Z...
    return 0;
}
```

Running the code produces the result: X!Y!Z!

It is very poor practice to define no constructors for a class. By default, C++ performs no default initialization of object members, while Java initializes members to 0 or null according to type. Neither provides a valid-state object for most classes. The purpose of the constructor is to have a way to perform initialization and operations on an object so that, at the time of its entry into the program domain, it is a fully formed, logically intact, safe-to-operate-on instance of its type.

If there are no start-of-life operations to be performed by a newly constructed object, Java allows nonzero default initializations to be performed within the class definition. In C++, initialization take place within a *member initialization list* that specifies initial values for members before entry into the constructor code block. Both languages allow assignment to members within the body of the constructor, although initialization should be preferred over assignment wherever possible.

In Java,

```
public class Account {
    private float balance = 0; // initialization
    ...
    public Account() {} // constructor need not assign
}
```

In C++,

```
class Account {
    float balance; // values not allowed
    ...
public:
    Account() : balance(0) {} // initialization via list
}
```

In C++, the system also supplies a copy constructor, that specifies the semantics of copying by assignment. Like the default (no-argument) constructor, if one is not written for the class, a constructor of the form *X(const X& x)* is provided, with the default value-based meaning of shallow (memberwise) copying. Java discourages object copying by requiring the programmer to specify that a class implements the *Cloneable* interface and override *Object's clone()* method.

18.4.2 Object Lifetime

Statically allocated (created at compile time) objects, which may be any type in C++ and primitive types and reference variables in Java, exist within the scope of a code block, indicated by { }. They are automatically destroyed when program control passes out of their scope. Dynamically allocated (*new*'d) objects persist in memory from the time of their creation until they are explicitly destroyed in C++, or no longer in use by the program in Java (see object destruction below).

Both C++ and Java allow class members to be qualified as **static**. Static members belong not to an instance of a class, but to the class itself, and (if public) can be accessed in the absence of any instance of the class: (C++) *X::StaticMethod( )* or (Java) *X.StaticMethod( )*. As a convenience, both static data and methods can be addressed through a particular object, but neither are instance members of that object.

Static data members come into existence before any particular object of the class type is created—at program entry in C++ or at class loading in Java—and remain in existence throughout the program. In C++, static members exist as independent objects (memory allocations), while in Java each class itself has an independent instantiation (the **class instance**), of which statics are considered members. Although statics may also be accessed within the scope of their class during method definition or through particular object instances, there is only one instance of a static data member per class, and its life cycle is entirely independent of any object through which it is accessed. Because static methods are not members of a particular object, the notion of *this* (and *super* in Java) has no meaning within the context of a static method, and regular instance data cannot be referenced without qualification with a specific object reference.

In C++, variables defined at global scope (not within a function, including *main*, method, or as a member of another object) have a life cycle much like class-based statics. They are created before the program starts, and are destroyed at program termination. While global data is discouraged as poor practice, global functions are commonly used in C++. Although Java does not allow free-standing functions to be defined at global scope, global functions are regularly emulated in utility library classes that contain groups of static methods. Several of Java's library classes, such as *Integer* or *Collections*, are predominantly or wholly composed of static methods.

Because static members and class instances are created apart from object instances, the initialization of statics occurs independently. Statics in C++ are declared within, but defined and initialized outside, the class, while Java static fields may be initialized conventionally or within a static initialization block. Both C++ and Java statics are guaranteed to be initialized only at some point before use in a program, but neither language specifies a relative instantiation or initialization order.

18.4.3 Object Destruction

When an object is no longer needed, it may be destroyed and its storage returned to the memory pool. With statically allocated (compile-time) objects, this happens as they fall out of scope. If, for some reason, you retain a handle to an object that has fallen out of scope, using it would be an error, somewhat analogous to calling the telephone number for someone who has moved and is no longer available at the number you called.

For dynamically allocated objects, with their potentially unconstrained lifetimes, the problem becomes one of eliminating objects that are no longer of interest, or whose existence is no longer logically valid, and recycling their space in memory. For this, C++ and Java each pursue one of two basic strategies: Either the programmer takes responsibility for explicitly removing objects that are no longer needed or sensible (C++), or the system keeps an eye out for whether an object is actually in use or not (Java). The latter approach, called **garbage collection**, is typically implemented in a way that the system tracks references to the object. When there are no remaining references (no valid handles to the object exist any more), the system tags the object as eligible for recycling. The system periodically runs a *garbage collector* that reclaims tagged objects' space for the memory pool.

Manual disposal of objects, as C++ practices, places a burden on the programmer to be aware of allocations and responsible for object cleanup. However, it also allows tight control of the object life cycle and the ability to fully model object events, including exit or termination of an object from its domain. Garbage collection frees the programmer from memory management chores, but restricts the ability to exercise end-of-life-cycle control.

C++ classes can have **destructors**, analogous to constructors, that run automatically at the destruction of an object. Destructors take the form of a no-argument constructor, with the ~ before the class name: *X::~X() { ... }*. They never take arguments and have no return value.

Because C++ object destruction can be explicitly invoked and predictably executed, it is common for the destructor to undo things a constructor has done. Most common is the allocation and deallocation of dynamically created object members, but this pairing of functionality may include increment/decrement of counts, acquisition and release of resources, and so forth. Destructors can also be used to predictably invoke any logically necessary (often cleanup) behaviors that are required at end of object life.

```
Window :: ~Window ()
{
    // erase the window and repaint the underlying region
}
```

The process of destruction is the inverse of construction: First, the destructor code runs, then any members that themselves require destruction are in turn destructed (starting with their destructors), and finally the whole of the memory is returned to the heap.

To explicitly destroy a dynamically allocated object, the **delete** operator is used. Empty array brackets [ ] are used to differentiate the deletion of individual objects from the deletion of a dynamically allocated array.

```
class X { ... }
...
X x1 = new X;
X* *x2 = new X[20];
...
delete x1;
delete [] x2;
```

After deleting a C++ object, it is advisable to immediately assign 0 to any pointers that were pointing to it. *Delete* is implemented to have no effect when (accidentally) called on a null pointer, whereas "double deleting" an object results in undefined—and often disastrous—behavior.

Java objects are not explicitly destroyed by the programmer. Java discerns when there are no more references to an object in use, at which time the object becomes eligible to be destroyed at the garbage collector's convenience. The programmer can attempt to induce destruction, by explicitly setting reference variables to *null* to detach them from objects, and may even suggest garbage collection, but cannot guarantee timely destruction of an object.

Java does allow classes to override *Object's finalize()* method, which acts in a manner similar to the C++ destructor. However, because the exact time of object destruction cannot be triggered, you cannot rely on any operations within *finalize()* to occur at a predictable time.

18.4.4 Link Creation

Links are forged and destroyed (valued or set to null) as objects interact with one another. Referential links should be created in the course of whatever behavior (method) initiates an association between objects, and destroyed in the course of whatever behavior terminates the association. In general, you should avoid direct *set* methods in favor of operations that encapsulate data and forge links only under validated conditions.

To create a link in a one-way association, an object retains a handle to a parameter object. For bidirectional links, handles can be exchanged, although it is usually preferable to initiate the exchange from one side and encapsulate the other to ensure consistent logic and full link updates. Which class governs the exchange is a matter of application logic.

In the following simplified Java example, *Students* maintain a list of current *Courses*, and *Courses* maintain class lists of current *Students*. Because the decision to take a course is generated by a student and conditioned on the student's status, the creation of links is governed by the *Student.addClass(Course)* method. The *addClass* method in turn calls the *Course's enroll(Student)* method, which is accessible to *Student* due to the class's shared package. However, package access prevents public access to clients (in this case, the class *EnrollmentApplication*), thereby restricting link creation to the orderly process prescribed by *Student's addClass* method.

```
// file Course.java
package school;
public class Course {
    private String title;
    private HashSet students = new HashSet();

    public Course (String nm) { title = nm; }
    public String courseName() { return title; }

    boolean enroll(Student stu) {
        // check that course isn't already full, etc.
        // if ok, return result of HashSet.add method
        return students.add(stu);
    }
```

```java
    public void printClassList() {
        System.out.println("Class List for " + courseName() +
            ":");
        Iterator it = students.iterator();
        while (it.hasNext())
            System.out.println(
                ((Student)it.next()).studentName());
    }
}

//file Student.java
package school;
public class Student {
    private String name;
    private HashSet classes = new HashSet();

    public Student(String nm) { name = nm; }
    public String studentName() { return name; }
    public boolean addClass(Course crs) {
        // validate student's ability to take this course;
        // if ok, request course to enroll student;
        // if course returns true, add course to list
        return ( crs.enroll(this)) ?
            classes.add(crs) : false ;
    }

    public void printCourses() {
        System.out.println("Courses for " + studentName() +
            ":");

        Iterator it = classes.iterator();
        while (it.hasNext())
            System.out.println(
                ((Course)it.next()).courseName());
    }
}

// file EnrollmentApplication.java
import local.school.*
public class EnrollmentApplication {
    public static void main(String [] args) {

        Student mike = new Student("mike");
        Student bill = new Student("bill");
        ...
        Course tt = new Course("Type Theory");
```

```
        mike.AddClass(tt);
        bill.AddClass(tt);

        tt.PrintClassList();
        mike.PrintCourses()
    }
}
```

Objects can be constructed with knowledge of their collaborators, and so establish links at the time of object creation. Often, it is desirable to condition object creation on establishment of links. In such cases, it is necessary to delegate construction to "factory" techniques that examine criteria before invoking construction, as neither Java nor C++ constructors can return an error, nor can they abort the construction process. Factories may be classes, or simply static methods (see Section 18.4.2).

Here (in C++), a *Transaction* will not be constructed until an account number is validated and a handle to the associated account obtained.

```
class Transaction {
    ...
    protected:
        // private or protected constructor to prevent
        // public construction
        Transaction(Account& acct) { ... }

    public:
        ...
        static Transaction* MakeTransaction
            ( const char* acctNumber) {
            Account* acct;
            // null pointer return indicates no transaction
            if (  /* account is not ok */ )   return 0;
            // return a  transaction for valid account
            return new Transaction(*acct);
            ...
        }
};
```

18.4.5 Link Destruction

Link destruction is generally the inverse of link creation. The activity that dictates the dissociation of objects is the method where a referential link is typically broken. In most cases, this simply means the handle attribute is set to a null value, or an entry is removed from a collection of links. A *Student* might drop a *Course*,

```
// Student.dropClass(Course):
    public boolean dropClass(Course crs) {
        if (!classes.contains(crs)) return false;
        if (!crs.drop(this)) return false;
        classes.remove(classes.indexOf(crs));
```

```
            return true;
        }

    // Course.drop(Student):
        boolean drop(Student stu) {
            if (!students.contains(stu)) return false;
            students.remove(students.indexOf(stu));
            return true;
        }
```

When links involving independently existing objects have been created, typically each object is intended to continue existence beyond the life of the link. Care must be taken that the referenced object is accessible through other references, or that a handle to a referenced object is captured from a link-destroying method. Failure to do so can result in a memory leak (C++) or an inaccessible object that may be garbage-collected in Java.

In C++, a common idiom is to pair constructor-destructor activity to implement the creation and destruction of links. Those links often reflect the acquisition and release of resources.

Links involving objects that are existentially dependent on one another may require destruction of one of the linked objects. This, in turn, may imply the updating or destruction of other objects that may be linked to the dependent object, or suggest that the link sustaining the dependent object not be destroyed. This is analogous to database operations, where record deletion may be propagated (cascaded) to related records or prohibited in order to preserve the integrity of existing records.

18.4.6 *Derived Attributes*

For accuracy and currency, it is always desirable to calculate fresh values from independent data at the time of use. Usually the time required to compute fresh values is negligible when weighed against the costs of managing updates and redundancy for stored derived data.

It is a common mistake to include redundant state data in objects. States can often be determined by examining other attributes (in Java).

```
public class Account {
        // wrong: redundant state data for overdrawn
    private boolean overdrawn;
    private float balance;
    ...
        // compute state upon request instead
    public boolean isOverdrawn() { return balance < 0; }
    ...
}
```

States can also be determined via links (here C++):

```
class Customer {
    ...
    List<Account> accts;
public:
```

```
        ...
    bool hasOverdrawnAccount() {
        // iterate through all accounts;
        // return true if any are overdrawn
    }
}
```

or may be implied by the presence of links (again, in C++):

```
class Telephone {
    Telephone* connectedTo;
    ...
    public:
        // are we connected to another phone?
        // if our link isn't null, we are...
    bool isBusy() { return connectedTo != 0; }
        ...
}
```

18.5 Practical Tips

Here are tips for using C++ and Java to implement an OO design.

- **Enumerations**. Use enumerated types for clarity and enforcement of domain values. (Section 18.3.1)

- **Java packages**. Avoid the default package and instead use named packages to manage access control. (Section 18.3.3)

- **Access control**. Declare all attributes and nonpublic methods as *private*. Relax encapsulation only if it is essential to do so. (Section 18.3.3)

- **C++ friend**. Use the friend declaration sparingly, because it can compromise encapsulation. (Section 18.3.3)

- **Java interfaces**. Consider using Java interfaces as a workaround for multiple inheritance in a model. An interface declares methods and constant fields and also provides a type for accessing objects. (Section 18.3.4)

- **C++ private inheritance**. Avoid private inheritance of classes in C++. Delegation is a better strategy. (Section 18.3.4)

- **One-way associations**. Use a one-way association when two-way association traversal is not needed. One-way associations are easier to maintain and reduce object interdependencies. (Section 18.3.5)

- **C++ reference and Java final**. Note association ends that must be bound at initialization and cannot be changed. C++ references can fully enforce these semantics, and the Java *final* property can partially enforce them. (Section 18.3.5)

- **Constructors**. It is a very poor practice to define no constructors for a class. A constructor should always initialize an object to a valid initial state. (Section 18.4.1)

■ **C++ deletion**. When deleting a C++ object, it is advisable to immediately set its pointer(s) to 0. Delete has no effect for a null pointer, but accidental deletion of an already deleted object can be disastrous. (Section 18.4.3)

■ **Link destruction**. When a link is destroyed, make sure the associated objects are accessible through other handles or intentionally destroyed. Otherwise you have a memory leak (C++) or an object that is inadvertently garbage collected (Java). (Section 18.4.5)

18.6 Chapter Summary

It is relatively easy to implement an OO design with an OO language, since language constructs are similar to design constructs. C++ and Java are the two dominant OO languages, and hence the subject of this chapter.

The first step in implementing an OO design is to implement the structure specified by the class model. Begin by assigning data types to attributes. Where possible, use numeric values instead of strings. Numeric types typically allow better storage and processing efficiency, as well as easier maintenance of attribute integrity.

Next define classes. It is best to work "outside in" by starting with the public interface. Then add internal methods, attributes, and lesser classes as needed to support the interface methods.

You should pay careful attention to access control—it provides the means to encapsulate attributes and methods and limit access to them. The most basic specifiers are the same for both C++ and Java. Only methods of the class can access private members. Any client can access public members. The *protected* specifier in C++ limits member access to the class and its subclasses. Java is more permissive, letting attributes and methods in the same package also access protected attributes and methods. Java packages are important both for organizing code and controlling access. The C++ *friend* declaration allows selective access to private members.

OO languages provide robust support for generalization through inheritance. C++ supports multiple inheritance, but Java is limited to single inheritance. However, Java does provide some of the benefits of multiple inheritance through the use of interfaces. A Java interface is a class specification with no implementation.

In Java polymorphism is automatic, though you can prevent further subclassing by declaring a class as *final*. Similarly, a *final* qualifier applied to a method prevents the method from being overridden. In contrast, polymorphism is not automatic in C++. To activate polymorphism, a method must be declared as *virtual*.

OO languages lack direct support for associations. However, you can readily implement links with pointers/references or distinct association objects. One-way associations reduce interdependencies among classes, so you should use them when traversal is needed in only one direction. C++ offers two options for implementing association ends. A pointer lets a link be changed or set to null. In contrast, a reference must be bound at initialization and cannot be changed. Java lacks the full equivalent to the C++ reference—you can define an object-type attribute as final, which ensures that a reference variable cannot be changed but does not require binding at initialization.

When you need to traverse an association in both directions, you should use a two-way implementation. You can bury a pointer/reference (or set of pointers/references) in each related class or use an association object. With two-way pointers/references, you have redundancy and must be careful to keep both directions mutually consistent.

Once you have the structure in place, you can start implementing methods. You should carefully define constructors for new objects and be sure to initialize them to a valid state. Similarly, you should pay attention to destructors, being sure to release any system or program resources that are no longer needed upon the end of the object.

You should seldom include redundant data in objects; for accuracy and reliability it is usually better to calculate fresh values from independent data at the time of use.

abstract	derived data	interface	private
access modifier	destructor	namespace	protected
access specifier	enumeration	new	public
association	final	overloading	reference
concrete	friend	package	static
constructor	garbage collection	pointer	virtual
data type	generalization	polymorphism	

Figure 18.2   Key concepts for Chapter 18

Bibliographic Notes

[Stroustrup-94] provides an interesting discussion of language-design issues.

References

[Arnold-00] Ken Arnold, James Gosling, and David Holmes. *The Java Programming Language, Third Edition.* Boston: Addison-Wesley, 2000.

[Gosling-00] James Gosling, Bill Joy, Guy Steele, and Gilad Bracha. *Java Language Specification, Third Edition.* Boston: Addison-Wesley, 2000. (Available online: http://java.sun.com/docs/books/jls/)

[Liskov-88] Barbara Liskov. Data abstraction and hierarchy. *SIGPLAN Notices, 23,* 5 (May 1988).

[Stroustrup-94] Bjarne Stroustrup. *The Design and Evolution of C++.* Boston: Addison-Wesley, 1994.

[Stroustrup-97] Bjarne Stroustrup. *The C++ Programming Language, Third Edition.* Boston: Addison-Wesley, 1997.

Exercises

18.1 (1) Assign a data type to each attribute in Figure E18.1.

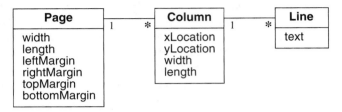

Figure E18.1 Portion of a class diagram of a newspaper

18.2 (4) Consider the model in Figure E18.2. For now, ignore the attributes, methods, and association. See Exercise 15.10 for an explanation of the model.

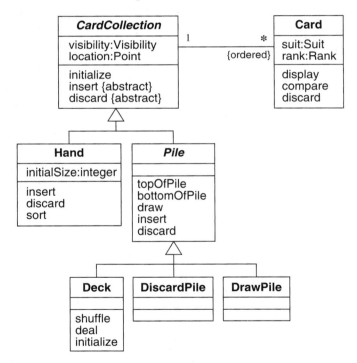

Figure E18.2 Portion of a class diagram of a card playing program

a. Prepare C++ declarations for the classes and the inheritance. Pay careful attention to access control.

b. Prepare Java declarations for the classes and the inheritance. Pay careful attention to access control and packages.

18.3 (6) In Figure E18.2 *visibility* controls whether the front or the back of a card is displayed. Add to your answer for Exercise 18.2 but, for now, continue to ignore the methods and association. [Instructor's note: You may want to give the students our answer to Exercise 18.2.]
a. In C++, add declarations for all attributes, except location. Also define the enumerations.
b. In Java, add declarations for all attributes, except location. Also define the enumerations.

18.4 (7) Add the *CardCollection—Card* association to your C++ and Java answers from Exercise 18.3. [Hint: You can use a template which is not explained in this book. You can answer the exercise by considering the implementation of associations and reading about the standard library and templates on the Web or in a C++ language book.]

18.5 (6) Declare methods for your answer for Figure E18.2 for both C++ and Java. See Exercise 15.10 for an explanation of the methods.

18.6 Write C++ or Java code, including class declarations and methods, to implement the following using pointers.
a. (9) One-to-one association that is traversed in both directions.
b. (6) One-to-many association that is traversed in the direction from one to many. The association is unordered.
c. (6) One-to-many association that is traversed in the direction from one to many. The association is ordered.
d. (8) Many-to-many association that is traversed in both directions. The association is ordered in one direction, and unordered in the other direction.

18.7 (7) Describe strategies for managing memory, assuming that automatic garbage collection is not available. Your answer should provide guidelines that a programmer could use during coding.
a. **A system for text manipulation**. The system often creates one large string in contiguous memory from several smaller strings. You cannot waste memory and cannot set an upper bound on string length or the number of strings to combine. Write pseudocode for a method that combines strings, recovering memory that is no longer used.
b. **A multipass compiler**. Objects are created dynamically. Each pass examines the objects created on the previous pass and produces objects to be used on the next pass. The computer system on which the compiler will run has a practically unlimited virtual address space and an operating system with a good swapping algorithm. The methods in the run-time library for allocating and deallocating memory dynamically are inefficient. Discuss the relative merits of two alternatives: (1) Forget about garbage collection and let the operating system allocate a large amount of virtual memory. (2) Recover deallocated objects with garbage collection.
c. **Software that runs for a long time, such as banking software or an air traffic control system**. You have the same computer system and run-time library as described in Exercise 18.7(b). Discuss the relative merits of the two approaches.
d. **A method which may create and return an object that uses a large block of memory**. Discuss the relative merits of the following two approaches: (1) Each time the method is called, it destroys the object created the last time it was called, if any. (2) Each time the method is called, it may create a new object. It is up to the calling method to destroy the object when it is no longer needed. Comment on these two approaches.

18.8   (6) How might you organize Figure E12.4 into Java packages?

18.9   (7) Write C++ and Java declarations for the model in Figure E18.3. Implement the entire model. Be sure to consider access control and Java packages. Pay attention to constructors and destructors. Implement all associations as bidirectional. See the exercises in Chapter 12 for an explanation of the model.

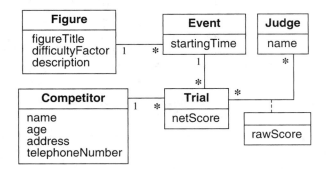

Figure E18.3 Partially completed class diagram for a scoring system

18.10 (6) Write C++ or Java code that corresponds to the pseudocode for Exercise 15.11. Make sure that your code respects encapsulation. [Instructor's note: You may want to give the students our answer to Exercise 15.11.]

18.11 (8) Write C++ or Java code for each of the OCL expressions in Section 3.5.3. Assume that there is a bidirectional implementation of associations. A specification, such as an OCL expression, need not respect encapsulation, but the code you write should.

18.12 (6) Using C++ or Java, implement all associations involving the classes *Box, Link, LineSegment,* or *Point* in Figure E18.4. Note that the editor allows links only between pairs of boxes.

18.13 (7) Implement the *cut* operation on the class *Box* in Figure E18.4 using C++ or Java. For simplicity, *cut* simply deletes the things that are cut and does not store them in a buffer. Propagate the operation from boxes to attached link objects. Update any associations that are involved. Be sure to recover any memory that is released by the operation (for C++ only). You may assume another method will update the display.

18.14 (7) Write a method using C++ or Java that will create a link between two boxes. Inputs to the method are two boxes and a list of points. The method should update associations and create object instances as needed. You may assume another method will update the display. Also write a method to destroy a link.

18.15 (8) Using C++ or Java, implement the following queries on Figure E18.4:
   a. Given a box, determine all other boxes that are directly linked to it.
   b. Given a box, find all other boxes that are directly or indirectly linked to it.
   c. Given a box and a link, determine if the link involves the box.
   d. Given a box and a link, find the other box logically connected to the given box through the other end of the link.

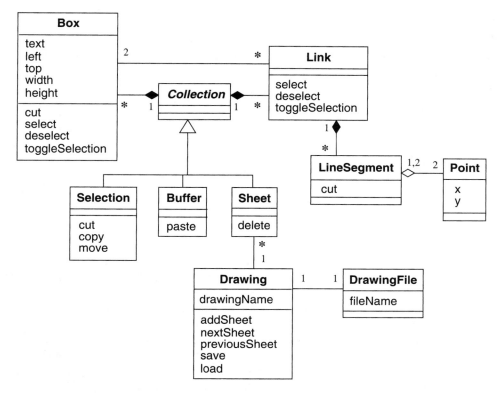

Figure E18.4 Class diagram for a diagram editor

e. Given two boxes, determine all links between them.
f. Given a selection and a sheet, determine which links connect a selected box to a deselected box.
g. Given two boxes and a link, produce an ordered set of points. The first point is where the link connects to the first box, the last point is where the link connects to the second box, and intermediate points trace the link.

19

Databases

The OO paradigm is versatile and applies to databases as well as programming code. It might surprise you, but you can implement UML models not only with OO databases but also with relational databases. The resulting databases are efficient, coherent, and extensible.

You prepare a database by first performing the analysis steps described in Chapter 12 and constructing a domain model. The remaining methodology chapters in Part 2 apply mostly to design of programming code and to a lesser extent to databases. This chapter resumes where Chapter 12 ends. How can we map a model to database structures and tune the result for fast performance? How can we couple the resulting database to programming code? This chapter also includes a brief introduction to databases for new readers.

The chapter emphasizes relational databases because they dominate the marketplace. OO databases are practical only for niche applications and are discussed at the end of the chapter.

19.1 Introduction

19.1.1 Database Concepts

A *database* is a permanent, self-descriptive store of data that is contained in one or more files. Self-description is what sets a database apart from ordinary files. A database contains the data structure or *schema*—description of data— as well as the data.

A *database management system (DBMS)* is the software for managing access to a database. One major objective of OO technology is to promote software reuse; for data-intensive applications DBMSs can replace much application code. You are achieving reuse when you use generic DBMS code, rather than custom-written application code. There are additional reasons for using a DBMS.

- **Data protection**. DBMSs protect data from accidental loss due to hardware crashes, disk media failures, and application errors.

- **Efficiency**. DBMSs have efficient algorithms for managing large quantities of data.

- **Sharing between users**. Multiple users can access the database at the same time.

- **Sharing between applications**. Multiple application programs (presumably related) can read and write data to the same database. A database is a neutral medium that promotes communication among programs.

- **Data quality**. You can specify rules that data must satisfy. A DBMS can control the quality of its data over and above facilities that application programs may provide.

- **Data distribution**. You can partition data across various sites, organizations, and hardware platforms. The DBMS keeps the fragmented data consistent.

- **Security**. A DBMS can restrict reading and writing of data to authorized users.

19.1.2 Relational Database Concepts

A *relational database* has data that is perceived as tables. A *relational DBMS (RDBMS)* manages tables of data and associated structures that increase the functionality and performance of tables. RDBMSs have benefitted from a clear definition by an authoritative figure (EF Codd, the inventor of relational databases) and a standard access language (SQL [Melton-93]). All RDBMSs support a common core of SQL for defining tables, manipulating data in tables, and controlling access to tables. Variations exist for data types, performance tuning, programming access, and system data, though the standard is gradually subsuming these areas. An RDBMS has three major aspects: data structure, operators, and constraints.

- **Data structure**. A relational database appears as a collection of tables. Tables have a specific number of columns and an arbitrary number of rows with a value stored at each row-column intersection. Figure 19.1 shows two sample tables. The *Person* table has five columns and four rows; the *Company* table has three columns and three rows. The column names in boldface are primary keys (to be explained). Note that Jane Brown lacks an employer. *Null* means that an attribute value is unknown or not applicable for a given row.

    RDBMSs use special techniques—such as indexing, hashing, and sorting—to speed access, because literal tables are much too slow for practical needs. These tuning techniques are transparent and not visible in the commands for reading and writing to tables. The RDBMS decides when tuning structures are helpful in processing a query, and if so, automatically uses them. The RDBMS automatically updates tuning structures whenever the corresponding tables are modified.

- **Operators**. SQL provides operators for manipulating tables. The SQL *select* statement reads the data in tables. The syntax looks something like (keywords are capitalized):

```
SELECT columnList
FROM tableList
WHERE predicateIsTrue
```

Person table

personID	lastName	firstName	address	employer
1	Smith	Jim	314 Olive St.	1001
5	Brown	Moe	722 Short St.	1002
999	Smith	Jim	1561 Main Dr.	1001
14	Brown	Jane	722 Short St.	NULL

Company table

companyID	companyName	address
1001	Ajax Widgets	33 Industrial Dr.
1002	AAA liquors	724 Short St.
1003	Win-more Sports	1877 Broadway

Figure 19.1 Sample tables. A relational DBMS presents data as tables.

Logically (the actual implementation is more efficient) the RDBMS combines the various tables into one temporary table. The column list specifies the columns to retain. The predicate specifies the rows to retain. The RDBMS returns the resulting data as the answer to the query. SQL has additional commands for inserting, deleting, and updating data in tables.

Interactive SQL commands are set-oriented; they operate on entire tables rather than individual rows or values. SQL provides a similar language for use with application programs that has a row-at-a-time interface.

■ **Constraints**. An RDBMS can enforce many constraints (such as candidate, primary, and foreign keys) that are defined as part of the database structure. An RDBMS refuses to store data that violates constraints, returning an error to the user or requesting program.

A *candidate key* is a combination of columns that uniquely identifies each row in a table. The combination must be minimal and include only those columns that are needed for unique identification. No column in a candidate key can be null.

A *primary key* is a candidate key that is preferentially used to access the records in a table. A table can have at most one primary key; normally each table should have a primary key. The boldface in Figure 19.1 indicates the primary key of each table.

A *foreign key* is a reference to a candidate key (normally a reference to a primary key) and is the glue that binds tables. In Figure 19.1 *employer* is a foreign key in the *Person* table that refers to *companyID* in the *Company* table. It would not be permissible to change Moe Brown's *employer* to 1004, since the *Company* table does not define 1004. If the row for Ajax Widgets were deleted in the *Company* table, then both Jim Smith rows would have to be deleted or have their *employer* set to null. The foreign-to-primary-key binding forms a frequent navigation path between tables.

19.1.3 Normal Forms

A *normal form* is a guideline for relational database tables that increases data consistency. As tables satisfy higher levels of normal forms, they are less likely to store redundant or contradictory data. Developers can violate normal forms for good cause, such as to increase performance for a database that is read and seldom updated. Such a relaxation is called *denormalization*. The important issue with normal forms is to violate them deliberately and only when necessary.

Normal forms were first used in the 1970s and 1980s. At that time, developers built databases by creating a list of desired fields, which they then had to organize into meaningful groups before storing them in a database. That was the purpose of normal forms. Normal forms organize fields into groups according to dependencies between fields. Unfortunately, it is easy to overlook dependencies. If any are missed, the resulting database structure may be flawed.

UML models provide a better way to prepare databases. Instead of focusing on the fine granularity of fields, developers think in terms of groups of fields—that is, classes. UML models do not diminish the validity of normal forms—normal forms apply regardless of the development approach.

However, UML modeling does eliminate the need to check normal forms. If developers build a sound model, it will intrinsically satisfy normal forms. The converse also holds—a poor model is unlikely to satisfy normal forms. Furthermore, if developers cannot build a sound model, they will probably be unable to find all the dependencies that are required for checking normal forms. It is less difficult to build models than to find all the dependencies.

The bottom line is that developers can still check normal forms if they want to after modeling, but such a check is unnecessary.

19.1.4 Choosing a DBMS Product

In order to build an application, you must choose a specific DBMS product. Because the core features have been set by the SQL standard, you should choose an RDBMS vendor according to pragmatic concerns.

- **Market share**. Oracle, IBM, and Microsoft are the major market players. The staying power of other vendors is less clear. You may also want to consider an open-source DBMS such as MySQL or PostgreSQL.

- **Vendor and third-party support**. DBMSs are a big commitment for an organization and require ongoing help.

- **Other applications**. You reduce administrative and license costs if you use the same vendor or a small number of vendors for your applications.

With each new product release the major vendors tend to jump ahead of the competition's features and performance benchmarks, only to be surpassed themselves when a competitor has its own new release. Over the long term there tends to be little difference in features and performance, so you should not dwell on them when choosing a product.

19.2 Abbreviated ATM Model

Figure 19.2 shows the portion of the ATM model that this chapter will use as an example. We added *CheckingAccount* and *SavingsAccount* so that we can discuss generalization. We also added the *Address* class to assist our explanation.

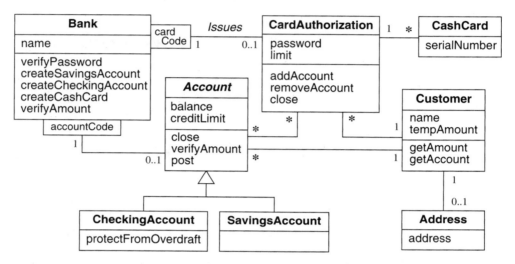

Figure 19.2 Abbreviated ATM implementation class model used in this chapter

19.3 Implementing Structure—Basic

You can readily translate the class model into SQL code. Many tools will do this, but you should still know the rules. Then you understand what the tools are doing and can spot check their results. RDBMSs provide good support for classes and associations but lack support for inheritance, so you must use a workaround. You should perform the following initial tasks.

- ■ Implement classes. [19.3.1]
- ■ Implement associations. [19.3.2]
- ■ Implement generalizations. [19.3.3]
- ■ Implement identity [19.3.4]

19.3.1 Classes

Normally you should map each class to a table and each attribute to a column (Figure 19.3). You can add columns for an object identifier and associations (to be explained). The boldface indicates the primary key. Keywords are in uppercase. Note that operations do not affect table structure. We have chosen data types and *not-null* constraints that seem appropriate for the

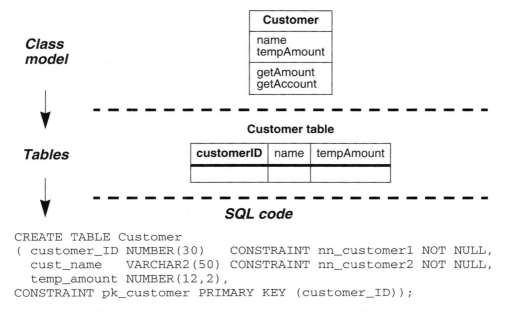

Class
model

Customer

name
tempAmount

getAmount
getAccount

Tables

Customer table

customerID	name	tempAmount

SQL code

```
CREATE TABLE Customer
( customer_ID NUMBER(30)    CONSTRAINT nn_customer1 NOT NULL,
  cust_name    VARCHAR2(50) CONSTRAINT nn_customer2 NOT NULL,
  temp_amount NUMBER(12,2),
CONSTRAINT pk_customer PRIMARY KEY (customer_ID));
```

Figure 19.3 Implementing classes. Make each class a table.

problem. All our examples use Oracle syntax. The *nn_customer1* and *nn_customer2* are names of the not-null constraints. The *pk_customer* is the name of the primary key constraint.

19.3.2 Associations

The implementation rules for associations depend on the multiplicity.

■ **Many-to-many associations**. Implement the association with a table and make the association's primary key the combination of the classes' primary keys (Figure 19.4). If the association has attributes, they become additional columns.

■ **One-to-many associations**. Each one becomes a foreign key buried in the table for the "many" class (Figure 19.5). If there had been a name on the "one" end of the association, we would have used it as the foreign key name. We presume that *serialNumber* is unique for *CashCard*.

■ **One-to-one associations**. These seldom occur. You can handle them by burying a foreign key in either class table (Figure 19.6).

■ **N-ary associations**. They also seldom occur. You can treat them like many-to-many associations and create a table for the association. Typically, the primary key of the n-ary association combines the primary keys of the related tables.

■ **Association classes**. An *association class* is an association that is also a class. It is easier to establish the proper dependencies if you make each association class into a table, regardless of the multiplicity.

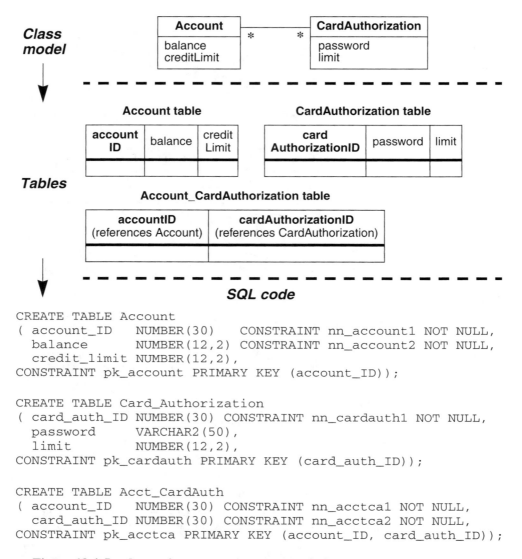

Figure 19.4 Implementing many-to-many associations. Make each one a table.

- **Qualified associations**. Qualified associations follow the same rules as the underlying association without the qualifier. Thus we treat Figure 19.7 like a one-to-many association (a bank has many accounts). The notation *ckn* (*n* is a number) denotes a candidate key. Many qualified associations have a candidate key involving the qualifier.

- **Aggregation, composition**. Aggregation and composition follow the same implementation rules as association.

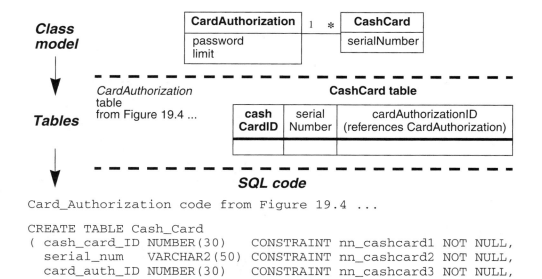

Figure 19.5 Implementing one-to-many associations. Bury each one as
a foreign key in the "many" class table.

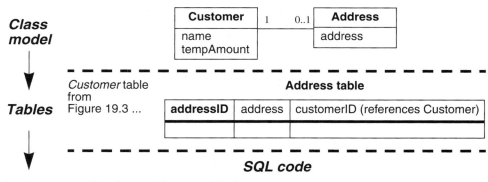

```
Customer code from Figure 19.3 ...

CREATE TABLE Address
( address_ID   NUMBER(30)     CONSTRAINT nn_address1 NOT NULL,
  address      VARCHAR2(200)  CONSTRAINT nn_address2 NOT NULL,
  customer_ID  NUMBER(30)     CONSTRAINT nn_address3 NOT NULL,
CONSTRAINT pk_address PRIMARY KEY (address_ID));
```

Figure 19.6 Implementing one-to-one associations. Bury a foreign
key in either class table.

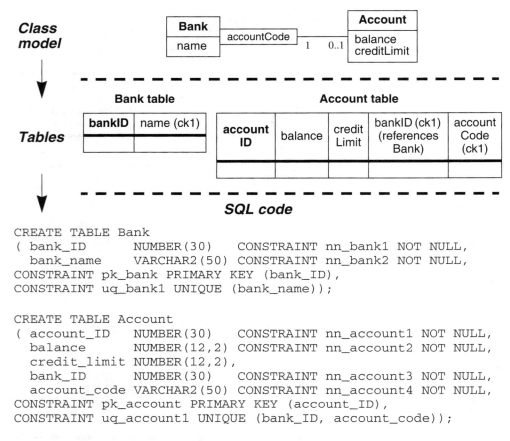

Figure 19.7 Implementing qualified associations. Treat each one like
the association without the qualifier.

19.3.3 Generalizations

The implementation rules for generalization depend on whether there is single or multiple inheritance.

- **Single inheritance**. The simplest approach is to map the superclass and subclasses each to a table, as Figure 19.8 shows. The generalization set name (*accountType*) indicates the appropriate subclass table for each superclass record. For a multilevel generalization, you apply the mappings one level at a time.

    In the figure, note that the primary key names vary, but an object should have the same primary key value throughout an inheritance hierarchy. Thus "Joe's checking account" may have one row in the *Account* table with *account_ID* 101 and another row in

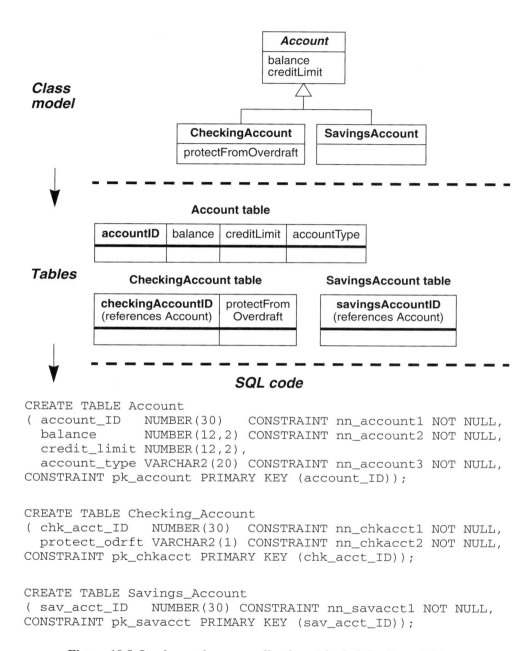

Figure 19.8   Implementing generalizations (single inheritance). Map
the superclass and subclasses each to a table.

the *Checking_Account* table with *chk_acct_ID* 101. We prefer to tie ID names to class names (*account_ID*, *chk_acct_ID*, and *sav_acct_ID*), rather than use the same name (*account_ID*) for all the tables that implement a generalization—this makes it easier to handle multilevel generalizations.

Note that you should not eliminate subclasses that have no attributes, such as *SavingsAccount* in Figure 19.8. Such a performance optimization is seldom important and it complicates the enforcement of foreign key dependencies (Section 19.4.1).

■ **Multiple inheritance**. You can handle multiple inheritance from disjoint classes with separate superclass and subclass tables. For multiple inheritance from overlapping classes, you should use one table for each superclass, one table for each subclass, and one table for the generalization.

19.3.4 Identity

Aside from special situations, such as temporary tables, every table should have a primary key. Without any explanation, we have been using object identity. This is our preferred approach, but we should mention another approach that is also common in the database literature. Figure 19.9 shows the two options.

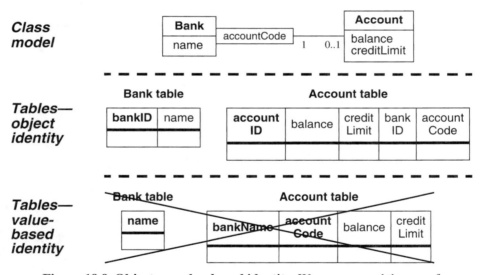

Figure 19.9 Object vs. value-based identity. We recommend the use of object identity.

■ **Object identity**. Add an artificial number attribute (an object ID) to each class table and make it the primary key. The primary key for each association table consists of identifiers from the related classes.

Object identifiers have the advantage of being a single attribute, small, and uniform in size. Most RDBMSs can efficiently allocate identifiers. However, object identifiers can make a database more difficult to read during debugging and maintenance. IDs also complicate database merges; ID values may contend and need to be reassigned. You should not display artificial numbers to users.

■ **Value-based identity**. Identify each object with some combination of real-world attributes. The primary key for each association table consists of primary keys from the related classes.

Value-based identity has different trade-offs. Primary keys have intrinsic meaning, making it easier to debug the database. On the downside, value-based primary keys can be difficult to change. A change may propagate to other tables. Some classes do not have natural real-world identifiers.

We recommend that you use object identity for RDBMS applications. The resulting uniformity and simplicity outweighs any additional debugging effort. Furthermore, object identity is more consistent with the spirit of object orientation—that objects have intrinsic identity apart from their properties. OO languages implement identity with pointers or look-up tables into pointers; an ID is the equivalent database construct.

19.3.5 Summary of Basic Rules for RDBMS Implementation

Table 19.1 summarizes the basic rules for implementing RDBMS structure.

Concept	UML construct	Recommended implementation rule
Class	Class	Map each class to a table and each attribute to a column in the table
Association (End names become foreign key names.)	Many-to-many	Use distinct table
	One-to-many	Use buried foreign key
	One-to-one	
	N-ary	Use distinct table
	Association class	
	Qualified	Same rules as underlying nonqualified association
Aggregation	Aggregation	Same rules as association
	Composition	
Generalization	Single inheritance	Create separate tables for the superclass and each subclass
	Disjoint multiple inheritance	
	Overlapping multiple inheritance	Same as disjoint multiple inheritance + generalization table to bind superclass and subclass records

Table 19.1   Summary of basic rules for implementing relational databases. These rules are embedded in most database generation tools.

19.4 Implementing Structure—Advanced

The prior section explained how to define tables for each construct in the UML class model. Now we cover advanced aspects that boost performance and ensure data quality. You should perform the following additional tasks.

■ Implement foreign keys. [19.4.1]

■ Implement check constraints. [19.4.2]

■ Implement indexes. [19.4.3]

■ Consider views. [19.4.4]

19.4.1 Foreign Keys

Foreign keys arise from generalizations and associations. When a foreign key is defined, the RDBMS *guarantees* that there will be no dangling references—the RDBMS refuses to perform any updates that would cause a dangling reference. Since an application knows that defined foreign keys will always be intact, it need not include error checking for them.

In addition, many RDBMSs can propagate the effects of deletions and updates that affect foreign keys. When you use object identity, as we have suggested, there is no need to propagate updates—IDs are invariant and never change. However, it is helpful to declare the response to deletions, as we will now explain.

For generalizations you should specify *on delete cascade* for each subclass table. Figure 19.10 shows the foreign-key statements that we would add to Figure 19.8. Recall that generalization structures the description of an object, with each level providing part of the description. An application must combine superclass and subclass records to reconstitute an entire object. Accordingly, with *on delete cascade*, deletion of a superclass record causes the deletion of the corresponding subclass record, and this deletion propagates downward for each generalization level.

```
ALTER TABLE Checking_Account ADD CONSTRAINT fk_chkacct1
   FOREIGN KEY chk_acct_ID
   REFERENCES Account ON DELETE CASCADE;

ALTER TABLE Savings_Account ADD CONSTRAINT fk_savacct1
   FOREIGN KEY sav_acct_ID
   REFERENCES Account ON DELETE CASCADE;
```

Figure 19.10 Maintaining foreign keys for generalization. Each subclass table should specify *on delete cascade* for the foreign key to the superclass.

In a similar manner we would like to propagate deletion of a subclass record upward to the superclass, but SQL unfortunately does not support this reverse direction. To compensate, you must write programming code to propagate deletions up a generalization hierarchy.

You should also declare foreign keys to enforce associations, as Figure 19.11 shows. The appropriate deletion action—cascade or no action—depends on the model's meaning. For example, we might want the deletion of a customer record to cause the deletion of the corresponding address record—this is *on delete cascade* (the first statement in Figure 19.11). Alternatively, you might want to prevent the deletion of a customer who has accounts (to avoid accidental loss of extensive data). The user must first delete all the accounts and only then can delete the customer. In the SQL standard you prevent deletion by specifying *on delete no action*; the Oracle equivalent is to omit a delete action (the second statement in Figure 19.11).

```
ALTER TABLE Address ADD CONSTRAINT fk_address1
    FOREIGN KEY customer_ID
    REFERENCES Customer ON DELETE CASCADE;


ALTER TABLE Account ADD CONSTRAINT fk_account2
    FOREIGN KEY customer_ID
    REFERENCES Customer;
```

Figure 19.11 Maintaining foreign keys for association. There are two possibilities, which depend on the model's meaning.

19.4.2 Check Constraints

SQL also has general constraints that can enforce the values of an enumeration. Such enforcement is especially helpful for implementing a generalization set name. Figure 19.12 adds a check constraint to the example of Figure 19.8.

```
ALTER TABLE Account ADD CONSTRAINT enum_account1
    CHECK (account_type IN ('Checking_Account',
    'Savings_Account'));
```

Figure 19.12 Enforcing a generalization set name. An SQL check constraint can enforce the values of an enumeration.

19.4.3 Indexes

Most RDBMSs create indexes as a side effect of SQL primary key and candidate key (*unique*) constraints. (An **index** is a data structure that maps column values into database table rows.) You should also create an index for every foreign key that is not covered by a primary key or candidate key constraint. For example, the primary key for *Acct_CardAuth* (Figure 19.4) causes an RDBMS to build an index that ensures fast access to *account_ID* as well as *account_ID + card_auth_ID*. An additional index on *card_auth_ID* (Figure 19.13) ensures that this field accessed alone is also fast.

These indexes are *critically* important. Foreign-key indexes enable quick combination of tables. A lack of indexes can cause RDBMS performance to degrade by orders of magni-

```
CREATE INDEX index_acctca1 ON Acct_CardAuth (card_auth_ID);
```

Figure 19.13 Defining indexes. Every foreign key should be covered by an index.

tude. Foreign-key indexes should be an integral part of a database because they are straight-forward to include and there is no good reason to defer them.

The database administrator (DBA) may define additional indexes for frequent queries and use product-specific tuning mechanisms.

19.4.4 Views

You may wish to define a view for each subclass to consolidate inherited data and make object access easier. A *view* is a table that an RDBMS dynamically computes. Figure 19.14 shows an example for the *CheckingAccount* subclass. You can freely read an object through a view, but RDBMSs only partially support writing through views. The restrictions vary across products.

```
CREATE VIEW view_checking_account AS
   SELECT chk_acct_ID, balance, credit_limit, protect_odrft
   FROM Account A, Checking_Account CA
   WHERE A.account_ID = CA.chk_acct_ID;
```

Figure 19.14 A sample RDBMS view. You can use a view to consolidate the object fragments that are stored for each generalization level.

19.4.5 Summary of Advanced Rules for RDBMS Implementation

Table 19.2 summarizes the advanced rules for implementing RDBMS structure.

Concept	Advanced implementation rule
Class	■ Define a check constraint for each enumerated attribute.
Association, Aggregation, Composition	■ Enforce foreign keys. Specify *on delete cascade* or *on delete no action*, depending on the model's meaning. ■ Define a check constraint for each enumerated attribute. ■ Define indexes for any buried foreign keys not covered by primary and candidate key constraints.
Generalization	■ Enforce foreign keys. Specify *on delete cascade* for each subclass table. ■ Define a check constraint for each generalization set name. ■ Consider defining a view to consolidate inherited data and to ease reading of objects.

Table 19.2 Summary of advanced rules for implementing relational databases.
These rules are embedded in most database generation tools.

19.5 Implementing Structure for the ATM Example

Figure 19.15 puts together all the rules and shows the tables for Figure 19.2. Figure 19.16 shows SQL code that creates Oracle database structures. Each *sequence* statement creates a counter that is used to allocate an ID. For example, *seq_bank* is used to allocate *bank_ID* as each *Bank* object is created. We have organized the code logically, and it must be reordered before execution. First execute the create table and create sequence statements, then the create index statements, and finally the alter table statements. We have omitted the optional views on *CheckingAccount* and *SavingsAccount*.

Bank table

bankID	name (ck1)

Customer table

customerID	name	tempAmount

Account table

account ID	balance	credit Limit	bankID (ck1) (references Bank)	accountCode (ck1)	account Type	customerID (references Customer)

CardAuthorization table

card AuthorizationID	password	limit	bankID (ck1) (references Bank)	cardCode (ck1)	customerID (references Customer)

CashCard table

cashCardID	serialNumber	cardAuthorizationID (references CardAuthorization)

Account_CardAuthorization table

accountID (references Account)	cardAuthorizationID (references CardAuthorization)

SavingsAccount table

savingsAccountID (references Account)

CheckingAccount table

checkingAccountID (references Account)	protectFrom Overdraft

Address table

address ID	address	customerID (references Customer)

Figure 19.15 RDBMS tables for the abbreviated ATM model

```
CREATE TABLE Bank
( bank_ID     NUMBER(30)     CONSTRAINT nn_bank1 NOT NULL,
  bank_name   VARCHAR2(50)   CONSTRAINT nn_bank2 NOT NULL,
CONSTRAINT pk_bank PRIMARY KEY (bank_ID),
CONSTRAINT uq_bank1 UNIQUE (bank_name));

CREATE SEQUENCE seq_bank;

CREATE TABLE Customer
( customer_ID NUMBER(30)     CONSTRAINT nn_customer1 NOT NULL,
  cust_name   VARCHAR2(50) CONSTRAINT nn_customer2 NOT NULL,
  temp_amount NUMBER(12,2),
CONSTRAINT pk_customer PRIMARY KEY (customer_ID));

CREATE SEQUENCE seq_customer;

CREATE TABLE Card_Authorization
( card_auth_ID NUMBER(30)    CONSTRAINT nn_cardauth1 NOT NULL,
  password     VARCHAR2(50),
  limit        NUMBER(12,2),
  bank_ID      NUMBER(30)     CONSTRAINT nn_cardauth2 NOT NULL,
  card_code    VARCHAR2(50) CONSTRAINT nn_cardauth3 NOT NULL,
  customer_ID  NUMBER(30)     CONSTRAINT nn_cardauth4 NOT NULL,
CONSTRAINT pk_cardauth PRIMARY KEY (card_auth_ID),
CONSTRAINT uq_cardauth1 UNIQUE (bank_ID, card_code));

CREATE SEQUENCE seq_cardauth;
CREATE INDEX index_cardauth1 ON Card_Authorization
   (customer_ID);

ALTER TABLE Card_Authorization ADD CONSTRAINT fk_cardauth1
   FOREIGN KEY bank_ID
   REFERENCES Bank;

ALTER TABLE Card_Authorization ADD CONSTRAINT fk_cardauth2
   FOREIGN KEY customer_ID
   REFERENCES Customer;


CREATE TABLE Checking_Account
( chk_acct_ID   NUMBER(30)  CONSTRAINT nn_chkacct1 NOT NULL,
  protect_odrft VARCHAR2(1) CONSTRAINT nn_chkacct2 NOT NULL,
CONSTRAINT pk_chkacct PRIMARY KEY (chk_acct_ID));

ALTER TABLE Checking_Account ADD CONSTRAINT fk_chkacct1
   FOREIGN KEY chk_acct_ID
   REFERENCES Account ON DELETE CASCADE;

ALTER TABLE Checking_Account ADD CONSTRAINT enum_chkacct1
   CHECK (protect_odrft IN ('Y', 'N'));
```

Figure 19.16 SQL code for the abbreviated ATM model

```
CREATE TABLE Account
( account_ID    NUMBER(30)    CONSTRAINT nn_account1 NOT NULL,
  balance       NUMBER(12,2)  CONSTRAINT nn_account2 NOT NULL,
  credit_limit  NUMBER(12,2),
  bank_ID       NUMBER(30)    CONSTRAINT nn_account3 NOT NULL,
  account_code  VARCHAR2(50)  CONSTRAINT nn_account4 NOT NULL,
  account_type  VARCHAR2(20)  CONSTRAINT nn_account5 NOT NULL,
  customer_ID   NUMBER(30)    CONSTRAINT nn_account6 NOT NULL,
CONSTRAINT pk_account PRIMARY KEY (account_ID),
CONSTRAINT uq_account1 UNIQUE (bank_ID, account_code));

CREATE SEQUENCE seq_account;

CREATE INDEX index_account1 ON Account (customer_ID);

ALTER TABLE Account ADD CONSTRAINT fk_account1
  FOREIGN KEY bank_ID
  REFERENCES Bank;

ALTER TABLE Account ADD CONSTRAINT fk_account2
  FOREIGN KEY customer_ID
  REFERENCES Customer;

ALTER TABLE Account ADD CONSTRAINT enum_account1
  CHECK (account_type IN ('Checking_Account',
  'Savings_Account'));


CREATE TABLE Acct_CardAuth
( account_ID    NUMBER(30) CONSTRAINT nn_acctca1 NOT NULL,
  card_auth_ID NUMBER(30) CONSTRAINT nn_acctca2 NOT NULL,
CONSTRAINT pk_acctca PRIMARY KEY (account_ID, card_auth_ID));

CREATE INDEX index_acctca1 ON Acct_CardAuth (card_auth_ID);

ALTER TABLE Acct_CardAuth ADD CONSTRAINT fk_acctca1
  FOREIGN KEY account_ID
  REFERENCES Account;

ALTER TABLE Acct_CardAuth ADD CONSTRAINT fk_acctca2
  FOREIGN KEY card_auth_ID
  REFERENCES Card_Authorization;


CREATE TABLE Savings_Account
( sav_acct_ID NUMBER(30) CONSTRAINT nn_savacct1 NOT NULL,
CONSTRAINT pk_savacct PRIMARY KEY (sav_acct_ID));

ALTER TABLE Savings_Account ADD CONSTRAINT fk_savacct1
  FOREIGN KEY sav_acct_ID
  REFERENCES Account ON DELETE CASCADE;
```

Figure 19.16 (continued) **SQL code for the abbreviated ATM model**

```
CREATE TABLE Cash_Card
( cash_card_ID NUMBER(30)    CONSTRAINT nn_cashcard1 NOT NULL,
   serial_num    VARCHAR2(50) CONSTRAINT nn_cashcard2 NOT NULL,
   card_auth_ID NUMBER(30)    CONSTRAINT nn_cashcard3 NOT NULL,
CONSTRAINT pk_cashcard PRIMARY KEY (cash_card_ID),
CONSTRAINT uq_cashcard1 UNIQUE (serial_num));

CREATE SEQUENCE seq_cashcard;

CREATE INDEX index_cashcard1 ON Cash_Card (card_auth_ID);

ALTER TABLE Cash_Card ADD CONSTRAINT fk_cashcard1
   FOREIGN KEY card_auth_ID
   REFERENCES Card_Authorization;

CREATE TABLE Address
( address_ID  NUMBER(30)    CONSTRAINT nn_address1 NOT NULL,
   address       VARCHAR2(200) CONSTRAINT nn_address2 NOT NULL,
   customer_ID NUMBER(30)    CONSTRAINT nn_address3 NOT NULL,
CONSTRAINT pk_address PRIMARY KEY (address_ID));

CREATE SEQUENCE seq_address;

CREATE INDEX index_address1 ON Address (customer_ID);

ALTER TABLE Address ADD CONSTRAINT fk_address1
   FOREIGN KEY customer_ID
   REFERENCES Customer ON DELETE CASCADE;
```

Figure 19.16 (continued) **SQL code for the abbreviated ATM model**

19.6 Implementing Functionality

Most often your purpose in using a database will be to build an application. Structural concerns dominate a database, but the application's functionality—the user interface, complex logic, and other behavior—is also important. The use of UML models is an important first step toward combining database and programming capabilities—UML models provide a uniform way for thinking about both aspects. However, there are some additional functionality issues to consider.

- Coupling a programming language to a database. [19.6.1]
- Converting data. [19.6.2]
- Encapsulation vs. query optimization. [19.6.3]
- Use of SQL code. [19.6.4]

19.6.1 Coupling a Programming Language to a Database

Relational databases and conventional programming languages have divergent styles that make them difficult to couple. Relational databases are declarative; developers describe the data they want instead of how to get it. In contrast, most programming languages are imperative and require that logic be reduced to a sequence of steps. Many techniques are available for combining databases and programming languages, and it is important that you consider all of your options.

- **Preprocessor and postprocessor**. Preprocessors and postprocessors can be helpful for batch applications. The basic idea is simple: Query the database and create an input file, run the application, and then analyze the output and store the results in the database.

  The downside is that database interaction via intermediate files can be awkward. The preprocessor must request all database information before executing the application, and output files with complex formats can be difficult to parse. This technique is useful for old software or certified software that cannot be altered.

- **Script files**. Sometimes all you need is a file of DBMS commands. For example, typing @*filename* into interactive SQL (SQL Plus) of Oracle causes the commands in *filename* to execute. Developers can use an operating system shell language to execute multiple script files and to control their execution.

  Script files are helpful for simple database interaction, such as creating database structures. They are also useful for prototyping.

- **Embedded DBMS commands**. Another technique is to intersperse SQL commands with application code.

  Many database books emphasize this technique. Unfortunately, such programs can be difficult to read and maintain. The essential problem is that the conceptual basis for an RDBMS is different than that for most programming languages. We discourage the use of this approach.

- **Custom application programming interface (API)**. A better alternative to embedded DBMS commands is to encapsulate database read and write requests within dedicated application methods that collectively provide a database interface. You can write these methods using a proprietary database-access language, such as Oracle's PL/SQL, or a standard language, such as ODBC or JDBC.

  A custom API isolates database interaction from the rest of the application. An API can help you partition the tasks of data management, application logic, and user interface consistent with the spirit of encapsulation.

- **Stored procedures**. A *stored procedure* is programming code that is stored in a database.

  Some RDBMSs, such as SQL Server, require stored procedures for maximum efficiency. Stored procedures also let applications share general-purpose functionality. However, you should try to avoid placing application-specific functionality in stored procedures—once the logic is placed in the database, any application can use it, compromising encapsulation. Stored procedures also vary widely across products.

- **Fourth-generation language (4GL)**. A *fourth-generation language* is a framework for database applications that provides screen layout, simple calculations, and reports.

  4GLs are widely available and can greatly reduce application development time. They are best for straightforward applications and prototyping. They are not suitable for applications with complex programming.

- **Generic layer**. A generic layer hides the DBMS and provides simple data access commands (such as *getRecordGivenKey* and *writeRecord*) [Blaha-98]. You can write application code in terms of the layer and largely ignore the underlying DBMS.

  A well-conceived generic layer can simplify application programming. However, it can also impede performance and restrict access to database functionality.

- **Metadata-driven system**. The application indirectly accesses data by first accessing the data's description (the metadata) and then formulating the query to access the data. For example, an RDBMS processes commands by accessing the system tables first and then the actual data.

  Metadata-driven applications can be quite complex. This technique is suitable for frameworks (see Chapter 14) and applications that learn.

Sometimes it is helpful to mix techniques. For example, a developer could use an API and implement some functionality with stored procedures. Table 19.3 summarizes the coupling techniques.

Data interaction technique	Recommendation
Preprocessor and postprocessor	Consider for old batch software or certified software that cannot be altered.
Script files	Consider for simple database interaction and prototyping.
Embedded DBMS commands	Use only when necessary. An API provides a better approach.
Custom API	Often a good choice.
Stored procedures	Good for general-purpose logic. Try to avoid placing application-specific logic in stored procedures.
4GL	Consider for straightforward applications and prototyping.
Generic layer	Consider when performance is not demanding and simple database functionality is needed.
Metadata driven	Consider for frameworks and other special situations.

Table 19.3 Data interaction techniques. It is important to consider all options for combining databases and programming languages.

19.6.2 Data Conversion

Legacy data processing is important for seeding new applications and exchanging data among applications. Many applications are poorly conceived, so it can be challenging and time consuming to rework their data. There are several key issues.

■ **Cleansing data**. You must repair errors in source data. Errors arise from user mistakes, modeling flaws, database flaws, and application program errors. For example, an application program may have missed some addresses with illegal postal codes. A combination of fields might be intended to be unique, but the data may have errors if the database structure does not enforce uniqueness.

■ **Handling missing data**. You must decide how to handle missing data. Can you find it elsewhere, do you want to estimate it, or can you use null values? You might want users to help resolve missing data.

■ **Moving data**. It is common to migrate data from one application to another, either on a one-shot or a recurring basis. A standard language, such as XML, can be helpful for handling such data interchange.

■ **Merging data**. Data sources may overlap. For example, one system may contain account information and another may contain address data. A new application may need both. For complex sources, it is best to model them first and then decide how to merge them.

■ **Changing data structure**. Typically, source structures differ from target structures, so you must adjust the data. For example, one application may store a phone number in a single field; another may split country code, area code, and local phone number into separate fields. Corresponding fields may have different names, data types, and lengths. There may be different data encodings; for example, sex can be encoded as male or female, M or F, 1 or 2, and so on.

You should begin processing by loading the data into staging tables that mirror the original structure. For example, if the old application uses files and the new application uses a relational database, create one staging table for each file. Each column in a file maps to one column in a table with the same data type and length. Most RDBMSs have commands that readily perform this kind of loading.

The staging tables get the data into the database so that it can be operated upon with SQL commands. It is often better (less work, fewer errors, easier modification) to use SQL commands than to write custom programming code. Staging tables enable the full power of database queries to convert data from the old to the new format.

Often you can find alternative data sources. Customer data may be available from sales records, customer service records, and an external marketing firm, for example. To resolve redundancy, load the most accurate source first and then load the next most accurate and so on. Before loading each source, place it in a staging table so that SQL can eliminate already existing records. If you do not do this, you could load the same customer twice, for example. This approach is a simple way to resolve conflicts in data, and it biases the database toward the best sources.

19.6.3 Encapsulation vs. Query Optimization

Section 15.10.1 emphasized the importance of encapsulation (information hiding) and consequently the need to limit class-model traversals. Unfortunately, there is a conflict between the goals of encapsulation and the goals of RDBMS query optimization.

According to the principle of encapsulation, an object should access only directly related objects. Indirectly related objects should be accessed indirectly via the methods of intervening objects. Encapsulation increases the resilience of an application; local changes to an application model cause local changes to the application code.

On the other hand, RDBMS optimizers take a logical request and generate an efficient execution plan. If queries are broadly stated, the optimizer has greater freedom for devising an efficient plan. RDBMS performance is usually best if you join multiple tables together in a single SQL statement, rather than disperse logic across multiple SQL statements.

Thus encapsulation boosts resilience but limits optimization potential. In contrast, broadly stating queries enables optimization, but a small change to an application can affect many queries. For RDBMS applications, there is no simple resolution of this conflict. There are three different situations.

- **Complex programming**. You should encapsulate your code if the programming is intricate and performance degradation is not too severe.

- **Easy programming and good query performance**. You should broadly state queries if doing so improves RDBMS performance and the programming code and queries are relatively easy to write—and rewrite if the class model changes.

- **Easy programming and poor query performance**. Somewhat paradoxically, you can sometimes improve performance by fragmenting queries. Query optimizers are imperfect, and occasionally you will need to guide the optimizer manually.

19.6.4 Use of SQL Code

You can always write programming code for methods, but sometimes SQL provides a better alternative. A skilled developer can write SQL code faster than programming code. Furthermore, SQL code can execute faster, has fewer defects (bugs), and is easier to extend. The performance of SQL code benefits from reduced communication traffic (computation is confined to the server) and robust internal RDBMS algorithms.

For example, referring to the full ATM model in Chapter 17, we might want to prepare a monthly statement of transactions for each account. We could query the database and bring the various pieces of data into memory. Alternatively, Figure 19.17 shows a SQL command that provides the core data for a statement all at once. The names preceded with a colon are programming variables that are passed into the SQL command.

19.7 Object-Oriented Databases

An *object-oriented database* is a persistent store of objects that mix data and behavior. With an ordinary programming language, objects cease to exist when the program ends; with an object-oriented database, objects persist beyond the confines of program execution. An *object-oriented DBMS (OO-DBMS)* manages the data, programming code, and associated structures that constitute an object-oriented database. In contrast to RDBMSs, OO-DBMSs vary widely in their syntax and capabilities.

```
SELECT T.date_time, U.amount, U.kind
FROM Bank B, Account A, Update U, Remote_Transaction T
WHERE B.bank_ID = A.bank_ID AND
      A.account_ID = U.account_ID AND
      U.transaction_ID = T.transaction_ID AND
      B.bank_name = :aBankName AND
      A.account_code = :anAccountCode AND
      T.date_time >= :aStartDate AND
      T.date_time <= :anEndDate
ORDER BY T.date_time;
```

Figure 19.17 Offloading functionality to SQL code. Sometimes it is better to use SQL to implement a method than to write programming code.

OO-DBMSs are a relative newcomer to the database market. RDBMSs were commercialized in the 1970s, but OO-DBMSs were not introduced until the 1990s. Two major motivations led to the development of OO-DBMSs.

- **Programmer frustration with RDBMSs.** Many programmers don't understand RDBMSs and want something more familiar. RDBMSs are declarative (queries describe properties that requested data must satisfy), while most languages are imperative (stated as a sequence of steps). Furthermore, RDBMSs awkwardly combine with most languages, and programmers prefer a DBMS with a more seamless interface.

  This is a poor reason for choosing an OO-DBMS. The reality is that RDBMSs dominate the marketplace now and will for the foreseeable future. Programmers should not be using an OO-DBMS out of frustration; they should learn to deal with RDBMSs. RDBMS products are more mature and have proven features for reliability, scalability, and administration.

- **Need for special features**. RDBMSs lack the power that some advanced applications need. OO-DBMSs offer advanced features, like rich data types and quick access to low-level primitives.

  This is a good reason for considering an OO-DBMS. If you have an advanced application that is critical to your business, an OO-DBMS may ease development. Engineering applications, multimedia systems, and artificial intelligence software can sometimes benefit from the use of an OO-DBMS.

You should be selective about deciding to use an OO-DBMS. OO-DBMSs are not popular in the marketplace. OO-DBMS sales are only about 2% of RDBMS sales and have hit a plateau [Leavitt-00]. Consequently, you should use OO-DBMSs only for compelling situations.

19.8 Practical Tips

Here are tips for using a relational database to implement an OO design.

■ **Normal forms**. Normal forms apply regardless of the development approach. However, it is unnecessary to check them if you build a sound OO model. (Section 19.1.3)

■ **Classes**. Map each class to a table and each attribute to a column. (Section 19.3.1)

■ **Associations**. For simple one-to-one and one-to-many associations, use a buried foreign key. For all other associations, use a distinct table. (Section 19.3.2)

■ **Generalizations**. For single inheritance, map the superclass and subclasses each to a table. (Section 19.3.3)

■ **Identity**. We strongly advise that you use object identity. Doing so has several advantages and little disadvantage. (Section 19.3.4)

■ **Foreign keys**. Define constraints to enforce all foreign keys. For each subclass, specify *on delete cascade* for the foreign key to the superclass. For some association foreign keys, you may also want to specify *on delete cascade*. (Section 19.4.1)

■ **Enumerations**. Use SQL check constraints to enforce them. (Section 19.4.2)

■ **Indexes**. Create an index for every foreign key that is not covered by a primary key or candidate key constraint. You may want to define additional indexes for frequent queries and use product-specific tuning mechanisms. (Section 19.4.3)

■ **Views**. You may want to define views to reconstitute objects that are fragmented across generalization tables. Such views are convenient for reading, but RDBMSs only partially support writing through views. (Section 19.4.4)

■ **Coupling to a programming language**. Be deliberate about coupling a programming language to a database. Consider all your options. (Section 19.6.1)

■ **Data conversion**. It is often helpful to load data into temporary staging tables. Then you can write SQL code to do much of the data processing. SQL code is easier and faster to write than programming code. (Section 19.6.2)

■ **Encapsulation vs. query optimization**. Be aware of the intrinsic conflict between these two goals and make your best resolution on a case-by-case basis. (Section 19.6.3)

■ **Object-oriented databases**. Consider them only when application needs are compelling. (Section 19.7)

19.9 Chapter Summary

A database management system (DBMS) is software that provides general-purpose functionality for storing, retrieving, and controlling access to data. A DBMS protects data from accidental loss and makes it available for sharing. Several paradigms are available, but the development of new applications is dominated by relational DBMSs (RDBMSs). OO-DBMSs are also available but pragmatic concerns limit their use.

OO models provide an excellent basis for thinking about databases. Developers can think about a problem abstractly and defer the details of design and implementation. With a proper implementation, sound OO models lead to extensible, efficient, and understandable databases. Table 19.1 and Table 19.2 summarize the implementation rules for RDBMS structure.

You should be deliberate in coupling a programming language to a database. Furthermore, you should look for opportunities to substitute SQL code for programming effort.

candidate key	implementing generalizations
coupling a language to a database	index
data conversion	normal form
database	null
database management system (DBMS)	object-oriented DBMS (OO-DBMS)
foreign key	primary key
identity	relational DBMS (RDBMS)
implementing associations	SQL
implementing classes	view

Figure 19.18 Key concepts for Chapter 19

Bibliographic Notes

Many good books explain DBMS and RDBMS principles. [Elmasri-00] is a premier textbook that explains database concepts. [Chaudhri-98] has thoughtful examples of applications that use OO databases.

[Blaha-98] elaborates the material in this chapter and provides more details for files, RDBMSs, and OO-DBMSs (specifically ObjectStore). Our approach to databases is consistent with that of other authors, such as [Muller-99].

[Chang-03] presents middleware for combining databases with GUIs via intermediate text files.

References

[Blaha-98] Michael Blaha and William Premerlani. *Object-Oriented Modeling and Design for Database Applications*. Upper Saddle River, NJ: Prentice Hall, 1998.

[Chang-03] Peter H. Chang. A platform independent middleware architecture for accessing databases on a database server on the Web. *IEEE Conference on Electro/Information Technology*. Indianapolis, 2003.

[Chaudhri-98] Akmal B. Chaudhri and Mary Loomis. *Object Databases in Practice*. Upper Saddle River, NJ: Prentice Hall PTR, 1998.

[Elmasri-00] Ramez Elmasri and Shamkant B. Navathe. *Fundamentals of Database Systems, Third Edition*. Redwood City, CA: Benjamin/Cummings, 2000.

[Leavitt-00] Neal Leavitt. Whatever happened to object-oriented databases? *IEEE Computer*, August 2000, 16–19.

[Melton-93] Jim Melton and Alan R. Simon. *Understanding the New SQL: A Complete Guide*. San Francisco: Morgan Kaufmann, 1993.

[Muller-99] Robert J. Muller. *Database Design for Smarties: Using UML for Data Modeling*. San Francisco: Morgan Kaufmann, 1999.

Exercises

19.1   (8) Figure E19.1 shows four different class models for directed graphs. A directed graph consists of a set of edges and a set of nodes. Each edge connects two nodes and has an arrow indicating direction of flow. Any number of edges may connect to the same node. More than one edge may connect a pair of nodes. An edge may connect a node to itself.

In Figure E19.1a a graph is a many-to-many association between nodes with directionality indicated by *from* and *to* ends. In Figure E19.1b a graph is a many-to-many association between edges. The qualifiers, *end1* and *end2*, are enumerated types with possible values of *to* and *from* indicating which ends of the edges connect. Figure E19.1c treats both nodes and edges as objects. Two associations, *to* and *from*, store connections, one for each end of an edge. Figure E19.1d represents each connection as a qualified association. Each end of an edge connects to exactly one node, and *end* is an enumerated type.

Which diagram most accurately models a graph? Explain the relative merits of each diagram. What happens if more than one edge connects a given pair of nodes? Can an edge connect a node with itself? What happens if only one edge connects to a node?

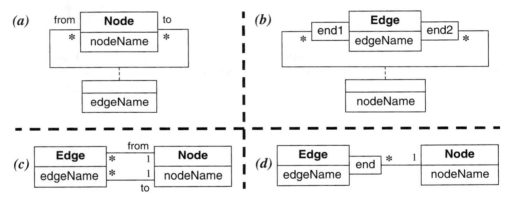

Figure E19.1   Alternative class models for a directed graph

19.2   (6) Prepare tables for each model from the previous exercise. Be sure to show primary, candidate, and foreign keys. Use object identity.

19.3   (4) Write SQL code to create an empty database for the tables for Figure E19.1c and Figure E19.1d from the previous exercise. Use your judgment to supply any missing information.

19.4   (3) Populate the database tables created by the SQL commands of Exercise 19.3 for the directed graph in Figure E19.2.

19.5   For the class model in Figure E19.1d, prepare SQL queries for the following. For part (d) you will need to augment SQL with pseudocode.
   a. (3) Given the name of an edge, determine the two nodes that it connects.
   b. (3) Given the name of a node, determine all edges connected to or from it.
   c. (5) Given a pair of nodes, determine the edges, if any, that directly connect them in either direction.

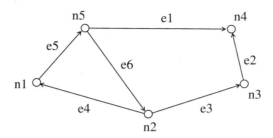

Figure E19.2 Sample directed graph

  d. (8) Given a node, determine the nodes that can be visited directly or indirectly from the given node by traversing one or more edges (transitive closure). Each edge must be traversed from its *from* end to its *to* end.

19.6 (6) Prepare tables for Figure E19.3. An expression is a binary tree of terms that is formed from constants, variables, and arithmetic operators. Unary minus is not allowed.

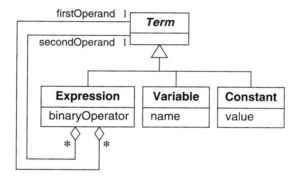

Figure E19.3 Class model for expressions

19.7 (4) Write SQL code to create an empty database for the tables from the previous exercise.

19.8 (5) Show populated database tables created by the previous exercise for the expression $(X + Y/2)/(X/3 - Y)$. Consider the parentheses in establishing the precedence of operators; otherwise, ignore them in populating the database tables.

19.9 (7) Prepare tables for Figure E19.4. A document consists of numbered pages. Each page contains many drawing objects—ellipses, rectangles, polylines, textlines, and groups of objects. Ellipses and rectangles are embedded within a bounding box. A polyline is a series of line segments defined by vertex points. Textlines originate at a point and have a font. Treat all associations and aggregations as unordered. For this exercise disregard the ordering of points in a polygon.

19.10 (7) Revise your tables from the previous exercise to treat the *Polyline_Point* association as ordered. That is, given a polyline, the database must be able to retrieve the points in the correct

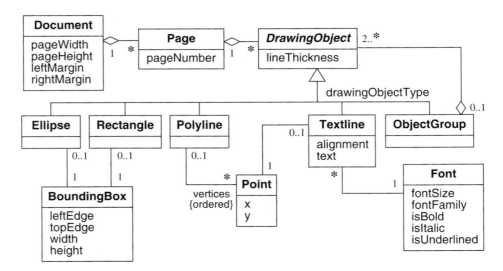

Figure E19.4 Class model for a desktop publishing system

order. [Instructor's note: You may want to give the students the answer to the previous exercise.]

19.11 (6) Modify your answer to Exercise 19.9 to reflect the revised class model in Figure E19.5. Discuss the merits of the revision. Disregard the ordering of *Points* in this exercise.

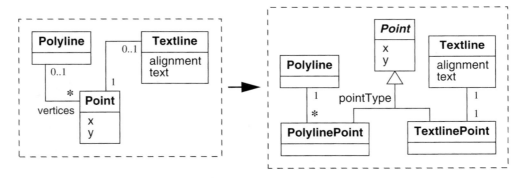

Figure E19.5 Generalization of point to eliminate zero-or-one multiplicity

19.12 (5) Write SQL code to create an empty database for the tables from Exercise 19.9.

19.13 (5) Convert the SQL commands in Figure E19.6 into a class model. The tables store the straight-line distances between pairs of cities.

19.14 (4) Using the tables from Exercise 19.13, write an SQL query that will determine the distance between two cities, given the names of the two cities.

```
CREATE TABLE City
( city_ID      NUMBER(30)     CONSTRAINT nn_city1 NOT NULL,
  city_name    VARCHAR2(255)  CONSTRAINT nn_city2 NOT NULL,
CONSTRAINT pk_city PRIMARY KEY (city_ID),
CONSTRAINT uq_city1 UNIQUE (city_name));

CREATE SEQUENCE seq_city;


CREATE TABLE Route
( route_ID  NUMBER(30)        CONSTRAINT nn_route1 NOT NULL,
  distance  NUMBER(20,10))    CONSTRAINT nn_route2 NOT NULL,
CONSTRAINT pk_route PRIMARY KEY (route_ID));

CREATE SEQUENCE seq_route;


CREATE TABLE City_Distance
( city_ID    NUMBER(30)  CONSTRAINT nn_dist1 NOT NULL,
  route_ID   NUMBER(30)  CONSTRAINT nn_dist2 NOT NULL,
CONSTRAINT pk_dist PRIMARY KEY (city_ID, route_ID));

CREATE INDEX index_dist1 ON City_Distance (route_ID);

ALTER TABLE City_Distance ADD CONSTRAINT fk_dist1
  FOREIGN KEY city_ID
  REFERENCES City;

ALTER TABLE City_Distance ADD CONSTRAINT fk_dist2
  FOREIGN KEY route_ID
  REFERENCES Route;
```

Figure E19.6 SQL commands for creating tables to store distances between cities

19.15 (5) Convert the SQL commands in Figure E19.7 into a class model. The tables store the straight-line distances between pairs of cities.

19.16 (6) Using the tables in Exercise 19.15, write an SQL query that will determine the distance between two cities, given their names. Assume that the distance between a given pair of cities is stored exactly once in the *CityDistance* table. (The application must enforce a constraint such as *city1ID* < *city2ID*, so that the distance is entered only once.)

19.17 (6) Discuss the relative merits of the two approaches in the previous four exercises for storing distance information.

19.18 (5) Discuss the similarities and differences between the database tables used to store edge and node information in Exercises 19.1–19.5 and the tables used to store distance information between cities in Exercises 19.13–19.17. How does fact that there is exactly one straight-line distance between a pair of cities simplify the problem? Is the problem of storing distances between cities more nearly like a directed graph or an undirected graph? Why?

```
CREATE TABLE City
( city_ID   NUMBER(30)    CONSTRAINT nn_city1 NOT NULL,
  city_name VARCHAR2(255) CONSTRAINT nn_city2 NOT NULL,
CONSTRAINT pk_city PRIMARY KEY (city_ID),
CONSTRAINT uq_city1 UNIQUE (city_name));

CREATE SEQUENCE seq_city;


CREATE TABLE City_Distance
( city1_ID   NUMBER(30)    CONSTRAINT nn_dist1 NOT NULL,
  city2_ID   NUMBER(30)    CONSTRAINT nn_dist2 NOT NULL,
  distance   NUMBER(20,10) CONSTRAINT nn_dist3 NOT NULL,
CONSTRAINT pk_dist PRIMARY KEY (city1_ID, city2_ID));

CREATE INDEX index_dist1 ON City_Distance (city2_ID);

ALTER TABLE City_Distance ADD CONSTRAINT fk_dist1
  FOREIGN KEY city1_ID
  REFERENCES City;

ALTER TABLE City_Distance ADD CONSTRAINT fk_dist2
  FOREIGN KEY city2_ID
  REFERENCES City;
```

Figure E19.7 SQL commands for creating tables to store distances between cities

19.19 (7) Prepare tables and SQL commands to create an empty relational database for the model in
      Figure E19.8.

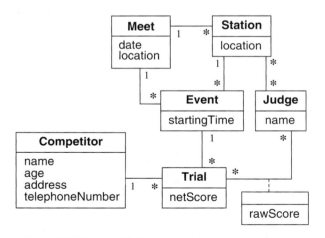

Figure E19.8 Partial class model for a scoring system

19.20 (6) Build a class model of forks and philosophers for the dining philosophers problem. (See Exercise 3.28.) Prepare tables and SQL code to create an empty database for your model. Show database contents for the situation in which each philosopher has exactly one fork.

19.21 (7) Prepare tables and SQL commands to create an empty relational database for the model in Figure 3.27.

19.22 (8) Write an SQL query for each of the OCL expressions in Section 3.5.3.

20

Programming Style

As any chess player, cook, or skier can attest, there is a great difference between knowing something and doing it well. Writing programs is no different. It is not enough to know the basic constructs and to be able to assemble them. The experienced programmer follows principles to make readable programs that live beyond the immediate need. These principles include programming idioms, rules of thumb, tricks of the trade, and cautionary advice. Good style is important in all programming, but it is even more important in OO programming, because much of the benefit of the OO approach is predicated on producing reusable, extensible, and understandable programs.

20.1 Object-Oriented Style

Good programs do more than simply satisfy their functional requirements. Programs that follow proper coding guidelines are more likely to be correct, reusable, extensible, and quickly debugged. Most style guidelines that are intended for conventional programs also apply to OO programs. In addition, facilities such as inheritance are peculiar to OO languages and require new guidelines. We present OO style guidelines under the following categories, although many guidelines contribute to more than one category.

- Reusability [20.2]
- Extensibility [20.3]
- Robustness [20.4]
- Programming-in-the-Large [20.5]

20.2 Reusability

Reusable software reduces design, coding, and testing cost by amortizing effort over several applications. Reducing the amount of code also simplifies understanding, which increases the likelihood that the code is correct. Reuse is possible in conventional languages, but OO languages greatly enhance the possibility of code reuse.

20.2.1 Kinds of Reusability

There are two kinds of reuse: sharing of newly written code within an application and reuse of previously written code on new applications. Similar guidelines apply to both kinds of reuse. Sharing of code within an application is a matter of discovering redundant code sequences and using programming-language facilities to consolidate them (refactoring). This kind of code sharing almost always produces smaller programs and faster debugging.

Planning for future reuse takes more foresight and represents an investment. It is unlikely that a class in isolation will be used for multiple applications. Programmers are more likely to reuse carefully thought out subsystems, such as abstract data types, graphics packages, and numerical analysis libraries. Patterns and frameworks can be helpful in this regard (see Chapter 14).

20.2.2 Style Rules for Reusability

There are a number of rules that you can follow to promote reusability within your application and across applications.

- **Keep methods coherent**. A method is coherent if it performs a single function or a group of closely related functions. If it does two or more unrelated things, break it apart into smaller methods.

- **Keep methods small**. If a method is large, break it into smaller methods. A method that exceeds one or two pages is probably too large. By breaking a method into smaller parts, you may be able to reuse some parts even when the entire method is not reusable.

- **Keep methods consistent**. Similar methods should use the same names, argument order, data types, return value, and error conditions. Maintain parallel structure when possible. The methods for an operation should have consistent signatures and semantics.

  The Unix operating system offers many examples of inconsistent functions. For example, in the C library, there are two inconsistent functions to output strings, *puts* and *fputs*. The *puts* function writes a string to the standard output, followed by a newline character; *fputs* writes a string to a specified file, without a newline character. Avoid such inconsistency.

- **Separate policy and implementation**. Policy methods make decisions, shuffle arguments, and gather global context. Policy methods switch control among implementation methods. Policy methods should check for status and errors; they should not directly perform calculations or implement complex algorithms. Policy methods are often application dependent, but they are simple to write and easy to understand.

  Implementation methods perform specific detailed logic, without deciding whether or why to do them. If implementation methods can encounter errors, they should only return status, not take action. Implementation methods perform specific computations on fully specified arguments and often contain complicated algorithms. Implementation methods do not access global context, make decisions, contain defaults, or switch flow of control. Because implementation methods are self-contained algorithms, they are likely to be meaningful and reusable in other contexts.

Do not combine policy and implementation in a single method. Isolate the core of the algorithm into a distinct, fully specified implementation method. This requires abstracting out the particular parameters of the policy method as arguments in a call to the implementation method.

For example, a method to scale a window by a factor of 2 is a policy method. It should set the target scale factor for the window and call on an implementation method that scales the window by an arbitrary scale factor. If you decide later to change the default scale factor to another value, such as 1.5, you just have to modify the parameter in the policy method, without changing the implementation method that actually does the work.

- **Provide uniform coverage**. If input conditions can occur in various combinations, write methods for all combinations, not just the ones that you currently need. For example, if you write a method to get the last element of a list, also write one to get the first element. By providing uniform coverage you not only boost reusability, but you also rationalize the scope of related methods.

- **Broaden the method as much as possible**. Try to generalize argument types, preconditions and constraints, assumptions about how the method works, and the context in which the method operates. Take meaningful actions on empty values, extreme values, and out-of-bounds values. Often a method can be made more general with a slight increase in code.

- **Avoid global information**. Minimize external references. Referring to a global object imposes required context on the use of a method. Often the information can be passed in as an argument. Otherwise store global information as part of the target object so that other methods can access it uniformly.

- **Avoid methods with state**. Methods that drastically change behavior depending on previous method history are hard to reuse. Try to replace them with stateless methods. For example, a text-processing application requires insert and replace operations. One approach is to set a flag to *insert* or *replace,* then use a *write* operation to insert or replace text depending on the current flag. A stateless approach uses two operations, *insert* and *replace,* that do the same operations without a state setting. The danger of method states is that an object left in a state in one part of an application can affect a method applied later in the application.

20.2.3 Using Inheritance

The preceding guidelines improve the chance of sharing code. Sometimes, however, methods on different classes are similar but not similar enough to represent with a single inherited method. There are several techniques of breaking up methods to inherit some code.

■   **Factor out commonality**. The simplest approach is to factor out the common code into a single method that is called by each method. The common method can be assigned to an ancestor class. This is effectively a subroutine call, as Figure 20.1 shows.

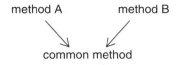

Figure 20.1 Code reuse via factoring out commonality. Place the common code into a method that is called by the original methods.

■   **Factor out differences**. In some cases the best way to increase code reuse between similar classes is to factor out the differences between the methods of different classes, leaving the remainder of the code as a shared method. This approach is effective when the differences between methods are small and the similarities are great. As Figure 20.2 shows, the common portion of two methods is made into a new method. The new method calls an operation that is implemented by different methods containing the code differences for each subclass. Sometimes an abstract class must be added to hold the top-level method. This approach makes it easier to add new subclasses, because only the difference code need be written.

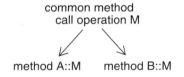

Figure 20.2 Code reuse via factoring out differences. Place the difference code in polymorphic methods of a common operation.

A package for plotting numerical data illustrates factoring. *DataGraph* is an abstract class that organizes common data and operations for its subclasses. One of *DataGraph's* methods is *draw,* consisting of the following steps: draw border, scale data, draw axes, plot data, draw title, and draw legend.

Subclasses of *DataGraph,* such as *LineGraph, BarGraph,* and *ScatterGraph,* draw borders, titles, and legends the same way but differ in the way they scale data, draw axes, and plot data. Each subclass inherits the methods *drawBorder, drawTitle,* and *drawLegend* from abstract class *DataGraph,* but each subclass defines its own methods for *scaleData, drawAxes,* and *plotData.* The method *draw* need be defined only once, on class *DataGraph,* and is inherited by each subclass. Each time the draw method is invoked, it applies *drawBorder, drawTitle,* and *drawLegend* inherited from the superclass and *scaleData, drawAxis,* and *plotData* supplied by the subclass itself. To add a new subclass, only the three specialized methods need be written.

- **Delegate**. Sometimes it appears that use of inheritance would increase code reuse within a program, when a true superclass/subclass relationship does not exist. Do not give in to the temptation to use this *implementation inheritance*; use delegation instead. Inheritance should be used only when the generalization relationship is semantically valid. Inheritance means that each instance of a subclass truly is an instance of the superclass; thus all operations and attributes of the superclass must uniformly apply to the subclasses. Improper use of inheritance leads to programs that are hard to maintain and extend. OO languages are permissive in their use of inheritance and will not enforce the good programming practice that we recommend.

  Delegation provides a proper mechanism to achieve the desired code reuse. The method is caught in the desired class and forwarded to another class for actual execution. Since each method must be explicitly forwarded, unexpected side effects are less likely to occur. The names of methods in the catching class may differ from those in the supplier class. Each class should choose names that are most appropriate for its purposes.

- **Encapsulate external code**. Often you will want to reuse code that may have been developed for an application with different interfacing conventions. Rather than inserting a direct call to the external code, it is safer to encapsulate its behavior within a method or a class. This way, the external routine or package can be changed or replaced, and you will have to change your code in only one place.

  For example, you may have a numerical analysis application but, knowing that reliable matrix-inversion software already exists, you do not want to reimplement the algorithm. You could write a matrix class to encapsulate the functionality provided by the external subroutine package. The matrix class would have, for example, an inverse method that takes the tolerance-for-singularity as an argument and returns a new matrix that is the inverse of the method's target.

20.3 Extensibility

Most software is extended in ways that its original developers never expect. The reusability guidelines enhance extensibility, as do the additional guidelines listed below.

- **Encapsulate classes**. A class is encapsulated if its internal structure is hidden from other classes. Only methods on the class should access its implementation. Many compilers are smart enough to optimize methods into direct access to the implementation, but the programmer should not. Respect the information in other classes by never reaching inside the class for data.

- **Specify visibility for methods**. Public methods are visible outside a class and have published interfaces. Once a public method is used by other classes, it is costly to change its interface, so carefully define and limit the number of public methods. In contrast, private methods are internal to a class—they can be deleted or changed with impact limited to other methods on the class. Protected methods have intermediate visibility—see Section 18.1.

Careful use of visibility (see Section 4.1.4) makes your classes easier to understand and increases code resilience. Private and protected methods suppress unnecessary details from the user of a class, avoiding confusion. Unlike a public method, a private method cannot be applied out of context, so it can rely on preconditions or state information of the class.

- **Hide data structures**. Do not export data structures from a method. Internal data structures are specific to a method's algorithm. If you export them, you limit flexibility to change the algorithm later.

- **Avoid traversing multiple links or methods**. A method should have limited knowledge of a class model. A method must be able to traverse links to obtain its neighbors and must be able to call methods on them, but it should not traverse a second link from the neighbor to a third class because the second link is not directly visible to it. Instead, call a method on the neighbor object to traverse nonconnected objects; if the association network changes, the method can be rewritten without changing the call.

  Similarly, avoid applying a second method to the result of a method call unless the class of the result is already known as an attribute, argument, or neighbor, or the result class is from a lower-level library. Instead, write a new method on the original target class to perform the combined method itself. The principles in this bullet were proposed in [Lieberherr-89] as the "Law of Demeter."

- **Avoid case statements on object type**. Use polymorphism instead. Case statements can be used to test internal attributes of an object but should not be used to select behavior based on object type. The dispatching of operations based on object type is the whole point of polymorphism, so don't circumvent it.

- **Design for portability**. Limit system dependencies to a few basic methods. You can then more easily port software to other hardware platforms and software environments. For example, if you are using a database, you might isolate database access. This would make it easier to switch database vendors and possibly enable switching paradigm (such as from relational to OO database).

20.4 Robustness

You should strive for efficient methods but not at the expense of robustness. A method is robust if it does not fail even if it receives improper parameters. In particular, you should never sacrifice robustness against user errors.

- **Protect against errors**. Software should protect itself against incorrect user input and never let it cause a crash. Methods must validate input that could cause trouble.

  There are two kinds of errors. Analysis uncovers errors that exist in the problem domain and determines an appropriate response. For example, an ATM should handle errors for the card scanner and communications lines. On the other hand, low-level system errors concern programming aspects. These low-level errors include memory allocation errors, file input/output errors, and hardware faults. Your program should check for system errors and at least try to die gracefully if nothing else is possible.

Try to guard against programming bugs as well, and give good diagnostic information. During development, it is often worthwhile to insert internal assertions into the code to uncover bugs, even though the checks will be removed for efficiency in the production version. A strongly typed OO language provides greater protection against type mismatches, but you can insert assertions in any language. In particular, you should check array bounds.

- **Optimize after the program runs**. Don't optimize a program until you get it working. Many programmers spend too much time improving code that seldom executes. Measure the performance within the program first; you may be surprised to find that most parts consume little time. Study your application to learn what measures are important, such as worst-case times and method frequencies. If a method may be implemented in more than one way, assess the alternatives with regard to memory, speed, and implementation simplicity. In general, avoid optimizing more of the program than you have to, since optimization compromises extensibility, reusability, and understandability. If methods are properly encapsulated, you can replace them with optimized versions without affecting the rest of the program.

- **Always construct objects in a valid state** [Vermeulen-00]. Otherwise, you create a situation where someone might use the constructor and not call the right subsequent method. As a matter of good software practice, your code should always be logically sound.

- **Validate arguments**. Public methods, those available to users of the class, must rigorously check their arguments, because users may violate restrictions. Private and protected methods can improve efficiency by assuming that their arguments are valid, since the implementor can rely on the public methods that call them for error checking.

Don't write or use methods whose arguments can't be validated. For example, the infamous *scanf* function in Unix reads a line of input into an internal buffer without checking the size of the buffer. This loophole has been exploited to write virus programs that force a buffer overflow in system software that did not validate its arguments.

- **Avoid predefined limits**. When possible use dynamic memory allocation to create data structures without predefined limits. It is difficult to predict the maximum capacity expected of data structures in an application, so don't set any limits. The day of fixed limits on symbol table entries, user names, file names, compiler entries, and other things should be long over. Most OO languages have excellent dynamic memory allocation facilities.

- **Instrument the program for debugging and performance monitoring**. Just as a hardware circuit designer instruments an IC board with test points, you should instrument your code for testing, debugging, statistics, and performance. The level of debugging that you must build into your code depends on your language's programming environment. You can add debug statements to methods that conditionally execute depending on the debug level. The debug statements print a message on entry or exit and selective input and output values.

You can better understand the behavior of classes by adding code to gather statistics. Some operating systems, such as Unix, offer tools to create execution profiles of an application. Typically, these tools report the number of times each method was called and the amount of processor time spent in each method. If your system lacks comparable tools, you can instrument your code for gathering statistics much like for debugging.

20.5 Programming-in-the-Large

Programming-in-the-large refers to writing large, complex programs with teams of programmers. Human communication becomes paramount on such projects and requires proper software engineering practices. You should observe the following guidelines.

- **Do not program prematurely**. Think long and carefully before you commit to code. Ultimately, of course you must have code to deliver your application. But code is tedious to write and difficult to change. In contrast, models are much more malleable, because they are high level and suppress details. It is much better to work out your ideas with models, gain a full understanding, and only then write the code.

- **Make methods readable**. Meaningful variable names increase readability. Typing a few extra characters costs less than the misunderstanding that can come later when another programmer tries to decipher your variable names. Avoid confusing abbreviations, and use temporary variables instead of deeply nested expressions. Do not use the same temporary variable for two different purposes within a method, even if their usage does not overlap; most compilers will optimize this anyway. Minor improvements to efficiency are not worth compromising readability.

- **Keep methods understandable**. A method is understandable if someone other than the creator can understand the code (as well as the creator after a time lapse). Keeping methods small and coherent helps to accomplish this.

- **Use the same names as in the class model**. The names used within a program should match those in the class model. A program may need to introduce additional names for implementation reasons, but you should preserve the names for concepts that carry forward. This practice improves traceability, documentation, and understandability. It is reasonable to adopt conventions such as uniform prefixes for consistency across applications, thereby avoiding name clashes.

- **Choose names carefully**. Make sure that your names accurately describe the operations, classes, and attributes that they label. Follow a uniform style in devising names. For example, you may name operations as *"verbObject,"* such as *addElement* or *drawHighlight*. Be sure to define a vocabulary of verbs that are often used. For example, don't use both *new* and *create* unless they have different meanings. Many OO languages automatically build method names from the class and operation names.

  Similarly, do not use the same method name for semantically different purposes. As Figure 20.3 shows, all methods with the same name should have the same signature (number and types of arguments) and meaning.

Circle::area()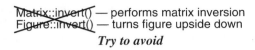
Rectangle::area()
Correct   *Try to avoid*

Figure 20.3 Method names. All methods with the same name should have the same signature and meaning.

■ **Use programming guidelines**. Project teams should use programming guidelines available in their organizations or external guidelines, such as [Vermeulen-00]. Guidelines address issues such as the form of variable names, indentation style for control structures, method documentation headers, and in-line documentation.

■ **Use packages**. Group closely related classes into a package. (See Section 4.11.)

■ **Document classes and methods**. The documentation of a method describes its purpose, function, context, inputs, and outputs as well as any assumptions and preconditions about the state of the object. You should describe not only the details of an algorithm, but also why it was chosen. Internal comments within the method should describe major steps.

■ **Publish the specification**. The specification is a contract between the producer and the consumer of a class. Once a specification is written, the producer cannot break the contract, for doing so would affect the consumer. The specification contains only declarations, and the user should be able to use the class just by looking at the declarations. On-line descriptions of a class and its features help promote the correct use of the class. Figure 20.4, Figure 20.5, and Figure 20.6 show sample specifications.

Class name: Circle

Version: 1.0

Description: Ellipse whose major and minor axes are equal

Super classes: Ellipse

Features:
   Private attributes:
      center: Point — location of its center
      radius: Real — its radius
   Public methods:
      draw (Window) — draws a circle in the window
      intersectLine (Line): Set of Points — finds the intersection of a line and a circle,
         returns set of 0–2 points
      area (): Real — calculates area of circle
      perimeter (): Real — calculates circumference of circle
   Private methods: none

Figure 20.4 Class specification

Operation: intersectLine (line: Line) : Set of Points

Origin Class: GeometricFigure

Description: Returns a set of intersection points between the geometric object and the line. The set may contain 0, 1, or more points. Each tangent point appears only once. If the line is collinear with a line segment in the figure, only the two end points of the segment are included.

Status: Abstract operation in the origin class, must be overridden.

Inputs:

   self: GeometricFigure — figure to be intersected with line
   line:Line — line to be intersected with circle

Returns:

   A set of intersection points. Set may contain 0 or more points.

Side Effects: none

Errors:

   If the figures do not intersect, returns an empty set.
   If the line is collinear with a line segment in the figure, the set includes only the end points of the segment.
   If the figure is an area, then its boundary is used

Figure 20.5 Operation specification

Method: Circle::intersectLine (line: Line) : Set of Points

Description: Given a circle and a line, finds the intersection, returns a set of 0–2 intersection points. If the line is tangent to the circle, the set contains a single point.

Inputs:

   self:Circle — circle to be intersected with line
   line:Line — line to be intersected with circle

Returns:

   A set of intersection points. Set may contain 0, 1, or 2 points.

Side Effects: none

Errors:

   If the figures do not intersect, returns an empty set.
   If the line is tangent to the circle, returns the tangent point.
   If the circle's radius is 0, returns a single point if the point is on the line.

Figure 20.6 Method specification

■ **Avoid duplicated code**. [Baker-95] cites two applications with one million lines of code. (One was X-Windows.) She found that at least 12% of the code was gross duplication that could be easily eliminated. Such duplication comes from programmers copying and editing code when making bug fixes and other reasons of expedience. The side effect is that the code swells in size, making it more difficult to maintain and understand.

20.6 Chapter Summary

Good style is important to maximize the benefits of OO programming; most benefits come from greatly reduced maintenance and enhancement costs and the reuse of the new code for future applications. OO programming style guidelines include conventional programming style guidelines as well as principles uniquely applicable to OO concepts such as inheritance.

A major goal of OO development is maximizing reusability of classes and methods. Reuse within a program is a matter of looking for similarities and consolidating them. Planning for reuse by future applications takes more time and effort up front. Reusability is enhanced by keeping methods small, coherent, and local. Separation of policy and implementation is important. One way to use inheritance is by factoring a generic method into submethods, some inherited from the origin class and some provided by each subclass. Delegation should be used when methods must be shared but classes are not in a true generalization relationship.

Most software is eventually extended. Extensibility is enhanced by encapsulation, minimizing dependencies, using methods to access attributes of other classes, and distinguishing the visibility of methods.

Do not sacrifice robustness for efficiency. Because objects contain references to their own classes, they are less vulnerable to mismatched typing than conventional programming variables and can be checked dynamically to see that they match the assumptions within a method. Programs should always protect against user and system errors. Assertions are important, because they can catch programming bugs and can be removed during production.

Writing large programs with teams of programmers requires more discipline, better documentation, and better communication than one-person or small applications. Writing readable, well-documented methods is essential.

delegation	optimization	robustness
documentation	programming-in-the-large	visibility
encapsulation	refactoring	
extensibility	reusability	

Figure 20.7 Key concepts for Chapter 20

Bibliographic Notes

OO programming must render application concepts into language constructs in a correct and maintainable way, so good style is important. Most conventional programming principles apply to OO programming. [Kernighan-99] is a well-written style guide for programming.

[Brooks-95] has excellent advice for programming in the large. [Vermeulen-00] has detailed programming guidelines for Java, but many of the ideas transcend Java.

References

[Baker-95] Brenda S. Baker. On finding duplication and near-duplication in large software systems. *Second IEEE Working Conference on Reverse Engineering*. July 1995, Toronto, Ontario, 86–95.

[Brooks-95] Frederick P. Brooks, Jr. *The Mythical Man-Month, Anniversary Edition*. Boston: Addison-Wesley, 1995.

[Kernighan-99] Brian W. Kernighan, Rob Pike. *The Practice of Programming*. Boston: Addison-Wesley, 1999.

[Lieberherr-89] Karl J. Lieberherr, Arthur J. Riel. Contributions to teaching object-oriented design and programming. *OOPSLA'89* as *ACM SIGPLAN 24*, 11 (November 1989) 11–22.

[Vermeulen-00] Allan Vermeulen, Scott W. Ambler, Greg Bumgardner, Eldon Metz, Trevor Misfeldt, Jim Shur, Patrick Thompson. *The Elements of Java Style*. Cambridge, UK: Cambridge University Press, 2000.

Exercises

20.1 (4) One technique for code reuse is to use a method as an argument for another method. For example, one operation that can be performed on a binary tree is ordered printing. The subroutine *print(node)* could print the values in a tree rooted at *node* by a recursive call to *Print(node.leftSubtree)* if there is a left subtree, followed by printing *node.value*, followed by a recursive call for the right subtree. This approach could be generalized for other operations. List at least three operations that could be performed on the nodes of a binary tree. Prepare pseudocode for a subroutine *orderedVisit(node, method)* that applies *method* to the nodes of the tree rooted at *node*, in order.

20.2 (3) Combining similar methods into a single operation can improve code reuse. Revise, extend, or generalize the following two methods into a single operation. Also list the attributes needed to track both types of accounts.

   a. *cashCheck (normalAccount, check)* If the amount of the *check* is less than the balance in *normalAccount*, cash the check and debit the account. Otherwise, bounce the check.

   b. *cashCheck (reserveAccount, check)* If the amount of the *check* is less than the balance in *reserveAccount,* cash the check and debit the account. Otherwise, examine the reserve balance. If the check can be covered by transferring funds from the reserve without going over the reserve limit, cash the check and update the balances. Otherwise, bounce the check.

20.3 (4) Figure E20.1 is a function coded in C to create a new sheet for a computer-aided design application. A sheet is a named, displayable, two-dimensional region containing text and graphics. Several sheets may be required to completely represent a system. The function given in the fig-

```
Sheet createSheet (sheetType, rootName, suffix)
SheetType sheetType;
char *rootName, *suffix;
{ char *malloc(), *strcpy(), *strcat(), *sheetName;
  int strlen(), rootLength, suffixLength;
  Sheet sheet, vertSheetNew(), horizSheetNew();
  rootLength = strlen(rootName);
  suffixLength = strlen(suffix);
  sheetName = malloc(rootLength + suffixLength + 1);
  sheetName = strcpy(sheetName, rootName);
  sheetName = strcat(sheetName, suffix);
  switch(sheetType)
  { case VERTICAL:
        sheet = vertSheetNew();
        break;
    case HORIZONTAL:
        sheet = horizSheetNew();
        break;
  }
  sheet->name = sheetName;
  return sheet;
}
```

Figure E20.1 Function to create a new named sheet

ure creates a new vertical or horizontal sheet and constructs a name from a root and a suffix. The C functions it calls are *strlen* to compute the length of a string, *strcpy* to copy a string, *strcat* to concatenate two strings, and *malloc* to allocate memory. The data types *SheetType* and *Sheet* are defined outside of the function in the same module. The functions *strlen*, *strcpy,* and *strcat* will cause a crash if they are called with 0 for any argument. As it stands, the subroutine is exposed to several types of errors. The arguments *rootName* and *suffix* could be zero and *sheetType* could be an illegal enumerated value. The call to *malloc* could fail to allocate memory.

a. Prepare a list of all the ways the function could fail. For each way, describe the consequences.

b. Revise the function so that it does not crash as a result of any of the errors you listed in part *a* and so that it prints out a descriptive error message for each kind of error as an aid in debugging programs in which it is called.

Part 4

Software Engineering

At this point, you have read and hopefully have learned from the first three parts of the book. You are now familiar with OO concepts and the UML notation for expressing them. Furthermore, you have a process for applying the concepts and know how to handle the implementation details with the C++ and Java languages as well as databases. Part 4 builds on this basic knowledge and elaborates some software engineering considerations.

We have stressed throughout the book that software development should be an iterative process. Our presentation is confined by the medium of a book to be linear, but we do not want to give readers the wrong impression. Software development rarely proceeds in a straight line. Chapter 21 elaborates this theme of the iterative nature of software development.

We find that most organizations are truly interested in OO technology, and especially OO modeling. However, many organizations find it difficult to inject the technology in their ranks and are unsure how to proceed. Chapter 22 has advice for how you can capitalize on the potential of OO technology and assimilate it within your organization.

Lastly, few applications are truly new and created from scratch. In practice, new development efforts build on the experiences of predecessor applications. Legacy systems can be a rich source of requirements for their successor systems. Additional issues arise with legacy systems such as data conversion and integration of related systems. Chapter 23 touches upon these topics.

Part 4 completes the content of this book and prepares you to proceed with OO modeling and its application on your own. As always, we welcome your comments and experiences to deepen our own understanding. Please send us email (blaha@computer.org) if you have any questions or comments.

21

Iterative Development

A written presentation, such as this book, might seem to imply a linear process, but that is an unintended artifact of the medium. Software development is by its very nature iterative—early stages lack perfect foresight and must be revisited to correct errors and make improvements. *Iterative development* is the development of a system by a process broken into a series of steps, or iterations, each of which provides a better approximation to the desired system than the previous iteration [Rumbaugh-05].

21.1 Overview of Iterative Development

We favor an iterative approach to software development. In this chapter, we start by comparing iterative development with two other common approaches: waterfall development (Section 21.2) and rapid prototyping (Section 21.3). Then we explore the following issues of iterative development.

- Iteration scope. [21.4]
- Performing an iteration. [21.5]
- Planning the next iteration. [21.6]
- Modeling and iterative development. [21.7]
- Identifying risks. [21.8]

21.2 Iterative Development vs. Waterfall

In the 1980s and early 1990s the waterfall approach was the dominant life-cycle paradigm [Larman-03]. As Figure 21.1 shows, with this approach, developers perform the software stages in a rigid linear sequence with no backtracking. Each stage must complete before the next stage begins.

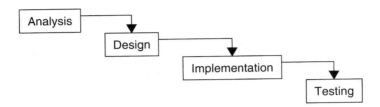

Figure 21.1 Waterfall approach. The waterfall approach is inflexible and unsuitable for most application development.

From experience, the software development community has found that the waterfall approach is not effective for building most applications [Sotirovski-01]. A waterfall is suitable for well-understood applications with predictable outputs from analysis and design, but such applications seldom occur. Most applications have substantial uncertainties in their requirements. Furthermore, a waterfall approach does not deliver a useful system until completion. This makes it difficult to assess progress and correct a project that has gone awry.

In contrast, iterative development provides frequent milestones and uncovers pitfalls early in development. When you catch difficulties early, a system is more malleable and amenable to change; revisions are easier to make and less costly than if they are deferred. Iterative development is clearly a better approach.

21.3 Iterative Development vs. Rapid Prototyping

With rapid prototyping (Figure 21.2) you quickly develop a portion of the software, use it, and evaluate it. You then incorporate what you have learned and repeat the cycle. Eventually, you deliver the final prototype as the finished application or, after a few prototypes, switch to another approach.

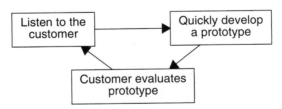

Figure 21.2 Rapid prototyping. Rapid prototyping has similar strengths to iterative development. The difference is that rapid prototyping often throws away code, while iterative development seeks to accumulate code.

Iterative development differs from rapid prototyping. Prototyping is proof of concept and often throwaway by intent. In contrast, iterative development is not throwaway; subsequent iterations build on the progress of prior ones. With iterative development, some code may be discarded due to revisions, but such throwaways are not the intent.

The strength of rapid prototyping is that it promotes communication with the customer and helps to elicit requirements. Rapid prototyping can also be helpful to demonstrate technical feasibility, where there is a potentially difficult technology. The downside of rapid prototyping is that it can be difficult to discard code. Customers often confuse a successful prototype with a product, not realizing that a prototype is just a demonstration and may lack a robust infrastructure. There is a natural reluctance to discard code; some customers regard throwing away code as throwing away money and do not realize that the true value of the prototype code is the lessons that are learned.

Iterative development has this same benefit, as long as iterations are kept small and are shown often to the customer. Both rapid prototyping and iterative development provide frequent checkpoints for assuring customers that development is going well. They also let developers resolve troublesome issues early in application development.

21.4 Iteration Scope

Iterative development consists of a series of iterations. The number of iterations and their duration depends on the size of a project. For a short project (six months or less) you might have iterations of two to four weeks. For a large multiyear project, iterations of three to four months may be more effective. If iterations are too small, the overhead of iterations is too high. If iterations are too large, there are insufficient checkpoints to assess the progress of an application and make midstream corrections. You should strive for a uniform length of iterations, but may occasionally need a longer length for deep infrastructure or difficult features.

Define the scope of an iteration—a good target is the minimum amount of work that represents material progress. Build mission-critical pieces early, as well as core pieces of code that are frequently executed by the application. Also, make sure that you balance functionality across a system. Developers will have their favorite technologies and prefer different aspects, but your overall plan must be balanced and targeted at realizing meaningful chunks of the application as quickly as possible. Each iteration must provide at least one of the following: economic payback, added functionality, improved user interaction, better efficiency, higher reliability, or strengthened infrastructure (for maintenance and future iterations).

Use cases provide a good basis for assignment. Each iteration can focus on a few use cases. However, an iteration need not complete a use case, and a use case can be spread across several iterations. For example, you might implement the core functionality in one iteration, more advanced functionality in another, and error handling in another. Don't break a use case across too many iterations, however. In addition to use cases, you must also assign internal services—mechanisms and services that provide infrastructure or support for implementing higher-level operations. These services will be identified during architectural planning and class design.

If something must be increased in priority, then something else must be decreased. This prevents the syndrome of "everything is equally important." Everything is never equally important, but managers and developers are frequently unwilling to make hard choices or to admit that there is not enough time. By maintaining the timing of iterations and adjusting their content, you are forced to be realistic about what you can do and where you are on the schedule.

You need not release the results of each iteration to the customer. From a development perspective, it is important to maintain momentum, stay on schedule, and make sure the different components of an application actually fit together. From the customer's perspective, it may be too much effort to install each iteration. A business may combine several increments before deployment to simplify logistics.

21.5 Performing an Iteration

Each iteration must start from a common baseline and finish with a new common baseline. Developers must integrate all versions of system artifacts and check them in at the end of an iteration. This permits everybody to work with a common set of assumptions and to keep up to date with system changes. Following this rule is absolutely essential to success.

Some developers may find this rule inconvenient. It may seem more efficient to continue development of a subsystem, without having to stop and integrate it with the rest of the system. It is certainly less convenient for a development team to have to work in small pieces and frequently coordinate with others. But it is crucial to the success of the project as a whole. If teams keep to themselves for a long time, they tend to drift apart on assumptions, interfaces, and other things. When integration does occur, it can be difficult and expensive. Worse, it often happens that different subsystems have used incompatible assumptions; then changes must be backed away or hacks put in place to paper over the differences.

A team must structure its work on an iteration to be able to finish it, check it in, test it, and integrate it with the rest of the system. This requires some planning, but it pays off in the long run with the whole system.

The second rule is that each iteration must produce an executable release. It is not enough to write code that doesn't run. Code that runs can be tested. Integration of subsystems can be tested and incompatibilities discovered and corrected early. Moreover, executable code is the best measure of progress. It is very easy to delude oneself and others about the progress of design if nothing has to run. It is easy to overlook major omissions and to underestimate the difficulty of debugging and integrating subsystems.

Each iteration must include time for all of the development stages. You perform a mini-waterfall within an iteration. That is, you step through analysis, design, implementation, testing, and integration. The waterfall approach is a viable option on a small scale, permitting the systematic development of functionality. The waterfall is a problem only if decisions cannot be changed later. In the iterative process, bad decisions can be revisited in the next iteration, so they do not threaten the project.

Make sure that you plan and allow enough time for testing. It is important to test as you go, and not to defer tests until later iterations. The point of iterative development is to build a reliable system in small steps.

21.6 Planning the Next Iteration

After each iteration you should assess your progress and reconsider your plan for the next iteration. Did the iteration take more or less time than estimated? Did you have the right mix of developer skills available? Is the customer happy with the progress of the work? Have any specific problems or issues surfaced for the next iteration? Is the software stable, or must you allow for additional rework and refactoring in the next iteration?

Of course, if the prior iteration succeeded, you can continue with your plan. Otherwise, do not be afraid to discard bad decisions and make midcourse corrections. Your application will only be extensible, maintainable, and viable if it has a sound construction. You should get feedback from users early and often—you want them to internalize what you are doing and be thinking about its implications for their day-to-day business. Furthermore, they can help you detect whether the scope of the software or the path of the iterations is getting off track.

21.7 Modeling and Iterative Development

Modeling is a natural complement to iterative development. One purpose of iterative development is to discover problems in software early, and so too with modeling. [Sotirovski-01] expresses this eloquently as a "fail fast" philosophy of iterative development. Problems are inevitable, so you should root them out early. With skillful modeling, you can discover some problems in models and reduce the amount of iteration—the net result is faster and better development. Iterative development certainly is not an excuse for hacking code and foregoing the careful thought of modeling.

As Figure 21.3 shows, you should begin by carefully modeling an application to elicit requirements and then building the model for the first iteration. Then you revisit the model and do another iteration, and so on, continuing to proceed by interleaving modeling with iterative development. Modeling uncovers errors early and gives a sense of direction and continuity to a sequence of iterations. Modeling can be, and must be, done quickly so that it does not slow the project timetable.

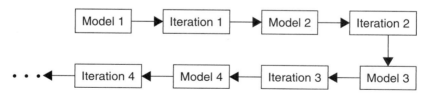

Figure 21.3 Modeling and iterative development. Modeling can improve the quality and productivity of incremental development.

Table 21.1 compares modeling with iterative development. Both promote requirements capture, but they do so in different ways. Modeling helps customers think about the potential

	Modeling	**Iterative development**
Requirements capture	Excellent. Models help customers understand software's capabilities and limitations before it is even built.	Excellent. Iterations show customers the software so that they can give frequent feedback.
Application quality	Excellent. Modeling fosters abstraction and deep thought.	Good. Thorough and frequent testing improves quality.
Development productivity	Excellent. The deep thought reduces rework.	Excellent. Frequent integration reduces rework.
Project tracking	Not applicable.	Excellent. Code deliveries provide frequent milestones.

Table 21.1 Comparing modeling with iterative development. Modeling and iterative development have different trade-offs. They complement each other.

of the software before it is even built. In contrast, iterative development shows customers the evolving software so that they can comment and redirect development efforts.

Modeling is unmatched in its ability to improve application quality. [Brooks-87] contends "that conceptual integrity is *the* most important consideration in system design." (The italics are his.) Modeling focuses on understanding and improving the essence of an application. Iterative development involves frequent testing, and this also contributes to quality, but the effect is less dramatic than with modeling.

Modeling improves productivity by quickly "failing" through thought experiments that preclude wasted code. Iterative development also makes a major contribution to productivity by forcing early integration, avoiding mismatched components and awkward revisions.

By definition, modeling does not deal with project tracking. Modeling concerns the early part of software development, so it is unable to have much bearing on the tracking of an entire project. Iterative development provides a great way for tracking projects—frequent deliveries of executable code leave little room for argument about what work is complete and what work remains. Consequently the schedule for a project becomes more predictable.

21.8 Identifying Risks

The key to planning an iteration is to mitigate risk. You should confront risks early, rather than defer them to the end of the project (as might otherwise occur). There are many kinds of risk to consider.

- **Technical risks.** The proposed technical solution may fail or prove unacceptable. If you address technical issues early, another solution can be found before it is too late and before the rest of the system is built on a faulty base.

- **Technology risks.** External technology that you plan to use may not be available or may not measure up to its claims. Resolve this by trying the necessary technology early in the critical parts of the system.

- **User acceptance risks.** The users may not like the user interface or the functionality of the system. Iterative development lets users try part of the system early while its style can be readily changed.

- **Schedule risks.** There is always the chance the project will not finish on time. Iterative development helps by providing an accurate measure of progress. If the schedule slips, you can trim functionality. Furthermore, even if the project finishes late, you will have an executable system to show at the deadline. A system with 90% functionality is much better than a waterfall system with 90% of the system implemented but nothing operational.

- **Personnel risks.** Key persons may leave the project at an inopportune time. Iterative development provides frequent checkpoints with delivery of a stable system. Models ensure that the iterations are carefully considered and documented. It still will be difficult to lose key personnel, but at least you have a chance of assimilating their replacements.

- **Market risks.** The requirements for an application can always change. Modeling and iterative development give you the flexibility and speed to respond.

At each iteration, you should identify risks, prioritize them, and address the highest-priority risks first. In this way, you mitigate the biggest risks early in a project, when you have time and the wherewithal to fall back to alternate approaches. Iterative plans *must* be prepared to change. This requires both a managerial climate and a working environment that understands and accepts change.

21.9 Chapter Summary

Software development is prone to miscommunication, oversights, misestimation, and unforeseen changes. Skillful modeling gives you a resilient application. Iterative development gives you a resilient process for building the application. Iterative development provides frequent milestones and uncovers pitfalls early in development.

Iterative development is different than a waterfall approach. A waterfall assumes perfect foresight and a strict development sequence. The waterfall is a failed approach that has been overemphasized in the literature.

Iterative development is also different than rapid prototyping. Rapid prototyping addresses difficult issues by exploring with throwaway code. In contrast, iterative development divides progress into small increments that intrinsically have less chance of failure. Both are valuable techniques.

The number of iterations and their duration depends on the size of a project. If iterations are too small, the overhead of iterations is too high. If iterations are too large, there are insufficient checkpoints to assess the progress of an application and make midstream corrections. Several weeks or months is usually an appropriate length. Define the scope of an iteration by prioritizing risks. Attack high-priority risks first and reevaluate your priorities based on the results of each iteration. It is important not to slip the schedule of an iteration by increasing functionality once it is underway (scope creep), unless offsetting functionality is removed.

It is important that you integrate subsystems throughout development, rather than waiting to the end. If development teams keep to themselves, they tend to drift apart on assumptions and interfaces. With late integration, changes may have to be backed away or differences hacked away. Also make sure each iteration delivers an executable release and that it is tested. Executable code is the best measure of progress.

Modeling is a natural complement to iterative development. Both improve the quality, productivity, and predictability of software development. Some developers seem to think that modeling slows down development and gets in the way. But this is certainly not the case if you model deeply and quickly.

There are a number of risks that threaten development of an application. You should structure iterations to deal with the most serious risks first.

development risk	iterative development	rapid prototyping
integration	modeling	testing
iteration scope	prototype	waterfall

Figure 21.4 Key concepts for Chapter 21

Bibliographic Notes

[Larman-03] provides a thorough history of iterative development with many literature references.

References

[Brooks-87] Frederick P. Brooks, Jr. No silver bullet: Essence and accidents of software engineering. *IEEE Computer,* April 1987, 10–19.

[Larman-03] Craig Larman and Victor R. Basili. Iterative and incremental development: a brief history. *IEEE Computer,* June 2003, 47–56.

[Rumbaugh-05] James Rumbaugh. *The Unified Modeling Language Reference Manual, Second Edition.* Boston: Addison-Wesley, 2005.

[Sotirovski-01] Drasko Sotirovski. Heuristics for iterative software development. *IEEE Software,* May/June 2001, 66–73.

22

Managing Modeling

Modeling is essential for developing quality software, but it can be difficult to put into practice. Many organizations genuinely want to use models, but stumble when it comes to actually building them. Modeling requires a change in culture that an organization must actively foster.

22.1 Overview of Managing Modeling

In practice we find that many organizations are interested in using modeling but are unsure of how to proceed. This chapter provides advice for assimilating modeling into an organization and covers the following topics:

- Kinds of models. [22.2]
- Modeling pitfalls. [22.3]
- Modeling sessions. [22.4]
- Organizing personnel. [22.5]
- Learning techniques. [22.6]
- Teaching techniques. [22.7]
- Tools. [22.8]
- Estimating modeling effort. [22.9]

22.2 Kinds of Models

In practice there are several categories of models, each having different motivations, characteristics, and content. We often see practitioners confuse these different kinds of models and forget why they are building a particular model.

- **Application model**. This is the most common reason for modeling and this book's primary focus. An application model helps developers understand requirements and provides a basis for building the corresponding software. The ATM case study is an example.

- **Metamodel**. Metamodels are similar to application models but are more complex. They are often used for advanced applications. Frameworks (Chapter 14) and a class-model editor are examples.

- **Enterprise model**. An *enterprise model* describes an entire organization or some major aspect of it. Application models and metamodels are used for building software; enterprise models are not. Instead, enterprise models are used for reconciling concepts across applications and understanding the enterprise. By nature enterprise models have a broad scope (over multiple applications) but they are seldom deep—they need cover only the common concepts. A model of all of a bank's software would be an example.

- **Product assessment**. Models are also relevant when you are purchasing software. You should prepare multiple models—a model of your requirements and a model of the software for each of the most promising products. The requirements model is the same as an application model, except that it can lack fine detail (you are not building it). Only some vendors provide models for their products, but you can often construct your own via reverse engineering [Blaha-04]. A model helps you assess the quality of the application and understand its strengths and weaknesses as well as its scope. As an example, you might decide to buy an ATM package rather than build one, and product assessment models can clarify your decision making.

22.3 Modeling Pitfalls

The benefits of modeling are compelling, but there can be drawbacks that you should try to mitigate.

- **Analysis paralysis**. Some persons become so focused on modeling that they never finish. This situation is most likely to arise with analysts who are not developers. It can also arise with beginning modelers who are inefficient and unsure when modeling is complete.

  Resolution. A project plan can help you avoid analysis paralysis by allotting time to tasks. The plan should specify the effort for modeling and the intended deliverables. Formal reviews can give you an indication of progress and model quality. It is helpful if modelers have development experience.

- **Parallel modeling**. On several occasions, we have seen organizations construct redundant models with different paradigms. We often find OO and database modeling occurring in parallel with no communication between the respective teams. OO teams tend to be dominated by programmers who do not understand databases. Similarly, database professionals have their accustomed techniques and are often unfamiliar with OO technology. This chasm in practice mirrors the chasm in the literature. The OO and database communities have their own style and jargon, and few persons operate in both camps. The current limitations of tools exacerbate the divide.

Resolution. Oddly enough, the schism is more a matter of terminology and style, rather than substance. Your best course of action is to be aware of culture gaps. Let developers construct models for both programming and databases if they find it helpful. This is one way to cope with the limitations of current tools. In short, tolerate almost anything to get developers to model, but if there are multiple models, insist that they be frequently reconciled. Iterative development helps here—developers should reconcile at each iteration.

■ **Failure to think abstractly**. Many persons cannot think abstractly and fail to learn the skill of modeling. They quickly slip into programming mode and have trouble stepping back from a problem. With models you indirectly realize an application, rather than just directly write code.

Resolution. About the only cure is a lot of practice. Inexperienced modelers should practice solving exercises. They should work on actual applications under the guidance of a mentor. Those who are still not able to model should be assigned other tasks.

■ **Excessive scope**. The purpose of modeling is to represent the real world, but only the portion relevant to your business objectives. Some people lose focus and model extraneous information. It can be reasonable to model a bit beyond your needs—after all, the exact scope of an application is seldom known up front and is partially a matter of negotiation. However, you do not want to reach way beyond application needs, because such a model is speculative and may never lead to something useful.

Resolution. You can mitigate this pitfall with a project plan and regular reviews. Business experts need to understand what the modelers are doing, as this is their window into the capabilities and limitations of the forthcoming application.

■ **Lack of documentation**. Much too often we encounter undocumented models. Diagrams alone are not sufficient; they need an explanation. A narrative should lead the reader through each diagram and define terminology. It should explain subtleties and the rationale for any controversial decisions as well as include examples to illustrate fine points.

Resolution. You should insist on documentation, such as a model narrative or a data dictionary, and carefully read it.

■ **Lack of technical reviews**. Similarly, we often encounter a lack of technical reviews. Each person or small group works on its own application in isolation and does not share experiences, knowledge, and talent. Developers do not discuss their projects, because discussion is not relevant to their immediate deliverables and there is no management encouragement. Just as business experts are a source of application requirements, development peers are a source of computing techniques and lessons from related applications. Formal reviews help to remove errors prior to testing.

Resolution. All projects should receive at least one formal technical review, and several reviews are ideal. If there is one review, it should take place after completion of the core model and architecture. If there are several reviews, they should happen after completion of the model and architecture for each major development iteration. Management should set the tone for a critical, uninhibited, and constructive discussion. They should make continued project funding contingent on holding a review. Keep in mind that these are *technical* reviews, not *management* reviews—the purpose of the reviews is to deepen technology, not to inform management. [Boehm-01] notes that peer reviews catch 60% of software defects, so technical reviews are clearly important. We advise that the size of technical reviews be kept small (less than ten persons) and confined to developers who are actively interested in the project.

22.4 Modeling Sessions

Chapter 12 explains domain analysis—the building of real-world models to clarify application requirements. Once you become experienced at modeling, you can consider different ways of engaging users and obtaining their input. We will characterize three alternatives— back-room, round-robin, and live modeling—and discuss their trade-offs.

22.4.1 Back-Room Modeling

The most popular way to build a model is to talk to business experts, record their comments (such as with a requirements statement or use cases), and then go off-line and model. Many analysts prefer this **back-room modeling** approach, because they can focus on what the user is saying and wrestle with the model later when they are alone. Over a series of meetings, users answer questions and volunteer information that they think may be helpful. After each meeting, the analyst incorporates the users' comments, and the model gradually improves. Typically, the model stays in the background and users do not see it.

It is better to meet with several users at once rather than have one-on-one meetings. A multiuser meeting has a better chemistry, because users stimulate each other's memory. Also there is a risk of intimidation in a one-on-one session, which is less likely with multiple users. Most analysts prefer to meet with a group of users who share an interest. For example, an analyst might meet separately with salespersons and engineers.

Back-room modeling has the following trade-offs.

■ **Advantages**. It requires the least skill and is appropriate for analysts who are tentative with modeling.

■ **Disadvantages**. The painstaking cycle of interaction with users is cumbersome for skilled modelers. The slow interaction can also be troublesome for users, because multiple interviews are required. Analysts must carefully transcribe information, or it will be forgotten.

22.4.2 Round-Robin Modeling

Round-robin modeling is more complex than back-room modeling, but more efficient at gathering requirements. The analyst still meets with small groups of users, segmented by interest or functional area, but in round-robin modeling, the users see the model. As users express requirements, the analyst traverses the model and tries to resolve them. An analyst can resolve simple issues during a meeting and complex issues afterward.

We call this approach ***round-robin modeling***, because an analyst shows the model to each group in a series of meetings until all concerns are addressed. Several iterations are required, because one group might surface an issue that an analyst needs to confirm with a previous group. Back-room modeling also parades from group to group, but users don't see the model.

We initiate round-robin modeling with a seed model that is based on existing business documentation. We don't like to start with a blank sheet of paper, because it wastes time and tries the patience of users. In contrast, a seed model stimulates discussion. Users see the analyst as well prepared and can focus on deeper issues.

In the meetings, we tell the users that they are the business experts and that we need their help in capturing requirements; we are the computer experts, and they should let us handle the details. Generally, users heave a sigh of relief. We don't dwell on formalisms and explain notation as we go. Participants don't have a problem, because we continually explain the model.

Round-robin modeling has the following trade-offs.

- ◼ **Advantages**. It requires fewer meetings than back-room modeling. Because the model is prominent, an analyst can resolve some issues during meetings. In contrast, with back-room modeling, the analyst just takes notes and may overlook needed details.

- ◼ **Disadvantages**. It still requires several iterations, and it is inefficient to shuttle ideas across the user groups. If there is contention, it can be difficult to reach agreement. The analyst is in the uncomfortable position of being an intermediary among conflicting user groups. Back-room modeling also shares this flaw. Some users do not understand models or may fear them, so the analyst must take care to allay their concerns.

22.4.3 Live Modeling

Live modeling is appropriate for expert modelers. We arrange a meeting of 10–20 persons with a range of interests—developers, managers, and various kinds of business experts. During the meeting, we build a model on the fly, listening to suggestions, volunteering comments, resolving names, and agreeing on scope. Usually, we can keep pace with the dialogue; we pause a moment when we get overloaded. A projector displays the model, which we draw with a modeling tool. A typical session lasts about two hours, and three sessions can usually elicit 80 percent of the structure for a model with 50 classes. Large and complex models take additional sessions. In between sessions, the modeler cleans up diagrams, documents the model, and resolves open issues.

The process is stimulated by the size and variety of the group; reluctant participants see others react and want to get involved to air their point of view. Comments from one person tend to trigger comments from another. We have been especially successful with skeptics.

It is acceptable to start live modeling with a clean sheet of paper, but the analyst should prepare and learn about the application in advance. The ideas will come quickly, and the analyst must be ready. Sometimes we prepare a seed model if we have prior information. Normally, we request that our client prepare a requirements statement to stimulate discussion if there are any lulls.

We are active facilitators, not just passive recorders; we ask questions and probe the attendees when answers seem unsatisfactory. We make suggestions on the basis of our experience. Ultimately, business experts make the final decisions. Occasionally, we encounter a deep modeling issue that we defer until the next meeting.

Often there are animated discussions over names. These can be helpful. Good names avoid misunderstandings. Also the discussions stimulate related information. We press business experts to devise good names—names that are brief, crisp, and not subject to confounding interpretations.

Live modeling has the following trade-offs.

- **Advantages**. This is clearly the best way to obtain user input for proficient modelers. We practice live modeling all the time, and clients are delighted by the rapid progress. The participants have different areas of knowledge and different perceptions; by working together in the same meeting, they can reconcile their views.

  A major side benefit is that the meetings induce the participants to talk to each other. Persons from different backgrounds who usually don't have the time or inclination are brought together and converse.

- **Disadvantages**. An analyst has to be highly confident of modeling, able to run a meeting, and adept with a modeling tool. Few developers have this combination of skills. Live modeling is good at eliciting structure—classes and relationships. It is less effective at finding attributes, because it is difficult to coordinate a large group for fine detail. Other input sources can provide attributes.

  Live modeling is not suitable for difficult applications, such as applications with intense metamodeling. For these situations we recommend back-room modeling.

Table 22.1 summarizes the trade-offs for the three kinds of modeling sessions.

	Back-room modeling	Round-robin modeling	Live modeling
Explanation	Record user comments and build model offline	Show model to user groups, but still build it offline	Build model during a meeting with all the users
Required skill level	Low	Medium	Very high
Productivity (for a model with 50 classes)	Low (about 15 meetings, each 2 hours long)	Medium (about 12 meetings each 2 hours long)	Very high (about 3 meetings, each 2 hours long)
Net recommendation	Best for a novice modeler	Best for a modeler with some application experience	Best for a very experienced modeler

Table 22.1 Trade-offs for different approaches to modeling sessions. Consider different approaches to modeling and their trade-offs.

22.5 Organizing Personnel

As Figure 22.1 shows, a large organization can most effectively service demand by placing a few experts in a technology-oriented group that supports groups of developers organized by business area. Table 22.2 clarifies the respective roles of the technology and application groups.

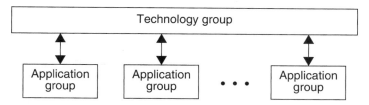

Figure 22.1 Corporate structure. A technology group can provide expertise for groups of developers organized by business area.

	Technology group	**Application group**
Perspective	The entire organization	A business area
Appropriate tasks	Promulgate standards and computing techniques; maintain enterprise models; support the application groups	Build applications; evaluate products for potential purchase
Required modeling skill	Expert	Fluent
Number of groups	One per organization	Many per organization
Size of group	Small to limit overhead	As many as needed to serve business area

Table 22.2 Technology vs. application groups. A large organization needs both kinds of groups.

The technology group takes the perspective of the entire organization. It promulgates standards and computing techniques and supports the application groups. You should place the best modelers and experts in the technology group, so that their skills are available to everyone. The technology group should not build applications; this is the purpose of the application groups. Rather, the technology group should be the custodian of advanced skills. Keep this group small to limit overhead.

Application groups have a different role. Their purpose is to learn about the business and transfer knowledge across related applications. Application group members should work closely with their business counterparts. Developers should be fluent with modeling, even though the best modelers belong to the technology group.

Some firms use a different organization; they place all modelers in a technology group and loan them out to perform modeling for application developers. We advise against this arrangement. Modeling is such a stimulus to insight and dialog that it should be dispersed across an entire computing organization. (For that matter, it is also beneficial if some business and marketing staff learn about models.) Modeling is the lingua franca for software development, and application developers should build models for themselves.

22.6 Learning Techniques

There are various actions that a person can take to learn about modeling. Some of these actions individuals can take on their own. Other actions require organizational support. This advice pertains to students in universities as well as practitioners in industry.

- **Training and mentoring**. Universities and commercial training houses both offer courses that explain modeling concepts and how to apply them. It is best to receive training shortly before (ideally a few weeks ahead of) its use on an actual project. Try not to receive training far in advance, or you will forget too much.

   Reinforce training with mentoring. Developers will need active help as they seek to apply the training material. Novice modelers will lack confidence that they are modeling correctly and need experience on which to draw. It will not suffice to bring in outside resources to service a project. There must be a transition of knowledge from the outside resources to in-house developers.

- **Teaming**. Application models should be constructed by small teams that initially consist of developers, business experts, and external consultants. After several applications, an organization should no longer need the external consultants, and the best in-house modelers can provide expertise. The purpose of teaming is to disseminate knowledge within a firm about both computing technology and the business.

- **Seminars**. Periodic seminars provide cost-effective education. A firm should encourage developers to present technical seminars. Seminars get developers talking and exchanging ideas. They learn about the various projects and can leverage related efforts. Seminars provide peer support for dealing with the difficulties of modeling.

- **Continual learning**. Developers should strive to find new ideas and adopt the best practices of the larger software community. Periodic attendance at technical conferences and professional meetings is helpful. Books and magazines can provide useful ideas.

- **Technical reviews**. Formal technical reviews promote conversation and become a learning experience for both the presenters and the reviewers. The reviews provide a forum for technical staff members to help one another. (See Section 22.3.)

22.7 Teaching Techniques

There are different ways to teach modeling that have various trade-offs.

- **Induction**. A person learns to model only by *doing* it, not by *talking* about it. Over the years we have tried a number of techniques and have found induction to be the quickest way to start modeling. When we run modeling sessions (see Section 22.4), we forego the preamble of a modeling tutorial (even though many attendees have never experienced a model before) and jump right into modeling the application problem. After several sessions, attendees have a good start on their application and have at the same time started to learn about modeling.

- **Practice**. Students should receive extensive hands-on practice and exercises. They should solve problems from disparate domains, with different kinds of input, different levels of abstraction, and varying difficulty.

- **Correction**. Students often make modeling mistakes, and it is difficult to anticipate all the possibilities. Part of the process of learning is for students to make mistakes and receive correction. They can learn both from their mistakes and the mistakes of their peers—through joint work with other students and class presentations. An academic setting can coerce the presentations, but in industrial courses we normally make presentations voluntary.

- **Implementation**. It is important that students understand that models can be readily implemented. They must realize that any model they can express can be implemented in a robust, predictable, and efficient manner. However, once they grasp that point, they need to set aside implementation concerns and think directly in terms of models.

- **Apprenticeship**. Another way of teaching is individually rather than en masse with a class. A new modeler can learn by forging a close working relationship with a skilled modeler. This form of teaching is best for someone who has already started to learn.

- **Patterns**. When we model, we always think in terms of patterns (Chapter 14). We encounter application situations, recognize their abstract mathematical underpinnings, and then jump to a pattern. A pattern provides a tried and true solution to a standard problem that has been studied by experts and is known to work well. There are many kinds of patterns: analysis, architecture, design, and implementation. One problem with patterns is recognizing when to apply them. Also even though they are important, patterns cover only part of a model.

22.8   Tools

Any serious software development effort requires tools—tools for modeling, configuration management, code generation, simulation, compiling, debugging, performance profiling, and so forth. We do not attempt to cover tools completely here, because there are so many kinds and such a variety of products. Instead, we focus on tools directly relevant to modeling and mention some prominent vendors.

22.8.1   Modeling Tools

Large applications (50 classes or more) require a heavyweight modeling tool. The minor benefit of a tool is that it increases productivity. The major benefit is that it can deepen thinking. Tools help experts build models more quickly and organize information about classes in a form that is easy to search. Tools help novices observe syntax and avoid common mistakes. IBM Rational Rose XDE, Rhapsody, Magic Draw, Together/J, and Enterprise Architect are heavyweight tools for the UML notation.

Small applications are less demanding and do not absolutely require a heavyweight modeling tool. Nevertheless, it is still a good idea to use a tool for small applications—modeling is essential to clear thinking, and the use of a tool eases model construction. Given the availability of inexpensive tools, as well as site licenses, there is seldom a good reason for not using a modeling tool.

22.8.2 Configuration Management Tools

Serious applications involve a number of files—files for programs (source code, compiled code, and executable code), documentation (for users, administrators, and maintainers), and data (configuration data, metadata, and test data). In practice it is difficult to coordinate all these files, and that is the purpose of configuration management tools. The tools improve developer efficiency and reduce the risk of losing useful work.

[Pressman-97] lists five major tasks that constitute configuration management.

- **Identification**. A configuration management tool must provide a mechanism for identifying each configuration file and relating it to other files.

- **Version control**. An organization must be able to track copies of a file as it evolves over time. Sometimes it is necessary to revert to old files (such as when trying to find the cause of a bug).

- **Change control**. An organization must determine who can approve changes as well as synchronize the work of collaborating developers. Check-in and check-out of files is a popular protocol.

- **Auditing**. A configuration management tool keeps a log of access activity. Users can access the log and determine the precise revisions to particular files, who made the changes, and the date of changes.

- **Status accounting**. There must be a means for reporting changes to others.

You can get by without configuration management for models if a single person is doing modeling and that person is disciplined about backups. However, an ad-hoc approach becomes increasingly difficult as the number of models and modelers increases. When you must manage many models and coordinate multiple persons, you should use configuration management software.

Prominent configuration management tools include IBM Rational's ClearCase, Merant PVCS, Microsoft's Visual SourceSafe, and the public-domain tool CVS.

22.8.3 Code Generators

Many modeling tools can generate application code. The typical modeling tool can generate data declarations for a program and a database, if you are using one. Some tools can generate algorithmic code, but that is more difficult. For example, a tool might generate programming code for a state diagram.

Regardless of the tools used, developers should be careful with generated code and spot-check it for correctness and efficiency. Some tools generate bad code with flaws that are subtle and difficult to catch. Also, to our surprise, some tools have had gross errors in their outputs. If your developers pay attention to tool output, they will better understand what the tool is doing.

22.8.4 Simulation Tools

Tools can also be used to predict the behavior and performance of a finished application. Some modeling tools can simulate the performance and behavior of the finished software in advance of building it. For example, i-Logix's Statemate can simulate state diagrams.

22.8.5 Repository

Repositories are also important to application development, because they store metadata that lets the various tools communicate. A repository sits at the center of tool usage. Because they involve metadata, repositories are difficult to deploy, but effective use of a repository can leverage your usage of the individual tools. Allen System Group, Computer Associates, IBM, and Microsoft have repository products.

22.9 Estimating Modeling Effort

Any software development effort is an economic proposition. Business people estimate the cost of building the software along with the resulting revenues and cost savings. Modeling is generally a small part (much less than 10%) of the overall application effort. The following factors affect modeling effort.

- **Application complexity**. Tangible applications are simpler; highly abstract applications take longer. For example, it is easier to build software for handling customer calls than to build a system for all kinds of customer interaction.

- **Proficiency**. A skilled modeler can work an order of magnitude faster than an inexperienced one. In addition, a skilled modeler is more likely to produce a quality model with thoughtful abstractions.

- **Tools**. It helps if the developer has access to a powerful modeling tool and is skilled with it.

- **Model size**. The time to construct a model is not linear with its size. Modeling time is roughly proportional to the number of classes to the one-and-one-half power. Thus, construction for a model with 500 classes takes about 30 times longer than for one with 50.

- **Reviews**. Thorough review reduces the number of iterations needed for a model.

Given all these factors, most models require from two weeks to six months of effort.

22.10 Chapter Summary

This chapter has covered several topics to help an organization assimilate the technology of modeling.

In practice, there are several categories of models—application, meta, enterprise, and product assessment—with different motivations, characteristics, and content. Many developers overlook how to properly use modeling for the various categories. For example, an enterprise model cannot contain all the details of the covered applications, or it will become unwieldy. Models can also be used to guide purchase evaluations.

Models have many benefits, but like any technology they also entail risks. We identified some major risks and noted actions that an organization can take to mitigate them.

There are different ways that you can engage users in the process of modeling. We listed several kinds of interactions—back room, round robin, and live—along with their trade-offs.

There are various actions that a person can take to learn about modeling, including training, mentoring, teaming, seminars, continual learning, and technical reviews.

Similarly, there are different ways to teach modeling. One of the most successful is induction—a person learns to model only by doing it, not by talking about it. Teachers should give students extensive practice with models and give them the opportunity to have their mistakes corrected. Students must understand that models can be readily implemented but they should directly think in terms of models. Advanced modelers will recognize patterns and apply them.

Any serious software development effort requires tools. We listed tools relevant to modeling and gave some criteria for choosing tools. We also gave some guidelines for estimating modeling effort.

abstraction	estimation	peer support
application model	induction	product assessment
apprenticeship	live modeling	repository
back-room modeling	mentoring	round-robin modeling
code generation	metamodel	seminar
configuration management	model review	simulation tools
continuing education	modeling pitfall	teaming
documentation	modeling tool	technical review
enterprise model	pattern	training

Figure 22.2 Key concepts for Chapter 22

Bibliographic Notes

This book says little about management issues, such as project planning, project estimation, costing, metrics, personnel assignment, and team dynamics. These are all important topics, but other books cover them, such as [Pressman-97] and [Blaha-01].

In [Colwell-03] Bob Colwell recalls some of his first-hand experiences with design reviews and stresses their importance to high-quality work.

[Berndtsson-04] describes his experiences with teaching three configurations of OO analysis and design courses over a nine-year period. He presents data for the following conclusions.

- **Programming success is not an indicator of modeling success**. 65% of students who did well in an OO programming course performed poorly in an OO modeling course.
- **Modeling success is an indicator of programming success**. 84% of students who did well in an OO modeling course also did well in an OO programming course.
- **Abstraction is the key difficulty with modeling**. There is a strong correlation in grades between an OO modeling course (high abstraction) and a distributed systems course (also high abstraction).

[Box-00] concludes that OO technology involves more abstraction than the older technique of structured technology. The authors consider abstraction to be the difficult learning action.

References

[Berndtsson-04] Mikael Berndtsson. Teaching object-oriented modeling and design. *Draft paper*, 2004.

[Blaha-01] Michael R. Blaha. *A Manager's Guide to Database Technology: Building and Purchasing Better Applications*, Upper Saddle River, NJ: Prentice Hall, 2001.

[Blaha-04] Michael Blaha. A copper bullet for software quality improvement. *IEEE Computer*, February 2004, 21–25.

[Boehm-01] Barry Boehm and Victor R. Basili. Software defect reduction top 10 list. *IEEE Computer*, January 2001, 135–137.

[Box-00] Roger Box and Michael Whitelaw. Experiences when migrating from structured analysis to object-oriented modeling. *Fourth Australasian Computing Education Conference*, Melbourne, Australia, December 4–6, 2000, 12–18.

[Colwell-03] Bob Colwell. Design reviews. *IEEE Computer*, October 2003, 8–10.

[Pressman-97] Roger S. Pressman. *Software Engineering: A Practitioner's Approach, Fourth Edition*. New York: McGraw-Hill, 1997.

23

Legacy Systems

Most development does not involve new applications but rather evolves existing ones. Rarely can you build an application completely from scratch. Even if you do get to build a new application, you will often need to gather information from existing applications and integrate with them. You can salvage requirements, ideas, data, and code.

It is difficult to modify an application if you don't understand its design. If an application was previously designed using OO models and they are accurate, you can use the models to understand and evolve the application. If the models are lacking or have been lost, you should start by building a model of the existing design.

23.1 Reverse Engineering

Reverse engineering is the process of examining implementation artifacts and inferring the underlying logical intent. Reverse engineering has its origins in the analysis of hardware—where the practice of deciphering designs from finished products is commonplace [Rekoff-85]. Models facilitate reverse engineering, because they can express both abstract concepts and implementation decisions.

When building new applications, the purpose of reverse engineering is to salvage useful information. It is not intended to perpetuate past flaws. The reverse engineer must determine what to preserve and what to discard. You should regard reverse-engineered models as merely one source of requirements for a new application.

Reverse engineering requires judgment—interpretative decisions by the developer—and cannot be fully automated. Tools can assist with the sheer volume of code to be reverse engineered and the rote. However, it is difficult for the current tools to accept human decisions. Many modeling tools can generate an initial model, but this model is little more than a visual representation of the program structure. The reverse engineer must overcome at least two problems with the program code: retrieving obscure or lost information and uncovering implicit behavior.

23.1.1 Reverse Engineering vs. Forward Engineering

As Table 23.1 shows, reverse engineering is the inverse to normal development (forward engineering); you start with the actual application and work backward to deduce the requirements that spawned the software.

Forward engineering	Reverse engineering
Given requirements, develop an application.	Given an application, deduce tentative requirements.
More certain. The developer has requirements and must deliver an application that implements them.	Less certain. An implementation can yield different requirements, depending on the reverse engineer's interpretation.
Prescriptive. Developers are told how to work.	Adaptive. The reverse engineer must find out what the developer actually did.
More mature. Skilled staff readily available.	Less mature. Skilled staff sparse.
Time consuming (months to years of work).	Can be performed 10 to 100 times faster than forward engineering (days to weeks of work).
The model must be correct and complete or the application will fail.	The model can be imperfect. Salvaging partial information is still useful.

Table 23.1   Forward engineering vs. reverse engineering. Reverse engineering is the opposite of forward engineering and requires a different mindset.

23.1.2 Inputs to Reverse Engineering

When performing reverse engineering, you must be resourceful and consider all inputs. The available information varies widely across problems.

■ **Programming code**. The programming source code can be a rich information source. Tools can help you understand the flow of control and the data structure. Comments and suggestive names of variables, functions, and methods can deepen your understanding.

■ **Database structure**. If the application has a database, you can also learn from it. The database specifies the data structure and many constraints—precisely and explicitly.

■ **Data**. If data are available, you can discover much of the data structure. A thorough application program or disciplined users may yield data of better quality than the data structure enforces. For large systems, you may have to sample the data to reach tentative conclusions, and then explore further for verification. Examination cannot prove many propositions, but the more data you encounter, the more likely will be the conclusion.

■ **Forms and reports**. Suggestive titles and layouts can clarify data structure and processing logic. Form and report definitions are especially helpful if their binding to variables is available. An empirical approach is to enter known, unusual values to establish the binding between forms and the underlying variables.

- **Documentation**. Problems vary in their quality, quantity, and kind of documentation. Documentation provides context for reverse engineering. User manuals are especially helpful. Data dictionaries—lists of important entities and their definitions—may be available. Be careful with all documentation, because it can become stale and inconsistent with application code.

- **Application understanding**. If you understand an application well, you can make better inferences. Application experts may be available to answer questions and explain rationale. You may be able to leverage models from related applications.

- **Test cases**. Test cases are intended to exercise the normal flow of control and unusual situations. Sometimes they provide useful clues.

23.1.3 Outputs from Reverse Engineering

Reverse engineering has several useful outputs.

- **Models**. The model conveys the software's scope and intent. It provides a basis for understanding the original software and building any successor software.

- **Mappings**.You can tie model attributes to variables. Less precisely, you can bind programming code to state and interaction models.

- **Logs**. Reverse engineers should record their observations and pending questions. A log documents decisions and rationale.

23.2 Building the Class Model

Begin by constructing a class model of the application so that you can understand the classes and relationships. We suggest building the class model using three distinct phases: implementation recovery, design recovery, and analysis recovery.

23.2.1 Implementation Recovery

First quickly learn about the application and create an initial class model. If the program is written in an OO language, you can recover classes and generalizations directly. Otherwise you must study the data structures and operations and manually determine classes. The system may lack a proper design, so the result may not be pleasing. Try to avoid making any inferences other than determining classes at this point. It is helpful to have an initial model focused on the implementation.

23.2.2 Design Recovery

Next probe the application to recover associations. The typical implementation of an association is as a single pointer attribute. The multiplicity in the forward direction is usually clear.

In contrast, the multiplicity in the reverse direction is typically not declared, and you must determine it from general knowledge or examination of the code.

Many implementations use a collection of pointers to implement an association with "many" multiplicity. Then the initial generated model points to the collection class, rather than the class of the elements. You should move the association to the class of the elements and adjust the multiplicity accordingly. Collection classes are mechanisms and should not appear in most analysis or design models. You can mark them on associations as recommended implementation for a "many" direction.

Sometimes pointers will implement both association directions. In those cases, you must identify the matching pointers and consolidate them. You should suspect any two classes that have pointer attributes to each other. If you reverse engineer the initial model with a tool, it will have one association for each pointer. You should remove one association and move its information to the reverse direction of the other.

Multiplicity typically has a lower limit of 0 or 1. The lower limit is '0' if the target object is initialized somewhere in the source code, but it is uncertain when initialization will happen. The lower limit is '1' if the target object is initialized at object creation time, such as in the constructor or the class initialization block.

23.2.3 Analysis Recovery

Finally, you interpret the model, refine it, and make it more abstract. Remove any remaining design artifacts and eliminate any errors. Be sure to get rid of all redundant information or mark it as such. It's also a good time to reconsider the model. Is it readable and coherent? Reconcile the reverse engineering results with models of other applications and documentation. Show your model to application experts and incorporate their advice.

If your source code is not object oriented, you will have to infer generalizations by recognizing similarities and differences in structure and behavior. Similarly, you will have to use your application understanding and careful study of the code to determine aggregations and compositions. For example, objects with coincident lifetimes suggest composition. You will also need to understand the application and code to determine qualifiers and association classes.

You can add packages to organize the classes, associations, and generalizations. You can combine the classes in several code files into one package or split a large code file across multiple packages.

23.3 Building the Interaction Model

The purpose of each method is usually clear enough, but the way that objects interact to carry out the purposes of the system is often hard to understand from the code. The problem is that code is inherently reductionist: it describes how each piece works by itself. But the meaning of the system as a whole is holistic: the emergent interactions among objects give it meaning. The interaction model can give you a broad understanding.

You can add methods to the class model by using slicing. A *slice* is a subset of a program that preserves a specified projection of its behavior [Weiser-84]. You can perform slicing by marking some initial code to retain. Then, recursively, mark all statements used by the retained code. The accumulated code lets you project an excerpt of behavior from the original program. Thus slicing provides a means for converting procedural code into an OO representation that is centered about objects.

Programmers naturally think in terms of slicing as [Weiser-82] notes. The power of slices comes from four facts: 1) they can be found automatically, 2) slices are generally smaller than the program from which they originated, 3) they execute independently of one another, and 4) each reproduces exactly a projection of the original program's behavior [Weiser-84].

You can use an activity diagram to represent an extracted method so that you can understand the sequence of processing and the flow of data to various objects. You can then construct sequence diagrams from the activity diagrams for simplification.

23.4 Building the State Model

If you are studying a user interface, a state model can be quite helpful. Otherwise, state models are not prominent in most other kinds of application code.

If you do need to construct a state model, you can proceed as follows. As an input, you have sequence diagrams from building the interaction model. You need to fold the various sequence diagrams for a class together, by sequencing events and adding conditionals and loops as Chapter 13 describes.

You can augment the information in the sequence diagrams by studying the code and doing dynamic testing. It is helpful to find all the possible states for each class that has a state model. Initiation and termination correspond to construction and destruction of objects.

23.5 Reverse Engineering Tips

As you perform reverse engineering and build class, interaction, and state models, it will help if you keep in mind the following tips.

- **Distinguish suppositions from facts**. Reverse engineering yields hypotheses. You must thoroughly understand the application before reaching firm conclusions. As reverse engineering proceeds, you may need to revisit some of your earlier decisions and change them.

- **Use a flexible process**. We adjust the reverse engineering process to fit the problem. Problem styles and the available inputs vary widely. You must use your wits for reverse engineering. You are solving a large puzzle.

- **Expect multiple interpretations**. There is no single answer as in forward engineering. Alternative interpretations can yield different models. The more information that is available, the less judgments should vary among reverse engineers.

- **Don't be discouraged by approximate results**. It is worth a modest amount of time to extract 80 percent of an application's meaning. You can use the typical forward engineering techniques (such as interviewing knowledgeable users) to obtain the remaining 20 percent. Many people find this lack of perfection uncomfortable, because it is a paradigm shift from forward engineering.

- **Expect odd constructs**. Developers, even the experts, occasionally use uncommon constructs. In some cases, you won't be able to produce a complete, accurate model, because that model never existed.

- **Watch for a consistent style**. Software is typically designed using a consistent strategy, including consistent violations of good design practice. Usually, you can look at an excerpt of the software and deduce the underlying strategy.

23.6 Wrapping

Some applications are brittle and poorly understood—they may have been written long ago, have missing documentation, and lack guidance from the original developers. Changes can threaten their viability and risk introducing bugs. Consequently, many organizations limit changes to such applications. They prefer to isolate the code and build a wrapper around it.

A *wrapper* is a collection of interfaces that control access to a system. It consists of a set of boundary classes that provide the interfaces, and it should be designed to follow good OO principles. The boundary classes' methods call the existing system using the existing operations. A boundary method may involve several existing operations and bundle data from several places. Often the calls to legacy code are messy, but the boundary classes hide the details from the outside. The source code can either be OO or non-OO. Wrapping preserves the form of legacy software and accesses its functionality.

Many existing applications have functionality that is confusing, unpredictable, or complex. Often it is possible to extract a core of functionality that is more fundamental, simpler to use, and better tested. In this case, a wrapper provides a clean interface for exposing the core functionality. Some features of the original application are lost, but they are usually the most dubious ones.

If you are adding new functionality, it can usually be added as a separate package. Design this package using good OO principles. Try to minimize interactions with the existing system, and keep them as uniform as possible.

For an example consider a Web application. The original code may be a legacy banking application written in Cobol and running on old hardware. Wrapping can expose the Cobol logic as OO methods that can then be attached to a modern Web interface. The legacy code still must be maintained, but its maintenance is little affected by the existence of the Web interface. The actual code that executes for the Web application is ugly, but it works as long as maintenance on the underlying Cobol logic does not disrupt the wrapper's methods.

Wrapping is usually just a temporary solution, because a wrapper is heavily constrained by the organization (often accidental) of the legacy software. Eventually the combination of the original old code, the wrapper, and new code in a different format become so unwieldy that it must be rewritten.

Sneed suggests the use of XML as a gateway for communication between the legacy software on the inside and the modern world on the outside. Programmers with different levels of sophistication and modernity can interact via the intermediary of XML [Sneed-01]. He also observes that wrapping serves both a technological and a social purpose. The maintainers of the old code do not have their artifacts disrupted with wrapping. Wrapping lets program maintainers keep their mental models of the software intact. This helps with the day-to-day maintenance of the wrapped code.

23.7 Maintenance

Much of the software literature treats maintenance as being monolithic, but we think the viewpoint of Rajlich and Bennett is more perceptive. According to [Rajlich-00], software moves through five stages.

- **Initial development**. Developers create the software.
- **Evolution**. The software undergoes major changes in functionality and architecture. Refactoring can be used to maintain software quality.
- **Servicing**. The available technical talent has been reduced, either by circumstances or by deliberate decision. Software changes are limited to minor fixes and simple functionality changes. At this stage the software begins its inexorable slide to obsolescence. Wrapping becomes an appropriate technology during this stage.
- **Phaseout**. The vendor continues to receive revenue from the product but is now planning its demise.
- **Closedown**. The product is removed from the market, and customers are redirected to other software.

These five stages do not have a rigid wall between them, but there is a continual decline in the technical quality of the software as it proceeds through its lifetime. Also the authors note that individual versions of software can experience these life stages, only to be replaced by successor versions.

The software engineering goal is to slow the decline and keep software in the evolution and servicing stages as long as possible. In any case, management wants to avoid an accidental slippage of the software and only let the transitions proceed with forethought.

23.8 Chapter Summary

Most development does not involve new applications but rather evolves existing ones. Accordingly, as a software engineer you must be able to evolve existing applications and integrate with them. You can salvage requirements, ideas, data, and code from existing applications. Reverse engineering is a critical technology when dealing with legacy applications.

The purpose of reverse engineering is to salvage information from old systems and carry it forward. Reverse engineering is *not* intended to perpetuate past flaws—you discard any flaws that you find. Reverse engineering provides merely one source of requirements for new applications, but it is an important source. There can be a variety of inputs to reverse engineering, all of which you should be prepared to exploit. The primary outputs from reverse engineering are models.

Begin by building the class model, emphasizing classes, associations, and generalizations. We suggest building the class model using three distinct phases—implementation recovery, design recovery, and analysis recovery—that involve increasing amounts of decisions and interpretation about the software.

Next build the interaction model, being sure to tie your understanding of behavior to the class model. You can start with procedural code and use slicing to extract portions of the logic that are centered about objects. Hence slicing provides a means for taking the content of procedural code and restructuring it as OO code. Ultimately you express the interaction model as a collection of activity and sequence diagrams.

Finally, if you need it, build the state model. The sequence diagrams provide a helpful intermediary to state diagrams.

Reverse engineering is much different than forward engineering and consequently requires a different mindset. We provided a number of tips to help with the changed mindset.

Wrapping is another technique for dealing with legacy applications. You can regard the legacy application as a black box and build interfaces around it. New applications then access the legacy logic via the intermediary of the wrapper.

forward engineering	re-engineering	slice
maintenance	reverse engineering	wrapper

Figure 23.1 Key concepts for Chapter 23

Bibliographic Notes

[Bachman-89] explains that most information systems build on past work and only the occasional project truly involves new work. We note that this claim applies not only to information systems but also to software in general.

[Chikofsky-90] has been influential in standardizing reverse engineering terminology. [Kollmann-01] explains how to recover a class model from source code and test executions. The test executions often do not prove hypotheses about the class model, but they can help understanding and are suggestive. [Sneed-96] presents a basic approach to taking a procedural COBOL program and converting it to an OO representation.

References

[Bachman-89] Charles W. Bachman. A personal chronicle: Creating better information systems, with some guiding principles. *IEEE Transactions on Knowledge and Data Engineering 1*, 1 (March 1989), 17–32.

[Chikofsky-90] Elliot J. Chikofsky and James H. Cross II. Reverse engineering and design recovery: A taxonomy. *IEEE Software*, January 1990, 13–17.

[Kollmann-01] Ralf Kollmann and Martin Gogolla. Application of UML associations and their adornments in design recovery. *IEEE Eighth Working Conference on Reverse Engineering*, October 2001, Stuttgart, Germany, 81–90.

[Rajlich-00] Vaclav T. Rajlich and Keith H. Bennett. A staged model for the software life cycle. *IEEE Computer*, July 2000, 66–71.

[Rekoff-85] MG Rekoff, Jr. On Reverse Engineering. *IEEE Transactions on Systems, Man, and Cybernetics SMC-15*, 2 (March/April 1985), 244–252.

[Sneed-96] Harry M. Sneed. Object-oriented COBOL recycling. *IEEE Third Working Conference on Reverse Engineering*, November 1996, Monterey, CA, 169–178.

[Sneed-01] Harry M. Sneed. Wrapping legacy COBOL programs behind an XML interface. *IEEE Eighth Working Conference on Reverse Engineering*, October 2001, Stuttgart, Germany, 189–197.

[Weiser-82] M. Weiser. Programmers use slices when debugging. *Communications of the ACM 25*, 7 (July 1982), 446–452.

[Weiser-84] M. Weiser. Program slicing. *IEEE Transactions on Software Engineering 10*, 4 (July 1984), 352–357.

Appendix A

UML Graphical Notation

The inside covers of the book summarize the graphical notations for the class, state, and interaction models. You can use these four pages as a quick reference while constructing or reading diagrams. However, we must caution you that a novice cannot simply take these four pages and understand them. To understand the concepts represented by the notation, refer to the chapters of Part 1. To learn how to apply the notation and concepts within the software development life cycle, consult the chapters in Part 2 and 3. The index can also help you find relevant material in the book.

With the exception of the label for each construct and a few descriptive comments, all of the diagram elements, text names, and punctuation symbols shown are part of the notation. The names in these diagrams (such as *Class*, *attribute1*, *operation*, and *event2*) indicate what kind of element they are examples of. You may wish to modify the syntax of names and the declarations of attributes and signatures to make them consistent with the syntax of your implementation language.

Most of the items shown are optional, especially during early stages of modeling. Even in design, it is unwise to overspecify by including superfluous names and notations. For example, when an association is labeled by end names, it is usually not necessary to give the association itself a name. We have not indicated which elements are optional, because we wanted to show only the actual UML notation wherever possible, without obscuring it with an additional metanotation.

Please feel free to copy the notation summaries on the inside covers. You can obtain an electronic copy at www.modelsoftcorp.com.

Appendix B

Glossary

The following terms are used in OO modeling for analysis, design, and implementation.

abstract class a class that has no direct instances. The UML notation is to italicize an abstract class name or place the keyword *{abstract}* below or after the name. (Contrast with *concrete class.*)

abstract operation an operation that lacks an implementation. A concrete descendant class must provide a method to implement the operation. The UML notation is to italicize an abstract operation name or place the keyword *{abstract}* after its name.

abstraction the ability to focus on essential aspects of an application while ignoring details.

access modifier (in Java) the means of controlling access to methods and data via *public*, *private*, *protected*, and *package* visibility.

access specifier (in C++) the means of controlling access to methods and data via *public*, *private*, and *protected* visibility as well as a *friend* declaration.

activation the period of time for an object's execution. The UML notation is a thin rectangle. (Synonymous with *focus of control.*)

active object an object that has its own thread of control. (Contrast with *passive object.*)

activity a specification of executable behavior.

activity diagram a diagram that shows the sequence of steps that make up a complex process.

activity token a token that can be placed on an activity symbol to show the progress of an execution.

actor a direct external user of a system. The UML notation is a "stick man" icon.

aggregation a kind of association in which a whole, the assembly, is composed of parts. Aggregation is often called the "a-part-of" or "parts-explosion" relationship and may be nested to an arbitrary number of levels. Aggregation bears the transitivity and antisymmetry properties. The UML notation is a small *hollow* diamond superimposed on the association end next to the assembly class. (Contrast with *composition*.)

analysis the development stage in which a real-world problem is examined to understand its requirements without planning the implementation.

ancestor class a class that is a direct or indirect superclass of a given class. (Contrast with *descendant class*.)

API (acronym) *application programming interface*.

application analysis the second substage of analysis that addresses the computer aspects of the application that are visible to users.

application programming interface a collection of methods that provide the functionality of an application.

architecture the high-level plan or strategy for solving an application problem.

assembly (for an aggregation) a class of objects that is composed of part objects.

association a description of a group of links with common structure and common semantics. The UML notation is a line between classes that may consist of several line segments.

association class an association that is also a class. Like the links of an association, the instances of an association class derive identity from instances of the related classes. Like a class, an association class can have attributes, operations, and participate in associations. The UML notation is a box (a class box) attached to the association by a dashed line.

association end an end of an association. A binary association has two ends, a ternary has three ends, and so forth.

attribute a named property of a class that describes a value held by each object of the class. The UML notation lists attributes in the second compartment of the class box.

automatic transition an unlabeled transition that automatically fires when the activity associated with the source state is completed.

bag an unordered collection of elements with duplicates allowed. The UML notation is to annotate an association end with *{bag}*.

base class (in C++) a superclass.

batch transformation (architectural style) a sequential input-to-output transformation, in which inputs are supplied at the start and the goal is to compute an answer. There is no ongoing interaction with the outside world. (Contrast with *continuous transformation*.)

boundary class a class of objects that provide a staging area for communications between a system and an external source.

call-by-reference (in a programming language) a mechanism that passes arguments to a method by passing the address of each argument. (Contrast with *call-by-value*.)

call-by-value (in a programming language) a mechanism that passes arguments to a method by passing a copy of the data values. If an argument is modified, the new value will not take effect outside of the method that modifies it. (Contrast with *call-by-reference*.)

candidate key (in a relational database) a combination of columns that uniquely identifies each row in a table. The combination must be minimal and include only those columns that are needed for unique identification. No column in a candidate key can be null.

cardinality the count of elements that are in a collection. (Contrast with *multiplicity*.)

change event an event that is caused by the satisfaction of a boolean expression. The intent of a change event is that the expression is continually tested—whenever the expression changes from false to true the event happens. The UML notation is the keyword *when* followed by a parenthesized boolean expression. (Contrast with *guard condition*.)

changeability an indication whether a property (such as an association end) can be modified after the initial value is created. The possibilities are *changeable* (can be updated) and *readonly* (can only be initialized).

class a description of a group of objects with similar properties (attributes), common behavior (operations and state diagrams), similar relationships to other objects, and common semantics. The UML notation is a box with the name in the top compartment.

class design the development stage for expanding and optimizing the analysis models so that they are amenable to implementation.

class diagram a graphic representation that describes classes and their relationships, thereby describing possible objects. (Contrast with *object diagram*.)

class model a description of the structure of the objects in a system including their identity, relationships to other objects, attributes, and operations.

classification a grouping of objects with the same data structure and behavior.

client a subsystem that requests services from another subsystem. (Contrast with *server*.)

coherence a property of an element, such as a class, an operation, or a package, such that it is organized on a consistent plan and all its parts fit together toward a common goal.

completion transition a transition that automatically fires when the activity associated with the source state is completed.

composite state a state that provides shared behavior for nested states. (Contrast with *nested state*.)

composition a form of aggregation with two additional constraints. A part can belong to at most one assembly. Furthermore, once a part has been assigned an assembly, it has a coincident lifetime with the assembly. The UML notation is a small *solid* diamond superimposed on the association end next to the assembly class. (Contrast with *aggregation*.)

concrete class a class that can have direct instances. (Contrast with *abstract class*.)

concurrent two or more activities or events whose execution may overlap in time.

condition (see *guard condition*).

constraint a boolean condition involving model elements such as objects, classes, attributes, associations, and generalization sets. The UML notation for simple constraints is a text string enclosed in braces or placed in a "dog-eared" comment box. For complex constraints, you can use the Object Constraint Language.

constructor (in C++ and Java) an operation that initializes a newly created instance of a class. (Contrast with *destructor*.)

container class a class of *container objects*. Examples include sets, arrays, dictionaries, and associations.

container object an object that stores a collection of other objects and provides various operations to access or iterate over its contents.

continuous transformation (architectural style) a system in which the outputs actively depend on changing inputs and must be periodically updated. (Contrast with *batch transformation*.)

control the aspect of a system that describes the sequences of operations that occur in response to stimuli.

controller an active object that manages control within an application.

database a permanent, self-descriptive store of data that is contained in one or more files. Self-description is what sets a database apart from ordinary files.

database management system the software for managing access to a database.

data dictionary the definition of all modeling elements (classes, associations, attributes, operations, and enumeration values) and an explanation of the rationale for key modeling decisions.

DBMS (acronym) *database management system*.

default value the value used to initialize an attribute or method argument.

delegation an implementation mechanism in which an object, responding to an operation on itself, forwards the operation to another object.

denormalization the violation of normal forms. Developers should violate normal forms only for good cause, such as to increase performance for a bottleneck. (See *normal form*.)

derived class (in C++) a subclass.

derived element (in UML) an element that is defined in terms of other elements. Classes, attributes, and associations can all be derived. Do not confuse the UML term *derived* with the C++ *derived class*. A C++ derived class refers to the subclass of a generalization and has nothing to do with UML's meaning of derived element. The UML notation is a slash preceding the element name.

descendant class a class that is a direct or indirect subclass of a given class. (Contrast with *ancestor class*.)

destructor (in C++) an operation that cleans up an existing instance of a class that is no longer needed. (Contrast with *constructor*.)

development the construction of software.

development life cycle an approach for managing the process of building software.

development stage a step in the process of building software. This book covers the following sequence of development stages: system conception, domain analysis, application analysis, system design, class design, implementation modeling, and implementation. Even though the development stages are ordered, all portions of an application need not proceed in tandem. We do not mean to imply waterfall development.

dictionary an unordered collection of object pairs with duplicates allowed. Each pair binds a key to an element. You can then use the key to look up the element.

direction whether an argument to an operation/method is an input (*in*), output (*out*), or an input argument that can be modified (*inout*).

do-activity an activity that continues for an extended time. The UML notation is *"do /"* followed by the do-activity name.

domain analysis the first substage of analysis that focuses on modeling real-world things that carry the semantics of an application.

dynamic binding a form of method resolution that associates a method with an operation at run time, depending on the class of one or more target objects.

dynamic simulation (architectural style) a system that models or tracks objects in the real world.

effect a reference to a behavior that is executed in response to an event. The UML notation for an effect is a slash ("/") followed by the activity name.

encapsulation the separation of external specification from internal implementation. (Synonymous with *information hiding*.)

enterprise model a model that describes an entire organization or some major aspect of an organization.

Entity-Relationship (ER) model a graphical approach to modeling originated by Peter Chen that shows entities and the relationships between them. The UML class model is based on the ER model.

entry activity an activity that is executed upon entry to a state. The UML notation is to list an entry activity within a state preceded by *"entry /"*. (Contrast with *exit* activity.)

enumeration a data type that has a finite set of values. The UML notation is the keyword «*enumeration*» above the enumeration name in the top section of a box. The second section lists the enumeration values.

ER (acronym) *Entity-Relationship model*.

event an occurrence at a point in time. (Contrast with *state*.)

event-driven control an approach in which control resides within a dispatcher or monitor that the language, subsystem, or operating system provides. Developers attach application methods to events, and the dispatcher calls the methods when the corresponding events occur ("callback"). (Contrast with *procedure-driven control*.)

exit activity an activity that is executed just before exit from a state. The UML notation is to list an exit activity within a state preceded by *"exit /"*. (Contrast with *entry* activity.)

extend (use case relationship) a relationship that adds incremental behavior to a use case. Note that the extension adds itself to the base; in contrast, for an *include* relationship the base explicitly incorporates the inclusion. The UML notation is a dashed arrow from the extension use case to the base use case. The keyword *«extend»* annotates the arrow. (Contrast with *include*.)

extensibility a property of software such that new kinds of objects or functionality can be added to it with little or no modification to existing code.

extent (of a class) the set of objects for a class.

feature an attribute or an operation.

final (for a Java class) a directive that prevents further subclassing.

final (for a Java method) a directive that prevents the method from being overridden.

fire to cause a transition to occur.

focus of control the period of time for an object's execution. The UML notation is a thin rectangle. (Synonymous with *activation*.)

foreign key (in a relational database) a reference to a candidate key (normally a reference to a primary key). It is the glue that binds tables.

forward engineering the building of an application from general requirements through to an eventual implementation. (Contrast with *reverse engineering*.)

fourth-generation language a framework for straightforward database applications that provides screen layout, simple calculations, and reports.

framework a skeletal structure of a program that must be elaborated to build a complete application.

friend (in C++) a declaration that permits selective access to members. The class containing the *friend* declaration grants access to a named function, method, or class.

garbage collection (in a programming language) a mechanism for automatically deallocating data structures that can no longer be accessed and are therefore not needed.

generalization an organization of elements (such as classes, signals, or use cases) by their similarities and differences. The UML notation is a triangle with the apex next to the superelement. (Contrast with *specialization*.)

generalization set name an enumerated attribute that indicates which aspect of an object is being abstracted by a particular generalization.

guard condition a boolean expression that must be true in order for a transition to occur. A guard condition is checked only once, at the time the event occurs, and the transition fires if the condition is true. The UML notation is to list a guard condition in square brackets after an event.

identifier one or more attributes in an implementation that unambiguously differentiate an object from all others.

identity the inherent property of an object which distinguishes each object from all others.

implementation the development stage for translating a design into programming code and database structures.

implementation inheritance an abuse of inheritance that seeks to reuse existing code, but does so with an illogical application structure that can compromise future maintenance.

implementation method (style) a method that implements specific computations on fully specified arguments, but does not make context-dependent decisions. (Contrast with *policy method*.)

implementation modeling the development stage for adding fine details to a model that transcend languages. Implementation modeling is the immediate precursor to the actual implementation.

include (use case relationship) a relationship that incorporates one use case within the behavior sequence of another use case. The UML notation is a dashed arrow from the source (including) use case to the target (included) use case. The keyword *«include»* annotates the arrow. (Contrast with *exclude*.)

index a data structure that maps one or more attribute values into the objects or database table rows that hold the values. Indexes are used for optimization (to quickly locate objects and table rows) and to enforce uniqueness.

information hiding (see *encapsulation*)

inheritance the mechanism that implements the generalization relationship.

integration testing testing of code from multiple developers to determine how the classes and methods fit together. (Contrast with *unit testing* and *system testing*.)

interaction model the model that describes how objects collaborate to achieve results. It is a holistic view of behavior across many objects, whereas the state model is a reductionist view of behavior that examines each object individually.

interactive interface (architectural style) a system that is dominated by interactions between the system and agents, such as humans, devices, or other programs.

interface (in Java) an uninstantiable class specification the contains only constants and method declarations.

iterative development the development of a system by a process broken into a series of steps, or iterations, each of which provides a better approximation to the desired system than the previous iteration. (Contrast with *rapid prototyping* and *waterfall development*.)

iterator (in a programming language) a construct that controls iteration over a range of values or a collection of objects.

layer a subsystem that provides multiple services, all of which are at the same level of abstraction. A layer can be built on subsystems at a lower level of abstraction. (Contrast with *partition*.)

leaf class a class with no subclasses. It must be a concrete class. In Java, this is the same as a final class.

library a collection of classes that are reusable across applications.

life cycle (see *development life cycle*).

lifeline the period of time during which an object exists.

link a physical or conceptual connection among objects. A link is an instance of an association. The UML notation is a line between objects that may consist of several line segments.

lock a logical object associated with some defined subset of a resource that gives the lock holder the right to access the resource directly.

member (in C++) data or methods of a class.

metaclass a class describing other classes.

metadata data that describes other data.

method the implementation of an operation for a class. The UML notation lists methods in the third compartment of the class box. (Contrast with *operation*.)

method caching (in a programming language) an optimization of method searching in which the address of a method is found the first time an operation is applied to an object of a class and then stored in a table attached to the class.

method resolution (in a programming language) the process of matching an operation on an object to the method appropriate to the object's class.

methodology (in software engineering) a process for the organized production of software using a collection of predefined techniques and notational conventions.

model an abstraction of some aspect of a problem. We express models with various kinds of diagrams.

modularity the organization of a system into groups of closely related objects.

multiple inheritance a type of inheritance that permits a class to have more than one superclass and to inherit features from all ancestors. (Contrast with *single inheritance*.)

multiplicity (of an association end) the number of instances of one class that may relate to a single instance of an associated class. Multiplicity is a constraint on the size of a collection. The UML notation is a numeric interval or the special symbol "*" denoting "many" (zero or more). (Contrast with *cardinality*.)

multiplicity (of an attribute) the possible number of values for each instantiation of an attribute. The most common specifications ar a mandatory single value [1], an optional single value [0..1], and many [*].

namespace (in C++) a means for providing a semantic scope for symbols to alleviate name conflicts.

***n*-ary association** an association involving three or more association ends. The UML symbol is a diamond with lines connecting to the related classes. If the association has a name, it is written in italics next to the diamond.

navigability the direction of traversal of a binary association in an implementation. The possibilities are none, either direction, or both directions. The UML shows navigability with an arrowhead on the association end attached to the target class.

navigation a traversal of associations and generalizations in a class model to go from source objects to target objects.

nested state a state that shares behavior from its composite state and adds additional behavior of its own. (Contrast with *composite state*.)

new (in C++ and Java) the operator to create objects.

normal form (in a relational database) a guideline for relational database design that increases data consistency.

***n*-tier architecture** an extension of the three-tier architecture, permitting any number of application layers. (Contrast with *three-tier architecture*.)

null a special value denoting that an attribute value is unknown or not applicable.

object a concept, abstraction, or thing that can be individually identified and has meaning for an application. An object is an instance of a class.

Object Constraint Language (OCL) a language for defining constraints that is part of the UML. You can also use the OCL to navigate class models.

object diagram a graphical representation that shows individual objects and their relationships. (Contrast with *class diagram*.)

object identity (in a relational database) the use of an artificial number to identify each record in a table. (Contrast with *value-based identity*.)

Object Management Group (OMG) a standards forum that is the owner of the UML.

object-orientation (OO) a strategy for organizing systems as collections of interacting objects that combine data and behavior.

OCL (acronym) *Object Constraint Language*.

OMG (acronym) *Object Management Group*.

OO (acronym) *object-oriented*.

OO database a database that is perceived as objects that mix data and behavior. (Contrast with relational database.)

OO-DBMS a DBMS that provides persistent objects in addition to the transient objects provided by OO programming languages. (Contrast with relational DBMS.)

OO development a software development technique that uses objects as a basis for the construction of software.

OO programming language a language that supports objects (combining identity, data, and operations), method resolution, and inheritance.

operation a function or procedure that may be applied to or by objects in a class. (Contrast with *method.*)

ordered a sorted collection of elements with no duplicates allowed. The UML notation is to annotate an association end with *{ordered}*. (Contrast with *sequence.*)

origin class the topmost class in an inheritance hierarchy that defines a feature.

overloading (in a programming language) binding the same name to multiple methods whose signatures differ in number or types of arguments. A call to an overloaded operation is resolved at compile time based on the types of the calling arguments.

override to define a method for an operation that replaces an inherited method for the same operation.

package (class modeling construct) a group of elements (classes, associations, generalizations, and lesser packages) with a common theme. The UML notation is a box with a tab; the package name is placed in the box.

package (referring to visibility) accessible by methods of classes in the same package as the containing class.

partition a subsystem that provides a particular kind of service in parallel to other subsystems. A partition may itself be built from lower-level subsystems. (Contrast with *layer.*)

passive object an object that does not have its own thread of control. (Contrast with *active object.*)

pattern a parameterized excerpt of a model that is important and recurring. It is mathematical in nature and worthy of reuse across multiple applications.

peer two or more subsystems that are mutually interdependent for services. (Contrast with *client* and *server.*)

persistent object an object that is stored in a database and can span multiple application executions. (Contrast with *transient object.*)

policy method (style) a method that makes context-dependent decisions but calls on implementation methods for detailed computations. (Contrast with *implementation method.*)

polymorphism takes on many forms; the property that an operation may behave differently on different classes.

primary key (in a relational database) a candidate key that is preferentially used to access the records in a table. A table can have at most one primary key; normally each table should have a primary key.

private (referring to visibility) accessible by methods of the containing class only.

procedure-driven control an approach in which control resides within the program code. Procedures request external input and then wait for it; when input arrives, control resumes within the procedure that made the call. The location of the program counter and the stack of procedure calls and local variables define the system state. (Contrast with *event-driven control.*)

programming-in-the-large the creation of large, complex programs with teams of programmers.

protected (referring to C++ visibility) accessible by methods of the containing class and any of its descendant classes.

protected (referring to Java visibility) accessible by methods of the containing class, any of its descendant classes, and classes in the same package as the containing class.

public (referring to visibility) accessible by methods of any class.

qualified association an association in which one or more attributes (called qualifiers) disambiguate the objects for a "many" association end. The UML notation is a small box on the end of the association line near the source class.

qualifier an attribute that distinguishes among the objects at a "many" association end. The UML notation is to place a qualifier in a small box on the end of the association line near the source class.

race condition a situation in which the order of receiving concurrent signals can affect the final state of an object.

rapid prototyping the quick development of a portion of a system for experimentation and evaluation. Prototyping is proof of concept and often throwaway by intent. (Contrast with *iterative development* and *waterfall development.*)

real-time system (architectural style) an interactive system for which time constraints on actions are particularly tight or in which the slightest timing failure cannot be tolerated.

refactoring changes to the internal structure of software to improve its design without altering its external functionality.

reference an attribute value in one object that refers to another object.

reflection a property of a system such that it can examine its own structure dynamically and reason about its own state.

region a portion of a state diagram.

reification the promotion of something that is not an object into an object.

relational database a database in which the data are perceived as tables. (Contrast with OO database.)

relational DBMS a DBMS that manages tables of data and associated structures that increase the functionality and performance of tables. (Contrast with OO-DBMS.)

responsibility something that an object knows or something it must do. A responsibility is not a precise concept; it is meant to get the thought process going.

reverse engineering the process of examining implementation artifacts and inferring the underlying logical intent. (Contrast with *forward engineering*.)

robust a property of software such that it does not fail catastrophically when some of its design assumptions are violated.

scenario a sequence of events that occur during one particular execution of a system.

schema the structure of the data in a database.

scope an indication if a feature applies to an object or a class. An underline distinguishes features with class scope (static) from those with object scope.

sequence a sorted collection of elements with duplicates allowed. The UML notation is to annotate an association end with *{sequence}*. (Contrast with *ordered*.)

sequence diagram a diagram that shows the participants in an interaction and the sequence of messages among them.

server a subsystem that provides a service to other subsystems. (Contrast with *client*.)

service a group of related functions or operations that share some common purpose.

shopping-list operation an operation that is meaningful in its own right. Bertrand Meyer coined the term *shopping list* because discovery of such an operation is driven by the intrinsic meaning of a class and not by the needs of a particular application. Sometimes the real-world behavior of classes suggests operations.

signal an explicit one-way transmission of information from one object to another. The UML notation is the keyword «*signal*» above the signal class name in the top section of a box. The second section lists the signal attributes.

signal event the event of sending or receiving a signal.

signature the number and types of the arguments for an operation and the type of its result.

single inheritance a type of inheritance in which a class may have only a single superclass. (Contrast with *multiple inheritance*.)

software engineering a systematic, disciplined, and quantifiable approach to the development, operation, and maintenance of software.

specialization the refinement of a class into variants. Specialization has the same meaning as generalization but takes a top-down perspective. In contrast, generalization takes a bottom-up perspective. (Contrast with *generalization*.)

SQL the standard language for interacting with a relational database.

state an abstraction of the values and links of an object. The UML notation is a rounded box containing an optional state name. (Contrast with *event*.)

state diagram a graph whose nodes are states and whose directed arcs are transitions between states.

state model a description of those aspects of a system concerned with time and the sequencing of operations. The state model consists of multiple state diagrams, one state diagram for each class with important temporal behavior.

static (in C++ and Java) data and methods that belong not to an instance of a class, but to the class itself.

stored procedure (in a relational database) a method that is stored in a database.

strong typing (in a programming language) a requirement that the type of each variable must be declared. (Contrast with *weak typing*.)

subclass a class that adds specific attributes, operations, state diagrams, and associations for a generalization. (Contrast with *superclass*.)

submachine a state diagram that may be invoked as part of another state diagram. The UML notation for invoking a submachine is to list a local state name followed by a colon and the submachine name.

substate a state that expresses an aspect of concurrent behavior for a parent state.

subsystem a major piece of a system that is organized around some coherent theme. A system may be divided into subsystems using either *partitions* or *layers*.

superclass the class that holds common attributes, operations, state diagrams, and associations for a generalization. (Contrast with *subclass*.)

swimlane a column in an activity diagram that shows the person or organization who performs activities; a partition.

system an application that is the subject of interest.

system architecture (see *architecture*).

system boundary the outline of the scope of a system determining what the system includes and what the system omits.

system conception the development stage that deals with the genesis of an application.

system design the development stage during which the developer devises the architecture and establishes general design policies.

system testing the checking of an entire application. (Contrast with *unit testing* and *integration testing*.)

table (in a relational database) an organization of data that has a specific number of columns and an arbitrary number of rows.

ternary association an association among three association ends. The UML symbol is a diamond with lines connecting to the related classes. If the association has a name, it is written in italics next to the diamond.

this (in C++ and Java) the default name of the target object of a method.

thread of control a single path of execution through a program, a state model, or some other representation of control flow.

three-tier architecture an approach that separates data management, application functionality, and the user interface. The data management layer holds the database schema and data. The application layer holds the methods that embody the application logic. The user-interface layer manages the forms and reports that are presented to the user. (Contrast with *n-tier architecture*.)

time event an event caused by the occurrence of an absolute time or the elapse of a time interval. The UML notation for an absolute time is the keyword *when* followed by a parenthesized expression involving time. The notation for a time interval is the keyword *after* followed by a parenthesized expression that evaluates to a time duration.

transaction manager (architectural style) a database system whose main function is to store and access information.

transient object an object that exists only in memory and disappears when an application terminates execution. Thus a transient object is an ordinary programming object. (Contrast with *persistent object*.)

transition an instantaneous change from one state to another. The UML notation is a line (with possibly multiple line segments) from the origin state to the target state; an arrowhead points to the target state.

transitive closure (from graph theory) the set of nodes that are reachable by some sequence of edges.

UML (acronym, trademark of the OMG) *Unified Modeling Language*.

Unified Modeling Language (trademark of the OMG) a comprehensive suite of object-oriented models intended to represent software and other kinds of applications fully. The UML has been developed under the auspices of the OMG.

UML1 informal term for the first release of the UML approved in 1997.

UML2 informal term for the second release of the UML approved in 2004. This book is based on UML2.

unit testing testing by developers of their own code for classes and methods. (Contrast with *integration testing* and *system testing*.)

use case a coherent piece of functionality that a system can provide by interacting with actors. The UML notation is an ellipse with the use case name inside.

use case diagram a graphical notation for summarizing actors and use cases.

user interface an object or group of objects that provides the user of a system with a coherent way to access its domain objects, commands, and application options.

value a piece of data. A value is an instance of an attribute.

value-based identity (in a relational database) the use of some combination of real-world attributes to identify each record in a table. (Contrast with *existence-based identity*.)

view (in a relational database) a table that a relational DBMS dynamically computes.

virtual (in C++) an operation that can be overridden by a descendant class.

visibility the ability of a method to reference a feature from another class. The UML denotes visibility with the following prefixes. The possibilities are *public* ("+"), *protected* ("#"), *private* ("-"), and *package* ("~").

waterfall development the development life cycle of performing the software development stages in a rigid linear sequence with no backtracking. (Contrast with *iterative development* and *rapid prototyping*.)

weak typing (in a programming language) the lack of a requirement that the type of each variable be declared. (Contrast with *strong typing*.)

wrapper a collection of interfaces that allow access into a system.

Answers to Selected Exercises

We selected answers with the following criteria: exercises with short answers in the core chapters, exercises that extend chapters by introducing new material, key exercises in a series of questions, answers that clarify subtle or difficult points, and prototypes for real problems. Most exercises have multiple correct answers, so use our answers only as a guide and not as a test of correctness.

1.5b. Criminal investigations can use combinations of photographs, fingerprinting, blood-typing, DNA analysis, and dental records to identify people, living and/or deceased, who are involved in, or the subject of, a criminal investigation.

d. Telephone numbers are adequate for identifying almost any telephone in the world. In general a telephone number consists of a country code plus a province, city, or area code, plus a local number plus an optional extension number. Businesses may have their own telephone systems with other conventions. Depending on the relative location of the telephone that you are calling, parts of the number may be implied and can be left out, but extra access digits may be required to call outside the local region.

In North America most local calls require 7 digits. Long distance calls in North America use an access digit (0 or 1) + area code (3 digits) + local number (7 digits). Dialing Paris requires an access code (011) + country code (33) + city code (1) + local number (8 digits). The access code is not part of the identifier.

g. One way that employees are given restricted, after-hours access to a company is through the use of a special, electronically readable card. Of course, if an employee loses a card and does not report it, someone who finds it could use it for unauthorized entry. Other approaches include a picture ID which requires inspection by a guard, fingerprint readers, and voice recognition.

1.8a. Electron microscopes, eyeglasses, telescopes, bomb sights, and binoculars are all devices that enhance vision in some way. With the exception of the scanning electron microscope, all these devices work by reflecting or refracting light. Eyeglasses and binoculars are designed for use with two eyes; the rest of the objects on the list are designed for use with one eye. Telescopes, bomb sights, and binoculars are used to view things far away. A microscope is used to magnify something that is very small. Eyeglasses may enlarge or reduce, depending on whether the prescription is for a nearsighted or a farsighted person. Some other classes that could be included in this list are optical microscopes, cameras, and magnifying glasses.

b. Pipes, check valves, faucets, filters, and pressure gauges are all plumbing supplies with certain temperature and pressure ratings. Compatibility with various types of fluids is also a consideration. Check valves and faucets may be used to control flow. With the exception of the pressure gauge, all of the items listed have two ends and have a pressure-flow characteristic for a given fluid. All of the items are passive. Some other classes include pumps, tanks, and connectors.

2.3a. For a transatlantic cable, resistance to salt water is the main consideration. The cable must lie unmaintained at the bottom of the ocean for a long time. Interaction of ocean life with the cable and the effect of pressure and salinity on cable life must be considered. The ratio of strength/weight is important to avoid breakage while the cable is being installed. Cost is an important economic factor. Electrical parameters are important for power consumption and signal distortion.

c. Weight is very important for wire that is to be used in the electrical system of an airplane, because it affects the total weight of the plane. Toughness of the insulation is important to resist chafing due to vibration. Resistance of the insulation to fire is also important to avoid starting or feeding electrical fires in flight.

3.2 Figure A3.2 shows a class diagram for polygons and points. The smallest number of points required to construct a polygon is three.

The multiplicity of the association depends on how points are identified. If a point is identified by its location, then points are shared and the association is many-to-many. On the other hand, if each point belongs to exactly one polygon, then several points may have the same coordinates. The next answer clarifies this distinction.

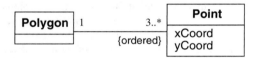

Figure A3.2 Class diagram for polygon and points

3.3a. Figure A3.3 shows objects and links for two triangles with a common side in which a point belongs to exactly one polygon.

b. Figure A3.4 shows objects and links for two triangles with a common side in which points may be shared.

3.20 Graphs occur in many applications. Several variations of the model are possible, depending on your viewpoint. Figure A3.23 accurately represents undirected graphs as described in the exercise. Although not quite as accurate, your answer could omit the class *UndirectedGraph*.

We have found it useful for some graph related queries to elevate the association between vertices and edges to the status of a class as Figure A3.24 shows.

3.23 Figure A3.27 shows a class diagram describing directed graphs. The distinction between the two ends of an edge is accomplished with a qualified association. Values of the qualifier end are *from* and *to*.

Figure A3.28 shows another representation of directed graphs. The distinction between the two ends of an edge is accomplished with separate associations.

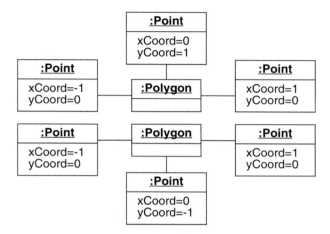

Figure A3.3 Object diagram where each point belongs to exactly one polygon

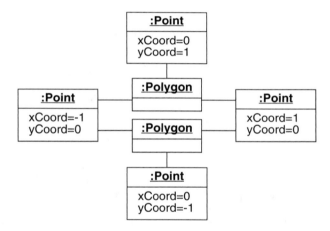

Figure A3.4 Object diagram where each point can belong to multiple polygons

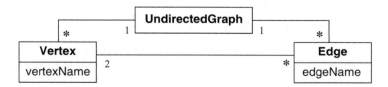

Figure A3.23 Class diagram for undirected graphs

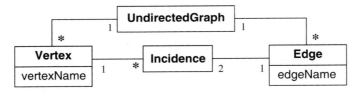

Figure A3.24 Class diagram for undirected graphs in which the incidence between vertices and edges is treated as a class

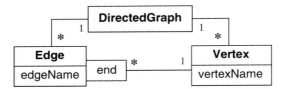

Figure A3.27 Class diagram for directed graphs using a qualified association

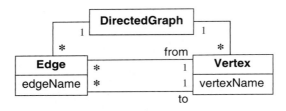

Figure A3.28 Class diagram for directed graphs using two associations

The advantage of the qualified association is that only one association must be queried to find one or both vertices that a given edge is connected to. If the qualifier is not specified, both vertices can be found. By specifying *from* or *to* for the *end* qualifier, you can find the vertex connected to an edge at the given *end*.

The advantage of using two separate associations is that you eliminate the need to manage enumerated values for the qualifier *end*.

3.25   Figure A3.30 shows a class diagram for car loans in which pointers are replaced with associations.

In this form, the arguably artificial restriction that a person have no more than three employers has been eliminated. Note that in this model an owner can own several cars. A car can have several loans against it. Banks loan money to persons, companies, and other banks.

3.28   Figure A3.34 shows a class diagram for the dining philosophers problem. The one-to-one associations describe the relative locations of philosophers and forks. The *InUse* association describes who is using forks. Other representations are possible, depending on your viewpoint. An object diagram may help you better understand this problem.

3.31   The following OCL expression computes the set of airlines that a person flew in a given year.

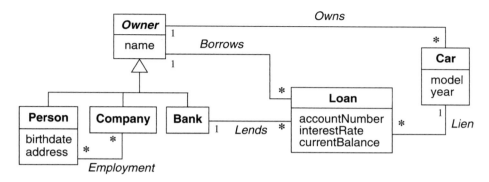

Figure A3.30 Proper class diagram for car loans

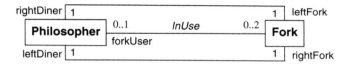

Figure A3.34 Class diagram for the dining philosopher problem

```
aPassenger.Flight->SELECT(getYear(date)=aGivenYear).
Airline.name->asSet
```
The OCL *asSet* operator eliminates redundant copies of the same airline.

3.34 Figure E3.13 (a) states that a subscription has derived identity. Figure E3.13 (b) gives subscriptions more prominence and promotes subscription to a class.

The (b) model is a better model. Most copies of magazines have subscription codes on their mailing labels; this could be stored as an attribute. The subscription code is intended to identify subscriptions; subscriptions are not identified by the combination of a person and a magazine, so we should promote *Subscription* to a class. Furthermore, a person might have multiple subscriptions to a magazine; only the (b) model can readily accommodate this.

4.2 The class diagram in Figure A4.2 generalizes the classes *Selection*, *Buffer*, and *Sheet* into the superclass *Collection*. This is a desirable revision. The generalization promotes code reuse, because many operations apply equally well to the subclasses. Six aggregation relationships in the original diagram, which shared similar characteristics, have been reduced to two. Finally, the structure of the diagram now captures the constraint that each *Box* and *Line* should belong to exactly one *Buffer*, *Selection*, or *Sheet*.

4.4 Figure A4.3 shows a class diagram for a graphical document editor. The requirement that a *Group* contain 2 or more *DrawingObjects* is expressed as a multiplicity of 2..* on *DrawingObject* in its aggregation with *Group*. The fact that a *DrawingObject* need not be in a *Group* is expressed by the zero-one multiplicity.

It is possible to revise this diagram to make a *Circle* a special case of an *Ellipse* and to make a *Square* a special case of a *Rectangle*.

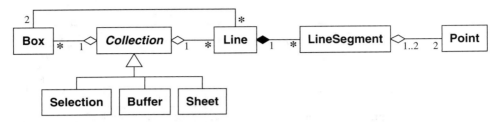

Figure A4.2 Generalization of the classes *Selection*, *Buffer*, and *Sheet* into the class *Collection*

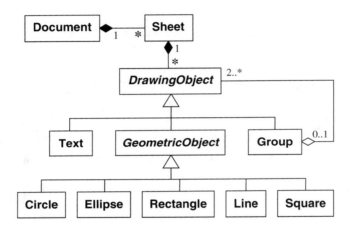

Figure A4.3 Class diagram for a graphical document editor that supports grouping

We presume that a *DrawingObject* belongs to a *Sheet* and has a coincident lifetime with it. Similarly, we presume that a *Sheet* belongs to one *Document* for its lifetime. Hence both are composition relationships.

4.5 Figure A4.4 shows a class diagram with several classes of electrical machines. We have included attributes that were not requested.

4.6 Figure A4.5 converts the overlapping combination of classes into a class of its own to eliminate multiple inheritance.

4.7 Figure A4.6 is a metamodel of the following UML concepts: class, attribute, association, association end, multiplicity, class name, and attribute name.

4.10 The class diagram in Figure E4.3 does support multiple inheritance. A class may have multiple generalization roles of subclass participating in a variety of generalizations.

4.11 To find the superclass of a generalization using Figure E4.3, first query the association between *Generalization* and *GeneralizationRole* to get a set of all roles of the given instance of *Generalization*. Then sequentially search this set of instances of *GeneralizationRole* to find the one with *roleType* equal to superclass. (Hopefully only one instance will be found with *role-*

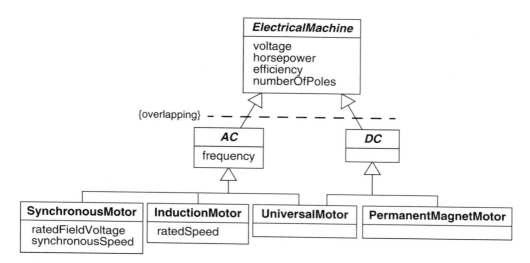

Figure A4.4 Partial taxonomy for electrical machines

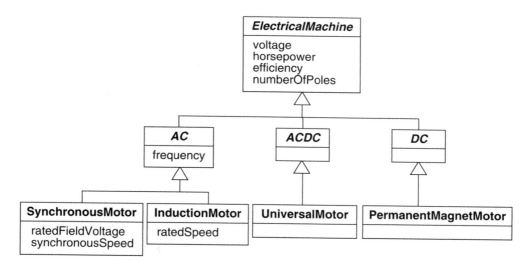

Figure A4.5 Elimination of multiple inheritance

Type equal to superclass, which is a constraint that the model does not enforce.) Finally, scan the association between *GeneralizationRole* and *Class* to get the superclass.

Figure A4.9 shows one possible revision which simplifies superclass lookup. To find the superclass of a generalization, first query the association between *Generalization* and *SuperclassRole*. Then query the association between *SuperclassRole* and *Class* to find the corresponding instance of *Class*.

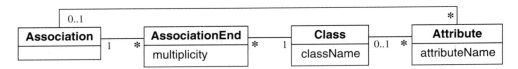

Figure A4.6 Metamodel for some UML concepts

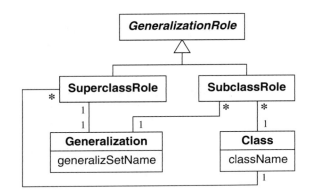

Figure A4.9 Metamodel of generalizations with separate subclass and superclass roles

Figure A4.10 shows another metamodel of generalization that supports multiple inheritance. To find the superclass of a generalization using this metamodel, simply query the *Superclass* association.

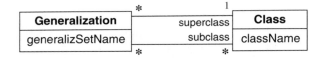

Figure A4.10 Simplified metamodel of generalization relationships

We do not imply that the metamodel in Figure A4.10 is the best model of generalization, only that it simplifies the query given in the exercise. The choice of which model is best depends on the purpose of the metamodel.

The following query finds the superclass, given a generalization for Figure E4.3.

■ aGeneralization.GeneralizationRole->SELECT(roleType='superclass').Class

The following query finds the superclass, given a generalization for Figure A4.9.

■ aGeneralization.SuperclassRole.Class

The following query finds the superclass, given a generalization for Figure A4.10.

■ aGeneralization.superclass

4.16 The simple class model in Figure A4.14 is sufficient for describing the given recipe data.

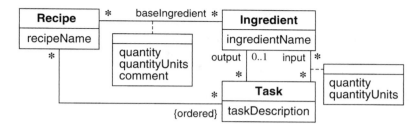

Figure A4.14 A simple class model for recipes

4.17   Figure A4.15 shows our initial solution to the exercise—merely adding an association that binds original ingredients to substitute ingredients. This model has two flaws.

   The first problem is that the model awkwardly handles interchangeable ingredients. For example, in some recipes you can freely substitute butter, margarine, and shortening for each other. Figure A4.15 would require that we store each possible pair of ingredients. Thus we would have the following combinations of original and substitute ingredients—(butter, margarine), (butter, shortening), (margarine, butter), (margarine, shortening), (shortening, butter), and (shortening, margarine).

   The second problem is that the substitutability of ingredients does not always hold, but can depend on the particular recipe.

   Figure A4.16 shows a better class model that remedies both flaws.

Initial inferior solution

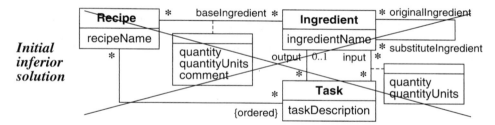

Figure A4.15 Initial class model for recipes with alternate ingredients

Correct solution

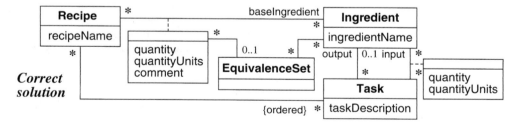

Figure A4.16 Correct class model for recipes with alternate ingredients

5.2   In Figure A5.2 the event *A* refers to pressing the *A* button. In this diagram, releasing the button
is unimportant and is not shown (although you must obviously release the button before you
can press it again). Note that a new button event cannot be generated while any button is
pressed. You can consider this a constraint on the input events themselves and need not show
it in the state diagram (although it would not be wrong to do so).

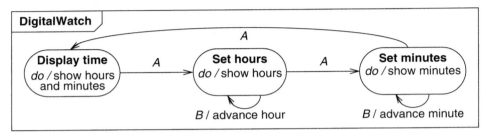

Figure A5.2 State diagram for a simple digital watch

5.6   Figure A5.6 shows the completed state diagram for the motor control.

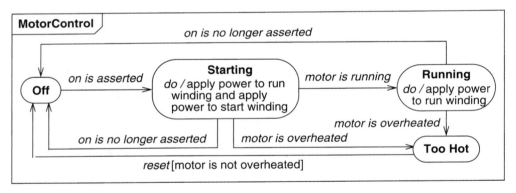

Figure A5.6 State diagram for a motor control

5.11   Figure A5.11 shows the state diagram. Note that even simple state diagrams can lead to complex behavior. A change event occurs whenever the candle is taken out of its holder or whenever it is put back. The condition at north is satisfied whenever the bookcase is behind the wall.
The condition at north, east, south, or west is satisfied whenever the bookcase is facing front,
back, or to the side.

     When you first discovered the bookcase, it was in the *Stopped* state pointing south. When
your friend removed the candle, a change event drove the bookcase into the *Rotating* state.
When the bookcase was pointing north, the condition at north put the bookcase back into the
Stopped state. When your friend reinserted the candle, another change event put the bookcase
into the *Rotating* state until it again pointed north. Pulling the candle out generated another
change event and would have caused the bookcase to rotate a full turn if you had not blocked
it with your body. Forcing the bookcase back is outside the scope of the control and does not
have to be explained.

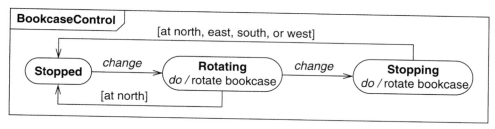

Figure A5.11 State diagram for bookcase control

When you put the candle back again, another change event was generated, putting the bookcase into the *Rotating* state once again. Taking the candle back out resulted in yet another change event, putting the bookcase into the *Stopping* state. After 1/4 turn, the condition at north, east, south or west was satisfied, putting the bookcase into the *Stopped* state.

What you should have done at first to gain entry was to take the candle out and quickly put it back before the bookcase completed 1/4 turn.

6.1 The headlight (Figure A6.1) and wheels (Figure A6.2) each have their own state diagram. Note that the stationary state for a wheel includes several substates.

We have shown default initial states for the headlight and wheels. The actual initial state of the wheels may be arbitrary and could be any one of the power off states. The system operates in a loop and does not depend on the initial state, so you need not specify it. Many hardware systems have indeterminate initial states.

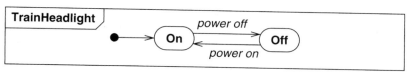

Figure A6.1 State diagram for a toy train headlight

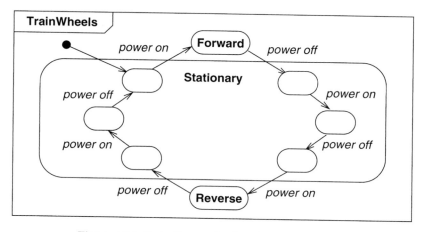

Figure A6.2 State diagram for the wheels of a toy train

6.3   Figure A6.4 adds *Motor On* to capture the commonality of the starting and running state. We
have shown a transition from the *Off* state to the *Starting* state. We could instead have shown
a transition from *Off* to *Motor On* and made *Starting* the initial state of *Motor On*. Note that the
activity *apply power to run winding* has been factored out of both starting and running states.

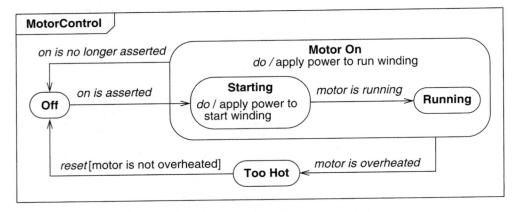

Figure A6.4 State diagram for a motor control using nested states

6.4   Figure A6.5 revises the motor state diagram. Note that a transition from *Off* to either *Forward*
or *Reverse* also causes an implicit transition to *Starting*, the default initial state of the lower
concurrent subdiagram. An off request causes a transition out of both concurrent subdiagrams
back to state *Off*.

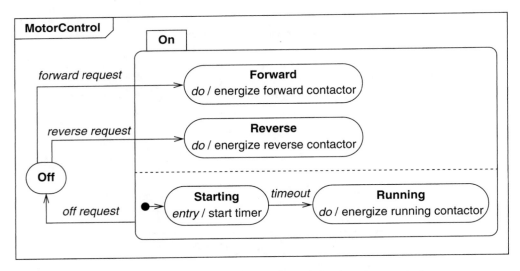

Figure A6.5 Revised state diagram for an induction motor control

7.1   Here are answers for a physical bookstore.

   a.   Some actors are:

- **Customer**. A person who initiates the purchase of an item.
- **Cashier**. An employee who is authorized to check out purchases at a cash register.
- **Payment verifier**. The remote system that approves use of a credit or debit card.

   b.   Some use cases are:

- **Purchase items**. A customer brings one or more items to the checkout register and pays for the items.
- **Return items**. The customer brings back items that were previously purchased and gets a refund.

   c.   Figure A7.1 shows a use case diagram.

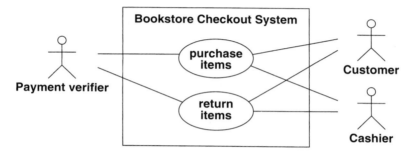

Figure A7.1 Use case diagram for a physical bookstore checkout system

   d.   Here is a normal scenario for each use case. There are many possible answers.

- **Purchase items**.
Customer brings items to the counter.
Cashier scans each customer item.
Cashier totals order, including tax.
Cashier requests form of payment.
Customer gives a credit card.
Cashier scans card.
Verifier reports that credit card payment is acceptable.
Customer signs credit card slip.

- **Return items**.
Customer brings purchased item to the counter.
Customer has receipt from earlier purchase.
Cashier notes that payment was in cash.
Cashier accepts items and gives customer a cash refund.

   e.   Here is an exception scenario for each use case. There are many possible answers.

- **Purchase items**.
Customer brings items to the counter.
Cashier scans each customer item.
An item misscans and cashier goes to item display to get the item price.

■ **Return items**.
Customer brings purchased item to the counter.
Customer has no receipt from earlier purchase.
Customer is given a credit slip, but no refund.

   f. Figure A7.2 shows a sequence diagram for the first scenario in (d). Figure A7.3 shows a sequence diagram for the second scenario in (d).

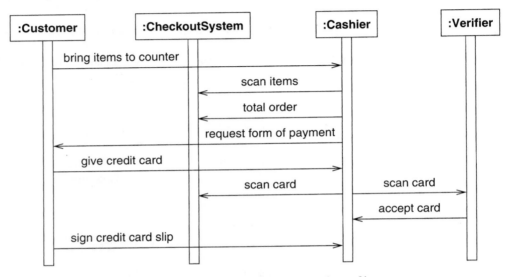

Figure A7.2 Sequence diagram for a purchase of items

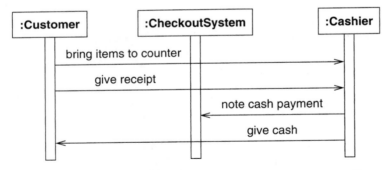

Figure A7.3 Sequence diagram for a return of items

  7.8   Figure A7.12 shows an activity diagram for computing a restaurant bill.

  8.1   Here are answers for an electronic gasoline pump.

    a. Figure A8.1 shows a use case diagram.

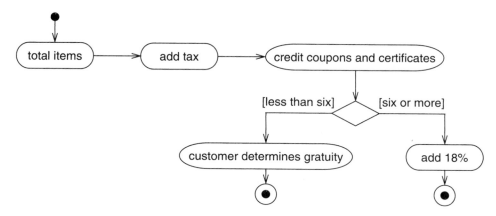

Figure A7.12 Activity diagram for computing a restaurant bill

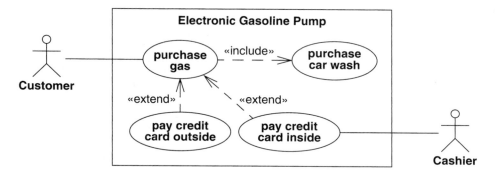

Figure A8.1 Use case diagram for an electronic gasoline pump

b. There are two actors:

- ■ **Customer**. A person who initiates the purchase of gas.

- ■ **Cashier**. A person who handles manual credit card payments and monitors the sale of gas.

c. There are four use cases:

- ■ **Purchase gas**. Obtain gas from the electronic gas pump and pay for it with cash.

- ■ **Purchase car wash**. A customer also decides to purchase a car wash and pays for it with cash.

- ■ **Pay credit card outside**. Instead of cash, pay for the gas and optional car wash with a credit card that is directly handled by the gas system.

- ■ **Pay credit card inside**. Instead of cash, pay for the gas and optional car wash with a credit card that is manually handled by the cashier.

8.6 Figure A8.6 computes the contents of a portfolio of stocks.

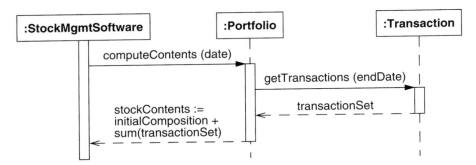

Figure A8.6 Sequence diagram for computing the contents of a portfolio of stocks

11.1 Here is elaboration for an antilock braking system for an automobile.

   a. An antilock braking system could target the mass market. If the antilock system was inexpensive and safer than current technology, it could be government mandated and installed on all cars. (Further study would be needed to determine what price is "inexpensive" and what would be a "significant" safety improvement.)

      There would be several stakeholders. Auto customers would expect improved safety and minimal detriment to drivability. Auto manufacturers would want to minimize the cost and quantify the benefit so they could tout the technology in their advertising. The government would be looking for a statistical safety improvement without compromising fuel efficiency.

      If the new system was inexpensive, worked well, and did not hurt drivability, all car owners could be potential customers. An expensive antilock system could be a premium option on high-end cars.

   b. Desirable features would include: effective prevention of brake locking, ability to detect excessive brake wear, and acquisition of data to facilitate auto maintenance. Some undesirable features would be: reduced fuel efficiency, reduced drivability, and greater maintenance complexity.

   c. An antilock system must work with the brakes, steering, and automotive electronics.

   d. There would be a risk that an antilock braking system could fail, leading to an accident and a lawsuit. Also it might be difficult to understand fully how the antilock system would interact with the brakes.

12.9 The following tentative classes should be eliminated.

- **Redundant classes.** *Child, Contestant, Individual, Person, Registrant* (all are redundant with *Competitor*).

- **Vague or irrelevant classes.** *Back, Card, Conclusion, Corner, IndividualPrize, Leg, Pool, Prize, TeamPrize, Try, WaterBallet.*

- **Attributes.** *address, age, averageScore, childName, date, difficultyFactor, netScore, rawScore, score, teamName.*

- **Implementation constructs.** *fileOfTeamMemberData, listOfScheduledMeets, group, number.*

- **Derived class.** *ageCategory* is readily computed from a competitor's age.

- **Operations.** *computeAverage, register.*

■ **Out of scope**. *routine*.

After eliminating improper classes we are left with *Competitor, Event, Figure, Judge, League, Meet, Scorekeeper, Season, Station, Team,* and *Trial*.

12.12 We use a combination of the OCL and pseudocode to express our queries.

[Some of our answers to these problems traverse a series of links. Chapter 15 explains that each class should have limited knowledge of a class model and that operations for a class should not traverse associations that are not directly connected to it. We have violated this principle here to simplify our answers. A more robust answer would define intermediate operations to avoid these lengthy traversals.]

a. Find all the members of a given team.

```
Team::retrieveTeamMembers ()
returns set of competitors
    return self.competitor;
```

c. Find the net score of a competitor for a given figure at a given meet. There are several ways to answer this question, one of which is listed below.

```
Competitor::findNetScore (figure, meet)
returns netScore
    event:= meet.event intersect figure.event;
        /* the above code should return exactly one   */
        /* event (otherwise there is an implementation */
        /* error). This is a constraint implicit in the */
        /* problem statement that is not expressed in   */
        /* the class model.                             */
    trial := event.trial intersect self.trial;
    if trial == NIL then return ERROR
    else return trial.netScore;
    end if
```

e. Find the average score of a competitor over all figures in a given meet.

```
Competitor::findAverage (meet) returns averageScore
    trials:= meet.event.trial intersect
        self.trial;
    if trials == NIL then return ERROR
    else
        compute average as in answer (d)
            return average;
    end if
```

g. Find the set of all individuals who competed in any events in a given season.

```
Season::findCompetitorsForAnyEvent ()
returns set of competitors
    return self.meet.event.trial.competitor;
```

12.14 The revised diagrams are shown in Figure A12.7–Figure A12.10. Figure A12.7 is a better model than the ternary because dateTime is really an attribute. Figure A12.8 is also better than the ternary because *UniversityClass* is likely to be a class with attributes, operations, and other relationships. The third ternary is not atomic because the combination of a *Seat* and a *Concert* determine the *Person*. The fourth ternary also is not atomic; this one can be restated as two binary associations.

13.14 The application manages data for competitive meets in a swimming league. The system stores swimming scores that judges award and computes various summary statistics.

13.15 Actors are competitor, scorekeeper, judge, and team.

Figure A12.7 Class diagram for appointments

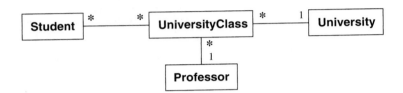

Figure A12.8 Class diagram for university classes

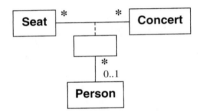

Figure A12.9 Class diagram for reservations

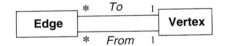

Figure A12.10 Class diagram for directed graphs

13.16 Here are definitions for the use cases. Figure A13.12 shows a use case diagram.

- **Register child**. Add a new child to the scoring system and record the name, age, address, and team name. Assign the child a number.

- **Schedule meet**. Assign competitors to figures and determine their starting times. Assign scorekeepers and judges to stations.

- **Schedule season**. Determine the meets that comprise a season. For each meet, determine the date, the figures that will be performed, and the competing teams.

- **Score figure**. A scorekeeper observes a competitor's performance of a figure and assigns what he/she considers to be an appropriate raw score.

- **Judge figure**. A judge receives the scorekeepers' raw scores for a competitor's performance of a figure and determines the net score.

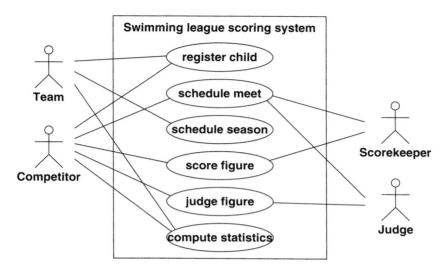

Figure A13.12 Use case diagram for the swimming league scoring system

- **Compute statistics**. The system computes relevant summary information, such as top individual score for a figure and total team score for a meet.

13.21 Figure A13.14 shows a partial shopping list of operations.

14.6 Figure A14.1 shows one possible partitioning.

14.7 A single program provides faster detection and correction of errors and eliminates the need to implement an interface between two programs. With a single program, any errors that the system detects in the process of converting the class diagram to a database schema can be quickly communicated to the user for correction. Also, the editing and the conversion portions of the program can share the same data, eliminating the need for an interface such as a file to transfer the class diagram from one program to another.

Splitting the functionality into two programs reduces memory requirements and decouples program development. The total memory requirement of a single program would be approximately equal to the sum of the requirements of two separate programs. Since both programs are likely to use a great deal of memory, performance problems could arise if they were combined. Using two separate programs also simplifies program development. The two programs can be developed independently, so that changes made in one are less likely to impact the other. Also, two programs are easier to debug than one monolithic program. If the interface between the two programs is well defined, problems in the overall system can be quickly identified within one program or the other.

Another advantage of splitting the system into two programs is greater flexibility. The editor can be used with other back ends, such as generating language code declarations. The relational database schema generator can be adapted to other graphical front ends.

14.10 Here is an evaluation of each solution.

   a.Do not worry about it at all. Reset all data every time the system is turned on. This is the cheapest, simplest approach. It is relatively easy to program, since all that is needed is an ini-

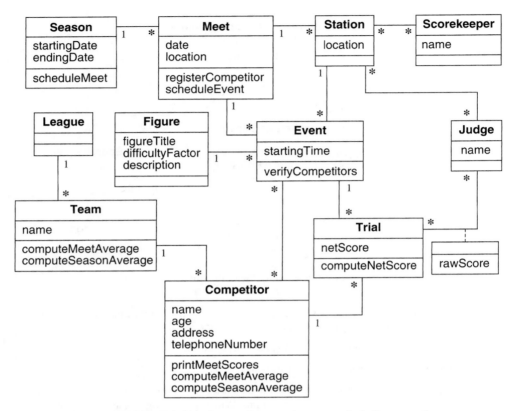

Figure A13.14 Partial class diagram for a scoring system including operations

command processing						
user interface	construct expression				file interface	
line semantics	apply operation	substitute	rationalize	evaluate	save work	load work
line syntax						
operating system						

Figure A14.1 Block diagram for an interactive polynomial symbolic manipulation system

tialization routine on power-up to allow the user to enter parameters. However, this approach cannot be taken for systems that must provide continuous service or that must not lose data during power loss.

c. Keep critical information on a magnetic disk drive. Periodically make full and/or incremental copies on magnetic tape. This approach is moderately expensive and bulky. In the event of a power failure, the system stops running. An operating system is required to cope with the disk and tape drive. An operator is required to manage the tapes, which would preclude applications where unattended operation is required.

e. Use a special memory component. This approach is relatively cheap and is automatic. However, the system cannot run when power is off. Some restrictions may apply, such as a limit on the number of times data can be saved or on the amount of data that can be saved. A program may be required to save important parameters as power is failing.

14.11a. Four-function pocket calculator. Do not worry about permanent data storage at all. All of the other options are too expensive to consider. This type of calculator sells for a few dollars and is typically used to balance checkbooks. Memory requirements are on the order of 10 bytes.

c. System clock for a personal computer. Only a few bytes are required, but the clock must continue to run with the main power off. Battery backup is an inexpensive solution. Clock circuits can be designed that will run for 5 years from a battery.

e. Digital control and thermal protection unit for a motor. On the order of 10 to 100 bytes are needed. This application is sensitive to price. An uninterruptable power supply is too expensive to consider. Tape and disk drives are too fragile for the harsh environment of the application. Use a combination of switches, special memory components, and battery backup. Switches are a good way to enter parameters, since an interface is required anyway. Special memory components can store computed data. A battery can be used to continue operation with power removed but presents a maintenance problem in this application. We would question the last requirement, seeking alternatives such as assuming that the motor is hot when it is first turned on or using a sensor to measure the temperature of the motor.

14.12a. A description of the diagram, ignoring tabs, spaces, and line feeds, is:

```
(DIAGRAM
  (CLASS
    (NAME "Polygon"))
  (CLASS
    (NAME "Point")
    (ATTRIBUTE "x")
    (ATTRIBUTE "y"))
  (ASSOCIATION
    (END (NAME "Polygon") ONE)
    (END (NAME "Point") MANY)))
```

14.13 The hardware approach is fastest, but incurs the cost of the hardware. The software approach is cheapest and most flexible, but may not be fast enough. Use the software approach whenever it is fast enough. General-purpose systems favor the software approach, because of its flexibility. Special-purpose systems can usually integrate the added circuitry with other hardware.

Actually, there is another approach, firmware, that may be used in hardware architectures. Typically, in this approach a hardware controller calculates the CRC under the direction of a microcoded program, which is stored in a permanent memory that is not visible externally. We will count this approach as hardware.

a. Floppy disk controller. Use a hardware approach. Flexibility is not needed, since a floppy disk controller is a special-purpose system. Speed is needed, because of the high data rate.

c. **Memory board in the space shuttle**. Use hardware to check memory. This is an example of a specific application, where the function can probably be integrated with the circuitry in the memory chips. The data rate is very high.

e. **Validation of an account number**. Use a software approach. The data rate is very low. (The system handling the account number is probably running on a general-purpose computer.)

15.6 Figure A15.1 enforces a constraint that is missing in Figure E15.1: Each *BoundingBox* corresponds to exactly one *Ellipse* or *Rectangle*. One measure of the quality of an class model is how well its structure captures constraints.

   We have also shown *BoundingBox* as a derived object, because it could be computable from the parameters of the graphic figure and would not supply additional information.

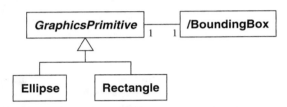

Figure A15.1 Revised class diagram for a bounding box

15.9 The derived association in Figure A15.3 supports direct traversal from *Page* to *Line*. Derived entities have a trade-off—they speed execution of certain queries but incur an update cost to keep the derived data consistent with changes in the base data. The *Page_Line* association is the composition of the *Page_Column* and *Column_Line* associations.

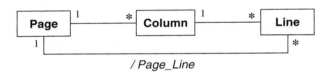

Figure A15.3 A revised newspaper model that can directly determine the page for a line

15.13 The code listed below sketches out a solution. This code lacks internal assertions that would normally be included to check for correctness. For example, error code should be included to handle the case where the end is a subclass and the relationship is not generalization. In code that interacts with users or external data sources, it is usually a good idea to add an error check as an else clause for conditionals that "must be true."

```
traceInheritancePath (class1, class2): Path
{
  path := new Path;
// try to find a path from class1 as descendant of class2
  classx := class1;
  while classx is not null do
      add classx to front of path;
      if classx = class2 then return path;
      classx := classx.getSuperclass();
```

```
// didn't find a path from class1 up to class2
// try to find a path from class2 as descendant of class 1
  path.clear();
  classx := class2;
  while classx is not null do
      add classx to front of path;
      if classx = class1 then return path;
      classx := classx.getSuperclass();
  // the two classes are not directly related
  // return an empty path
  path.clear();
  return path;
}

Class::getSuperclass (): Class
{
  for each end in self.connection do:
      if the end is a Subclass then:
          relationship := end.relationship;
          if relationship is a Generalization then:
              otherEnds := relationship.end;
              for each otherEnd in otherEnds do:
                  if otherEnd is a Superclass then:
                      return otherEnd.class
  return null;
}
```

15.16 Figure A15.5 shows the revised model. Political party membership is not an inherent property of a voter but a changeable association. The revised model better represents voters with no party affiliation and permits changes in party membership. If voters could belong to more than one party, then the multiplicity could easily be changed. *Parties* are instances, not subclasses, of class *PoliticalParty* and need not be explicitly listed in the model; new parties can be added without changing the model and attributes can be attached to parties.

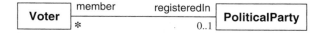

Figure A15.5 A revised model that reifies political party

15.18 The left model in Figure A15.6 shows an index on points using a doubly qualified association. The association is sorted first on the *x* qualifier and then on the *y* qualifier. Because the index is an optimization, it contains redundant information also stored in the *Point* objects.

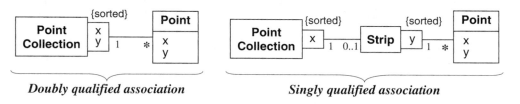

Doubly qualified association   *Singly qualified association*

Figure A15.6 Models for sorted collections of points

The right model shows the same diagram using singly qualified associations. We introduced a dummy class *Strip* to represent all points having a given *x*-coordinate. The right model would be easier to implement on most systems, because a data structure for a single sort key is more likely to be available in a class library. The actual implementation could use B-trees, linked lists, or arrays to represent the association.

The code listed below specifies search, add, and delete methods.

```
PointCollection::search (region: Rectangle): Set of Point
{
    make a new empty set of points;
    scan the x values in the association until x ≥ region.xmin;
    while the x qualifier ≤ region.xmax do:
        scan the y values for the x value until y ≥ region.ymin;
        while the y qualifier ≤ region.ymax do:
            add (x,y) to the set of points;
            advance to the next y value;
        advance to the next x value;
    return the set of points;
}


PointCollection::add (point: Point)
{
    scan the x values in the association until x ≥ point.x;
    if x = point.x then
        scan the y values for the x value until y ≥ point.y
    insert the point into the association at the current
        location;
}


PointCollection::delete (point: Point)
{
    scan the x values in the association until x ≥ point.x;
    if x = point.x then
        scan the y values for the x value until y ≥ point.y
        if y = point.y then
            for each collection point with the current x,y value
                if collection point = point
                    then delete it and return
    report point not found error and return
}
```

Note that the scan operation should be implemented by a binary search to achieve logarithmic rather than linear times. A scan falls through to the next statement if it runs out of values.

17.2 An arrow indicates that the association is implemented in the given direction.

- **Text <–> Box**. The user can edit text and the box must resize, so there should be a pointer from text to box. Text is allowed only in boxes, so we presume that a user may grab a box and move it, causing the enclosed text to also move. So there should be a pointer from box to text.

- **Connection <–> Box**. A box can be dragged and move its connections, so there must be pointers from box to connections. Similarly, a link can be dragged and move its connections to boxes, so there must also be a pointer from connection to box. There is no obvious ordering.

- **Connection <–> Link**. Same explanation as previous bullet.

- **Collection –> ordered Box**. Given a collection, we must be able to find the boxes. There does not seem to be a need to traverse the other way. There likely is an ordering of boxes, regarding their foreground / background hierarchy for visibility.

- **Collection –> ordered Link**. Same explanation as previous bullet.

18.6a. Here is Java code to implement a bidirectional, one-to-one association between classes *A* and *B*, using a pointer (reference variable) in each class. Each class maintains its own association end and calls on the associated class to maintain the other side. Each class contains an internal attribute, *_updateInProgress*, that breaks the potential infinite recursion. We show only the attributes and methods needed to implement the association.

 We demonstrate class *A*; class *B* would contain the same code, but classes *A* and *B* and objects *a* and *b* would be substituted with *B*, *A*, *b*, and *a*, respectively. Thus the field *private B b* would become *private A a*, and the method *A.SetB(B newB)* would become *B.SetA(A newA)*. Note that we have minimized error handling as well as omitted boolean or enumerated returns and proper exception handling.

 This code assumes the most rigid of access control. Classes are presumed to exist in separate packages and so can access only each other's public `elements`.

```java
// in Java
// class A with a one-to-one association to class B

import BPackage.*;

public class A {
   private B b = null;
   private boolean _updateInProgress = false;

   // Check if A has a B
   public boolean hasB () {
      return b != null;
   }

   // Given an A, bind newB to it with a one-to-one association.
   public void setB (B newB) {
      if (newB == null) return; // don't "associate" to null;
                  // caller should call RemoveB instead!
      if (_updateInProgress) return; // break mutual recursion
      if (b == newB) return; // this A already bound to newB
      if (newB.hasA()) return;
         // newB must lack an association
      if (hasB()) removeB();
         // remove current b, if any; only 1:1 allowed

      _updateInProgress = true;
      newB.setA(this);
         // request newB to update its end of association
      b = newB; // update this end of association
      _updateInProgress = false;
```

```
    }

    // Remove the one B that may be associated.
    // Note that a 1-to-1 assoc does not need a remove argument.
    public void removeB() {
        if ( hasB() == false ) return; // no B to remove!
        if (_updateInProgress) return; // break mutual recursion

        _updateInProgress = true;
        b.removeA();
            // request B to remove its end of association
        b = null; // remove this end of association
        _updateInProgress = false;
    }
};
```

Often, classes that mention one another in their interfaces are packaged together and may therefore have more extensive and privileged knowledge of one another. In such cases, it may reasonable for one side or another of an association to take responsibility for maintaining both association ends. This can provide optimization, centralize update code, and avoid the need for devices (see _updateInProgress_ in code) to terminate recursion. However, it may imply an increased level of code dependency among associated classes.

This is not necessarily "bad" or "disencapsulating." A logical dependency already exists, expressed in the interface(s). The ability to restrict operations to selected callers may result in safer, more accurate, more encapsulated (from the public view) code, even as it exposes selected internals to an associated class. Consider the case where the ability to trigger termination of a link should be restricted to the linked object itself. In Java, the publicly available _remove()_ methods would instead be given default package access, and by packaging A and B together, invocation of those methods would be reserved for call only across the link and not by those outside the package.

Alternatively, A and B might selectively expose their pointers and allow one end of the association to perform all update activities. We offer the essentials of such a C++ solution.

```
//in C++
class B; // forward declaration

class A {

    friend class B; // or per function if B has been declared:
    //    friend void B::setA(A&);
    //    friend void B::removeA();
    B* b;

    void removeB(); // B can ask A to remove B; others cannot

public:

    bool hasB () { return b != 0; }
```

```
        void setB (B& newB);
            // or use pointer parameter to allow null b
        };


    void A::setB(B& newB)
    {
        if (b == &newB) return; // this A already bound to newB
        if (newB.hasA()) return; // newB must lack an association
        if (hasB()) removeB();
            // remove current b, if any; only 1:1 allowed

        b = &newB; // update this end of association
        b->a = this;
    }

    void A::removeB()
    {
        if ( !hasB() ) return; // no B to remove!
        if (b->a != this) return; // whoops -- not bidirectional!

        b->a = 0; // remove old b's pointer to this A
        b = 0; // remove this end of association
    }
```

19.13 We infer that a *Route* has 2 *Cities* from the problem statement. We could not deduce that from the SQL code alone.

Figure A19.12 Class model for Figure E19.6

19.14 SQL code to determine distance between two cities for Figure E19.6.

```
SELECT distance
FROM Route R, City C1, City C2,
     City_Distance CD1, City_Distance CD2
WHERE C1.city_ID = CD1.city_ID AND
      CD1.route_ID = R.route_ID AND
      R.route_ID = CD2.route_ID AND
      CD2.city_ID = C2.city_ID  AND
      C1.city_name = :aCityName1  AND
      C2.city_name = :aCityName2;
```

19.15 Here is the class diagram.

19.16 SQL code to determine distance between two cities for Figure E19.7. We don't know which name is 1 and which name is 2, so the SQL code allows for either possibility.

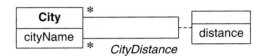

Figure A19.13 Class model for Figure E19.7

```
SELECT distance
FROM City C1, City C2, City_Distance CD
WHERE C1.city_ID  = CD.city1_ID AND
      CD.city2_ID = C2.city_ID   AND
      ((C1.cityName = :aCityName1 AND
        C2.cityName = :aCityName2) OR
       (C1.cityName = :aCityName2 AND
        C2.cityName = :aCityName1));
```

19.17 We make the following observations about Figure A19.12 and Figure A19.13.

- Figure A19.12 has an additional table. Figure A19.12 could store multiple routes between the same cities with different distances. Given the lack of explanation about route in the problem statement (is it a series of roads with different distances or is it the distance by air?), this may or may not be a drawback.

- Figure A19.13 is awkward because of the symmetry between city1 and city2. Either data must be stored twice with waste of storage, update time, and possible consistency problems, or special application logic must enforce an arbitrary constraint.

We need to know more about the requirements to choose between the models.

20.3a. This is an example of poor programming style. The assumption that the arguments are legal and the functions called are well behaved will cause trouble during program test and integration.

The following statements will cause the program to crash if the argument to *strlen* is zero:

```
rootLength = strlen(rootName);
suffixLength = strlen(suffix);
```

The following statement will assign zero to *sheetName* if the program runs out of memory, causing a program crash during the call to *strcpy* later in the function:

```
sheetName = malloc(rootLength + suffixLength + 1);
```

The following statements will cause the program to crash if any of the arguments are zero:

```
sheetName = strcpy(sheetName, rootName);
sheetName = strcat(sheetName, suffix);
```

If *sheetType* is invalid, the switch statement will fall through, leaving *sheet* without an assigned value. Also, it is possible that the call to *vertSheetNew* or the call to *horizSheetNew* could return zero for some reason. Either condition would make it possible for the following statement to crash:

```
sheet->name = sheetName;
```

Index

A

abstract class **69–70**, 81, 163, 326
    convention for 70
    notation for 69
abstract operation 69, 326
    notation for 70
abstract signal 114, 125, 163
abstract use case 149, 163
abstraction **16**, 22, 76, 93, 199–200, 405, 415
    exercise 212–213
access control 341
    in C++ 315, **322–325**
    in Java 317, **322–325**
accidents of software 3
activation **152**
active object 152
active value 283
activity **99–103**, **141–143**
    entry 100–101, 103, 113
    exit 100–101, 103, 113
    notation for 99, 140, 142
activity diagram **140–144**, **154–157**, 223
    notation for 140, 155, 156
    practical tips 143–144
activity token 143
actor **131–132**, 134–136
    finding 217
    notation for 134–135
Ada 288
aggregation 64, **66–69**, 163–164, 191

and concurrency 114–115
    exercise 83, 84
    implementing
        for a programming language 310
        for a relational database 354
    notation for 67
    vs. association 67
    vs. composition 67–68
agile programming 311
algorithm, design of 274–278
allocation
    of subsystems to processors 248–250
analysis 4, 167–169, **181–215**, **216–239**, 299
    application analysis 168–169, **216–239**
    building application class model 224–227
    building application interaction model 216–224
    building application state model 227–233
    building domain class model 183–201
    building domain interaction model 204
    building domain state model 201–204
    choosing packages 201
    data dictionary 187
    domain analysis 168, **181–215**
    finding associations 187–192
    finding attributes 192–194
    finding classes 183–186
    iteration of 196–199, 204–206
    shifting abstraction 199–200
    testing access paths 196